THE COMPLETE GUIDE TO THE

NATIONAL
PARK LODGES

SIXTH EDITION

DAVID L. SCOTT

KAY W. SCOTT

gpp®
travel
Guilford, Connecticut

The dollar cost of rooms and meals is for summer 2008. Taxes are not included unless noted. The prices and rates listed in this guidebook were confirmed at press time. We recommend, however, that you call establishments before traveling to obtain current information.

Maps provided are for reference only and should be used in conjunction with a road map or official park map. Distances suggested are approximate.

Other Globe Pequot Press books by
David L. Scott and Kay Woelfel Scott
Guide to the National Park Areas, Eastern States
Guide to the National Park Areas, Western States

Text design: Sheryl Kober
Text illustrations: Carole Drong

ISSN 1537-3312
ISBN 978-0-7627-4985-0

Printed in the United States of America

10 9 8 7 6 5 4 3 2 1

CONTENTS

CONTENTS

CONTENTS

CONTENTS

CONTENTS

CONTENTS

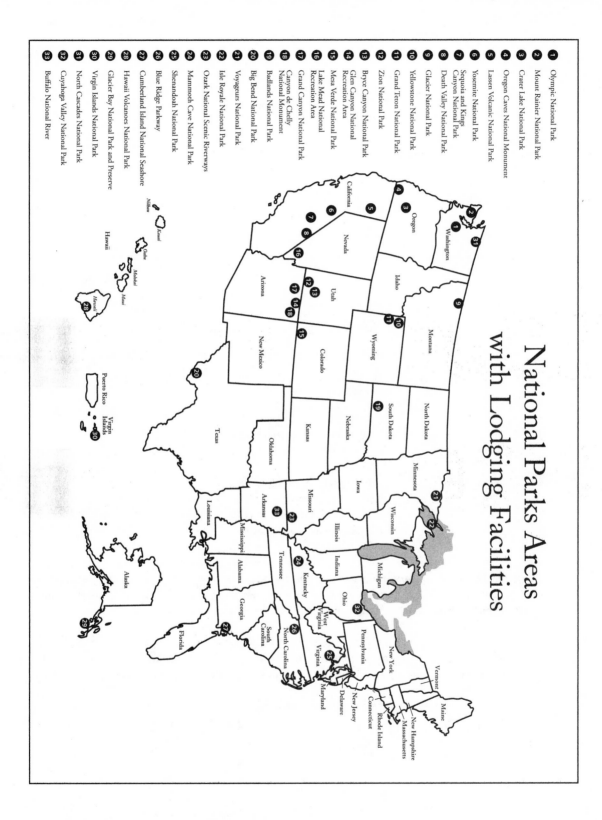

National Parks Areas with Lodging Facilities

1. Olympic National Park
2. Mount Rainier National Park
3. Crater Lake National Park
4. Oregon Caves National Monument
5. Lassen Volcanic National Park
6. Yosemite National Park
7. Sequoia and Kings Canyon National Park
8. Death Valley National Park
9. Glacier National Park
10. Yellowstone National Park
11. Grand Teton National Park
12. Zion National Park
13. Bryce Canyon National Park
14. Glen Canyon National Recreation Area
15. Mesa Verde National Park
16. Lake Mead National Recreation Area
17. Grand Canyon National Park
18. Canyon de Chelly National Monument
19. Badlands National Park
20. Big Bend National Park
21. Voyageurs National Park
22. Isle Royale National Park
23. Ozark National Scenic Riverways
24. Mammoth Cave National Park
25. Shenandoah National Park
26. Blue Ridge Parkway
27. Cumberland Island National Seashore
28. Hawaii Volcanoes National Park
29. Glacier Bay National Park and Preserve
30. Virgin Islands National Park
31. North Cascades National Park
32. Cuyahoga Valley National Park
33. Buffalo National River

HELP US KEEP THIS GUIDE UP TO DATE

Every effort has been made by the authors and editors to make this guide as accurate and useful as possible. However, many things can change after a guide is published—establishments close, phone numbers change, facilities come under new management, and so on.

We would love to hear from you concerning your experiences with this guide and how you feel it could be improved and be kept up to date. While we may not be able to respond to all comments and suggestions, we'll take them to heart, and we'll also make certain to share them with the authors. Please send your comments and suggestions to the following address:

The Globe Pequot Press
Reader Response/Editorial Department
P.O. Box 480
Guilford, CT 06437

Or you may e-mail us at:
editorial@GlobePequot.com

Thanks for your input, and happy travels!

INTRODUCTION

Have you ever thought about waking up, looking out your window, and viewing the morning sun shining on the north face of the Grand Canyon? How about a walk down a dirt road from the historic hotel where you just had a dinner of walleye pike, and standing where French fur trappers portaged their canoes around a waterfall? Maybe you would enjoy sitting on a wooden deck outside your room, listening to the roar of a mountain stream. Perhaps you are a closet cowboy who has always wanted to spend a week riding horses at a dude ranch. Maybe you would like to walk outside your lodge and view a dormant volcano. These are just a few of the dreams that can be brought to life by staying at a national park lodging facility.

The two of us have devoted thirty summers and numerous Christmas vacations to exploring America's national parks. Most of our trips took place in a series of four Volkswagen campers that accumulated nearly a quarter of a million miles. Trust us, twenty summers living in VW campers is marital devotion with a capital D. We dedicated six of the summers to experiencing the national park lodges. Our latest lodge trips during 2007 and 2008 included stays in fifty-six different national park lodges and visits to over a dozen more, many for the fourth or fifth time. At each lodge we walk the property, view as many different types of rooms as possible, talk with the employees, and sample the food. We gather information that we believe will be of value to you in planning a trip.

Most national park lodges are in the well-known and heavily visited parks, such as Grand Canyon, Death Valley, Yosemite, Yellowstone, Grand Teton, Olympic, and Glacier. However, some lesser-known park areas, including Oregon Caves National Monument, Isle Royale National Park, Big Bend National Park, and Lassen Volcanic National Park, each offer comfortable and interesting lodge facilities. Some of the biggest and busiest parks do not have lodges. For example, Great Smoky Mountains National Park, Rocky Mountain National Park, and Acadia National Park do not offer conventional lodging inside the park boundaries, although accommodations are available directly outside each of these parks.

Not all areas managed by the National Park Service are classified as national parks. In fact, only about 15 percent of the areas officially carry the title "national park." The National Park Service also manages many national monuments, national lakeshores, national historic sites, national recreation areas, national memorials, and several other categories of facilities. Each of these areas has something unique to offer or it wouldn't be included in the system. Some even have lodging.

Staying in a park lodge during your trip to a national park area will almost surely enhance your park experience. It certainly did ours. Spend some time talking to the employees and learning about the history of the building where you are staying. Most of all, travel and enjoy.

CONSIDERATIONS IN PLANNING A STAY AT A NATIONAL PARK LODGE

National park lodges provide a different kind of vacation experience. Most of the lodges are in close proximity to the things you want to see, the places you want to visit, and the facilities you will want to utilize when you visit a park. At Crater Lake Lodge, you can sleep in a room with windows that overlook the crater rim. In Yellowstone's Old Faithful Inn, you can walk out the entrance and view an eruption of Old Faithful geyser. At the Grand Canyon's El Tovar, you can walk a few steps outside the hotel and look down into the magnificent canyon. Many park lodges have large rustic lobby areas where you can relax with other guests in front of a blazing fireplace. Glacier Park Lodge in Montana's Glacier National Park is noted for its massive three-story lobby. The lodges are often near National Park Service visitor centers or campgrounds where guided walks originate and natural history programs are presented. Evening programs or other entertainment can be enjoyed in many of the lodges.

Most lodge facilities in national park areas are owned by the government but managed by private concerns subject to oversight by the park in which they are located. Managements of these lodges operate as concessionaires and are required to obtain the approval of the National Park Service for room rates, improvements, activities offered, and the prices charged for everything from food to gasoline. Some lodges remain under private ownership on private property within a park. In general, lodges under private ownership were in operation prior to the establishment or expansion of a park. Lodges on private property are subject to less government oversight regarding what they can offer and the prices they can charge.

Some basic information regarding reservations, facilities, and policies can be helpful if you have never stayed in a national park facility or have stayed in only one or two lodges. Most national park lodges experience large public demand for a limited number of rooms, especially during peak season, when you are most likely to want a room. Consider that no new accommodations have been added to many national parks in decades, and it is easy to see why there are not sufficient rooms to meet demand. Thus, you should make a reservation as early as possible, especially if your planned vacation coincides with the park's busiest period. Try to book rooms at a popular lodge at least six months before your expected arrival. Several lodges in very busy locations such as Yosemite Valley should, if possible, be booked nearly a year in advance, especially if you want to stay at the Ahwahnee. Choosing to vacation in off-peak periods, normally spring and fall, will make it much more likely that you are able to obtain a reservation on the dates you desire. Other important factors regarding national park lodges are discussed below.

Facilities. National park lodges range from luxurious and expensive facilities, such as Yosemite National Park's Ahwahnee and Death Valley National Park's Furnace Creek Inn, to very rustic cabins without bathrooms, such as those at Grant Grove in Kings Canyon National Park. Some facilities call themselves lodges but are not what most of us picture when we think of a lodge. For example, Old Faithful Lodge Cabins (not the more famous Old Faithful Inn that sits nearby) offers only cabins as overnight accommodations. Likewise, Signal Mountain Lodge in Grand Teton National Park does not have a main lodge building with overnight accommodations; rather, it has several types of cabins that rent at a fairly wide range of prices. The variation in facilities between and within parks makes it important that you understand exactly what types of accommodations are being discussed when you are making a reservation.

Most national park lodging facilities don't have amenities such as spas, exercise rooms, swimming pools, game rooms, and some of the other niceties you may expect to find at commercial facilities outside the parks. In fact, rooms in many park lodges don't have telephones or televisions, although public telephones are nearly always available somewhere in the facility. Several older lodges, including Old Faithful Inn in Yellowstone National Park, Wawona in Yosemite National Park, and Lake Crescent Lodge in Olympic National Park, offer some rooms without a private bathroom. Community bathrooms and shower rooms are available for occupants of these rooms. Some cabins do not have private bathrooms.

Rooms. Rooms in a lodge often vary considerably with regard to size, bedding, view, and rate. Likewise, a single lodging facility may offer rooms in the main lodge building, rooms in motel-type buildings, and a variety of cabin rooms. This is the case with Lake Crescent Lodge in Olympic National Park and with Big Meadows in Shenandoah National Park, for example. Potential differences in rooms mean that it is worthwhile to learn what options are available at a particular location where you plan to stay. If you wait to make a reservation near your planned arrival date, you are likely to find a limited variety of accommodations. For example, you may discover that all the rooms with private bathrooms are already taken. On the other hand, call early and you are likely to have a wide choice of rooms that are offered at a broad range of rates. Ask about a view room, for example. Sometimes rooms with an excellent view are more expensive, and sometimes they are not. Some multiple-story buildings do not have elevators, so the floor you are assigned may be important. Higher floors tend to offer better views but may require more climbing. Rooms near the lobby may be noisy. Some lodges allow you to reserve a particular room, but most lodges guarantee only a particular type of room. Even when a particular room won't be guaranteed, a lodge will often make note of your preferences and attempt to satisfy the request when rooms are assigned.

Wheelchair Accessibility. Most national park lodging facilities offer some type of wheelchair accessibility, but the degree of accessibility varies considerably among the lodges and among different types of accommodations at the same lodge. For example, Zion Lodge has two newer motel-type rooms that are fully wheelchair accessible with ramps, wide doorways, and roll-in showers. On the other hand, Western Cabins at the same lodge are only marginally wheelchair accessible. It isn't that the lodge operators don't care, but rather that many national park lodging facilities are historic and restrictions exist with regard to modifications that can be made. Keep in mind that lodging facilities are sometimes a distance from parking, and many facilities with two or more stories do not have elevators. In addition, some national park accommodations do not have telephones in the rooms. Be certain to have a clear understanding about the extent of wheelchair accessibility when booking a room.

Reservations. Reservations can generally be made by telephone, and increasingly via the Internet.

Either method allows you to immediately determine room availability and, if necessary, choose alternative dates. Using the telephone will also allow you to discuss with the reservation agent the types of facilities that are available. It is a good idea to study the lodge Web site so that you have a basic understanding of the facilities and rates prior to calling. This will allow you to know which type of room and building to request and what to expect regarding rates. Be aware that it is often difficult to get through to a reservation agent via telephone, especially if you call late in the spring, when everyone else in the country seems to be trying the same number. Try calling at odd hours, such as weekend mornings.

Most lodges require a deposit of at least one night's lodging when making a reservation. A few lodges permit you to guarantee the reservation with a credit card and to pay for the entire stay when you check out.

Grand Canyon. The park fee generally provides exit and entrance for three to seven days, depending on the park. Inquire about this at the entrance station if you may need to go outside the park during a stay of several days. The National Park Service sells three types of passes that provide free entrance at all national parks. The America the Beautiful–National Parks and Federal Recreation Lands Pass ($80) allows unlimited entry to all federal recreation sites (including those operated by the National Park Service) for one year from the month of purchase. For seniors (age sixty-two and over), the America the Beautiful Senior Pass provides lifetime free entrance for a one-time fee of $10. A lifetime pass is available at no charge to individuals who are disabled. Passes for seniors and the disabled also allow a 50 percent reduction in fees for parking, boat launching, and most tours. All three passes are available at most National Park Service entrance stations and visitor centers.

Getting the Most from a National Park Visit. Staying in a national park lodge should enhance your visit to a park, but don't let it be your main activity. National park areas offer numerous activities in which you can participate. Your first order of business should be to request information from the park areas you will be visiting. We have included addresses, phone numbers, and Web sites for each park that has lodging facilities. Parks are generally prompt in answering requests for information. Read about the parks so you will have a basic understanding of the history, geology, and activities prior to your arrival. At parks with an entry station you will be given a park newspaper and a mini-folder with a map of the park. These can be obtained at the visitor centers of parks without an entry station. Stop at a visitor center to determine what activities are scheduled during your stay. A visitor center may be near the lodge where you will be staying, or it may be on the way to your lodge. Visitor centers generally have excellent video presentations that provide either an overview of the park or a story about some particular facet of history or geology. Visitor centers also generally post a list of daily activities including talks, demonstrations, guided hikes, and campfire programs. Take advantage of as many of these activities as time permits, for they are nearly always enjoyable and educational. You will have an opportunity to ask questions of an expert at the same time that you share information with other visitors who have interests similar to yours. Many parks offer Junior Ranger programs for children. These programs allow kids to earn a Junior Ranger patch while they learn about the park and its environment. Information on these programs is available at the visitor center.

ALASKA

■ **State Tourist Information**
(907) 929-2200 | www.travelalaska.com

Glacier Bay National Park and Preserve

P.O. Box 140 • Gustavus, AK 99826 • (907) 697-2230 • www.nps.gov/glba

Glacier Bay National Park and Preserve comprises approximately 3.3 million acres that include some of the world's most impressive examples of tidewater glaciers, rivers of ice that flow to the sea. The park is rich in plant and animal life and is the home to moose, black bears, grizzly bears, mountain goats, sea lions, sea otters, puffins, bald eagles, humpback whales, and porpoises. A 9-mile paved road links the small town of Gustavus and its airport with the lodge, but most of the natural features of the park can be seen only by boat or airplane. The National Park Service visitor center is on the second floor of Glacier Bay Lodge. The park is in southeastern Alaska, approximately 60 miles northwest of Juneau. Access to the park is only via plane or boat. **Park Entrance Fee:** No charge.

Lodging in Glacier Bay National Park: Glacier Bay Lodge offers the only overnight accommodations in Glacier Bay National Park. The rustic fifty-six-room lodge is located in the southeastern section of the park near the mouth of Glacier Bay, approximately 9 miles from the small town of Gustavus. Several bed-and-breakfasts and other accommodations are outside the park in Gustavus.

GLACIER BAY LODGE

P.O. Box 179 • Gustavus, AK 99826 • (907) 697-4000 • www.visitglacierbay.com

Glacier Bay National Park and Preserve

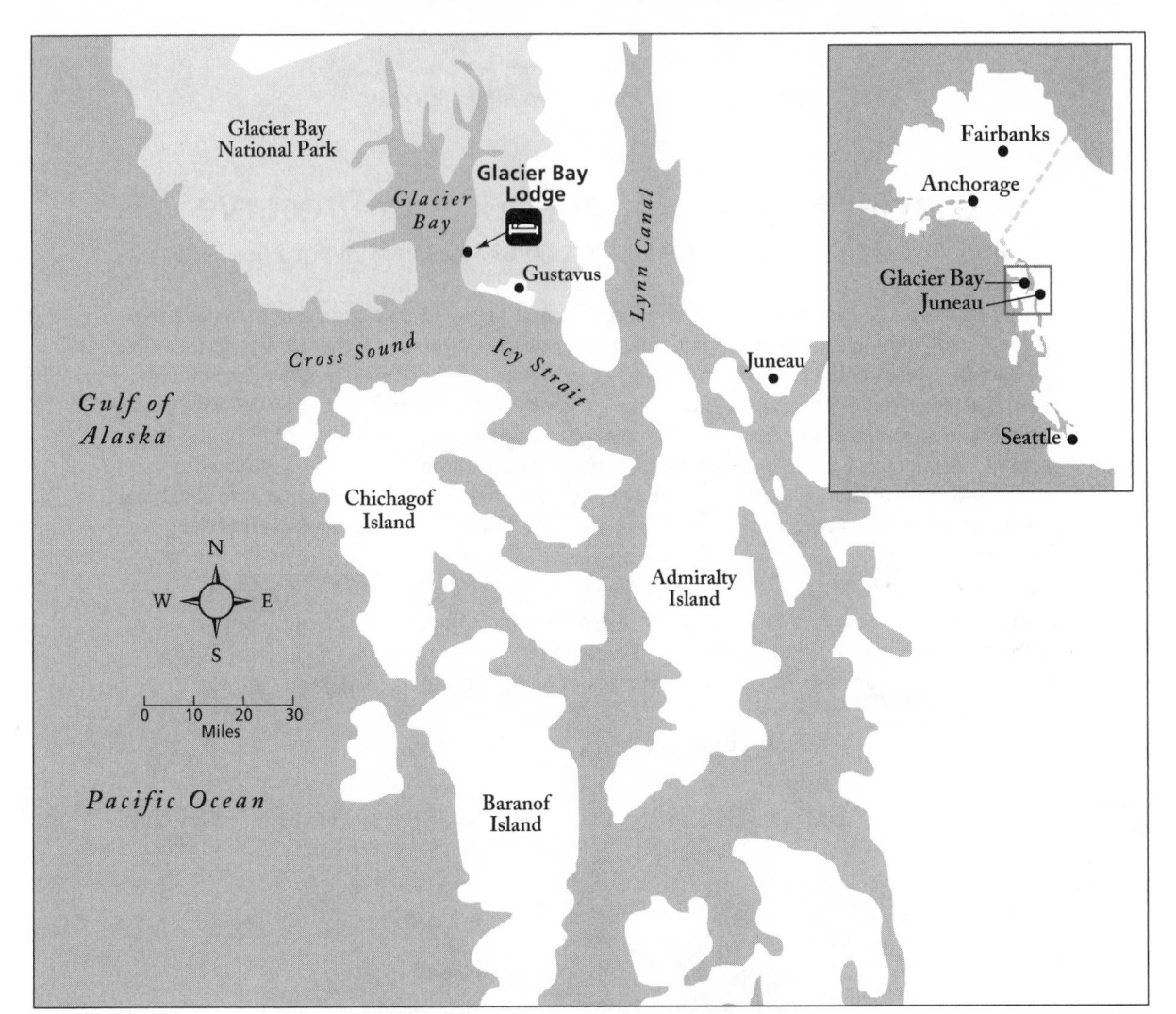

Glacier Bay Lodge is a wilderness resort situated on Bartlett Cove in a Sitka spruce rain forest. The complex includes an attractive two-story wooden chalet-type lodge building that houses a lobby that has a cathedral ceiling with wood beams, a large gas fireplace, registration desk, dining room with great views of the cove, and a gift shop. The lodge mezzanine is the location for the National Park Service visitor center with interpretive displays and an auditorium where films about Glacier Bay are shown during the day and programs are presented by park rangers each evening. Boardwalks connect the main lodge building to nineteen nearby one-story wooden structures that provide guest accommodations. The lodge is located on Bartlett Cove, 9 miles from the tiny town of Gustavus in the southeastern corner of the park. A road connects the lodge with the town of Gustavus and its small airport, but no roads lead from the mainland into the park.

Glacier Bay Lodge was constructed by the National Park Service from 1965 to 1966 and opened in June 1966 with the main lodge building plus twenty cabins. The concessionaire constructed an additional thirty-five cabins plus two utility cabins and a service building (the current shower and laundry) six years later. These added buildings were subsequently purchased by the National Park Service from the financially distressed concessionaire. During the winter of 1984 to 1985, the National Park Service enlarged the lodge basement and provided exhibit space on the second floor that currently houses the National Park Service visitor center. The lodge and its boat tours have been operated under a succession of firms, including one that filed for bankruptcy in 1989. The lodge contract was awarded in 2004 to a joint venture of Aramark Leisure Services and a subsidiary of HUNA Totem Native Corporation, which continues to hold the concession.

The lodge offers fifty-six rooms in nineteen one-story wooden buildings that are near but separate from the main lodge building. Approximately a dozen of these rooms are utilized as housing for management and interpreters. The buildings with accommodations each have from two to six rooms. The rooms all have radiant heat, a coffeemaker, a hair dryer, a telephone, and a private bathroom with a combination shower-tub. There are no televisions. All but four of the rooms are the same size, and most have one double bed plus a twin bed or two twin beds. A limited number of rooms have three twin beds. One room has one double bed, and another has two double beds. The rooms have attractive interiors with rough-hewn wood walls and a vaulted ceiling. A large back window offers views of Bartlett Cove or the surrounding forest. A few of the rooms don't have a particularly attractive window view.

About a third of the rooms are classified as "view rooms" that offer window views of Bartlett Cove. These rent for about $25 per night more than rooms that offer window views of the rain forest. If a water view is important to you, we suggest rooms 9 through 21. Keep in mind that water views are at least partially obscured by spruce trees. If you don't particularly care about a water view and want to save $25, ask for rooms 43 through 52. A number of steps are required to reach some of the rooms, especially those with a view. Be sure to mention if steps are a problem when making a reservation.

Glacier Bay Lodge is a place to enjoy spectacular scenery and abundant wildlife in a wild environment. Keep in mind that the lodge is in a rain forest with lots of moisture and cool temperatures. Pack rain gear and clothing that is appropriate for daytime summer temperatures that range from 45 to 65° Fahrenheit. We suggest you spend at least three nights at the lodge to allow sufficient time to enjoy this unique lodge and explore the surrounding area. If you are committing the time and money to travel to this remote location, you may as well have time to enjoy yourself. Most guests choose to take the daylong Glacier Bay cruise that leaves at 7:30 a.m. from the dock behind the lodge. We saw whales, mountain goats, wolves, sea otters, sea lions, puffins, and a grizzly bear during our cruise. We also witnessed a huge chunk of ice split off a tidewater glacier and crash into Glacier Bay. The next day can be spent kayaking Glacier Bay or hiking one or more of the four trails that begin near the lodge. The 1-mile Forest Loop Trail begins from the beach below the lodge and winds through the rain forest where the trees, ground, and logs are covered in green. Bicycle rentals are also available at the lodge. On the second evening consider the whale-watching tour that cruises outside the park into a popular feeding area for the humpback whales. The tour is available with or without dinner.

■   ■   ■

Nearly everyone visiting Glacier Bay, be it by boat or plane, comes by way of Juneau. Alaska's capital offers a variety of things to see and do that make a layover of several days worthwhile. As you might expect in a capital city, you can tour an interesting state museum and the state capitol. Perhaps you would enjoy a 1,800-foot tram ride up Mount Roberts. Scenic seaplane flights over the Juneau Icefield and its many glaciers leave from a downtown dock. A short distance north of Juneau, a U.S. Forest Service visitor center offers exhibits near a viewing area for the famous Mendenhall Glacier. Nearer to downtown a salmon hatchery and its small aquarium offer insights on one of the state's important industries. After all this, it may be time for a tour of the Alaska Brewing Company, where you can sample some fine brews without anyone trying to rush you out the door. My favorite is the somewhat bitter Alaska I.P.A. For information contact the Juneau Convention & Visitors Bureau. Call (800) 587-2201, visit www.traveljuneau .com, or e-mail info@traveljuneau.com.

■   ■   ■

Whale-watching tours are not offered every night, so it is important to inquire about tour schedules when making a lodge reservation.

Rooms: Singles, doubles, triples, and quads. Rollaways are available. All rooms in the lodge have private baths.

Wheelchair Accessibility: Two lodge rooms are ADA compliant, with grab bars in the shower and near the toilet.

An elevator is available to transport guests to the second floor of the lodge building where the National Park visitor center is located.

Reservations: Glacier Bay Lodge & Tours, 241 West Ship Creek Avenue, Anchorage, AK 99501. Phone (800) 229-8687. Rooms must be prepaid. Cancellation is required at least thirty days prior to arrival.

Rates: View rooms ($201); regular rooms ($174). Rates quoted are for two adults. Each additional person is $20 per night. Children under twelve years of age stay free with adults.

Location: Approximately 9 miles northwest of Gustavus, on the shore of Bartlett Cove.

Season: Mid-May through mid-September.

Food: A dining room specializing in fresh Alaskan seafood, such as Dungeness crab, halibut, and salmon, serves breakfast ($8–$14); lunch ($9–$11); and dinner ($14–$32). The lunch menu is served on the deck during the afternoon and evening hours. A small grocery is in the town of Gustavus.

Transportation: Alaska Airlines operates scheduled jet service to Gustavus during summer months. Charter airlines provide service between Glacier Bay and several Alaska towns. Charter air service between Juneau and Gustavus costs approximately $85 per person. Glacier Bay Lodge and Tours offers a ferry service between Glacier Bay and Juneau on Wednesday, Friday, and Saturday ($70 one way), departing Glacier Bay at 4:30 p.m. The return trip leaves Juneau at 8:00 p.m., arriving in Glacier Bay at 11:00 p.m. A lodge shuttle (fee charged) operates between the lodge and the town of Gustavus. A private taxi service ($15 per person one way) also operates between these two points. Service, schedules, and prices are subject to change, so check with the lodge or review Gustavus transportation information at www.gustavus.com/gethere.html.

Facilities: Restaurant, cocktail service, gift shop, bike and kayak rental, national park visitor center with an auditorium. A ranger station and boat dock are nearby.

Activities: Hiking, guided walks, biking, kayaking, guided kayak trips, fishing, fishing charters, all-day wildlife and glacier cruises, and whale-watching dinner cruises. A nine-hole golf course is in the town of Gustavus (rental clubs are available).

ARIZONA

▨ State Tourist Information
(888) 520-3434 | www.arizonaguide.com

Canyon de Chelly National Monument

P.O. Box 588 • Chinle, AZ 86503 • (928) 674-5500 • www.nps.gov/cach/

Canyon de Chelly (pronounced "d' SHAY") National Monument comprises nearly 84,000 acres of Navajo land that include ruins of Indian villages built between A.D. 350 and 1300 in steep-walled canyons. The visitor center is located near the park entrance. The canyon can be seen from scenic overlooks along North Rim Drive (36 miles round-trip) and South Rim Drive (34 miles round-trip). White House Ruin is accessible via a 2.5-mile (round-trip) trail that begins at a trailhead on South Rim Drive. All other trails and all four-wheel-drive travel within the park require a park ranger or authorized guide. Information is available at the visitor center. Canyon de Chelly is in northeastern Arizona, approximately 85 miles northwest of Gallup, New Mexico, near the town of Chinle, Arizona. **Monument Entrance Fee:** No charge.

Lodging in Canyon de Chelly National Monument: Thunderbird Lodge, near the monument entrance, is the only lodging facility in Canyon de Chelly National Monument. The lodge includes a cafeteria and gift shop. Guided tours of the canyons leave from the lodge. A Best Western and a Holiday Inn are a short distance outside the monument in the town of Chinle.

THUNDERBIRD LODGE

P.O. Box 548 • Chinle, AZ 86503 • (928) 674-5841 • www.tbirdlodge.com

Canyon de Chelly National Monument

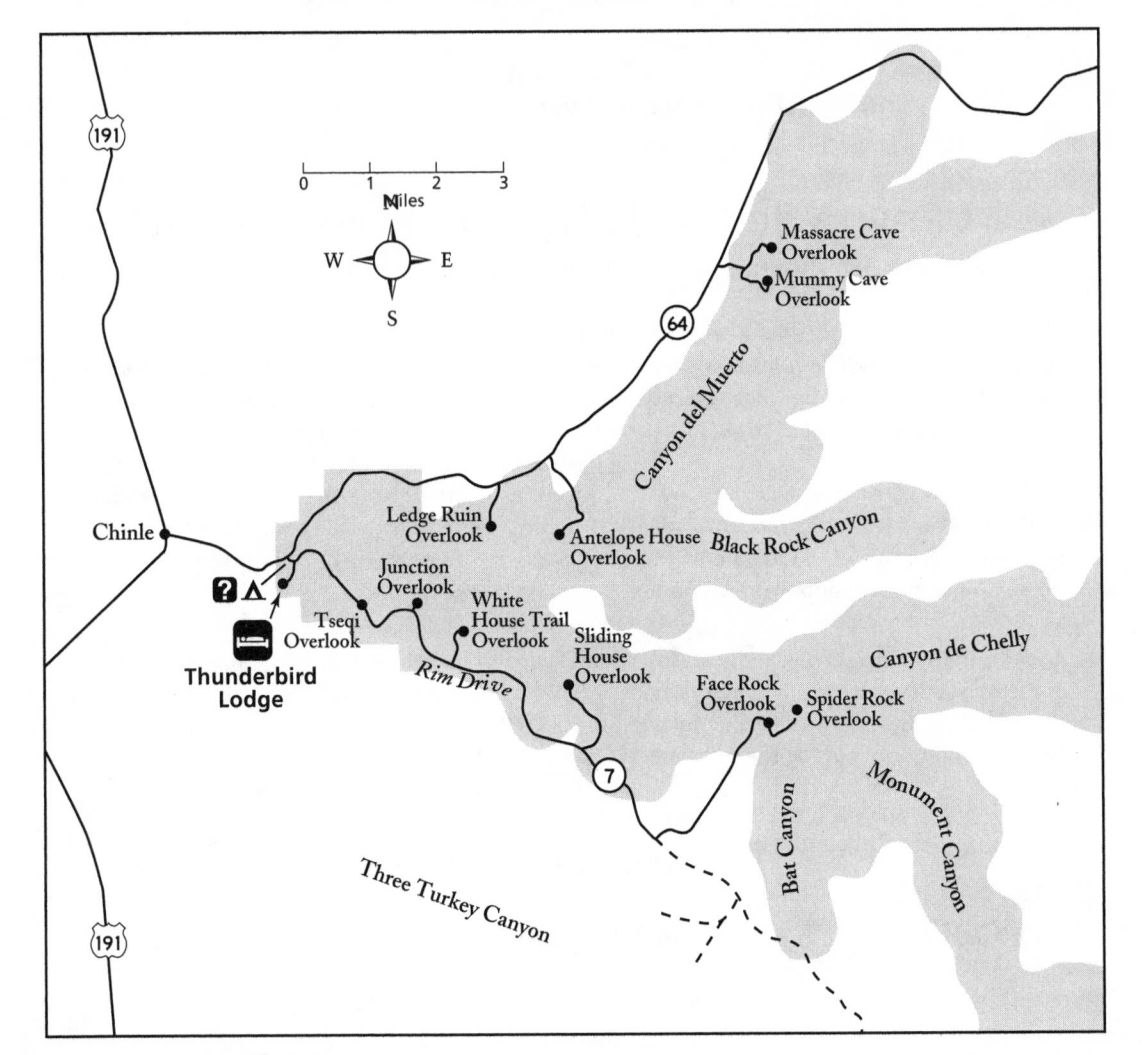

Thunderbird Lodge is an attractive, well-maintained motor lodge, offering seventy-four rooms just inside the entrance to Canyon de Chelly National Monument. The lodge, situated in a grove of cotton-wood trees, comprises a complex of several adobe and stone buildings, including four adobe units that contain most of the lodging rooms. The adobe registration building is separate but adjacent to the buildings containing the rooms. Separate stone buildings house a small number of rooms, a gift shop, and a cafeteria. Thunderbird Lodge is on Navajo Route 7, 3 miles east of the intersection with Highway 191 in the town of Chinle.

Thunderbird Lodge offers several types of rooms, although most are very similar. All rooms are decorated in an attractive Southwest style and have air-conditioning, heat, ceiling fans, a television, and a telephone.

■   ■   ■

Thunderbird Lodge was originally constructed in 1902 as a trading post on the Navajo Reservation. The post served as a store, bank, post office, community meeting place, and courtroom. The owner began offering rooms and food service to accommodate an increasing number of tourists, who came to view the cliff dwellings and spectacular scenery. The present-day cafeteria is in the original trading post, while the building housing the gift shop originally served as home for the trading post's owner.

■   ■   ■

Most of the forty-one Adobe motel-type rooms have two queen beds and a full bath. The Adobe Rooms have beamed ceilings and are housed in two long buildings built into the back of a hill. Adequate parking is directly in front of a covered walkway that runs across the front of the buildings. Most of the twenty-eight De Chelly Rooms each contain two double beds and a full bath, although one has three full beds, and a few are available with a king bed. All but four of the De Chelly Rooms are in two buildings constructed around a grassy courtyard filled with trees. Rooms in these buildings back up to one another, with half facing the courtyard and half facing the parking lot. Four De Chelly Rooms are in two buildings, one stone and one adobe, that sit in the center of the complex. One suite in a stone building has a separate bedroom with one king bed, a living room area with a queen sofa bed and a refrigerator, and a full bathroom. Four smaller rooms in one stone building each have one double bed and are rented only on-site. We recommend you choose from De Chelly Rooms 14 through 18 or 25 through 29, all of which face the courtyard. These are quiet and front on a nice grassy area.

Thunderbird Lodge is an exceptionally well-maintained facility offering a relaxing atmosphere where guests visit from porch chairs directly outside their rooms. The green lawns are immaculate and the building exteriors always appear as if they were recently redone. Guests from a neighboring room told us during our 2005 visit that Thunderbird Lodge was their favorite stay during a two-week trip to the Southwest. The lodge cafeteria has an attractive interior with decorative Navajo rugs and offers inexpensive food, including the house specialty Navajo taco, from early morning to evening. The lodge gift shop features a large selection of handwoven Navajo rugs. The National Park Service visitor center with a variety of exhibits, including a Navajo home called a *hogan,* is an easy half-mile walk from the lodge. Interpretive programs at the visitor center include ranger presentations and guided walks. The lodge is also near the monument's campground, where evening campfire programs are offered.

Half-day ($43 adults/$33 children) or full-day ($71) guided canyon tours are offered by the lodge. The half-day tours take approximately three and a half hours and cover the lower half of Canyon del Muerto and Canyon de Chelly. They depart at 9:00 a.m. and 2:00 p.m. April through October, and 1:00 p.m. the rest of the year. Full-day tours last approximately eight hours, departing at 9:00 a.m. The longer tour includes lunch and traverses Canyon del Muerto to Mummy Cave and Canyon de Chelly to Spider Rock. For reservations call (800) 679-2473. The Tseqi Guide Association offers guides to lead tours in your four-wheel-drive vehicle. Call (520) 674-5500 for information.

Rooms: Doubles, triples, and quads. All rooms offer a full private bath.

Wheelchair Accessibility: Seven De Chelly Rooms offer ramp access, one king bed, and a bathroom with a wide doorway, grab bars, and a combination shower-tub. These rooms are on the parking lot side of the building. The registration building and cafeteria also offer ramp access.

Reservations: Thunderbird Lodge, P.O. Box 548, Chinle, AZ 86503. Phone (800) 679-2473; fax (928) 674-5844. Reservations may be made up to a year in advance. Cancellation must be made twenty-four hours in advance for a full refund.

Rates: Summer rates (March 1 to October 31) for two people: Adobe units ($111); De Chelly units ($106); Suite ($152). Each additional person is $4 in rooms and $5 in suite. Winter rate for two persons: Adobe or De Chelly ($69); Suite ($95). Rollaway, crib, and each additional person is $6.50. Special packages are available during winter months. Senior discounts and government rates are offered.

Location: The lodge is a short distance inside the park entrance.

Season: The lodge is open year-round. Heaviest season is from April through October, when reservations are advised.

Food: A lodge cafeteria offers basic food at reasonable prices from 6:30 a.m. to 8:00 p.m. during the summer months, with shorter hours the remainder of the year. Most meals range from $6 to $15, with steak dinners from $11 to $20. Alternative eating facilities are in the town of Chinle.

Transportation: No public transportation serves Canyon de Chelly National Monument or the town of Chinle.

Facilities: Cafeteria, gift shop, stable, National Park Service visitor center. Three miles west the town of Chinle has fast-food outlets, service stations, grocery stores, laundries, and a bank.

Activities: Hiking, canyon tours, National Park Service interpretive programs, horseback riding.

Glen Canyon National Recreation Area

P.O. Box 1507 • Page, AZ 86040 • (928) 608-6200 • www.nps.gov/glca/

Glen Canyon National Recreation Area comprises 1.25 million acres of high desert surrounding and including Lake Powell and its nearly 2,000 miles of shoreline. Lake Powell is formed by the Glen Canyon Dam near Page, Arizona, which backs up the Colorado River for nearly 200 miles. Most of the activities here, including boating, fishing, and waterskiing, are water-related. Houseboat rental is available at several locations on Lake Powell. Although nearly all of the recreation area is in southern Utah, the most accessible section is along U.S. Highway 89 near Page, Arizona, where the Glen Canyon Dam is located. **Recreation Area Entrance Fee:** $15.00 per vehicle or $7.00 per person, good for seven days.

Lodging in Glen Canyon National Recreation Area: Four locations in Glen Canyon National Recreation Area offer overnight lodging facilities. The largest and nicest facility by far is Lake Powell Resort, 6 miles north of Page, Arizona, on US 89. The resort also has a large marina. Overnight accommodations are offered by the same concessionaire at three other locations on the same lake, but on a much smaller scale than Lake Powell Resort and at relatively remote locations. Bullfrog Resort and Halls Crossing are located in the central section of Lake Powell, and Hite, in the northern section. Reservations are made using the same address and phone number listed for Lake Powell Resort. All of the locations permit pets.

LAKE POWELL RESORT

Box 1597 • Page, AZ 86040 • (928) 645-2433 • lakepowell@aramark.com
www.lakepowell.com

Lake Powell Resort offers 350 rooms as part of an attractive marina resort complex on Lake Powell, just north of Page, Arizona. The resort comprises a registration building plus eight nearly identical two-story lodging buildings on a peninsula of Lake Powell. The landscaped stucco buildings are finished and decorated in a Southwestern design. The complex also includes two swimming pools, a well-equipped fitness room with sauna, a gas station, an upscale restaurant, a coffee bar, a lounge, a pizzeria, a sports shop, and a gift shop. A beach area has cabanas, food and beverage service, and water-related offerings including kayak rentals and waterskiing lessons. A variety of half- and full-day boat tours can be arranged in the lobby of the registration building. Special packages that include a boat tour and room at the lodge are available. A large marina complex is down the hill from the lodge, which is situated directly on Lake Powell.

All rooms other than the four suites are of identical size. The majority have two queen-size beds, while others have a king bed. All of the rooms have heat, air-conditioning, a television, a telephone, a refrigerator, a coffeemaker, a hair dryer, and a full bath. Each room has a private balcony or patio with a table and chairs. Interior corridors through each two-story building provide access to the rooms. Second-floor rooms require climbing a flight of stairs, as none of the buildings has an elevator.

The lodge offers four categories of rooms. The least expensive Standard rooms on both the first and second floors face the large parking area. Views from all these rooms are pretty much confined to asphalt, vehicles, and other buildings, especially from the first-floor rooms. The furnishings in Standard rooms are gradually being upgraded. A second category, Lakeview rooms, generally offer good views of the lake and surrounding mesas and buttes. These rooms were renovated in 2004 and 2005 with substantially nicer furnishings, tiled bathrooms, and upgraded porch furniture. Deluxe Lakeview rooms in the two newest buildings (the 700 and 800 buildings)

Glen Canyon National Recreation Area

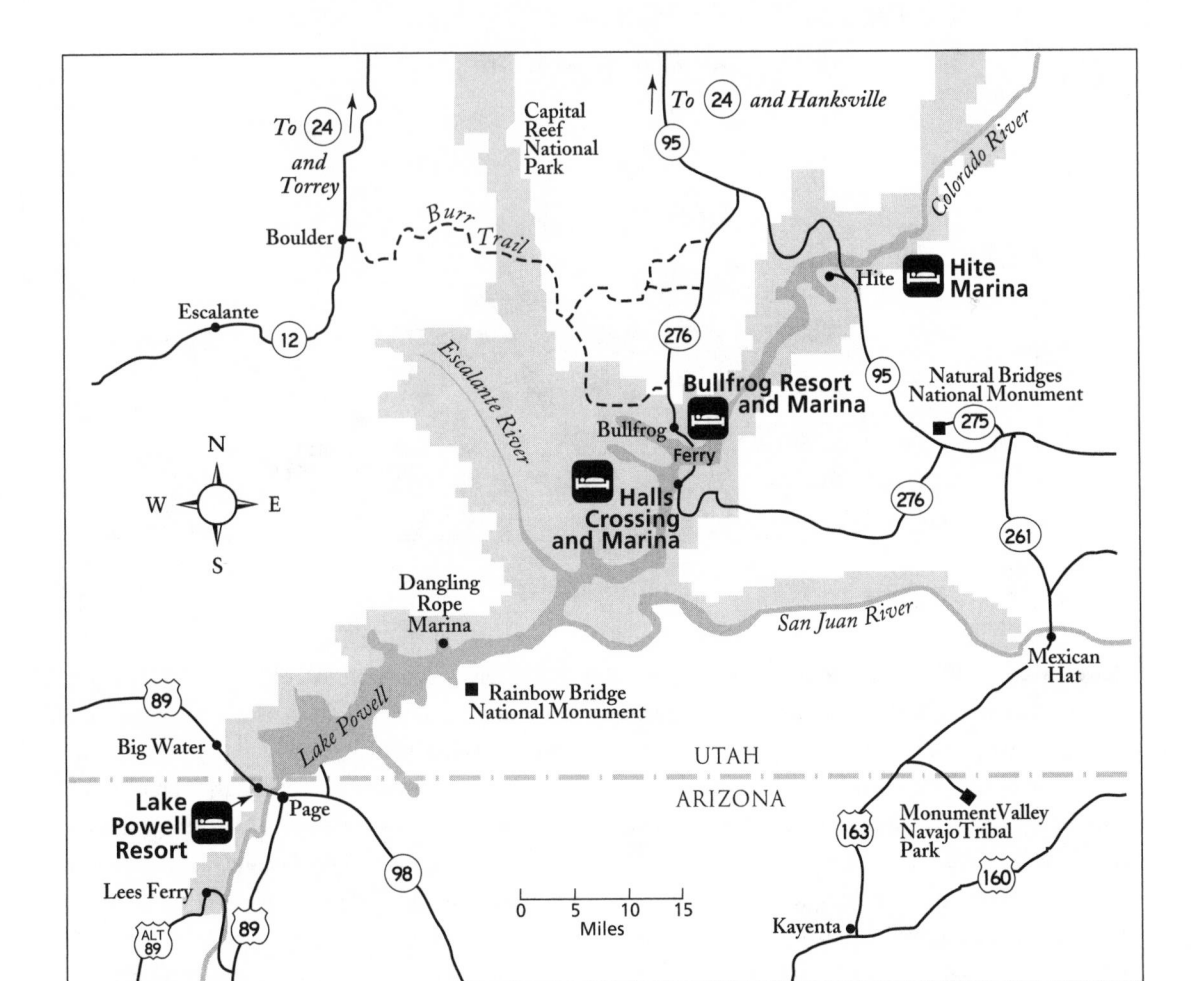

were completely refurbished in 2005 and 2006 with upmarket Southwestern-themed furnishings. These two buildings have superior balconies and patios that allow guests to more easily enjoy a view of the lake and surrounding landscape without standing. The other six buildings have relatively high outside balcony and patio walls that require second-floor guests to stand in order to view the landscape. The lodge offers one first-floor

and three second-floor Lakeview suites, each twice the size of a regular room. The suites include a wet bar, a 32-inch LCD television, and a king bed plus a sofa bed in the sitting room. Two suites each have a wraparound balcony and one has a whirlpool tub.

Lake Powell Resort is an upscale place to spend one or several nights in a scenic lakeside setting. The type of room to choose is best determined by how

Houseboat rentals are big business on Lake Powell, a huge body of water where boaters can wander at leisure and anchor in isolation among some of America's most spectacular landscape of brilliant red canyons, mesas, and buttes. Houseboats ranging from 59 to 75 feet, sleeping from ten to fifteen people, with multiple bedrooms, multiple bathrooms, a complete kitchen with full-size appliances, satellite television, upscale furniture, and a Jacuzzi on the top deck, are available for rent. Two major players in houseboat rentals near Page are Lake Powell Resort and Antelope Point Marina (800–255–5561; antelopepointlakepowell.com). Rentals range from $3,200 for three days to $14,000 for seven days, depending on season and boat size. Ski boats, kayaks, and deck cruisers are also available.

eroded sandstone arch is even more impressive than we imagined. The all-day tour includes a box lunch and narration by the boat captain. Half-day tours to Rainbow Bridge begin in June. Other offerings include a one-and-a-half-hour Antelope Canyon Cruise, a three-hour Navajo Tapestry Cruise, and breakfast and dinner cruises. Boat tour information is available near the resort registration desk.

Rooms: Doubles, triples, and quads. All rooms have private baths with a combination shower-tub.

Wheelchair Accessibility: Twelve wheelchair-accessible rooms (no suites), some Lakeview and some Standard rooms have a wide bathroom door, a roll-in shower or combination shower-tub with grab bars, and a regular door, rather than a sliding door, connecting with the patio.

Reservations: Lake Powell Resorts & Marinas, P.O. Box 56909, Phoenix, AZ 85079. Phone (800) 528-6154 or, from the greater Phoenix area, (602) 278-8888; www.lakepowell .com. A deposit of one night's lodging is required. A cancellation notice of twenty-four hours is required for a refund.

Rates: Peak season: June 1–August 26; Value Season: August 27–September 21 and April 24–June 8; Budget Season: September 22–April 23. Rooms: Standard

you plan to spend your stay. Choose the less-expensive Standard room if you expect to arrive late in the day and leave early in the morning or immediately after a morning boat tour. On the other hand, spend the extra money for a Lakeview or a Deluxe Lakeview room if you will be staying a couple of days and plan to spend time enjoying the patio or balcony. It is best to request a second-floor room that provides better views if you don't mind climbing a flight of stairs. Relaxing on a Deluxe Lakeside balcony with a hot cup of coffee and watching the sun rise over the distant mesa was a high point we experienced during our last stay here.

Lake Powell Resort is a center for water-based recreation, and we suggest you consider at least one boat tour during your stay. The Rainbow Bridge Cruise provides access to the world's largest natural stone bridge at Rainbow Bridge Natural Monument. This giant water-

The stunning landscape surrounding Lake Powell Resort has served as a location for more than forty movies, including 1962's The Greatest Story Ever Told, *starring Charlton Heston, Carroll Baker, Pat Boone, and Jose Ferrer.* Maverick, *with Mel Gibson, Jodie Foster, and James Garner, was filmed here in 1993. Other movies filmed in the Lake Powell area include* Planet of the Apes, Sergeants Three, The Outlaw Josey Wales, Superman III, *and* Anasazi Moon. *John Travolta stayed in Lake Powell Resort suite 274 for a month during the 1995 filming of* Broken Arrow.

($149/$134/$69); Lakeview ($169/$143/$81); Deluxe Lakeview ($189); Suite ($239). Cribs are free and roll-a-ways are available for a fee. Children under eighteen years of age stay free.

Location: Lake Powell Resort is on US 89, 6 miles north of Page, Arizona.

Season: The lodge is open all year.

Food: A full-service restaurant with a tiered circular dining area and wall of windows offers diners a panoramic view of the lake and surrounding countryside. The restaurant serves breakfast ($7.00–$12.00), lunch ($5.00–$9.00), and dinner ($13.00–$30.00). Alcoholic beverages are available in the restaurant and an adjacent lounge that also serves appetizers, salads, and sandwiches ($7.00–$10.00). A coffee bar in the lobby serves gourmet coffee and pastries. A pizzeria with indoor/outdoor dining at the end of the complex serves pizza, pasta, sandwiches, salads, and ice cream from Memorial Day weekend through Labor Day. Room service is available from both the restaurant and pizzeria. The Canyon Princess offers breakfast and dinner cruises April through October depending on demand. Advance reservations are required.

Transportation: Regularly scheduled flights to Page, Arizona, operate from Phoenix. Charter flights are available to other cities within the region. Rental cars are available at the airport. From mid-May through mid-October, the lodge operates scheduled bus service between the lodge and the airport, as well as other destinations in the town of Page. This service is offered "on request" in the off-season. A courtesy shuttle service to various locations around the Lake Powell area is offered year-round to lodge guests.

Facilities: A sport shop (with limited groceries), cocktail lounge, gift shop, gas station, restaurant, pizza parlor, Adventure Cove Beach area, and marina. Two swimming pools, a hot tub, and a fitness room with top-of-the-line equipment and a sauna are at the lodge. A coin-operated laundry is at the nearby campground. Postal service and stamps are available at the marina.

Activities: Swimming (two pools and a beach); walking and hiking; boat rentals (all sizes); waterskiing; fishing; many water tours of from one hour to all day.

Pets: A fee of $10 per night per pet is charged in addition to a $75 deposit.

BULLFROG RESORT AND MARINA

Box 4055 • Lake Powell, UT 84533 • (435) 684-3000

■   ■   ■

Lake Powell was created by the Glen Canyon Dam, which is just south of Lake Powell Resort. The dam backs up the Colorado River for 200 miles and supplies water and electricity to California, Arizona, and Nevada. Concrete for the dam and power plant was poured around the clock for more than three years. Dam tours once offered have been discontinued indefinitely.

■   ■   ■

Bullfrog Resort and Marina offers forty-eight lodge rooms at Defiance House Lodge plus eight family units. The lodge rooms are in a single stucco building that sits atop a high bluff overlooking Bullfrog Bay. Both the building, constructed in the early 1980s, and the rooms within are almost identical in looks and room rates to those in Lake Powell Resort. Eight freestanding prefabricated family units (peak $266; off-peak $214; for one to six persons per unit) each contain three bedrooms, two full baths, a living room, a full kitchen, a microwave, a coffeemaker, a toaster, dishes and utensils for eight people, linens, and a television but no telephone.

A charcoal grill and picnic table area outside each unit. Pay phones are available. All of the units have heat and air-conditioning. The interiors are attractive and nicely furnished.

The resort is located at Bullfrog Basin on Utah Highway 276 on the west side of Lake Powell. A toll ferry at Bullfrog crosses the lake. Bullfrog Resort and Marina offers a restaurant, cocktail lounge, gift shop, liquor store, and gas station. Like the resort, the restaurant is open year-round. It offers cocktails and three meals a day (breakfast is seasonal). A fast-food restaurant at the marina is open from Memorial Day through Labor Day. The marina store sells basic food supplies and beverages. Ranger programs and a medical clinic operate during summer months. A National Park Service visitor center adjacent to the resort contains exhibits concerning the Colorado Plateau and the evolution of Glen Canyon plant and animal life. A concessionaire offers half- and full-day boat tours during the summer. Boat rental is available.

HALLS CROSSING AND MARINA

Box 5101 • Lake Powell, UT 84533 • (435) 684-7000

Halls Crossing and Marina is located on Utah Highway 276 between Blanding and Hanksville. It offers twenty freestanding family units identical to those at Bullfrog Resort and Marina. Halls Crossing and Marina has auto service, a marina, and a store with limited supplies. Boat rentals and tours are offered. A toll ferry provides continuation of UT 276. Transportation is available from a small airport 10 miles from Halls Crossing. Rates are the same as at Bullfrog Resort and Marina.

HITE MARINA

Box 501 • Lake Powell, UT 84533 • (435) 684-2278

Hite Marina is off Utah Highway 95 on the north end of Lake Powell between Blanding and Hanksville. This is the smallest of the four lodging complexes at Lake Powell, offering only five family units that are identical to those at Bullfrog Resort and Marina and Halls Crossing. One family unit is totally wheelchair accessible. Hite offers a gas station, a ranger station, a supply store, and a marina where boats can be rented. Rates for family units are the same as at Bullfrog Resort and Marina.

Grand Canyon National Park

P.O. Box 129 • Grand Canyon, AZ 86023 • (928) 638-7888 • www.nps.gov/grca

Grand Canyon National Park, covering 1,904 square miles, is one of the most popular parks operated by the National Park Service, especially the South Rim section. The Grand Canyon itself is so spectacular that first-time visitors are likely to think they are viewing a painting. The canyon has been created by massive uplift and the cutting effect of the Colorado River, which originates in the Rocky Mountains. The river now flows nearly a mile below the South Rim and even farther below the higher North Rim. Although the developed areas of the North Rim and the South Rim are separated by only about 10 miles, the distance by road is 215 miles. An alternative is the 21-mile Kaibab Trail, which leads from Yaki Point on the South Rim to within 2 miles of Grand Canyon Lodge on the North Rim. A daily shuttle service (fee charged) is offered between the South Rim and the North Rim.

North Rim or South Rim? The two sides of the Grand Canyon are so different that they share little other than the same canyon and river. The more popular South Rim is open year-round and has easier canyon access, more facilities, and many more visitors. The South Rim offers more eating facilities, more stores, more places to walk, and more people to bump into. Vehicles and people are in constant motion. Things seem to move much more slowly at the more isolated North Rim, where services and visitors are limited. The higher elevation of the North Rim results in cooler temperatures and more trees. Vistas from the North Rim seem more intimate, and fewer people will be standing next to you straining for the same view. The North Rim is closed in winter. If you are lucky, you will be able to sample both rims, perhaps on the same trip. **Park Entrance Fee:** $25 per vehicle or $15 per person, good for seven days on both sides of the rim.

Lodging in Grand Canyon National Park: Grand Canyon National Park has eight lodges, six at the popular South Rim, one on the floor of the canyon, and one at the North Rim. Lodging alternatives range from small lodge rooms without a private bath, to historic cabins, to rooms in a classic historical hotel building. Rates also vary a great deal depending on where you decide to stay (or are able to locate a room). The wide variation in accommodations means that you should have a basic understanding of the alternatives when you make your reservations. All the lodges on the South Rim are operated by the same concessionaire, and reservations are made using the same address, telephone number, or Web site. The North Rim lodge is operated by a different concessionaire. The lodges are all very popular, and reservations should, if possible, be made many months in advance. Keep in mind that several motels are a short distance outside the south entrance, which is only 7 miles from Grand Canyon Village and the South Rim.

South Rim (Six Lodges)

Most visitors reach the South Rim of the Grand Canyon via Arizona Highways 180 and 64 from Flagstaff, Arizona. An alternative route via AZ 89 to AZ 64, and the east entrance is longer and slower but offers numerous views of the canyon. The center of activity for the South Rim is Grand Canyon Village, where you will find lodges, cabins, gift shops, restaurants, a large National Park Service visitor center, and the start of numerous tours.

The South Rim has six lodging alternatives (actually eight because two have two separate sections). The classic El Tovar, the most expensive, is directly on the rim and is the South Rim's top-of-the-line hotel. This historic hotel is in an ideal location and offers recently remodeled rooms, but nearby parking is scarce. Next door are Thunderbird and Kachina, two identical lodges with nice rooms. North-facing rooms in both units have terrific canyon views. Bright Angel Lodge offers historic Grand Canyon cabins. Parking can be a problem, but we think Bright Angel's rim cabins with fireplaces may be among the best accommodations on the South Rim. Maswik is a large lodging complex with two very different sections. Both offer plentiful parking and a nearby cafeteria. Maswik North has nice motel-type rooms a moderate walk from the canyon rim. Maswik South has smaller, less expensive but less desirable rooms. Yavapai East offers relatively large rooms, plenty of parking, and proximity to Market Plaza, the South Rim's commercial center. Keep in mind that Yavapai is about a half-mile from the rim and 1 mile from the South Rim's other hotels and restaurants, although a free shuttle offers frequent service. Yavapai West is less expensive and less desirable than Yavapai East.

All of the lodges are served by a free park shuttle system that stops at various points in the village. The main shuttle operates year-round and connects with two other free shuttles that offer service to Hermits Rest on the West Rim and the Kaibab Trailhead on the East Rim. The village area can be quite congested, and it is best to park your vehicle and utilize the shuttle system. A map illustrating the shuttle routes is in the park newspaper provided at the entrance stations.

Reservations: (For South Rim hotels; see North Rim section for Grand Canyon Lodge reservations.) Grand Canyon National Park Lodges, Xanterra Parks and Resorts, 6312 S. Fiddlers Green Circle, Suite 600N, Greenwood Village, CO 80111. Phone (888) 297-2757; fax (303) 297-3175; www.xanterra.com or www.grandcanyonlodges.com. The cost of the first night's lodging is required as a deposit.

Cancellation notice of forty-eight hours is required for a full refund. Reservations may be made up to thirteen months in advance. Try to make reservations six or more months in advance for busy summer months, especially for the popular El Tovar. Space is often available on short notice because of cancellations. For same-day reservations phone (928) 638-2631.

Food: A variety of restaurants and snack bars are scattered around Grand Canyon Village. Inexpensive cafeterias are near the registration areas of Maswik and Yavapai Lodges, while a classy restaurant is in the El Tovar. Excellent steaks are served in the Arizona Room connected to Bright Angel Lodge. The Bright Angel complex also has a nice restaurant and a combination coffee shop/lounge. A deli/bakery and a full-service grocery store are at Market Plaza.

Transportation: Commercial air service is available to Grand Canyon Airport at Tusayan, 6 miles south of Grand Canyon Village. Private taxi service is available from the airport to the South Rim (928-638-6563). Many visitors to the Grand Canyon fly to either Las Vegas or Flagstaff, where rental vehicles are available. Open Road Tours (800-766-7117; www.openroadtours.com) and Flagstaff Express (800-563-1980; www.flagstaffexpress.com) provide daily shuttle service to Grand Canyon Village from both Flagstaff and Phoenix. Amtrak serves Flagstaff and Williams. The Grand Canyon Railroad (800-843-8724) operates between Williams and the historic Santa Fe station at Grand Canyon Village. Trans Canyon (928-638-2820) operates a daily shuttle between the North and South Rims.

Facilities: Grand Canyon Village is truly a village. It includes a full-service grocery and general store, a post office, a full-service bank, a laundry, gift shops, emergency medical and dental services, bookstores, film processing, an ice cream shop, and an array of restaurants. Emergency auto service is available, and gasoline is sold in Tusayan and at Desert View, but not in Grand Canyon Village.

Activities: A variety of activities begin in the village. Narrated motor coach tours of various sites along the South Rim are offered. Additional activities, some of which begin outside the village, include river raft excursions, hiking, mule rides to Plateau Point and to the canyon floor, horseback riding, and helicopter and airplane trips over the canyon. The National Park Service offers programs on the history and geology of the park throughout the day and evening. A fall chamber music festival is offered annually in September. Make the Canyon View Information Plaza an early stop so you can plan your visit.

Grand Canyon National Park

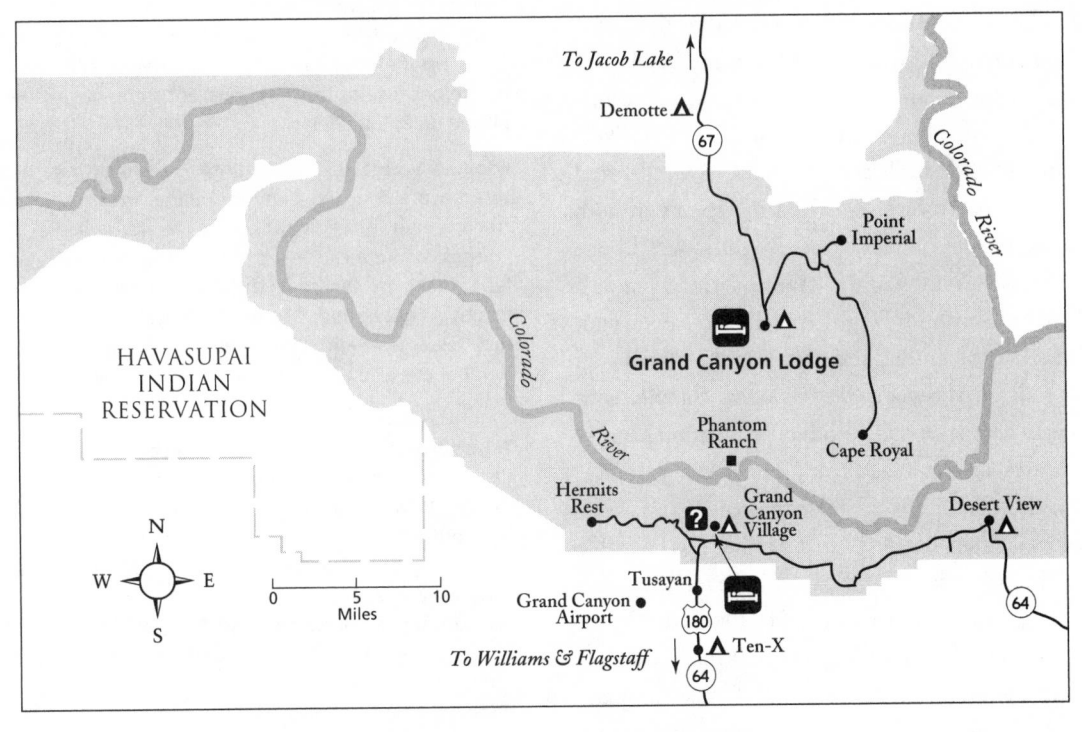

Grand Canyon Village

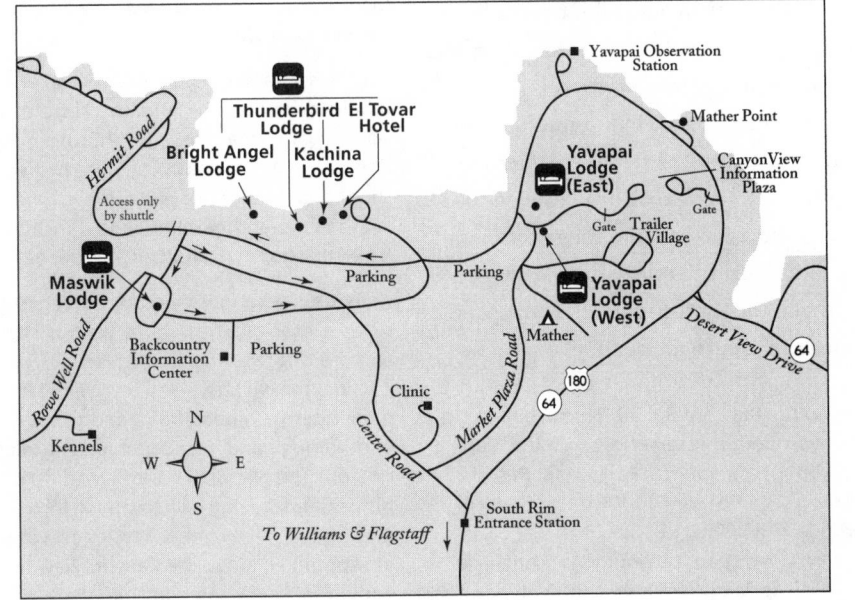

BRIGHT ANGEL LODGE

Bright Angel Lodge is a complex consisting of a main registration building plus eighteen cabins and dormitory-style buildings that provide a total of eighty-nine rooms. The buildings with lodging are separate from but adjacent to the main registration building, which also houses a tour desk, gift shop, coffee shop/lounge, steak house, and restaurant. The complex is at the center of South Rim activity and handy to the other hotels, eating facilities, and gift shops. This area of Grand Canyon Village is very busy with people and traffic, which makes it a hectic setting for individuals and families intent on discovering nature. On the plus side, Bright Angel provides some of the South Rim's least expensive rooms, which were totally remodeled in winter 2007. The remodeling included a refurbishing of the bathrooms with decorative tiles and pedestal sinks. Even with remodeling the cabins retain a flavor of the rim's historic past.

Bright Angel Lodge provides four types of rooms. All have heat but no air-conditioning. The least expensive "standard," or "lodge," rooms are in Powell Lodge and Buckey Lodge, two dormitory-style buildings. Most of the thirty-eight rooms offer one double bed, while five have a double plus a single and two have two double beds. Some of the rooms have a full bath, while others have a shower or tub. Likewise, some have a sink and a toilet, while some have only a sink. Common bath and shower facilities are in the hallway. These rooms are particularly popular with hikers who want a relatively inexpensive place to crash after returning from a trek through the canyon.

■   ■   ■

The oldest surviving structure on the South Rim is Buckey O'Neill's cabin, which was constructed in the early 1890s. O'Neill, a prospector-turned-tourism promoter, was killed in Cuba while serving as a member of Theodore Roosevelt's Rough Riders. The cabin was preserved by Mary Colter, architect of Bright Angel Lodge, who incorporated the structure into her design for one of the lodge buildings. Today the cabin is rented to guests as the "Buckey Suite."

■   ■   ■

One step up are thirty-five rooms in fifteen wooden or wood-and-stucco buildings with vaulted ceilings called historic cabins. Some of these buildings have a single cabin, while others have two, three, or four cabin-style rooms. Although the exteriors are rustic, the interiors are nicely furnished and comfortable. Each of the cabins has a queen bed, ceiling fan, refrigerator, coffeemaker, hair dryer, television, and telephone. Some have a full bath, while others have a shower only. The most expensive historic cabins in Bright Angel are fifteen rim cabins that offer a view of the Grand Canyon. Each of these rooms has a full bath and is situated in several buildings beside a paved walking trail along the rim. Four have gas fireplaces. Two rim cabins with fireplaces, 6151 and 6152, provide an outstanding view of the canyon and are two of our favorite accommodations on the South Rim.

The Bright Angel complex includes three suites. A two-room historic cabin has a living room and a bedroom with two queen beds. The Powell Semi-Suite has two double beds in one room, one double bed in the second room, and a bathroom with a claw-foot tub (no shower) in between. The Buckey Suite is the top of the line and sits on the rim of the canyon. It includes two large rooms, one bedroom with a king bed, and a living room with a large stone gas fireplace. This suite also includes a wet bar and two televisions. This is by far the nicest and most expensive lodging accommodation in Bright Angel and one of the most desirable lodging facilities on the South Rim.

Bright Angel Lodge is a handy location for all the activities and facilities the South Rim offers. Although none of the rooms is directly on the rim and most don't offer a view of it, spectacular vistas of the canyon are only a few steps from any of the buildings. Other dining facilities, including a cafeteria, two restaurants, and the most elegant dining room on the South Rim, are a reasonable walk from any of the rooms at Bright Angel. Parking can be a problem in the busy season, when a relatively large parking lot directly in front of the lodge is packed. Parking spaces scattered among the cabins

■   ■   ■

The original Bright Angel Hotel was constructed in 1895 to serve stagecoach passengers passing through this area. In 1905 the hotel became Bright Angel Camp, which eventually included cabins and an adjoining tent village to serve tourists who were attracted by the canyon's spectacular scenery. In 1935 the Fred Harvey Company replaced the camp with today's Bright Angel Lodge.

■   ■   ■

can generally be counted on to yield a few empty slots, although they may not be directly outside your room.

Rooms: Singles and doubles. One two-room cabin can sleep up to four, and rollaways are available. All but rooms in the two lodge buildings have full private baths. The two lodge buildings with standard rooms have some rooms with private baths. Other rooms use common baths and showers located in the hallway.

Wheelchair Accessibility: Four historic cabins and one rim cabin (with fireplace) are ADA compliant. The registration building, gift shop, and restaurants in this complex are wheelchair accessible.

Rates: Standard rooms ($66–$86); historic cabins ($106); two-room historic cabin ($166); rim cabins ($136–$166); suite ($317). Each additional person is $9.00 per night.

Location: On the South Rim at the center of activity in Grand Canyon Village.

Season: Rooms at Bright Angel Lodge are open year-round.

Food: A full-service restaurant is inside the main registration building and convenient to all the rooms. The restaurant is open for breakfast ($6.00–$12.00), lunch ($8.00–$11.00), and dinner ($11.00–$25.00), and alcoholic beverages are available. The coffee shop/lounge offers specialty coffees and continental breakfast items beginning at 5:30 a.m. Appetizers are available after 11:00 a.m. The Bright Angel Fountain, open May through September (10:00 a.m.–6:00 p.m.), directly outside the registration building, offers sandwiches, soft drinks, and ice cream. The Arizona Room, offering steaks, poultry, and fish, is attached to the east end of the Bright Angel registration building. It is open for lunch ($8.00–$13.00) and dinner ($16.00–$26.00).

EL TOVAR HOTEL

El Tovar is the regal hotel of the Grand Canyon's South Rim. Constructed in 1905 by the Santa Fe Railroad to promote the firm's transportation services, the hotel was named after Spanish explorer Pedro de Tovar, who led a 1540 expedition to this area. El Tovar is the type of hotel most people envision when they think about a national park lodge. It is a single large wood-and-stone four-story structure that commands a hilltop vista on the canyon rim. The two-story lobby area is complete with log beams, a large stone fireplace, and comfortable sofas and chairs for chatting with other guests. Several verandas and a large covered front porch have chairs for relaxing in the early morning or after dinner or an evening walk. A nice mezzanine with an overlook of the lobby area has tables, stuffed chairs, a television, and a piano. Complimentary coffee and tea are provided here each morning for hotel guests. No elevators are in the building, but bell service is available to assist with luggage. A circular drive directly in front of the hotel entrance can be used for registration and baggage drop-off, but parking near the hotel is very limited.

El Tovar offers seventy-eight rooms in five classifications. Like many historic hotels, rooms in the same classification have different sizes and shapes. An extensive 2005 renovation included new carpeting, furnishings, decorations, and bathroom fixtures. All of

The El Tovar has welcomed many famous guests, including Paul McCartney, who visited the hotel in the fall of 2001. With his room booked under a company name, the former Beatle spent the first night on the third floor in room 6474. The hotel upgraded him to the El Tovar Suite for the second and last night of his stay. One evening McCartney began playing the piano on the mezzanine until other guests, unaware the famous singer/songwriter was staying at the hotel, complained to the front desk about the noise. Instructed not to reveal that Mr. McCartney was staying at the El Tovar, employees were forced to ask that the famous musician stop playing. If the other guests had only known.

the rooms are attractively decorated and have heat, air-conditioning, a refrigerator, a coffeemaker, a telephone, a CD player/radio, a television, and a hair dryer. Although a number of rooms provide good window views, the siting of the hotel results in only a few rooms having an excellent view of the Grand Canyon. The least expensive lodging at El Tovar is a standard double with one double bed in a relatively small room. Standard queen rooms are also generally small but offer a variety of beds that includes one queen, one king, two doubles, and two queens. Deluxe rooms are larger and offer either a king or two queen-size beds with a small sitting area. Two deluxe rooms, 6463 and 6465, have small balconies with chairs. Suites in the El Tovar are named and decorated to a particular theme. For example, the Zane Grey Suite is decorated western style with movie posters, several of the author's books, and framed first edition book jackets. All of the twelve suites have a bedroom with either a king or two queen beds, a sitting room with chairs and a couch (some convert into a bed), a full bath, and a dressing area. Four view suites each offer stunning canyon views and have a large porch with tables and chairs. The two third-floor view suites are smaller but offer more privacy from their porches than the two second-floor view suites. Eight nonview suites on the south end of the hotel rent for slightly less than view suites. Four nonview suites have a porch and two have a Jacuzzi (the Roof Garden Suite has both). Porches off the nonview suites offer some views of the canyon, but not on the same scale as the more expensive view suites.

El Tovar provides most of the things you will want or need during a trip to the Grand Canyon. The ground floor has gift shops, a lounge, and the elegant El Tovar dining room, which offers an extensive menu in a formal setting. The dining room looks like it belongs in a national park. Murals on the walls reflect different Indian tribes, and a number of tables offer diners a view of the rim. A small private dining room that holds up to ten persons is available at no charge with a seventy-two-hour advance reservation. The lounge has a bar and windows that overlook the canyon. Travel information is available, and tours can be booked at a small tour desk in the lobby across from the registration desk. Service at El Tovar is a cut above that found at other lodging facilities at the Grand Canyon. For example, room service is available from the El Tovar dining room, and mints are placed on your bed each evening.

El Tovar, built at a cost of $250,000, was to be a first-rate lodging facility, and at its completion, in 1905, many considered it to be the most elegant hotel west of the Mississippi. Designed as a cross between a Swiss chalet and a Norwegian villa, the hotel was constructed of stone and Oregon pine. The building was equipped with a coal-fired steam generator to provide electric lighting, and Santa Fe railroad tank cars brought fresh water from a distance of 120 miles. Water from the tank cars was pumped into a large metal container in the El Tovar's famous cupelo, where gravity feed brought it to the rooms. Hens raised here supplied fresh eggs, and a dairy herd provided milk. Fresh fruit and vegetables were grown in greenhouses on the premises.

Rooms: Singles, doubles, triples, and quads. Some suites can sleep up to six, and rollaways are available. All rooms have full baths.

Wheelchair Accessibility: Two rooms on the first floor, one with a king bed and the other with two queen beds, are ADA compliant, with a combination shower-tub. The El Tovar restaurant is also wheelchair accessible.

Rates: Standard double ($166); standard queen ($196); deluxe ($256); suites (nonview $306–$356; view $406). Rates quoted are for two adults. Each additional person is $14 per night.

Location: Center of Grand Canyon Village, directly east of Kachina Lodge and just up the hill from the historic train depot.

Season: El Tovar Hotel is open year-round.

Food: A first-class dining room off the hotel's lobby serves breakfast ($9.00–$14.00), lunch ($8.00–$19.00), and dinner ($20.00–$33.00). Alcoholic beverages are available, and reservations are recommended for dinner. A lounge offering appetizers is open from 11:00 a.m. to 11:00 p.m. Other less expensive food service is within easy walking distance.

KACHINA LODGE/THUNDERBIRD LODGE

Kachina Lodge and Thunderbird Lodge are two virtually identical facilities that sit side by side on the South Rim of Grand Canyon Village between El Tovar Hotel and Bright Angel Lodge. The two-story stone buildings house a total of 104 rooms that, other than the view they provide, are identical. Approximately half the rooms face the rim, while the remainder face the road and parking lot. No registration facilities are in either of the lodges. Registration for Kachina Lodge is at the registration desk of El Tovar Hotel, and registration for Thunderbird Lodge is at the registration desk in the main building of Bright Angel Lodge.

The exteriors of Kachina and Thunderbird resemble upscale college dormitories, but the interiors with Southwestern decor have the appearance of fashionable hotel rooms. Each room has electric heat, a small refrigerator, a coffeemaker, a hair dryer, a CD player/radio, a television, and a full tiled bath. In addition, each building offers an evaporative cooling system with individual room controls. Most rooms have two queen beds, while a few offer one king bed. Rollaways are available but result in a crowded room. Rim-view rooms in both buildings rent for an extra $10 per day and are worth the additional cost. Two medium-size conference rooms in Thunderbird can be reserved.

Thunderbird and Kachina Lodges are in a convenient location at the center of South Rim activity. The central location results in insufficient parking during the busy summer season. No information desk or commercial facilities are in either building, but food service, gift shops, and anything else offered at the South Rim are just a short walk from any of the rooms at these two lodges. If you plan to stay at one of these two lodges, our choice would be a second-floor rim-view room in Kachina.

Rooms: Singles, doubles, triples, and quads. All rooms have full baths.

Wheelchair Accessibility: Two rooms in Thunderbird are ADA compliant and have roll-in showers. Two rooms in Kachina are ADA compliant with combination shower-tubs.

Rates: Park-side (nonview) rooms ($162); Canyon-side rooms ($172). An extra $9.00 per person per night is charged for more than two persons.

Location: On the Rim between El Tovar Hotel and Bright Angel Lodge.

Season: All rooms are available year-round.

Food: No eating facilities are available in either building. Restaurants and cafeterias are within easy walking distance.

MASWIK LODGE

Maswik Lodge (named for a Hopi kachina who guards the Grand Canyon) is a lodging complex of modern apartment-type buildings and older cabins that provide 278 rooms in two large areas on each side of a centrally located registration building. Maswik buildings with

■　　■　　　■

Grand Canyon Railway operates a vintage train that offers year-round daily service between Williams, Arizona, and Grand Canyon Village. The 62-mile trip (one way) from Williams to the canyon takes two and a quarter hours, with departure in the morning. Tours from Grand Canyon Village allow visitors to travel one way in a motorcoach and return on the train. Six classes of service, from coach ($65 round-trip) to a parlor car ($170 round-trip), are available. The railway offers package plans that include overnight accommodations and some meals. For information or reservations call (800) 843-8724 or visit www.thetrain.com.

■　　■　　　■

accommodations are clustered around the main lodge building that houses the registration desk, cafeteria, gift shop, sports lounge, and tour desk. All of the rooms and cabins at Maswik have heat, a telephone, a television, and convenient parking.

Maswik North, the section of this complex nearest the canyon rim, underwent an extensive renovation in 2006. These units each have air-conditioning, a refrigerator, a coffeemaker, a hair dryer, and a full bathroom with a combination shower-tub, and offer the largest, nicest, and most expensive rooms in Maswik. Rooms have either two queen beds or one king bed. The rooms are in a cluster of twelve attractive wooden and stone buildings. Most of the structures are two-story buildings (no elevators) typical of an upscale apartment complex. Most rooms run the depth of the building with a front window and either a window or a sliding glass door in back. Those with a sliding door have either a balcony or a patio. Eight end rooms are larger than average but rent for the same price as the other rooms in this section. The larger rooms include 6803 through 6806 and 6831 through 6834. Try for a larger room or, failing this, a room with a balcony or patio if you will be staying in Maswik North.

■   ■   ■

Many visitors to the Grand Canyon try a mule ride to the bottom of the canyon, where the views are spectacular and the temperature is considerably warmer than on the rim. Those with limited time are likely to choose the 12-mile, seven-hour round-trip to Plateau Point, 3,200 feet below the rim and 1,300 feet above the Colorado River. A lunch is included. More adventurous souls may prefer the two-day round-trip to Phantom Ranch on the canyon's bottom. The 10-mile ride down Bright Angel Trail takes five and a half hours. After an overnight at Phantom Ranch, the four-and-a-half-hour return trip follows the South Kaibab Trail. Advance reservations are required for mule trips and stays at Phantom Ranch. For information and reservations call (928) 638-2631.

■   ■   ■

Maswik South comprises six two-story, motel-type buildings (no elevators) at the end of the complex most distant from the rim. These relatively small rooms, renovated in 2001 and 2002, have two queen-size beds, a refrigerator, a coffeemaker, a hair dryer, a wall fan, and a full bathroom with a combination shower-tub, but no balcony or rear window. They rent for considerably less than the more spacious rooms in Maswik North. The Maswik complex also includes seven quad-style cabin buildings that house a total of twenty-eight rooms, each with a vaulted ceiling, bathroom with a tiled shower, two double beds, and a ceiling fan. The cabin interiors were totally remodeled in 2004 and offer some of the least expensive housing on the South Rim. Cabins with two queen beds are somewhat larger but rent for the same price as cabins with two full beds.

The lodge's location on the west side of the village, across the main road from the rim, is relatively peaceful. Staying in Maswik allows you to avoid the hustle and bustle of vehicles and crowds that roam over the rim area and yet remain within easy walking distance of the rim and most facilities in Grand Canyon Village. Of course, you are unable to view the Grand Canyon from the window of your room, but the same disadvantage exists with many rooms in other complexes closer to the rim. Maswik offers plentiful parking, a considerable advantage if you are driving, because other areas of the village are often very crowded.

Rooms: Singles, doubles, triples, and quads. Rollaways are available for all rooms except cabins. All rooms have private baths, most with a combination shower-tub.

Wheelchair Accessibility: ADA-compliant rooms are available in both Maswik North and Maswik South, but not the cabins. Two units at Maswik North have roll-in showers. The registration building housing the cafeteria and gift shop is wheelchair accessible.

Rates: Cabins ($86); South Unit ($86); North Unit ($162). Additional person: $9.00. Children sixteen and under stay free with an adult.

Location: West side of Grand Canyon Village, approximately a quarter-mile from the canyon rim.

Season: All rooms except for cabins (closed in winter) are open year-round.

Food: An attractive full-service cafeteria in the registration building serves a full breakfast ($5.00–$7.00), while lunch and dinner ($7.00–$9.00) offerings include Mexican dishes, hot and cold sandwiches, home-style meals, soups, salads, beer, wine, and ice cream. The cafeteria is within easy walking distance of all Maswik rooms. Additional dining facilities on the rim are also within walking distance of Maswik.

YAVAPAI LODGE

Yavapai Lodge is a complex of sixteen buildings a distance from a separate registration building that houses a gift shop and large cafeteria. Yavapai Lodge is located on the east side of Grand Canyon Village near Market Plaza. It is located about halfway between Yavapai Point and the rim hotels. It is a moderate walk from the rim of the Grand Canyon. Although the lodge is not in the center of Grand Canyon Village activity, free shuttle transportation to various points in the village is available.

Yavapai Lodge, with 358 rooms, is the largest lodging complex in Grand Canyon National Park. The facility is divided into two separate complexes containing very different styles of buildings. The newest (constructed in the mid-1970s) and slightly more expensive rooms are in Yavapai East. Six two-story wooden buildings (no elevators) each contain thirty-three spacious rooms that were renovated in 2003, have a king or two queen beds, a telephone, a television, a full bath, heat, air-conditioning, a small refrigerator, and a coffeemaker. The buildings have an outside staircase leading to an inside corridor with access to the rooms. A large window in each room provides a nice view of the pine and juniper woodlands in which the buildings sit. None of the rooms has a balcony or patio. The buildings, which

sit well back from large parking areas, have the appearance of a nice apartment complex.

Ten buildings in less-expensive Yavapai West were constructed in the late 1960s and remodeled in 2002. These one-story brick buildings have the appearance of a motel, but the remodeled interiors are quite attractive.

■   ■   ■

At the bottom of Grand Canyon, Phantom Ranch provides food and overnight accommodations for hikers, rafters, and mule riders. Cabin accommodations are included with two-day mule tours, while dormitory-style lodging and a limited number of cabins are available to backpackers. The ranch was originally constructed in 1922, and dormitories were added in 1976. Space is limited, so plan to make reservations (phone 888-297-2757; fax 303-297-3175) well in advance for both lodging and food service. Reservations are accepted up to one year in advance.

■   ■   ■

Each room has a full bath, heat, two queen beds, a telephone, a television, and a ceiling fan. The rooms are smaller than the rooms in Yavapai East. Plenty of parking is in front of each structure, and the buildings are widely spaced in two large circles and surrounded by woodlands. Rooms are accessed via a front door that faces the parking lot. Rooms in buildings 1 through 6 have front windows only, which seem to result in a darker interior. The rooms in buildings 7 through 10 have back windows that provide more light and a pleasant outside view.

Yavapai is convenient to the Canyon View Information Plaza and to Market Plaza, a large commercial complex with a post office, a bank, and a general store with a large grocery selection. Meals are available at a cafeteria connected to the registration building and at a deli/bakery in the general store. The major downside of staying at Yavapai is that the distance from rim facilities will require you to take the shuttle or walk a considerable distance each time you visit the main area of the village. If you stay in Yavapai East, try to get into one of the first two buildings that are nearest Market Plaza and the shuttle stop.

Rooms: Doubles, triples, and quads. Rollaways are available. All rooms have a full bath.

Wheelchair Accessibility: Yavapai East has four first-floor rooms that are ADA compliant. Two have roll-in showers. The cafeteria and store are wheelchair accessible.

Rates: Yavapai East ($146); Yavapai West ($102). Rates quoted are for two adults. Each additional person is $9.00 per night. Children sixteen and under stay free with an adult.

Location: On the east side of Grand Canyon Village, across from Market Plaza.

Season: Yavapai Lodge is open from mid-March through November. Rooms are also available seasonally at Thanksgiving and Christmas.

Food: A large and attractive cafeteria connected to the registration building serves breakfast ($3.00–$7.50), lunch/dinner ($4.00–$8.00). Food selections include salads, pasta, pizza, hamburgers, and chicken. Beer and wine are available. The general store has a deli/bakery that serves bakery items, soups, salads, pizza, and large sandwiches. A large selection of grocery items, beer, wine, and other alcoholic beverages is available in the general store.

■   ■   ■

Many visitors to Grand Canyon National Park decide to take an air tour of the canyon. Several airline and helicopter companies in the town of Tusayan and at the Grand Canyon Airport offer scenic flights over the canyon. The helicopter tours are generally shorter and somewhat more expensive than flights in fixed-wing aircraft but add extra excitement to the trip. Most firms offer several types of tours of various lengths. Any of the tours presents a very different perspective of the Grand Canyon. Prices begin at about $90 per person.

■   ■   ■

NORTH RIM

Visiting the North Rim of Grand Canyon National Park is an entirely different experience compared with a visit to the South Rim. You will actually feel you are in a different park, except, of course, for the Grand Canyon itself, which is the common thread dividing these two areas. With fewer visitors, the North Rim provides fewer facilities and a relatively short season. It is more relaxing to visit than the South Rim. The North Rim offers only a single lodge in which to stay and the facilities are operated by a different concessionaire than South Rim facilities. Staying on both rims will require separate reservations.

Grand Canyon Lodge

North Rim, AZ 86052 • (928) 638-2611 • www.grandcanyonforever.com

Grand Canyon Lodge is the only lodging facility at Grand Canyon National Park's North Rim. The lodge consists of a classic main lodge building that houses the registration desk, lobby, and dining room and more than one hundred cabin units scattered along a peninsula of the Kaibab Plateau. The peninsula is surrounded by two spectacular canyons that snake off the Grand Canyon, which can be viewed at the tip of the peninsula. All of the rooms are in buildings that are separate from, but within walking distance of, the main lodge, which itself has no overnight rooms. The lodge is at the end of Arizona Highway 67, which leads into the park from Jacob Lake.

The main lodge building at the North Rim was constructed in 1936, after the original lodge burned. It is what every national park lodge should look like. It was designed by Gilbert Stanley Underwood, who also served as architect for the Ahwahnee at Yosemite National Park and the lodge at Bryce Canyon National Park. The U-shaped building is constructed of massive limestone walls and timber beams and is situated on the canyon rim near Bright Angel Point. Large windows in the spectacular high–ceilinged dining room offer diners scenic vistas of the canyon. A large sunroom just off the registration area provides canyon views through three huge windows. A veranda next to the sunroom allows guests a place to enjoy equally spectacular views from wooden chairs and benches. The building has two huge stone fireplaces, one in the sunroom and the other outside on the veranda. The lodge also houses a tour desk, deli, gift shop, post office, and coffee shop/saloon.

More than a hundred rustic log cabins constructed in the 1920s provide the majority of the 218 rooms for visitors to the North Rim. Forty rooms are in two motel-style buildings. The four basic types of rooms each have heat, a telephone, a private bath, and carpeted floors, but no air-conditioning (you don't need it) or television. Fifty-six Western Cabins, by far the largest and nicest accommodations on the North Rim, are constructed either two or four to a building and were refurbished from 2000 to 2003. Each Western Cabin has a finished interior, a vaulted log-beam ceiling, and a private front porch with rocking chairs. These cabins have two queen beds, a full tiled bath with a combination shower-tub, a small dressing area, a small refrigerator, a coffeemaker, a hair dryer, and a gas fireplace. Four of the Western Cabins sit directly on the North Rim and rent for about $10 extra per day. Western Cabins 310, 320, and 332 offer a nice view and rent for the regular rate.

Eighty-three Frontier Cabins are constructed two units to a building. Each Frontier Cabin has one double and one single bed and a bath with a shower only. These cabins have an unfinished log interior, including a vaulted log ceiling, and are relatively small, so that the beds consume most of the interior space. The bathroom is also quite small. Thirty-nine Pioneer Cabins each have two bedrooms, one on each side of a central bathroom with a shower, toilet, and sink. One bedroom has two single beds plus a sink, and the other bedroom has a double and a single bed. The Pioneer Cabins farthest from the road (and parking) offer the best views. These are classified as Pioneer Rim Cabins and cost $10 extra per night compared to other Pioneer Cabins. A disadvantage of Frontier and Pioneer Cabins is neither has a porch or chairs where you can sit outside and read, relax, or visit with other guests.

Two motel-type buildings with forty rooms sit farthest from the main lodge and dining room. The rooms in each building back up to one another and are entered from an outside door. The room has a small front window and an outside bench beside the door. Each motel room has a queen bed, ceiling fan, hair dryer, coffeemaker, sink in the room, and small bathroom with a toilet and shower. These rooms are of modest size with a small front window and a relatively dark interior. Rooms on the back side (410 through 420 and 431 through 440) provide the best views. Rooms 415, 416, 432, and 433 sit on the back side and are considerably larger than other rooms in these two buildings. End rooms 400, 409, 410, 420, 421, 430, 431, and 440 have

◾   ◾   ◾

Construction of the original Grand Lodge using Mormon craftsmen from surrounding towns began in 1927. The two-story lodge was completed at a cost of $350,000 in June 1928 and dedicated three months later. One year later the rustic North Rim Inn was constructed 1 mile north to offer less expensive accommodations. The second inn is now utilized as the camp store. Grand Lodge burned in September 1932, and construction of the current one-story lodge commenced on the same site in June 1936. It was completed one year later. Pictures of the original Grand Lodge are in the lodge Sunroom. Only a couple of cabins were lost to the fire. The current motel units were built later in order to serve as employee housing. Interior corridors were later changed into small bathrooms when it was decided to convert employee housing into guest lodging.

◾   ◾   ◾

windows on two sides and provide for a brighter interior. These rooms are also a little larger than most other rooms in these buildings. Rooms in the motel units are larger than the Frontier Cabins.

The Western Cabins are by far the nicest and best value of all the rooms offered at Grand Canyon Lodge. They rent for more than the Frontier Cabins and motel units but offer more room, more privacy, nicer furnishings, and a better location. They are also the units in greatest demand, so reservations for Western Cabins should be made early. The four Western Cabins on the rim are usually reserved 13 months in advance. The Pioneer Cabins offer two bedrooms and are priced for four people. Thus, these cabins may offer the best value for families with children.

Most of the lodging units are some distance from parking. Getting to the motel units involves descending forty-five steps from the parking lot to the building. In addition, visitors (other than handicapped) are not permitted to drive to the main lodge that houses the registration desk. You should park in any open spot, walk down the road to the main lodge, and check in at the registration desk before removing any luggage from your vehicle. Once you determine the location of your assigned unit you may want to move your vehicle to a different parking place closer to where you will be staying. Porters are available to help with luggage.

The North Rim of the Grand Canyon is a special place. It is isolated, intimate, and unique. You may know of many friends who have visited the Grand Canyon, but how many have visited the North Rim? Staying on the rim will enhance the enjoyment of your visit. The facilities are old, historic, and a fun place to stay. The beauty of the lodge's dining room is surpassed only by that in Yosemite's Ahwahnee. On several mornings we have risen early, fixed a cup of coffee, and walked to the veranda to watch the sun rise over the canyon. Each time there were no more than half a dozen people with whom to share such a special experience.

Rooms: Doubles, triples, and quads in the Western Cabins. Doubles and triples in the Frontier Cabins. Pioneer Cabins can sleep up to five. Doubles only in the motel units. Rollaways are available for the Western Cabins and some motel units. All rooms have a private bath, although only Western Cabins offer a combination shower-tub.

Wheelchair Accessibility: Four Western Cabins with one queen bed offer ramp access, wide bathroom doorways, and bathroom grab bars. These units have either a combination shower-tub or a roll-in shower. All four units are some distance from disabled parking. Two Frontier Cabins with one queen bed have ramp access and grab bars in a bathroom with a shower. The main lodge building and restaurant are wheelchair accessible with lifts that have been installed.

Reservations: Forever Resorts, 7501 E. McCormick Parkway, Scottsdale, AZ 85258. Phone (877) 386-4383 or visit www .grandcanyonforever.com. Cancellations must be made at

least forty-eight hours prior to scheduled arrival for a full refund.

Rates: Western Cabins ($147); Western Rim Cabins ($157); motel units ($108). Western Cabin and motel unit rates are quoted for two adults. Frontier Cabins for up to three people ($112); Pioneer Cabins for up to four people ($120). Each additional person is $10 per night. Children sixteen and under stay free. Rollaways in Western Cabins and some motel rooms are $10.

Location: Forty miles south on AZ 67 from the town of Jacob Lake, Arizona.

Season: The lodge is open from mid-May to mid-October.

Food: An excellent restaurant with spectacular views offers three meals a day. Breakfast ($6.00 to $11.00 with a buffet available most mornings), lunch ($6.00 to $12.00), and dinner ($10.00 to $27.00). Mixed drinks, beer, and an extensive wine list are available. An evening Grand Canyon Cookout Experience ($35 per adult) offers guests a chance to ride a tram to Outfitter Station, where they enjoy entertainment and barbeque-style food. The deli serves breakfast each day from 7:00 to 10:30 a.m. and salads, sandwiches, pasta, pizza, ice cream, and beverages the rest of the day until closing at 9:00 p.m. The saloon offers gourmet coffee and fresh-baked rolls each morning beginning at 5:30 a.m. Alcoholic beverages are served in the saloon beginning at 11:30 a.m. A limited selection of groceries, prepackaged sandwiches, and beverages are in the general store at the campground 1 mile away. A microwave is available for heating frozen and canned goods purchased in the store.

Transportation: Scheduled air service is available to Kanab, Utah, and Page, Arizona, where rental cars are available. A daily shuttle (fee charged) is offered between the North Rim and the South Rim.

Facilities: A gift shop, information desk, post office, full-service restaurant, coffee shop/saloon, and deli are at the main lodge. A general store, bike rentals, laundry facilities, and combination gas-outfitters station are 1 mile north at the campground.

Activities: Hiking, mule rides, bicycling, horse rides, evening interpretive programs, and guided hikes and nature walks. Several short- and intermediate-length trails originate near the lodge. Information about horse and mule rides is available by calling (435) 679-8665 or visiting www.canyonrides .com.

ARKANSAS

■ **State Tourist Information**
(800) 628-8725 | www.arkansas.com

Buffalo National River

402 North Walnut, Suite 136 • Harrison, AR 72601 • (870) 741-5443
www.nps.gov/buff

Buffalo National River is one of the most scenic, unpolluted, and undeveloped free-flowing rivers remaining in the lower forty-eight states. The 135-mile river flows eastward through forested hill country dominated by oaks and hickories. The river is especially popular for canoeing or floating. The park is located in northwestern Arkansas in the Ozarks, across a three-county area. The nearest sizable community is Harrison, Arkansas.

Lodging at Buffalo National River: A single lodging facility is inside the river boundaries operated by the National Park Service. Buffalo Point Concessions offers cabins and a restaurant at Buffalo Point, 20 miles south of Yellville via Arkansas Highway 14 and an access road. Additional lodging facilities are in the area surrounding Yellville.

Buffalo National River

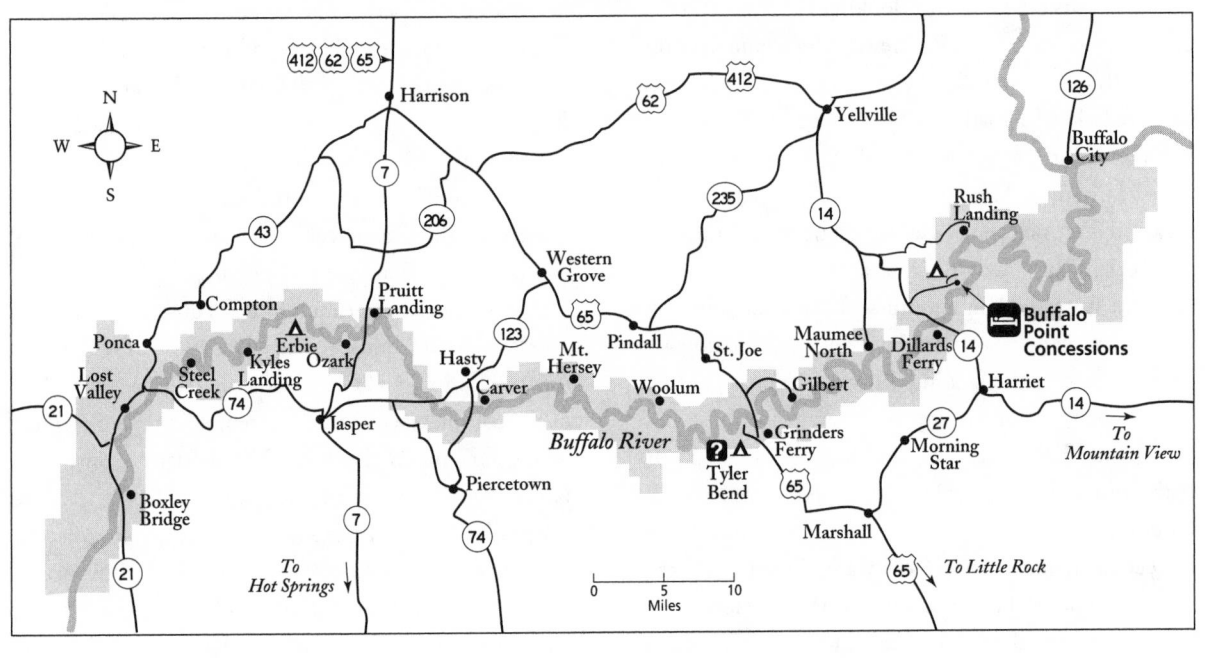

BUFFALO POINT CONCESSIONS

2261 Highway 268 East • Yellville, AR 72687 • (870) 449-6206 • www.buffalopoint.com

Buffalo Point is a relatively small lodging complex comprised of an office building, a restaurant, and ten wooden structures offering a total of seventeen cabins and lodge rooms. The complex is on a high ridge about a mile and a half from the Buffalo National River. The restaurant sits on a bluff overlooking the river, and diners are treated to a stunning view of the scenic river that snakes through the valley below. The lodging units are scattered along a road in a heavily wooded area. Four lodge units and two modern cabins offer an excellent view of the river. The other units back up to a wooded area and offer no direct river view. The restaurant, open Memorial Day to Labor Day, is a short drive or moderate walk from the lodging units. A National Park Service visitor center with exhibits and information is a short walk from the lodging office.

Three types of lodging units are available at Buffalo Point. Each has air-conditioning and a private bathroom with a shower but no tub. All units also offer a full kitchen with refrigerator, oven, stove, microwave, coffeemaker, and toaster. Cookware, dishes, and utensils are supplied. The units do not have a television or telephone, but cell phones work in this area. A picnic table and grill are outside each unit. The units vary in size, but each is set up to sleep from four to six people.

Five freestanding rustic cabins with wooden floors and beamed ceilings were built by the Civilian Conservation Corps (CCC) in the 1940s. Each of these cabins has a large screened porch with two single beds, a separate bedroom with a full bed, and a large living area with a full bed, table, and chairs. These are the only cabins at Buffalo Point with a fireplace (firewood provided without charge), which serves as the only source of heat. The rustic cabins are nearest the office but most distant from the restaurant. Rustic cabin 1 offers the most privacy and is our choice among these units.

Eight modern cabins were constructed in the 1960s as duplex units in four wooden buildings. Three of the buildings sit side-by-side on a hill in the middle of the complex, while the fourth building sits on a bluff at the far end of the road. The modern cabins have larger windows with brighter interiors than the rustic cabins. Each modern cabin has wooden floors, electric heat, a separate bedroom with a full bed, and a living area with a full bed, a futon, a table, chairs, and a nice back deck. Ample space is available in the living area

The last of the six rustic cabins at Buffalo Point constructed by the Civilian Conservation Corps (CCC) were completed in 1942 as part of Buffalo River State Park. CCC workers quarried the rock, finished the lumber, and crafted the furniture used in the construction. The cabins that retain their original design and most of the original material were placed on the National Register of Historic Places in 1988. Cabin 1, completed in 1940, is the only one of the six rustic cabins that was built using log construction.

for the rollaway kept in a closet. Especially popular are cabins 13 and 14 with decks that provide a spectacular view of the Buffalo River. These two units are within easy walking distance of the restaurant.

The least expensive lodging units at Buffalo Point are four lodge rooms that are in a CCC–constructed building that sits on a bluff above the river. They are smaller in size than the cabins and do not have a separate bedroom. Each lodge unit has a kitchen, electric heat, a double bed, a futon, a table with chairs, and a shared deck that spans the back of the building. The two end units, A and D, are considerably larger, have brighter interiors (due to a side window), and rent for the same price as units B and C. The four lodge units offer good river views and are close to the restaurant.

Buffalo Point is in a rural setting that offers nature, solitude, a beautiful river, dining at inexpensive prices, and friendly people. We would choose modern cabin units 13 or 14 for a party of three or more people. The view from the deck is outstanding, and the more isolated location at the end of the road offers more privacy than other units in the complex. One person or a couple might consider lodge units A or D that offer good

river views and are a little less expensive than the rustic or modern cabins. If an indoor fireplace is important, choose one of the rustic cabins, preferably cabin unit 1 if it is available. Our last choice would be lodge units B and C that have small, dark interiors. Don't forget to bring a book, some hiking shoes, and a canoe to paddle along one of America's most scenic rivers. Canoe rentals are available just outside the park.

Rooms: Lodge units can accommodate two occupants, while each cabin can hold four to six people. All units have a private bath with a shower but no tub. Each of the units also has a full kitchen with utensils supplied.

Wheelchair Accessibility: One modern cabin is fully wheelchair accessible with wide doorways and lowered counters. It has a bathroom that is also fully wheelchair accessible.

Reservations: Buffalo Point Concessions, 2261 Highway 268 E., Yellville, AR 72687. Phone (870) 449-6206. One night deposit required. Twenty days' cancellation notice required for a refund.

Rates: Rustic cabins ($86); modern cabins ($86); lodge units ($70). Rates are quoted for two adults. Extra persons are $5.00 each. Children four years and younger are free. Rates are reduced during the winter season.

Location: Twenty miles south of Yellville, Arkansas, on Arkansas Highway 14 and a paved access road.

Season: Four modern cabins, including those with a river view, are open year-round. The other cabins are open from mid-March through November.

Food: A full-service restaurant serves breakfast ($4.00–$6.00), lunch ($4.00–$5.00), and dinner ($7.00–$13.00) from Memorial Day weekend through Labor Day. Meals are inexpensive. Groceries and restaurants are available in Yellville. No alcoholic drinks are available at Buffalo Point.

Transportation: The nearest scheduled airline service is in Harrison, approximately 50 miles from Buffalo Point.

Facilities: Restaurant, National Park Service visitor center, pay phone at NPS visitor center.

Activities: Hiking, canoeing, horseback riding, guided hunting and fishing trips. Ranger-led walks and programs are held daily during the summer. The old mining town of Rush is nearby and can be accessed via automobile.

CALIFORNIA

Death Valley National Park

P.O. Box 579 • Death Valley, CA 92328 • (760) 786-3200 • www.nps.gov/deva/

Death Valley National Park comprises 3.3 million acres of harsh desert environment that includes the lowest point in North America. The park features a desert mansion, ruins of old mining towns, abandoned borax works, mountain peaks, volcanic craters, and some of the highest summer temperatures you have ever encountered. The visitor center is at Furnace Creek. The major part of Death Valley National Park is in southeastern California. The main road is California Highway 190, which provides access to many of the major features and activity areas. **Park Entrance Fee:** $10.00 per vehicle or $5.00 per person, good for seven days.

Lodging in Death Valley National Park: Four very different types of lodging facilities in Death Valley National Park provide accommodations that range from exquisite and expensive to quaint and moderately priced. Furnace Creek Inn and Furnace Creek Ranch near the park's visitor center are privately owned and operated by Xanterra Parks and Resorts. Stovepipe Wells is owned by the National Park Service but operated as a concession by Xanterra. On the park's west side, Panamint Springs Resort is privately owned and operated. We have stayed in all four locations, and each provides a different desert experience. Furnace Creek Inn allows you to experience the desert on your terms, with a very nice room plus excellent food and service. Nearby Furnace Creek Ranch offers motel-type rooms in a desert oasis. This facility is less expensive and appeals to families and tour groups. Stovepipe Wells sits isolated, with little surrounding vegetation, and provides a true desert experience. Keep in mind that all three of these facilities are at sea level and experience sweltering summer temperatures. Panamint Springs is one of the most unique places we have visited. The rooms are relatively small, and there is little to do other than hike and enjoy the desert. On the other hand, spending the evening sitting on the front porch nursing a cold beer and viewing the desert valley and distant mountains is an experience worth remembering. Panamint Springs sits approximately 2,000 feet higher than the three other lodging facilities, allowing guests to avoid some of the highest daytime temperatures.

DEATH VALLEY TEMPERATURE (°FAHRENHEIT) AND PRECIPITATION

	Jan.	Feb.	March	April	May	June	July	Aug.	Sept.	Oct.	Nov.	Dec.
Record high	89	97	102	111	122	128	134	127	123	113	97	88
Ave. daily high	65	72	80	90	99	109	115	113	106	92	76	65
Ave. daily low	39	46	53	62	71	80	88	85	75	62	48	39
Record low	15	25	30	35	42	49	52	64	41	32	24	19
Ave. precip.	.26"	.35"	.25"	.12"	.08"	.04"	.11"	.10"	.14"	.11"	.18"	.18"

Death Valley National Park

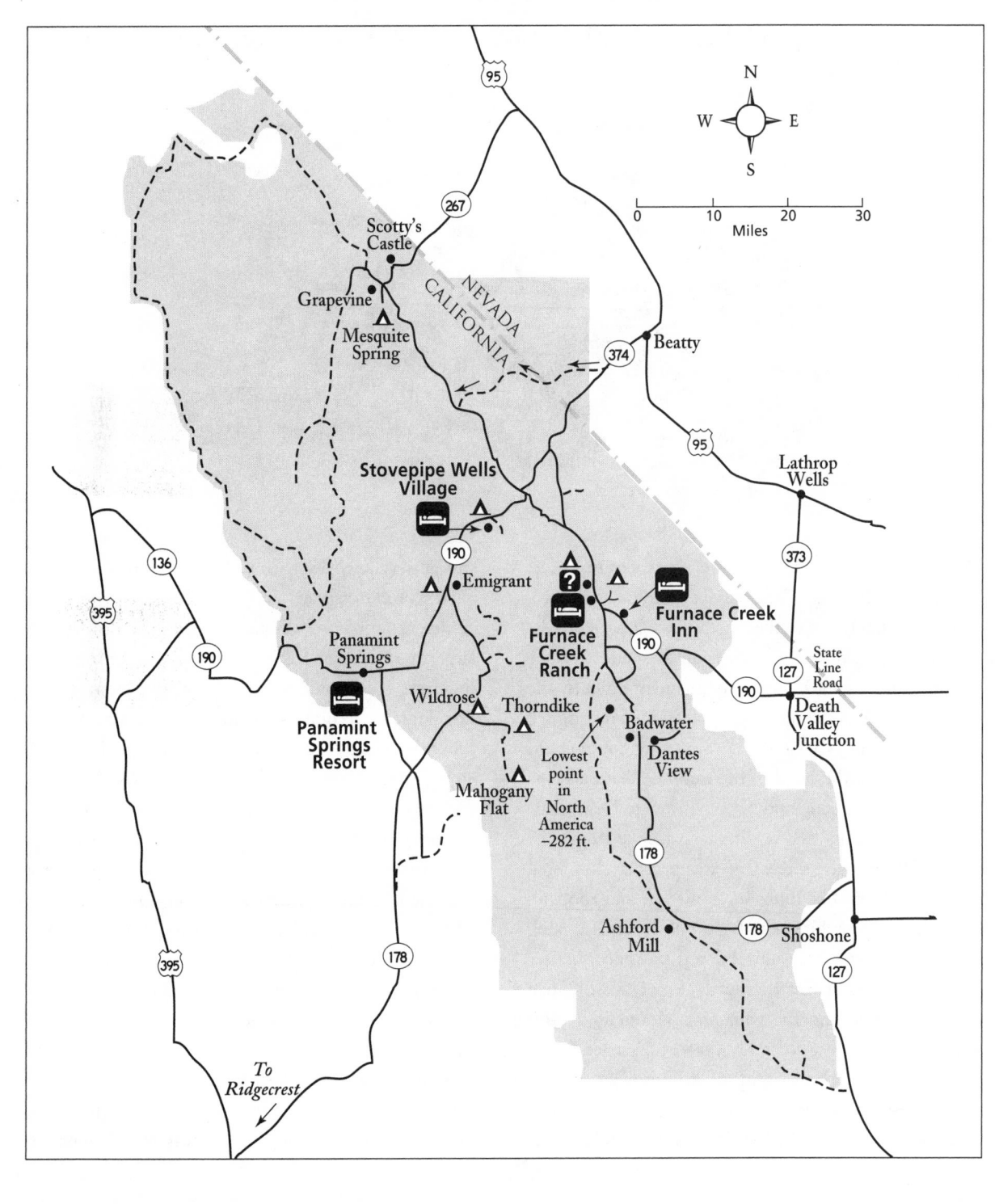

Furnace Creek Inn

P.O. Box 1 • Death Valley, CA 92328 • (760) 786-2345 • www.furnacecreekresort.com

Furnace Creek Inn may be the most elegant hotel located in a National Park Service–administered area, and it is certainly one of the most unique lodging facilities in the United States. Located in the middle of one of the country's most inhospitable environments, the AAA-rated, four-diamond inn has retained its original grandeur. Pacific Coast Borax Company commenced construction of the hotel in the early 1920s to accommodate the increasing number of visitors to Death Valley. Improvements and additions continued into the mid-1930s. Furnace Creek Inn was purchased by Fred Harvey in 1966. The inn is built of stone and adobe in a Mission-style architecture. It sits on a hill overlooking a desolate but starkly beautiful desert that encompasses both the lowest point in North America (282 feet below sea level) and the Panamint Mountain Range, which soars to more than 11,000 feet. Furnace Creek Inn is situated on the back side of an oasis of green grass and palm trees complete with stone walkways, a stream, and ponds on a terraced hillside. Services include free

shuttle service to Furnace Creek Ranch or the nearby airstrip, room service, and massage therapy. A large conference room with stone walls, beamed ceiling, and large windows that face the swimming pool has stone fireplaces at each end. Additional meeting rooms on the first floor can accommodate up to sixty people. A bar at the end of the pool serves beverages and snacks.

Furnace Creek Inn offers a total of sixty-six luxurious rooms of different shapes and sizes on four floors. An elevator is located in the main building. Each room has heat, air-conditioning, a ceiling fan, a refrigerator, a television, a coffeemaker, a hair dryer, and a telephone with data port and voice mail. The rooms are rented in five categories according to size, view, and amenities.

Eight relatively small hillside rooms on the back side of the hotel offer no view and are the least expensive accommodations at Furnace Creek Inn. All of these rooms have one king bed. Thirty-four standard-view rooms, slightly larger than hillside rooms, offer varying views depending upon location. All fourteen

■ ■ ■

A crew of Shoshone and Paiute working at Furnace Creek Ranch made adobe for the original Furnace Creek Inn that opened on February 1, 1927, three months after Bob Eichbaum's bungalows commenced business at Stove Pipe Wells. The first wing of twelve rooms, a dining room, and a kitchen were completed in two months. The twenty-room Terrace Wing was added during 1927 and 1928, and a swimming pool, tennis courts, golf course, and airfield were completed one year later. The twenty-room north wing was added in 1930. The female manager and staff from Yellowstone's Old Faithful Inn were brought down to manage Furnace Creek Inn during the winter.

■ ■ ■

standards in the main lodge building have a king bed, and those on the first or second floor have a terrace or deck. Twenty of the standards are on a U-shaped terrace above the pool. These rooms have either a king bed or a double bed plus a twin bed. Several of these rooms have connecting doors. Sixteen deluxe-view rooms with either a deck or terrace are larger than standards, and most have a king bed. Five large luxury rooms have a spa tub and either two double beds or one king bed. These are the largest rooms other than suites, and each has a deck or terrace. Two two-room suites each have a living room with a sofa bed plus a bedroom with a king bed. The suites have access to a very large deck.

One of the unique rooms at Furnace Creek Inn is the pool bungalow, which is isolated from the other rooms and can require descending several staircases. It is located on the second floor of a separate building with a private outside staircase to the swimming pool. The room has stone walls and a beamed ceiling. Rumor has it that the bungalow is haunted by a ghost, most likely the former chef.

Furnace Creek Inn has about anything you will need for a pampered and relaxing vacation. An attractive, spring-fed swimming pool, four lighted tennis courts, an exercise room, a men's and a women's sauna, a nearby eighteen-hole golf course, horseback riding, and hiking are all available for sports-minded visitors. An upscale dining room serves three meals a day. Two other restaurants at nearby Furnace Creek Ranch can be reached by a short drive or via the free hotel shuttle. A lounge is located off the lobby at the inn. The Death Valley National Park Service visitor center, with exhibits and naturalist talks, is about 2 miles from the inn.

Rooms: Doubles, plus a limited number of triples and quads. All rooms have a private bath, many with a combination shower-tub.

Wheelchair Accessibility: One standard view room with a king bed is wheelchair accessible. The room has a wide entrance door and grab bars around a combination shower-tub. An elevator operates from the hotel's first floor to the third floor, where the room is located. The registration area, gift shop, and restaurant are also on the third floor.

Reservations: Furnace Creek Inn & Ranch Resort, P.O. Box 1, Death Valley, CA 92328. Phone central reservations (800) 236-7916 or on-site (760) 786-2345; www.furnacecreek resort.com. Cost of the first night's lodging is required as a deposit. Cancellation of forty-eight hours required for full refund.

Rates: Hillside—no view ($275–$320); standard view ($295–$340); deluxe view ($320–$370); luxury view ($360–$410); suite ($375–$425). Two- and three-night minimums and higher rates apply during holidays and blackout periods. Rates are for two persons. Additional person is $20; cribs and rollaways, $20. Children seventeen and under stay free. Senior discounts are available. Check the Web site for special packages.

Location: Furnace Creek Inn is 120 miles northwest of Las Vegas and 300 miles northeast of Los Angeles.

Season: The inn is open mid-October to Mother's Day (May).

Food: Diners are treated to a scenic view of the Panamint Mountains from the elegant Inn Dining Room, which offers a complete menu for breakfast, lunch, and dinner. Entree prices range from $22 to $35. Afternoon tea ($17) is served in the lobby from 3:30 to 5:00 p.m. The Lobby Bar, open from noon to 11:00 p.m. daily, serves espresso, liquor, wine, and light hors d'oeuvres. Two less expensive restaurants at nearby Furnace Creek Ranch are described in the write-up of that facility.

Transportation: The nearest major airport is in Las Vegas, where rental cars are available. The resort has a concrete airstrip with lights for private planes. Transportation from the airstrip is available (contact the inn in advance).

Facilities: The inn has a large, spring-fed swimming pool (constant 82° Fahrenheit), a men's and a women's sauna, massage therapy, four lighted tennis courts, a restaurant, a lobby-bar, a gift shop, and four meeting rooms, two of which can be used as banquet rooms. A gas station and general store are at Furnace Creek Ranch.

Activities: Swimming, tennis, and golf (year-round); horseback riding, group hayrides, and carriage rides. The National Park Service offers interpretive programs throughout the park.

Furnace Creek Ranch

P.O. Box 1 • Death Valley, CA 92328 • (760) 786-2345 • www.furnacecreekresort.com

Furnace Creek Ranch is the family alternative to the more expensive and elegant Furnace Creek Inn. Located in an oasis area of Furnace Creek, about 1.5 miles from the inn, Furnace Creek Ranch offers a total of 224 rooms in three classifications of accommodations. The buildings sit amid tall palm and tamarisk trees, with an eighteen-hole golf course at one end. The ranch offers more activities and eating places than the more famous inn. A building just to the right of the stone entrance gate houses the registration desk. Inside the gate and to the left in a western-style wooden building are a general store, a saloon, and two restaurants. Lodging rooms are in six one- and two-story motel-type buildings behind the restaurant building, plus fourteen duplex wood cabins beside the registration building. All of the buildings

with overnight rooms are within walking distance of the registration building and restaurants. Plentiful parking is available near each of the buildings.

All of the rooms at Furnace Creek Ranch have heat, air-conditioning, a television, a refrigerator, a coffeemaker, a hair dryer, a ceiling fan, and a telephone. One hundred and sixty-four standard rooms are in four two-story wooden buildings constructed in the 1960s. These buildings do not have elevators. An entrance is at each end of the building, with access to the rooms through an interior corridor. Second-floor rooms each have a balcony, and rooms on the bottom floor have a patio. Each standard room has two queen beds, a refrigerator, and a ceiling fan. Half the 164 rooms face either the golf course or a grassy area surrounding the

* * *

Furnace Creek Golf Course, at Furnace Creek Ranch, is situated 214 feet below sea level, which qualifies it as the lowest grass golf course in the world. The course was opened in 1931 and, during the early years, closed each summer when it was leased to a cattle rancher. A small flock of sheep kept the course mowed during winter months. The 6,215-foot course was renovated in 1997 by Peter Dye. Although the course lies in the middle of a desert, nine of its eighteen holes have water hazards.

* * *

swimming pool. Rooms on the opposite side of each building face one another. All standard rooms rent for the same price, so try for one with a view toward the golf course. These include even-numbered rooms in the 600 and 800 buildings and odd-number rooms in the 700 and 900 buildings.

Two one-story wood buildings contain thirty-two deluxe rooms, which each have a sliding glass patio door on the back side that opens to a patio and large grassy area near the swimming pool. These rooms each have two queen beds. Deluxe rooms are larger than standard rooms, have parking directly in front of each room, and offer closer access to the swimming area.

Twenty-eight cabin units are constructed two to a building. Each has either one queen or two double beds and a bath with a shower but no bathtub. The cabin units are nicely done but quite a bit smaller than the deluxe or standard rooms.

Furnace Creek Ranch provides all the facilities you will need for a comfortable stay in Death Valley National Park. Best of all, the facilities are near the rooms. The golf course, the Borax Museum with interesting displays, and the National Park Service visitor center are within walking distance. If you desire a

special dinner, take the free shuttle or drive a little more than a mile to the Furnace Creek Inn (mid-October to Mother's Day). You can play golf in the morning, swim in the afternoon in a spring-fed pool, have a beer in the saloon, take a nap, and walk to a restaurant without ever getting in your vehicle. Keep in mind that some of these things are easier to handle in the spring, winter, and fall than in the heat of the summer. On the other hand, this is a great place to spend a spring weekend, when daytime temperatures are more reasonable.

Rooms: Doubles, triples, and quads. All rooms have a private bath with a combination shower-tub except the cabins, which have only a shower.

Wheelchair Accessibility: Two deluxe rooms are both fully wheelchair accessible, with a ramp and a roll-in shower. Four standard rooms each have a ramp and a bathroom with grab bars and a combination shower-tub. The main office, general store, and restaurants are wheelchair accessible.

Reservations: Furnace Creek Inn & Ranch Resort, P.O. Box 1, Death Valley, CA 92328. Phone central reservations (800) 236-7916 or visit the Web site at www.furnacecreek resort.com. Cost of the first night's lodging is required as a deposit. Cancellation of forty-eight hours required for full refund.

* * *

Water, the lifeblood for development in the Furnace Creek area, flows from two nearby hot water springs. The springs caused the forty-niners to camp here during their rush for riches and even resulted in ranchers giving this area a try. The water now flows from the springs to a holding tank that supplies Furnace Creek Inn, and eventually, Furnace Creek Ranch and the Furnace Creek Golf Course. The National Park Service sells the water to the lodging facilities for irrigation and drinking water, as well as for the two swimming pools. Take a swim and enjoy the warm water.

* * *

Rates: High season (mid-October to mid-May)/low season (mid-May to mid-October): cabins ($119–$139); standard ($149–$169); deluxe ($169–$189). Rates are higher during some holidays and special events. A three-night minimum stay is required during New Year's. Rates quoted are for two adults. Children under eighteen stay free when accompanied by an adult. Each additional person is $20 per night. Check the Web site for special packages.

Location: Furnace Creek Ranch is 120 miles northwest of Las Vegas and 300 miles northeast of Los Angeles. The ranch is approximately 1.5 miles north of Furnace Creek Inn.

Season: The ranch is open all year. The busiest seasons are mid-July through August, spring, and all holidays, when the hotel is frequently full.

Food: The Wrangler Steakhouse offers a buffet for breakfast ($10) and lunch ($12). Dinner (seasonally) is ordered from a menu that includes steaks, seafood, and poultry ($18–$35). The 49er Cafe offers breakfast (seasonally), lunch ($8.00–$14.00), and dinner ($10.00–$21.00). The Saloon offers hot dogs, pizza, and snacks. Beer, wine, other beverages, and limited groceries are sold in the general store. The 19th Hole Grill at the golf course serves hamburgers, hot dogs, sandwiches, and chili from 8:00 a.m. to 5:00 p.m. from mid-October to mid-May.

Transportation: The nearest major airport is in Las Vegas, where rental cars are available. The resort has a concrete airstrip with lights for private planes. Transportation from the airstrip is available (contact the ranch in advance).

Facilities: The ranch has a large, spring-fed swimming pool (constant 82° Fahrenheit), two lighted tennis courts, a basketball court, a children's playground, a horseshoe area, a volleyball court, an eighteen-hole golf course, the Borax Museum, a coin-operated laundry, two restaurants, a saloon, a gas station, and a general store.

Activities: Swimming, tennis, golf, basketball, volleyball, horseshoes, and hiking. Horseback riding, group hayrides, and carriage rides are offered from mid-October to mid-May. The National Park Service offers interpretive programs throughout the park except during summer.

Panamint Springs Resort

P.O. Box 395 • Ridgecrest, CA 93556 • (775) 482-7680 • www.deathvalley.com

Panamint Springs Resort is a small facility that, if not for the surrounding landscape, causes you to wonder if you are in Key West, Florida. In fact, walk in the front door of the main building that houses the registration area and dining room and you might expect to see Ernest Hemingway sitting on one of the stools at a bar made from a large slab of walnut supported by redwood roots. Most likely, he would be sampling one of many varieties of beer they offer at the resort. A large porch wraps around the building, with the front and east sides serving as an outside dining area. A small grassy area east of the building has chairs for relaxing. Four wooden buildings with shake roofs sit directly behind the main building and house the motel rooms.

The best-known man-made structure in Death Valley National Park is Scotty's Castle, which lies just inside the park's north entrance. This unique rock building, which cost nearly $2 million, was constructed in the 1920s as a vacation retreat for Albert Johnson, a partner and lifelong friend of Walter Scott, alias Death Valley Scotty, for whom the castle is named. Today you can take a fifty-minute tour conducted by Park Service rangers in period clothing. The tours are offered daily from 9:00 a.m. to 5:00 p.m., and waits of an hour or two can be expected during busy times of the year. The castle also includes a bookstore, a gift shop, an exhibit room, and a snack bar.

Panamint Springs offers fourteen motel-type rooms and one two-bedroom cottage. The motel rooms are of varying size, but all are relatively small. Room rates are based on the number of beds in a room, not the number of occupants. Rooms with one bed generally have a queen, although one has a king. Rooms with more than one bed have either two or three double beds. Each room has heat, air-conditioning, a ceiling fan, and a private bathroom with a shower but no tub. Only the cottage has a television, and the only pay telephone is a cellular unit in the registration building. Wireless access is available without charge.

The one cottage unit with a covered front porch sits to the side of the registration building and has a living room with a sofa, a television with satellite hookup, a refrigerator, a table and four chairs, but no cooking facilities. One large bedroom has a queen bed, and a second, smaller bedroom has a bunk bed with a double bottom and single top. The cottage has a full bathroom with a combination shower-tub.

Panamint Springs Resort is a small, quaint motel-type facility in a desert setting. The resort generates its own electricity, and water is piped from a spring 5 miles away. Panamint Springs isn't fancy, but it is a fun and unique place that you will remember. The dining room holds about twenty-five persons, and additional seating is outside on a covered patio. The homemade food is very good, and the steaks are exceptional. The bar is terrific, and the atmosphere of the whole place can't be beat. Stay here and you will think you are a thousand miles from civilization, which isn't too far from the truth.

Rooms: Two people in one double bed to six people in three double beds. All rooms have private baths with a shower but no tub.

Wheelchair Accessibility: No wheelchair-accessible rooms are available at Panamint Springs Resort. A ramp provides wheelchair access to the restaurant.

Reservations: Panamint Springs Resort, P.O. Box 395, Ridgecrest, CA 93556. Phone (775) 482-7680; fax (775) 482-7682; www.deathvalley.com. A credit card is required to guarantee a room. A cancellation notice of forty-eight hours is required.

Rates: One bed ($79–$84); two beds ($94); three beds ($109); cottage ($149). Rollaway ($5.00). A 10 percent discount is given for AAA and AARP.

Location: The resort is on the western edge of Death Valley on California Highway 190, 48 miles east of Lone Pine.

Season: The resort is open all year. The busiest season is mid-July through August.

Food: The attractive dining room serves breakfast ($6.00–$15.00), lunch ($6.00–$15.00), and dinner ($13.00–$30.00). Beer, wine, cocktails, and soft drinks are available from the bar or coolers just off the registration area. The bar remains open until the registration desk closes at midnight.

Transportation: The nearest airports are in Bakersfield, California (168 miles), and Las Vegas (174 miles), where rental cars are available.

Facilities: Dining room, bar, and gift shop area. Gasoline, diesel fuel, and propane are available. A campground with full hook-ups is across the road.

Activities: Hiking, four-wheel off-road vehicles, bird-watching, sightseeing.

Pets: Pet fee is $5.00 per night per pet.

STOVEPIPE WELLS VILLAGE

Death Valley, CA 92328 • (760) 786-2387 • www.stovepipewells.com

Stovepipe Wells Village is a complex of eleven wooden buildings that provide eighty-three overnight rooms and supporting services. A general store, a small gas station, and a National Park Service ranger station are directly across the road. The village has the appearance of a small western town, which in some respects it is. Six separate one-story buildings each contain from eight to twenty-three rooms. The guest registration area is in a building that also houses an auditorium/meeting room, a gift shop, and a small TV/game lobby. Employee housing is scattered around the back of the complex. Stovepipe Wells Village is situated in the middle of Death Valley National Park, on California Highway 190, approximately 25 miles northwest of Furnace Creek. It is about 33 miles southwest of Beatty, Nevada.

Stovepipe Wells offers three categories of rooms that range from a limited number of small, inexpensive patio rooms to deluxe rooms similar to those at Furnace Creek Ranch. All the rooms have heat, air-conditioning, and a private bath but no telephone.

Forty-seven deluxe rooms in three buildings each have either two double beds or one king bed. These rooms offer a full bathroom, television, refrigerator, and ceiling fan. Rooms in the Roadrunner and 49er buildings facing toward the east provide good views of the valley and distant mountains. Rooms on the west side have views obscured by other buildings. Less expensive and smaller standard rooms each have two double beds, a double plus a single, or two single beds. These rooms have a full bathroom but no television. Standard rooms rent for about $20 less per night than deluxe rooms. Eight even smaller patio rooms were constructed in 1927 as part of the original building. Each room has one double or one double plus a single bed, and a bath with shower but no tub. These rooms are attached to the front of the registration building near the highway. All of the buildings with rooms are a short walk from the registration building.

Stovepipe Wells is particularly appealing to someone seeking the solitude of the desert. Being located on

■ ■ ■

Stovepipe Wells served as the site for Death Valley's first tourist facility when, on November 1, 1926, Bob Eichbaum opened Stove Pipe Wells Hotel. Eichbaum built and operated a toll road franchise, and a daily stage line connected Los Angeles with various points in Death Valley. Often referred to as "Bungalette City," "Bungalow City," and "Stove Pipe Wells Hotel," the facility included twenty open-air bungalows and several larger buildings, supplemented by army tents, and a gas pump, all on the south side of the road. Later, additional bungalows were constructed along with another building on the north side of the road that served as the lobby, kitchen, and dining room.

■ ■ ■

CA 190, which passes through Death Valley, makes it a convenient stop for travelers crossing the park. Stovepipe Wells Village offers an attractive restaurant and saloon with a real western atmosphere. The dining room and saloon have vaulted ceilings and were built with timbers from an old Death Valley mining operation. In fact, staying at Stovepipe Wells is itself a bit of the Old West, even though the rooms are quite comfortable and modern. A general store across the road offers supplies, souvenirs, limited groceries, soft drinks, beer, liquor, wine, and a microwave. A pool with heated mineral water is available for guests. Stovepipe Wells is a short distance west of a large area of sand dunes that is easily accessible via vehicle or on foot. Parking is available beside the road adjacent to the dunes. The sand dunes are a fun place to explore, but be sure to carry plenty of water, especially when it is hot.

Rooms: Doubles, triples, and quads. All rooms have private baths, although the patio rooms have showers but no tubs.

Wheelchair Accessibility: Two standard rooms are fully wheelchair accessible, with a ramp and roll-in shower. Two deluxe rooms in the Tucki building each have a ramp and bathroom grab bars with a combination shower-tub. The restaurant and saloon are both wheelchair accessible.

Reservations: Stovepipe Wells Village, Death Valley, CA 92328. Phone (760) 786-2387; fax (760) 786-2389. The first night's lodging is required as a deposit. Cancellation of forty-eight hours is required for full refund.

Rates: Patio ($75), standard ($95), and deluxe ($115). Rates quoted are for two adults. Children twelve and under stay free when accompanied by an adult. Each additional person is $10 per night. A crib is $5.00, and a rollaway (deluxe rooms only) is $10.00.

Location: Stovepipe Wells Village is on CA 190, near the middle of Death Valley National Park. It is approximately 25 miles northwest of the Furnace Creek Ranch and about 33 miles southwest of Beatty, Nevada.

Season: The facility is open all year. The busiest season is mid-February through April, when it is frequently full.

Food: The Toll Road Restaurant offers a buffet for breakfast ($10) and dinner ($17) during summer. From mid-October to mid-May, breakfast ($6.00–$9.00), lunch ($6.00–$10.00), and dinner ($13.00–$25.00) are ordered from a complete menu. A children's menu is available. The Badwater Saloon just off the restaurant offers draft beer, cocktails, and appetizers. Beer, wine, other beverages, and limited groceries are sold in the general store.

Transportation: The nearest major airport is in Las Vegas, where rental cars are available. A concrete airstrip with lights for private planes is near Furnace Creek Ranch. Another airstrip without lights is next to Stovepipe Wells.

Facilities: Stovepipe has a heated well water swimming pool, restaurant, saloon, lobby with TV and board games, auditorium/meeting room (fee), gift shop (seasonal), gas station (regular only), and general store.

Activities: Swimming, walking, and hiking. The National Park Service offers interpretive programs throughout the park except during summer.

Pets: Pets are permitted with a $20 deposit.

Lassen Volcanic National Park

P.O. Box 100 • Mineral, CA 96063 • (530) 595-4444 • www.nps.gov/lavo

Lassen Volcanic National Park comprises 106,000 acres of a beautiful and relatively uncrowded mountainous area centered on Lassen Peak, a 10,457-foot plug-dome volcano that last erupted during a seven-year period beginning in 1914. The park has other evidence of geothermal activity, including boiling springs, mud pots, fumaroles, and sulfurous vents. A paved road connecting the southwest entrance station with the north entrance station provides scenic views and access to many features of this beautiful area. Road guides are sold at the information center. Lassen Volcanic National Park is located in north-central California, 42 miles east of Redding and 55 miles east of Red Bluff. **Park Entrance Fee:** $10.00 per vehicle or $5.00 per person, good for seven days.

Lodging in Lassen Volcanic National Park: Lassen Volcanic has only one lodging facility, and it is an out-of-the-way location for most visitors who will drive along the single paved road through the park. Drakesbad Guest Ranch is in the southeast part of the park, 17 miles north of the small town of Chester. Private accommodations are available in Chester, Mineral, Mill Creek, Shingletown, Old Station, and Hat Creek.

DRAKESBAD GUEST RANCH

End of Warner Valley Road • Lassen Volcanic National Park
Chester, CA 96020 • (Phone information in text.) • www.drakesbad.com

Lassen Volcanic National Park

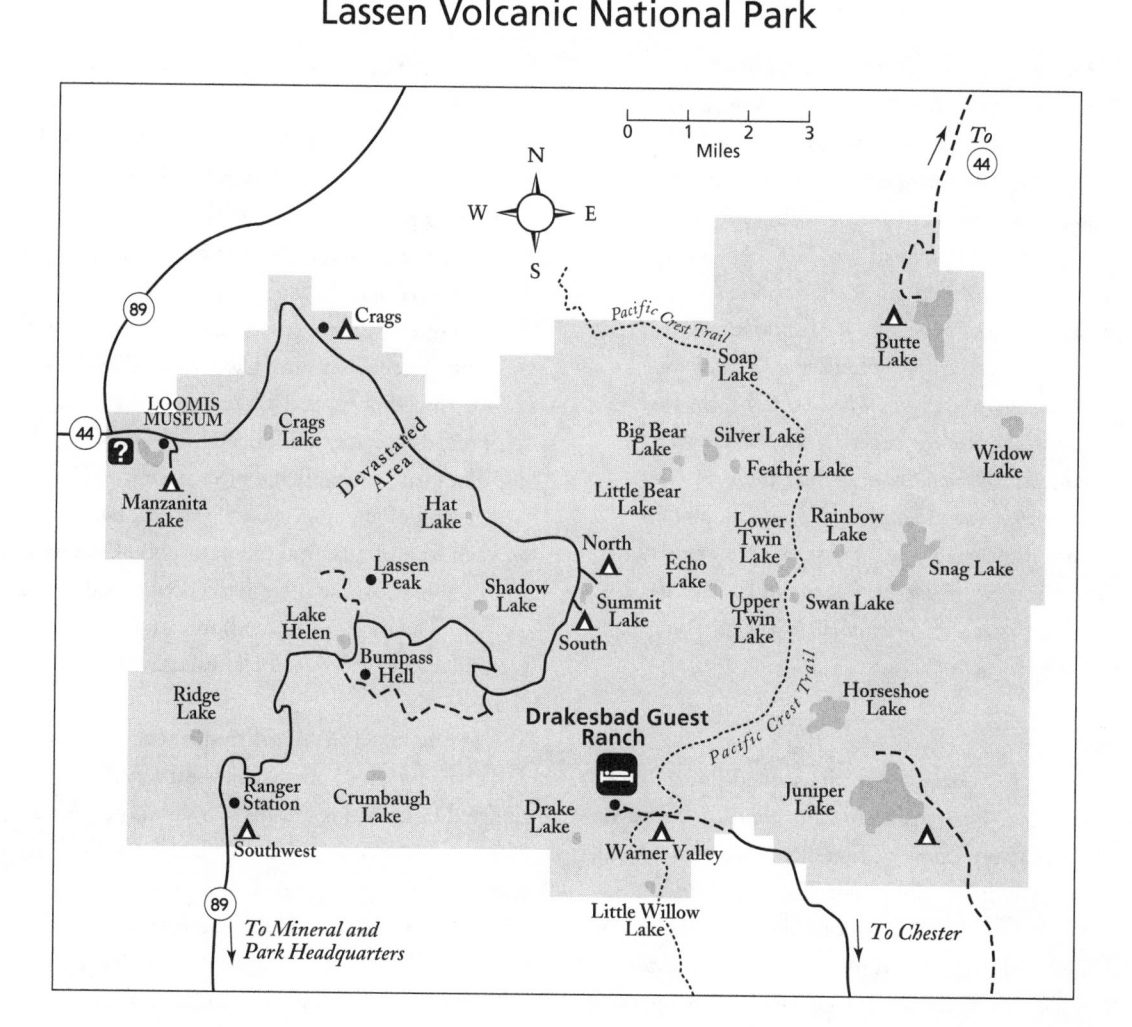

Drakesbad Guest Ranch provides a total of nineteen rooms in a relatively isolated complex of cabins, bungalows, and a two-story lodge. The ranch also has a central dining hall, a thermal heated swimming pool, and several service buildings. The complex lies beside a meadow in the southeast portion of Lassen Volcanic National Park. It is at an altitude of 5,700 feet and surrounded by trees, hills, and mountains. Drakesbad Guest Ranch is reached via a 17-mile road from the town of Chester, California. The first 14 miles are a winding but well-maintained paved road. The last 3

miles, through national park land, are on a relatively rough gravel road. Drakesbad can be called directly by asking the long-distance phone operator to connect you with Drakesbad Toll Station No. 2 at area code 530 (in season), or call (530) 529-1512, ext. 120, and leave a message.

Drakesbad Guest Ranch offers several types of accommodations, all of which are relatively small and nicely finished with pine paneling. All rooms have propane heat but no telephone, air-conditioning, television, or electrical outlets. The two-story rustic wooden lodge

▪ ▪ ▪

The valley in which Drakesbad Guest Ranch is located was first settled by Edward Drake, a trapper and guide who may have arrived here as early as 1875. Drake hosted occasional campers during summers but moved down the valley to Prattville during the harsh winters. In 1900 the seventy-year-old Drake sold his 400 acres to Alexander Sifford, a school teacher from Susanville who had traveled here to drink the healing soda water. Sifford later purchased an additional forty acres and in 1908 renamed the valley Drakesbad, the original owner's name in combination with the German term for warm-water bath. Sifford and his family spent sixty years improving the property and providing visitor services and in 1958 deeded the property to the National Park Service.

▪ ▪ ▪

building has six rooms, all on the second floor. Rooms are on each side of an inside corridor that is accessed via an inside stairway from the first-floor recreation room. No elevator is in the building. The three even-numbered lodge rooms each have one double bed and one single bed. Odd-numbered rooms on the opposite side of the building are somewhat smaller and have only one double bed. Each lodge room has electric lights and a private bath with a sink and toilet, but no tub or shower. Showers and bathtubs are in the swimming pool bathhouse, a short walk from the lodge building.

The northeast annex, directly behind the dining hall, is the only other accommodation with electric lights. The one-story wooden annex has two rooms, each with two double beds and a bathroom with a sink, a toilet, and a shower but no tub. A porch runs across the front of the building. These rooms are somewhat larger and rent for a little more than rooms in the main lodge building.

The remaining rooms at Drakesbad have no electricity, and light is by means of kerosene lanterns. Four freestanding wooden cabins sit at the base of a hill across from the parking lot and the stable. Each cabin has a double bed plus a single bed and a bathroom with a sink and toilet. Cabin guests must shower at the swimming pool bathhouse. Parking is directly in front of each cabin. The cabins rent for the same price and are somewhat larger than rooms in the lodge.

Six one-story bungalows are constructed two to a building. Each bungalow has two double beds, a full bath with a shower, and a back porch that overlooks a large meadow. Parking is directly in front of each building. These are probably the nicest rooms at Drakesbad.

A single one-story wooden duplex has two rooms on each side of a central full bathroom. One room has two double beds; the other has a double bed plus a single bed. The duplex is rented only as a single unit and is particularly desirable for families with two or more children.

For most travelers, even frequent visitors to national parks, staying at Drakesbad will be a very different experience. Drakesbad is not for people who expect a fancy lodge with room service; it is a place for individuals who want to get away from it all and experience nature, but without giving up good food and friendship. The facilities at Drakesbad are comfortable but basic. A dinner bell rings three times a day to announce that food is being served in a pine-paneled dining room. The entire bottom floor of the lodge building, filled with chairs, tables, and sofas, serves as a meeting place to read and chat with other guests. A wood stove is near the middle of the room, and a large stone fireplace occupies one end wall. Chairs are also on the outside porch, which wraps around the lodge. Short to all-day horseback rides are offered. The swimming pool has naturally heated spring water. Equipment is provided for a variety of activities, including table tennis, volleyball, badminton, croquet, and horseshoes. Fly-fishing for trout is excellent for anglers. A fly-fishing instructor is available with advance notice. Several trails, both short and long, lead from the lodge to some of Lassen's best spots. Massage therapy and yoga classes are available. Campfires are held each evening, and programs are frequently presented by the National Park Service. Best of all, both employees and guests seem to be family members who have found a good thing few other people have even heard about. The ease with which you will make friends with other guests is one of the great pleasures of staying at Drakesbad. Everyone eats together in the dining hall and guests sit with one another around the evening campfire or on the porch of the recreation hall of the main lodge building. Likewise, most children have an easy time making friends with the children of other guests. Best of all, Drakesbad is a place where you can wind down and push your worries to another day.

Rooms: Singles, doubles, triples, and quads. A single duplex holds up to seven individuals. Cabins and lodge rooms have half-baths. Other rooms have a full bath with shower.

Wheelchair Accessibility: One bungalow is wheelchair accessible, with an entry ramp to the back porch and double doors. A large bathroom has a combination shower-tub with grab bars.

Reservations: Drakesbad Guest Ranch, 2150 North Main Street, Suite 5, Red Bluffs, CA 96080. Phone (530) 529-1512, ext. 120; fax (530) 529-4511. Reservations can be made up to two years in advance and should be made no later than the end of February to ensure a choice of rooms and dates. Two nights' deposit is required, and a thirty-day cancellation is required for a full refund, less a 10 percent fee.

Rates: Rates quoted are per person and include three meals per day. Lodge and cabins (single, $176; double, $155; extra adult, $132; child, $85); bungalows and northeast annex (single, $201; double, $179; extra adult, $148; child, $85); duplex (double, $190; extra adult, $146; child, $85). Weekly rate is approximately six times the daily rate. Children age two and under are free; for ages three to eleven there is a child rate; twelve and over pay an adult rate.

Location: Seventeen miles north of Chester, California, at the end of Warner Valley Road.

Season: Open from the first Friday in June to the second Monday in October, depending on the weather.

Food: Three meals are served daily in an attractive dining room that is a short walk from all the lodging units. Breakfast includes fresh fruits, hot and cold cereals, and a hot entree. Lunch is buffet-style (sack lunches are available upon request), while dinner with a choice of two entrees is served at the table. An outdoor cookout is scheduled each Wednesday evening. Beer and wine are available for purchase.

Transportation: Scheduled airline service is available to Redding and Chico, California, and Reno, Nevada, where rental cars are available. Private planes may land at a small lighted airport at Chester, where rental cars are available. The lodge will pick up guests in Chester if prior arrangements are made. Amtrak serves Redding and Chico.

Facilities: Hot-spring-fed swimming pool, dining hall, and stables.

Activities: Horseback riding (fee), fishing, swimming, hiking, canoeing, and a variety of games, including volleyball, croquet, Ping-Pong, horseshoes, and badminton. Massage therapy (fee). Yoga classes (fee). Fly-fishing lessons are by reservation only (fee).

■ ■ ■

Lassen Volcanic National Park once housed a lodging facility other than Drakesbad, this one near Manzanita Lake in the northwest corner of the park. Manzanita Lake Lodge and nine cabins were built by Lassen National Park Camp, Ltd. (which later became Lassen National Park Company) in 1933. A dining room and ten wooden double housekeeping cabins were added in 1935. The lodging facility expanded yet again in 1940 when forty tent cabins and a cafeteria, grocery store/gift shop, and gas station were added. The entire area was closed in 1974 when this area of the park was declared hazardous because of a potential rock avalanche. The lodge, cabins, store, and service station were removed in 1977. Photos of the lodge are available in a loose-leaf binder kept at the Loomis Museum near the park's northwest entrance station.

■ ■ ■

Sequoia National Park/Kings Canyon National Park

47050 Generals Highway • Three Rivers, CA 93271 • (559) 565-3341 • www.nps.gov/seki

Sequoia and Kings Canyon are separate but adjoining national parks that are nearly always visited together. The two parks comprise more than 865,000 acres, including groves of giant sequoias on plateaus surrounded by the scenic High Sierra. The magnificent sequoias are immense trees that can live for up to 3,000 years and grow until trunk diameters reach 40 feet. The range in elevation from 1,300 feet to nearly 14,500 feet results in a wide variety of wildlife and vegetation. The parks are in central California. Access from the west is via California Highway 180 from Fresno, which leads through the Grant Grove section of Kings Canyon to Cedar Grove. From the south, California Highway 198 leads to the Giant Forest area of Sequoia National Park, then connects with CA 180 at Grant Grove. **Park Entrance Fee:** $20 per vehicle or $10 per person, good for seven days.

Lodging in Sequoia and Kings Canyon National Parks: Three locations within Sequoia and Kings Canyon National Parks offer overnight accommodations that range from rustic cabins to modern lodges. Wuksachi Village and Lodge is just north of Lodgepole and the only lodging facility in Sequoia National Park. Two lodging facilities in Kings Canyon National Park include rustic cabins and a new lodge at Grant Grove, as well as a nice motel unit at Cedar Grove. Private lodging facilities are at Mineral King in the southern end of Sequoia National Park and in Sequoia National Forest on the road to Cedar Grove from Grant Grove.

CEDAR GROVE LODGE

P.O. Box 909 • Kings Canyon National Park, CA 93633 • (559) 565-0100 • www.kcanyon.com

Sequoia National Park/Kings Canyon National Park

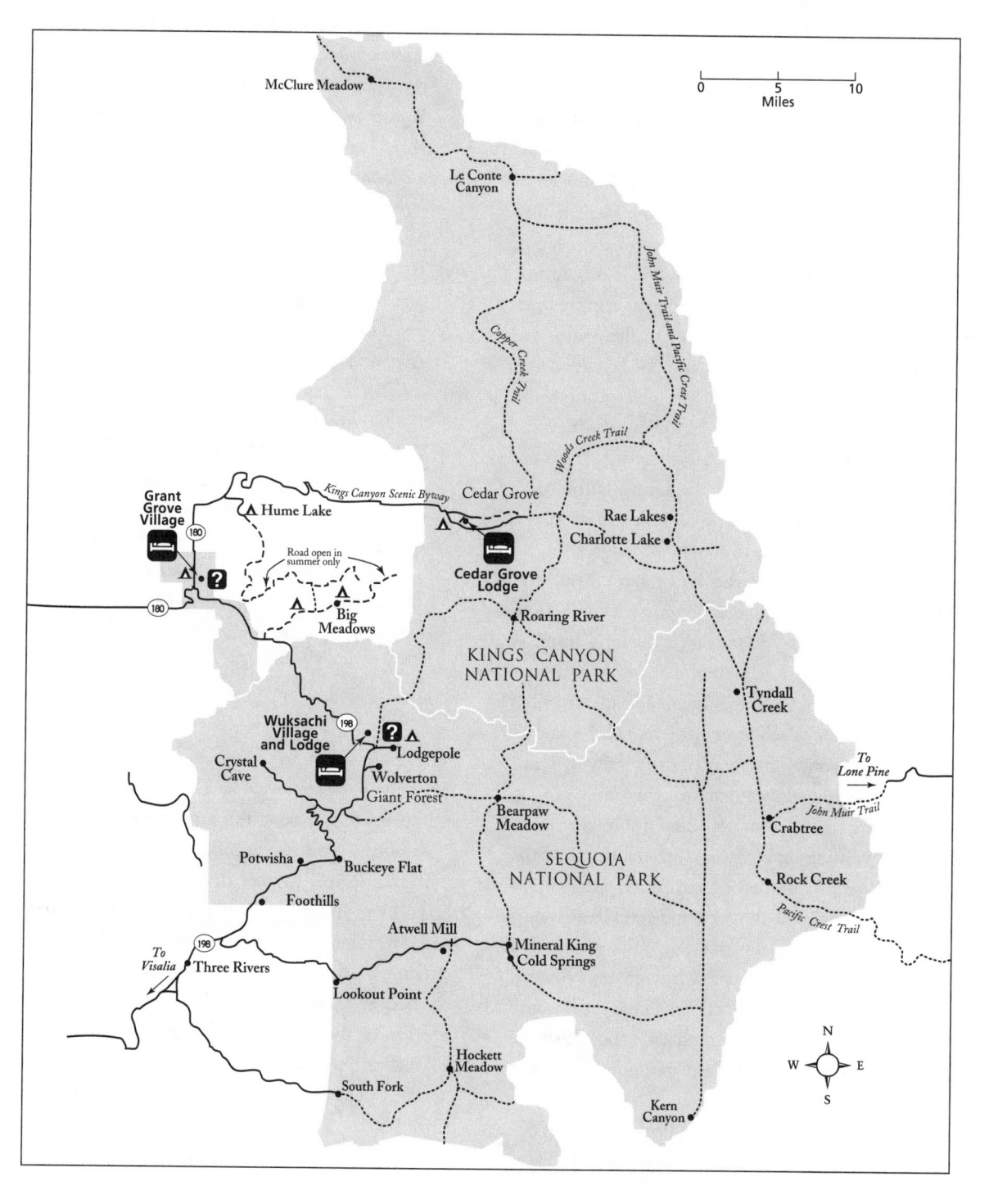

Cedar Grove Lodge is a modern two-story wooden building in the isolated Cedar Grove area of Kings Canyon National Park. The lodge has the appearance of a ski chalet, with eighteen rooms on the second floor and three rooms on the ground level. The first floor houses a combination market/gift shop, a cafe, and a small guest registration desk just inside the entrance to the market. The lodge sits among giant cedar and pine trees beside the South Fork of the Kings River. Picnic tables are scattered about the grounds, many near the river. A large, covered second-floor balcony provides a restful place to read and relax while viewing the surrounding tree-covered mountains and listening to the roar of the river. Another large deck area, one floor below on the same side of the building, has picnic tables just outside the cafe. Cedar Grove Lodge is 35 miles east of Grant Grove Village, 6 miles from the terminus of Kings Canyon Highway. The drive to Cedar Grove is the most scenic in either Sequoia or Kings Canyon and worth the time even if you don't plan to stay at the lodge.

All of the rooms at the lodge have heat, air-conditioning, and telephones, but no television. The second-story rooms are identical in size and furnishings, with two queen-size beds and a private bath that includes a shower but no tub. One handicap-accessible room has a bathtub. Each room has a modest back window but no balcony. The rooms have plenty of space for two people and adequate room for a family of four. Rooms on the second floor are entered through a relatively narrow inside corridor that runs the length of the building between a ramp at one end and a wide stairway at the opposite end. The three ground-level Patio rooms are smaller, with one queen-size bed, a full bath with a shower only, and a kitchen area with a sink, microwave, coffeemaker, and small refrigerator. These rooms have a private patio with a table and chairs a short distance from the river. Plentiful parking is in front of and beside the lodge.

Cedar Grove in Kings Canyon National Park is one of our favorite places to visit. Scenery along the drive

The Sequoia Field Institute, a department of the Sequoia Natural History Association, offers a variety of educational programs throughout the year in Sequoia and Kings Canyon National Parks. Programs include indoor and outdoor seminars, school programs, nature hikes, backpacking, cross-country skiing, and environmental education. For example, you can take snowshoe treks or enhance your ski skills in winter months, or learn about birding, backpacking, and photography in the spring and summer months. The Institute offers guided mountain treks of several days and programs for children. Instructors include park naturalists, college professors, and professional photographers. Participants are charged a fee that is reduced for members of the Sequoia Natural History Association. For a current catalog containing a program listing and registration form write: Sequoia Natural History Association, HCR 89, Box 10, Three Rivers, CA 93271. Similar institutes operate in other national park areas.

from Grant Grove to Cedar Grove is as spectacular as anywhere in the country. The Cedar Grove area is quiet and uncrowded, making this a perfect place to unwind in a beautiful setting.. The lodge is 2,000 feet lower and about ten degrees warmer than Grant Grove. It is off the park's main traffic artery, near the end of a 30-mile road. The remoteness and small size of the lodge reduce visitation to this area of the park that is not nearly as crowded as Grant Grove Village. The unpretentious cafe serves the usual sandwiches, hamburgers, fries, and soft drinks. It also offers other selections, including breakfast items, and dinner specials that might include fried chicken, trout, steak, and pasta. Eat on the deck and enjoy your meal while listening to the roar of the

Kings River. Afterward take a walk down the road and across the bridge to browse through the .small National Park Service visitor center. Park rangers conduct evening programs at the nearby campground amphitheater.

Rooms: Doubles, triples, and quads. All rooms have private baths with showers. One wheelchair-accessible room has a bathtub.

Wheelchair Accessibility: One second-floor room is wheelchair accessible, with a wide bathroom door and grab bars around the toilet and combination shower-tub. Access to the room is via a relatively long outside ramp. The registration area, cafe, and market are also wheelchair accessible.

Reservations: Kings Canyon Park Services, P.O. Box 907, Kings Canyon National Park, CA 93633. Telephone toll free (866) 522-6966; (559) 335-5500, ext #0; www.kcanyon.com. A deposit of two nights' lodging is required. Cancellation of forty-eight hours prior to scheduled arrival is required for a full refund.

Rates: Doubles ($119); patio rooms ($135). Rates quoted are for two adults. Children twelve and under stay free unless an extra bed is requested. Each additional person is $12 per night. Rollaways are $12.

Location: Cedar Grove Lodge is located near the terminus of CA 180, Kings Canyon Highway. It is 35 miles east of Grant Grove Village.

Season: The lodge is open from mid-May to early October, depending on the weather.

Food: The cafe serves breakfast ($5.00–$8.00), lunch ($5.00–$10.00) (seasonal), and dinner ($10.00–$20.00). Food items including milk, sandwiches, ice-cream treats, beer, wine, fresh vegetables and fruits, and drugstore items can be purchased in the market.

Transportation: Scheduled air, bus, and Amtrak serve Fresno, where rental cars are available.

Facilities: Laundry, cafe. Gift items are available in the market. A small National Park Service visitor center is a quarter mile away.

Activities: Hiking, fishing, evening campfire programs, horseback riding.

GRANT GROVE VILLAGE

P.O. Box 907 • Kings Canyon National Park, CA 93633 • (559) 335-5505, ext. 1603

www.kcanyon.com

Grant Grove Village, one of two lodging facilities in Kings Canyon National Park, includes fifty older wood cabins plus a modern two-story cedar lodge building with thirty-six rooms. Both the cabins and the lodge are just off Generals Highway behind a small commercial center that houses a post office, a market, a gift shop, a dining room, the lodging registration desk, plus a National Park Service visitor center. The lodge building and cabins are within walking distance of the registration area and dining room. Cabins are clustered in two separate but adjacent areas a short distance behind the commercial center. One cabin area, called Tent City, is on a hillside overlooking a meadow that separates the cabins from the dining room and registration building. The hillside is dotted with numerous big trees. The remainder of the cabins sit in an adjacent area called Meadow Camp, a more heavily wooded area across the road from the meadow and a little farther from the commercial center. The lodge is on a hillside a short distance behind and above the cabins. A National Park Service visitor center with exhibits and an information desk is directly across the road from the dining room and registration desk. The Grant Grove area can be quite busy in summer, so expect heavy traffic. Grant Grove Village is 3 miles from the Kings Canyon entrance on California Highway 180 from Fresno, California. It is 24 miles north of Lodgepole on a small peninsula of Kings Canyon National Park that juts from the northwest corner of adjoining Sequoia National Park.

Grant Grove offers four types of cabin accommodations plus lodge rooms. Nine cabins have a private bathroom, while occupants of the other forty-one cabins must use one of two central bathhouses. The bathhouse at Meadow Camp was newly constructed in 2008. All cabins have sheets, towels, and daily maid service. The least expensive rooms at Grant Grove are tent cabins with wooden walls and canvas roofs. These cabins each have two double beds in a dark and stark unfinished interior with a wooden floor. They have no heat or electricity, although a battery operated lamp is provided.

If you want something to tax your brain, think about this: The complex at Grant Grove spans two California counties. Tulare County on the south side levies a 10 percent hotel/motel tax, while Fresno County on the north side does not. Stay in a cabin on the south side of the complex and you will be charged the tax. Stay in an identical cabin on the north side of the complex and you will not be required to pay it. Occupants of the lodge are fortunate because the building sits in Fresno County, which does not levy the tax. Even the concessionaire was confused by this bizarre situation and was at one time charging tax on all the rooms. Guests in both the cabins and the lodge are charged a National Park Service impact fee of $3.50 per night. How can life on vacation become so complicated?

Parking at the bottom of the hill is some distance from these cabins. One step up (actually quite a large step) and about $15 more expensive are the somewhat larger camp cabins without a bathroom. Most camp cabins have two double beds (a few have three doubles), propane heat, and electricity. Each unit has an unfinished interior and a covered patio with a wood stove and picnic table. Grant Grove also offers rustic cabins that have a similar exterior but a much nicer interior than camp cabins. Rustics have finished paneled interiors with carpeting and rent for about $10 per night more than camp cabins. Parking is directly beside most of the camp cabins and rustic cabins, but keep in mind that some of the cabins are a long walk from the bathroom. Rustic cabin 510 is surrounded by tall shrubs and not far from the bathroom, which makes it a good choice. Rustic 508 is the only cabin to have an inside wood stove. The top cabin accommodations at Grant Grove are nine cabins with private bathrooms. These units have interiors similar in size to the rustics, and are constructed two to a building with a shared front porch. Of the nine cabins with a private bath, cabin 9 is freestanding and classified as deluxe. It has one queen-size bed, a sofa bed, a refrigerator, a coffeemaker, and a front porch. Cabins 1 through 4 are in two buildings that sit just up the hill from the parking area, while cabins 5 through 9 are farther up the hill and require more walking.

John Muir Lodge, which opened in May 1999, offers thirty-six rooms in an attractive two-story cedar building. The lodge building does not have an elevator. Each floor has a large balcony with chairs on the west end of the building. The lodge boasts an impressive lobby area with a vaulted beamed ceiling and a large stone fireplace. This is a good place to play board games, read a book, or visit with other guests. Furnishings were especially created for the lodge. The rooms have heat, two queen-size beds or a king plus a sofa bed, a full bath, a coffeemaker, and a telephone. No air-conditioning is in any of the rooms. Rooms with a king bed cost an additional $10 per night. The even-numbered rooms, which are on the south side of the building, offer a better view and less noise because they are on the opposite side of the building from the parking lot.

Grant Grove offers a choice of accommodations at a wide range of prices. Cabin 9 with a bath (also called the honeymoon cabin) is our favorite accommodation. We consider it superior to even the more expensive lodge rooms. If you don't mind using a community bathroom, rustics are the best value in the Grant Grove complex. These are especially desirable if you can make use of the outside wood stove that is available for cooking. If you desire modern accommodations, choose the lodge, which offers upscale rooms in an attractive cedar building. Grant Grove offers a convenient location for day trips to both Cedar Grove and Giant Forest. You will find horseback riding, guided hikes, and evening programs. Winter activities include cross-country skiing and snowshoeing. Equipment is available for rental at the market.

Rooms: Doubles, triples, and quads. Several of the cabins will accommodate six. Only nine of the cabins have a private bathroom.

Wheelchair Accessibility: Two first-floor rooms in the John Muir Lodge are ADA compliant with a combination shower-tub. None of the cabins is wheelchair accessible. The dining room, registration area, and gift shop are wheelchair accessible, as is the National Park Service visitor center.

Reservations: Kings Canyon Park Services, P.O. Box 907, Kings Canyon National Park, CA 93633. Telephone toll free (866) 522-6966; (559) 335-5500; www.kcanyon.com. A deposit of two nights' lodging is required. Cancellation of forty-eight hours prior to scheduled arrival is required for a refund.

Rates: Tent cabin ($62); camp cabin ($77); rustic cabin ($87); cabin with private bath ($129); deluxe cabin with private bath ($140); lodge room ($170–$180)). Rates quoted are for two adults. Children twelve and under stay free. Each additional person is $12 per night. Rollaways are $12. Rates are reduced from January to March.

Location: Three miles inside the entrance to Kings Canyon National Park on CA 180 from Fresno.

Season: Grant Grove Village is open all year, although the tent, camp, and rustic cabins close for winter.

Food: A nice dining room offers family dining with breakfast ($5.00–$9.00), lunch ($7.00–$10.00), and dinner ($9.00–$20.00). A children's menu is available. A pizza parlor is attached to the dining room. A market offers limited groceries.

Transportation: Scheduled air, bus, and Amtrak serve Fresno, California, 60 miles from Grant Grove. Rental cars are available in Fresno.

Facilities: Dining room, pizza parlor, market, gift shop, post office, and National Park Service visitor center.

Activities: Horseback riding, hiking, and interpretive programs. During winter months snowshoeing and cross-country skiing are popular.

Wuksachi Village and Lodge

P.O. Box 89 • Sequoia National Park, CA 93262 • (559) 565-4070 • www.visitsequoia.com

Wuksachi Village and Lodge, named for a Native American tribe that once lived in Sequoia, consists of an attractive cedar registration/dining building and three nearby cedar lodge structures that provide a total of 102 overnight rooms. Opened in May 1999, Wuksachi is one of the newest national park lodging facilities. The complex is on a hillside amid large cedar, sugar pine, and fir trees. Excellent mountain and forest views are available from the windows of most of the rooms. Parking is down a hill from the buildings, and transporting luggage may require more exercise than you desire. Luggage carts are in the lodge buildings, and bellstaff at the registration building are available to assist with luggage. Wuksachi is just north of Lodgepole, the commercial village in Sequoia National Park.

The registration building boasts a handsome lobby area under a beamed-vaulted ceiling where guests can talk, read, or just relax in front of a wood-burning stove. There is a small gift shop just off the registration area. The dining room on the backside of the building has a large stone fireplace and features a wall of windows providing excellent views of this beautiful area of the

park. A small lounge is situated just outside the dining room. Public telephones and conference rooms are downstairs. The entire complex is attractively done with first-class furnishings.

Paved walkways lead from a central parking lot to each of the three virtually identical lodge buildings. Each building has three floors in a split-level design in which rooms on each floor are accessed from central corridors that can be entered from either end of the buildings. Rooms on the bottom floor of each building face the mountains to the east, while rooms on the third floor face the forest to the west. The second floor of each building has rooms on each side of the corridor. There are no elevators in the three lodge buildings, which means guests may be required to climb one or two flights of stairs. Two of the buildings, Stewart and Silliman, are each entered on the second floor so guests do not have to climb more than one flight of steps. The third and largest building, Sequoia, is entered on the first floor, thus requiring third-floor guests to climb two flights of steps. If stairs are a problem, request a room on the entry floor of the building to which you are assigned.

The planning for Wuksachi Village and Lodge had been in the works for well over a decade before its May 1999 completion. The major activity and lodging center of Sequoia National Park was for many years at Giant Forest, 6 miles south of Wuksachi. Here there were cabins, motel-type units, and two two-story lodge buildings. The area also had a restaurant, market, gift shop, and pizza pub. For a variety of reasons, including an antiquated sewage system, danger from falling trees, high maintenance costs, and harm to reproduction of the area's sequoias, the National Park Service closed all commercial activities here in October 1998 and subsequently began removing most of the structures. The old restaurant/market building currently serves as the museum.

All of the 102 rooms at Wuksachi have heat, a ceiling fan, a full bathroom with combination shower-tub, a hair dryer, a refrigerator, a television, a telephone with data port, a coffeemaker, and very attractive furnishings. The rooms are not air-conditioned, but this is seldom needed. None of the rooms has a balcony. Each of the three lodge building offers rooms in three classifications. Twenty-four standard rooms, the lowest-priced alternative, and sixty deluxe rooms are similar except for a slight difference in room size and furnishings. Standard rooms, each with two queen beds, are at least as large as, if not larger than, most nice motel rooms. Deluxe rooms have about three feet of extra depth and come with two queen beds or a king plus a sofa bed. Eighteen superior rooms with either two queen-size beds or one king-size bed and a sofa bed also have a side room with a sofa bed and chair. The extra room can be closed off with two sliding wood doors. We suggest a standard room and request a mountain view. Rooms within each classification rent for the same price, so obtaining a room with a mountain view doesn't cost extra.

Wuksachi Village and Lodge is a comfortable and restful base from which to explore this impressive national park. The lodge sits alone without stores, a visitor center, or other attractions to serve as magnets to large numbers of park visitors. Despite the secluded location, the lodge is a short distance from several of the park's major attractions. Lodgepole, a major activity area with a large visitor center, market, laundry facilities, mountain shop, deli, and nature center, is only 2 miles away. Giant Forest, with an outstanding museum and trails that offer access to the park's namesake sequoias, is 4 miles south of Lodgepole. A free summer shuttle operates among Wuksachi, Lodgepole, the General Sherman Tree, and Giant Forest Museum. Another free shuttle connects the Giant Forest Museum with Moro Rock and Crescent Meadow.

Sequoia and Kings Canyon winter activities include cross-country skiing and snowshoeing during winter months when the area is typically buried in snowfall. Both Wuksachi in Sequoia National Park and Grant Grove Lodge in Kings Canyon National Park are open all year. Cedar Grove Lodge is closed during the winter. Keep in mind that Generals Highway is sometimes closed by snow during the winter, so access to Wuksachi may be limited to the south entrance from Ash Mountain and access to Grant Grove Lodge may be only via California Highway 180 from Fresno. Call the National Park Service or the lodge where you will be staying prior to leaving home to determine which road to take. Also keep in mind that chains may be required on your vehicle even when a road is open.

Rooms: Doubles, triples, and quads. Superior rooms can sleep up to six. All rooms have private baths with a combination shower-tub.

Wheelchair Accessibility: Eight rooms, several in each of the three price categories, are each fully wheelchair accessible, with one queen bed and a large bathroom that includes a roll-in shower. Ramp access is provided to each of the three lodge buildings. Keep in mind that rooms are up a hill and some distance from parking. The registration area, restaurant, and gift shop are also wheelchair accessible. Porters with electric carts are available to assist with luggage and transportation.

Reservations: Delaware North Park Services, P.O. Box 89, Sequoia National Park, CA 93262. Phone (888) 252-5757 or (559) 253-2199, or visit www.visitsequoia.com. One night's deposit required. Cancellation requires seventy-two hours' notice.

Rates: Peak season rates apply from mid-May to mid-October and during holidays. Off-season rates are applicable the remainder of the year: standard (peak $194/off-peak $99); deluxe ($215/$119); superior ($260/$149). Rates quoted are for two adults. Each additional person is $10 per night. Children twelve and under stay free unless an extra bed is required. Rollaways and cribs are $10 per night.

Location: Wuksachi Village and Lodge is just off Generals Highway in the northern section of Sequoia National Park. The lodge is approximately 2 miles west of Lodgepole.

Season: The lodge is open all year.

Food: The restaurant serves breakfast (Continental, $7.25 or full buffet, $11.50), lunch ($8.00–$16.00), and dinner ($17.00–$33.00) daily. Reservations are required for dinner. Two miles away, Lodgepole has a market and deli, as well as a snack bar that serves breakfast, sandwiches, and pizza. The lodge offers an evening all-you-can-eat barbecue dinner ($20) at Wolverton Recreation Area.

Transportation: Scheduled air service is available to Fresno, California, where cars may be rented. The National Park Service operates a free park shuttle from Memorial Day through Labor Day. One shuttle operates between Wuksachi and Giant Forest with stops at Lodgepole and the General Sherman Tree. Another shuttle operates between Giant Forest and Moro Rock.

Facilities: Restaurant, lounge, gift shop, conference rooms. Two miles away, Lodgepole offers a mountain shop, post office, laundry facilities, deli, market, snack bar, nature center, and a National Park Service visitor center. Most services at Lodgepole are seasonal.

Activities: Hiking, horseback riding, and fishing. Cave tours are at Crystal Cave, about 20 miles south of Wuksachi. Buy tickets at Lodgepole or Foothills visitor center. Winter activities include cross-country skiing, sledding, snowshoeing, and guided walks.

Yosemite National Park

P.O. Box 577 • Yosemite National Park, CA 95389 • (209) 372-0200 • www.nps.gov/yose

Yosemite National Park comprises 761,000 acres of scenic valleys, high-country meadows, and granite peaks and domes in one of America's most spectacular and popular national parks. The three major features of the park are beautiful Yosemite Valley, groves of giant sequoias at Crane Flat and Mariposa Grove, and the alpine wilderness reached via Tioga Road. The park's main activity area is in Yosemite Valley. Tioga Road is a paved road that winds through the High Sierra and connects on the east side of the park with U.S. Highway 395 at Lee Vining, California. Yosemite National Park is in east-central California, approximately 190 miles due east of San Francisco. The southern edge of the park is approximately 60 miles north of Fresno via California Highway 41. **Park Entrance Fee:** $25 per vehicle or $10 per person, good for seven days.

Lodging in Yosemite National Park: Yosemite has seven lodging facilities, four of which are in Yosemite Valley. These include the Ahwahnee, Yosemite Lodge at the Falls, Curry Village, and Housekeeping Camp. Accommodations in the valley range from the upscale and expensive Ahwahnee (many consider this the most elegant hotel in any national park) to downscale and relatively

Yosemite National Park

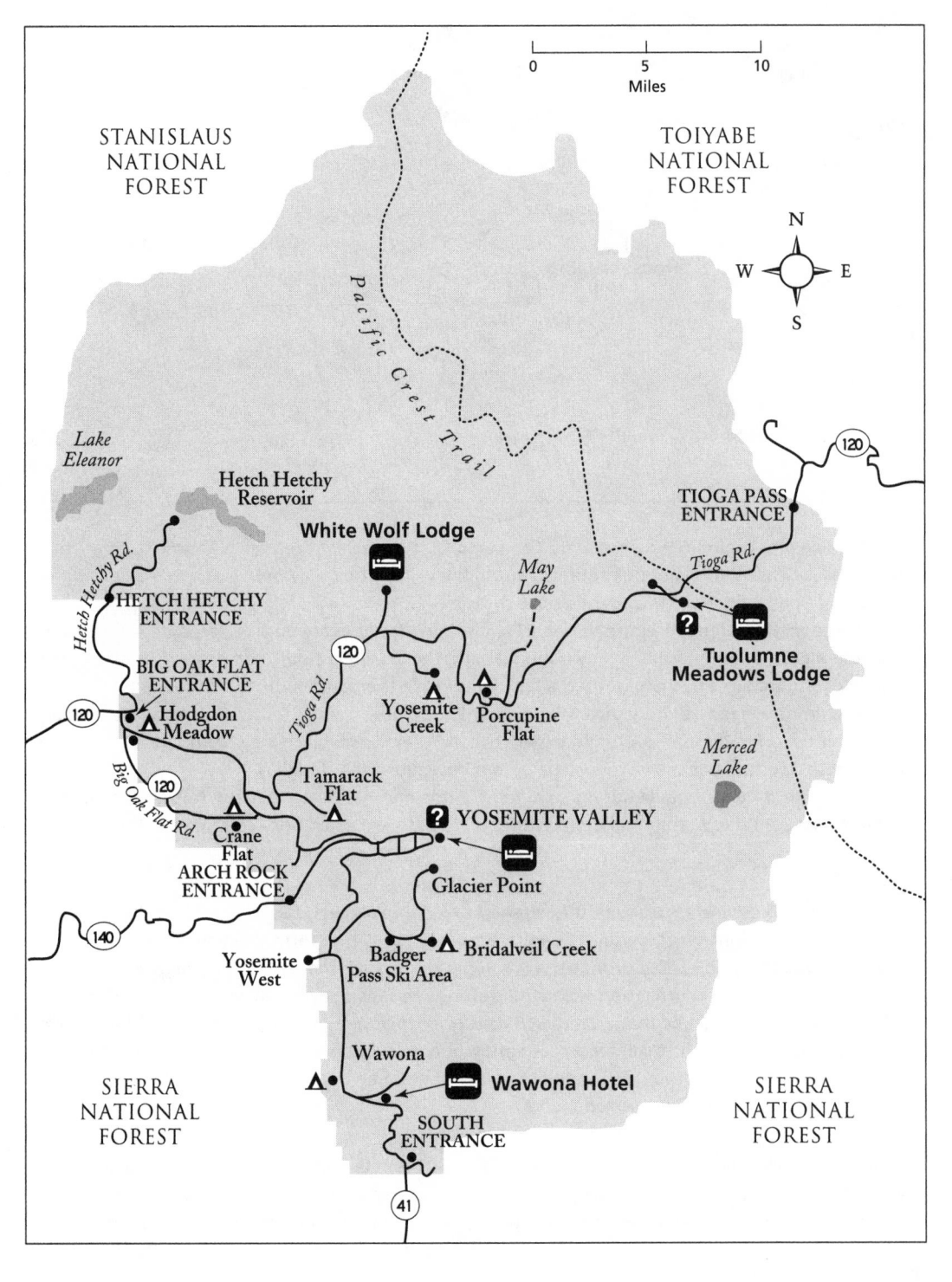

STANISLAUS NATIONAL FOREST

TOIYABE NATIONAL FOREST

0   5   10
Miles

N
W   E
S

Pacific Crest Trail

Lake Eleanor

Hetch Hetchy Reservoir

White Wolf Lodge

May Lake

TIOGA PASS ENTRANCE

Tioga Rd.

Hetch Hetchy Rd.

HETCH HETCHY ENTRANCE

120

?

Tuolumne Meadows Lodge

BIG OAK FLAT ENTRANCE

120

Hodgdon Meadow

Tioga Rd.

Yosemite Creek

Porcupine Flat

Merced Lake

Big Oak Flat Rd.

120

Tamarack Flat

Crane Flat

ARCH ROCK ENTRANCE

?   YOSEMITE VALLEY

Glacier Point

140

Badger Pass Ski Area

Bridalveil Creek

Yosemite West

Wawona

Wawona Hotel

SIERRA NATIONAL FOREST

SOUTH ENTRANCE

SIERRA NATIONAL FOREST

41

Yosemite National Park—Yosemite Valley

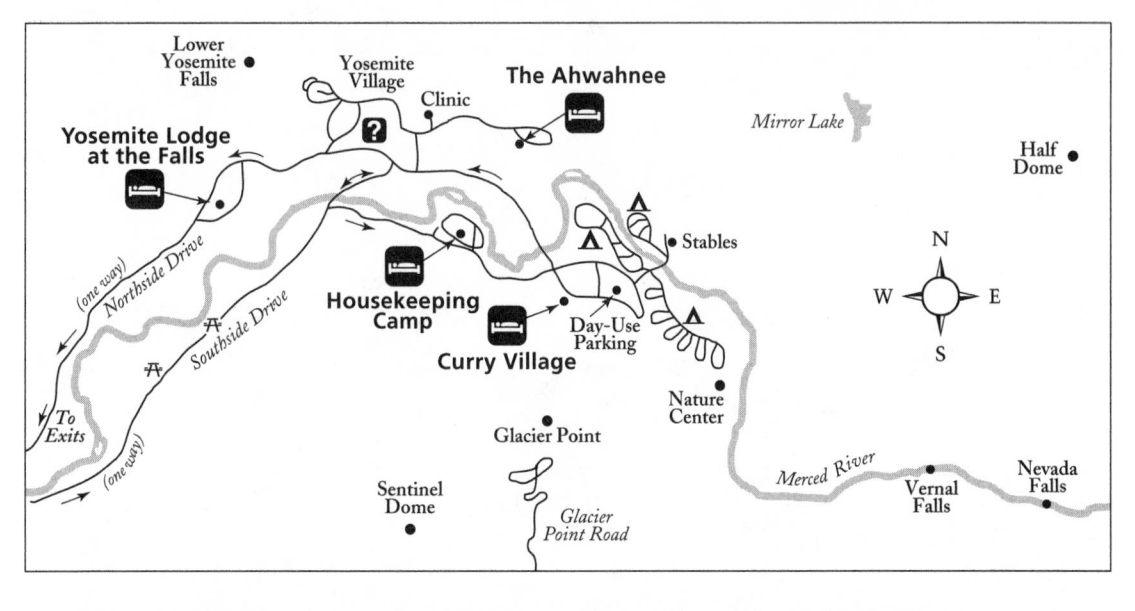

inexpensive tent cabins in Housekeeping Camp and Curry Village. A free valley shuttle stops at each facility as well as other major points of interest in the valley. The valley can be congested during the summer, so park your vehicle and utilize the shuttle.

Three very different Yosemite National Park lodging facilities are outside Yosemite Valley. Probably the oldest lodging facility in any national park, the Wawona Hotel, comprises six white frame buildings situated in a peaceful setting a few miles inside the park's south entrance.

Tuolumne Meadows Lodge and White Wolf Lodge offer canvas tent cabins and a few wood cabins on Tioga Road for an overnight experience in Yosemite's high country. Although in the same park, these two facilities seem worlds apart from Yosemite Valley lodging.

Yosemite is very popular during summer months and holidays, so make reservations at the earliest possible date. Accommodations with private bath are often booked a year and one day in advance.

Reservations: A central reservation office services all seven lodging facilities in Yosemite National Park. For reservations write or call Yosemite Reservations, 6771 North Palm Avenue, Fresno, CA 93704. Phone (801) 559-5000, or visit www.yosemitepark.com. The cost of one night's lodging is required as a deposit. Cancellation with a full refund requires a seven-day notice. Reservations for all Yosemite lodging can be made up to 366 days prior to your planned arrival date. If the hotel is fully booked when you first call for a reservation and you lack flexibility with regard to dates, try again thirty, fifteen, or seven days prior to your intended arrival, when previous reservations by others are most likely to be canceled.

Food in the Valley: Food service is available at several Yosemite Valley locations, including all of the lodging facilities other than Housekeeping. The free shuttle system makes any of the eating establishments easily accessible, so you can choose to have pizza at Curry Village even though you are staying at the Ahwahnee. Likewise, you can enjoy a memorable evening dining at the Ahwahnee when you have a room at Yosemite Lodge. Nearly every type of food is available somewhere in Yosemite Valley. Beer and wine are sold at most of these locations and at the markets. Yosemite Village offers a pizza loft, a deli, a cafe, and a grill. Yosemite Lodge and Curry Village both offer several different dining experiences that are listed under the respective lodge section in this book. Markets selling cold sandwiches, alcoholic beverages, soft drinks, snacks, and groceries are at several locations.

Transportation: Scheduled air service is available to Fresno, where rental cars are available. Amtrak serves Yosemite Valley through a combination train-bus service. Yosemite Area Regional Transportation System (YARTS) buses serve Yosemite Valley on a year-round basis from Mariposa, El Portal, and Merced (an Amtrak stop). Seasonal bus service to Yosemite Valley is available from the towns of Mammoth Lakes and Lee Vining. For information check www.yarts.com, or call (877) 989-2787. A free shuttle bus system within Yosemite Valley serves all the lodges and other popular points of interest. A free daily shuttle operates between the Wawona and Yosemite Valley. Another free shuttle offers frequent service between the Wawona and Mariposa Grove near the south entrance to the park.

Yosemite Valley

THE AHWAHNEE

Yosemite National Park, CA 95389 • (209) 372-1407 • www.yosemitepark.com

Many travelers assert that Yosemite's Ahwahnee is the finest lodging facility at any national park. This claim is difficult to dispute. The Ahwahnee, built in the late 1920s with a name that Native Americans gave to what is now Yosemite Valley, is both a National Historic Landmark and a world-class facility. Everything about this six-story hotel makes you want to stay, except perhaps the expense, which is rivaled by only a few other national park facilities including Death Valley's Furnace Creek Inn, Cumberland Island's Greyfield Inn, and Grand Teton's Jenny Lake Lodge. The Great Lounge, with a 24-foot-high beamed ceiling, stained

■   ■   ■

Guests who have enjoyed staying in the Ahwah-nee since its opening in 1927 can thank Stephen Mather, first superintendent of the National Park Service. Mather facilitated the merger of Yosemite's first concessionaires—Curry Company and the Yosemite Park Company—on the condition the new firm construct an upscale fireproof hotel with the capability of year-round operation. The luxurious hotel was expected to increase tourism (and the park's budget) and attract important people who would provide political and financial support for the National Park Service. The Ahwahnee's architect, Gilbert Stanley Underwood, had previously designed impressive lodges at Zion National Park and Bryce Canyon National Park, and would subsequently design Grand Canyon Lodge on the North Rim and Oregon's Timberline Lodge.

■   ■   ■

glass windows, and two massive stone fireplaces, is the hotel's focal point. The spectacular dining room, with its 34-foot-high vaulted beamed ceiling and floor-to-ceiling windows, is one of the most beautiful you will enter. Pottery, historic photos, paintings, and rugs are placed throughout the public rooms. The Ahwahnee offers a total of 123 rooms in both the main hotel building and several nearby secluded cottages. The hotel is located in the northeast section of Yosemite Valley, at the base of the Royal Arches. The location is remote enough to avoid the congestion that typifies much of the valley. Parking is nearby the entrance, and valet parking is available. Bellstaff will assist with luggage.

The Ahwahnee offers two types of lodging. The main hotel has ninety-nine rooms on six floors. Rooms have either one king-size bed or two double beds. A few rooms also have a sofa bed. The rooms are stylishly furnished and include heat, air-conditioning, a television, a

telephone, a small refrigerator, guest bathrobes, a coffee-maker, a hair dryer, and full tiled bath. Bedding consists of down mattresses, down pillows, and down blankets. One or more large windows in each hotel room offer differing views depending on room location. Vistas range from excellent views of Yosemite Falls or Glacier Point to rooms that look out at a loading dock or under a porch roof. The best views are from corner rooms, which each have windows on two sides. The hotel has two junior suites with extra large rooms. One has a sunken sitting area and offers the only Jacuzzi in Yosemite. The other has a four-poster bed that was used by Queen Elizabeth II when she stayed in this room during a 1983 visit. The top-of-the-line rooms are four suites that each have one bedroom plus a large, luxuriously furnished parlor with spectacular views. The suites offer varying amenities that can include a fireplace, library, large flat-screen television, and balcony. Each offers an option of adding a second adjoining bedroom.

The Ahwahnee has eight separate but nearby single-story frame buildings that house a total of twenty-four cottages. These cottages sit in a secluded and quiet wooded area of dogwoods and pines near the hotel but away from the hotel traffic. They are in a natural setting, but most provide minimal views. Each cottage has a patio with table and chairs. Cottages 720 and 721 and cottages 722 and 723 share common patio areas and are probably less desirable. The cottages vary in size and are decorated to highlight Yosemite's Native American heritage. Unlike the hotel rooms, the cottages have ceiling fans but no air-conditioning. Cottages 714 and 719 are the only two with wood-burning fireplaces (wood provided) and are slightly larger than average. Cottage 716 has a mountain view, and cottages 707 and 718 are more private and offer a view of the Merced River. Most cottages have one king-size bed, while five have two double beds. Amenities are the same as the hotel rooms.

The standard hotel rooms and cottages rent for the same price, and choosing between the two isn't easy. Our suggestion is that first-time visitors who plan to stay a day or two should choose a room in the hotel to appreciate the delight of staying overnight in such a wonderful place where you can wander downstairs to read or relax in the Grand Lounge. Standard rooms in the hotel are not quite as large as most of the cottage rooms, but the hotel's common areas are really wonderful. If you plan on staying for more than a couple of days and desire solitude, you may be happier in one of the cottages.

The Ahwahnee offers upscale lodging in a beautiful setting. If you are willing to splurge, it is a delightful place to spend several nights while exploring the beauty and enjoying the many activities offered by this spectacular national park. If spending your entire Yosemite stay here will break the bank, try to schedule at least one night's lodging in this unique hotel. Walk through the lobby and marvel at the Great Lounge. On through the lounge past the second fireplace is the Solarium, where massive windows furnish a sweeping view of a grassy

❖ ❖ ❖

The Ahwahnee has hosted many famous guests since the hotel's opening on July 14, 1927. President John F. Kennedy stayed overnight in August 1962 in what is now known as the Presidential Suite. Presidents Hoover, Eisenhower, and Reagan also stayed overnight, although not during their presidential terms. Winston Churchill, Will Rogers, and Eleanor Roosevelt were guests at the Ahwahnee. Among the numerous Hollywood stars who have stayed here are Shirley Temple, Bing Crosby, Ginger Rogers, Judy Garland, Lucille Ball, Clint Eastwood, Jack Benny, Greta Garbo, Red Skelton, and Humphrey Bogart. Among the hotel's most famous guests were Queen Elizabeth II and her husband, Prince Philip, who stayed three nights in March 1983.

❖ ❖ ❖

area surrounded by trees with a background of granite cliffs. A complimentary afternoon tea and cookies for Ahwahnee guests is a tradition. A free shuttle bus that operates throughout Yosemite Valley stops at the Ahwahnee entrance, allowing guests to enjoy activities and facilities in other valley locations.

Rooms: Singles, doubles, triples, and quads. All rooms can accommodate a rollaway and some have sofa beds. All rooms have a full tiled bath.

Wheelchair Accessibility: Two rooms in the main hotel are wheelchair accessible, with a wide bathroom door, an extra large bathroom, and a roll-in shower. Several other hotel rooms offer bathrooms with a combination shower-tub with grab bars. Two cottages have a bathroom with a wide doorway and a roll-in shower. Keep in mind that the cottages are some distance from parking, although bell service is available.

Rates: Hotel rooms and cottages ($439); junior suites ($499); suites ($955–$1,015). Children twelve and under stay free in the same room with an adult. Each additional person is $21 per night. A variety of packages are offered in the off season.

Location: North section of Yosemite Valley, at the end of a dead-end road.

Season: The Ahwahnee is open year-round. It is often fully booked a year ahead for busy periods such as holidays and summer months.

Food: An elegant dining room serves breakfast ($8.00–$19.00), lunch ($11.00–$15.00), and dinner ($25.00–$36.00). A children's menu is available. Dinner reservations are highly recommended, and appropriate attire is required; athletic clothing is not allowed. A Sunday brunch ($32) is served from 7:00 a.m. to 3:00 p.m. The cocktail lounge serves light meals including sandwiches, salads, and appetizers from 11:00 a.m. to 10:00 p.m. Room service is available. The famous Bracebridge Dinner, a three-hour Christmas pageant and feast, is presented during eight days of the Christmas holidays.

Facilities: Outdoor heated swimming pool, tennis courts, gift shop, cocktail lounge, sweetshop, and full-time concierge service. Wireless Internet access is available in the guest rooms, meeting rooms, and some public spaces.

Activities: Hiking, swimming, tennis, evening programs, guided hotel tours. Winter activities listed under Curry Village.

CURRY VILLAGE

Yosemite National Park, CA 95389 • (209) 372-8333 • www.yosemitepark.com

Curry Village is the largest lodging complex in Yosemite Valley, with a total of 628 rooms, mostly in canvas tents. The term *village* is certainly appropriate for this facility that is much like a small town, with tents, cabins, a buffet, fast-food restaurants, a bar, a sporting goods store, a market/gift shop, a guest lounge, a post office (summer only), a community shower building, and restrooms. The location, in the southeast section of Yosemite Valley, is near several campgrounds and a convenient place for campers to roam and eat.

Curry Village offers four types of accommodations. The least expensive lodging is 427 canvas tent cabins with a wooden platform and canvas walls and roof. These units are available in different sizes, with a variety of bedding options that range from two singles to a double and three singles. The bedding consists of metal cots, with linens, towels, soap, and maid service provided. A padlock is available for securing the front door. A light is in each tent, although there are no electrical outlets, plumbing, or heat; however, a few heated tent cabins are available at slightly higher cost. Restroom and shower facilities are centrally located.

Curry Village also has 183 wood-frame cabins, most of which are constructed as duplexes, although a few are quads and some are freestanding. Each cabin has carpeting, heat, and some have a front porch with a bench. Approximately a hundred of the cabins have private baths, mostly with showers but some with a combination shower-tub. The remaining cabins have no bath or running water. Excluding the bathrooms, both types of cabins have approximately the same amount of living space. Cabins with a bath rent for approximately $30 per night extra and are more widely spaced than cabins without a bath, which literally sit on top of one another. Most cabins have two double beds, but a few cabins with bath have a double plus a single. Curry Village also has one deluxe cabin (819) that has a living room with a fireplace, a bathroom, and a separate bedroom. This deluxe cabin has a king bed plus a sofa bed that will sleep up to four persons and is by far the nicest lodging facility at Curry Village. A single motel-type building, Stoneman House, has eighteen standard rooms with private bath and shower but no tub. These units have heat and a ceiling fan. Beds range from one to three

One of Yosemite's best-known activities was the evening Firefall, during which a massive pile of glowing red fir bark embers was pushed over the cliff at Glacier Point near Camp Curry. The practice was begun in the 1870s, abandoned several years later, then revived in 1899 by David Curry, proprietor of Camp Curry. The evening activity became so popular that everything in the valley would come to a halt when the time came for embers to be pushed over the side. The Firefall continued until 1968, when it was permanently halted by park management.

doubles; the three double beds are in units with a loft. The motel units with a loft are an especially desirable accommodation for families, as the loft can be used to separate children from parents, at least temporarily. In addition, they are a good value and rent for the same price as the other motel units.

Lodging facilities at Curry Village are tightly packed, and most of the units are some distance from parking. Porters with motorized carts can transport luggage to your room. When you are assigned a room, ask about the distance of the room from parking and whether help from a porter is advisable. Basically, Curry is a low-cost alternative to the Ahwahnee and Yosemite Lodge. The many tent cabins are among the cheapest of Yosemite's overnight offerings. Our choice would be the cabins with a bath that cost about $30 per night more than the more crowded cabins without a bath. If a cabin with a bath is unavailable choose a cabin without a bath, which is only $12 more than the more spartan tent cabins. Guests at Curry enjoy a variety of eating facilities including a dining pavilion that serves an all-you-can-eat-style buffet for breakfast and dinner, a Mexican-style food stand, a pizza deck,

and an ice cream/coffee corner. Evening programs are presented at an outside amphitheater. The decision on whether to stay here depends on how much you are willing to spend, what lodging facilities are available when your reservation is made, and, because this area can be very busy in the summer, how well you tolerate crowds.

Rooms: Doubles, triples, and quads; a few units will hold five or six persons. Most rooms, including all the tent cabins, do not have private baths.

Wheelchair Accessibility: Eight cabins with a bath, one motel room with a bath, and six cabins without a bath are ADA compliant. A paved path leads from cabins without a bath to the community bathroom, which has ramp access and a roll-in shower.

Rates: Canvas tent cabins ($85); cabins without bath ($97); cabins with bath ($126); deluxe cabin ($213); standard motel-type rooms ($152). Children twelve and under stay free except in the tent cabins, where an additional child is $6.00 per night. Rates for an additional person are from $10.00 to $13.75. Prices are slightly lower from mid-November through mid-March, excluding holidays.

Location: Southeast side of Yosemite Valley.

Season: All of the lodging facilities in Curry Village are open spring through fall. Some are also open during the winter.

Food: A dining pavilion serves a buffet breakfast and a buffet dinner from spring through fall. Mexican food and pizza are served on the patio as fast-food items. An inside coffee corner has specialty coffees, bakery items, and ice cream. A bar serves alcoholic beverages beginning at noon along with hamburgers and a few other items. A small market sells beer, wine, cold sandwiches, and limited grocery items.

Facilities: Gift shop, mountain shop, bicycle rental and river raft rental stands, camp store, outdoor swimming pool, and post office (summer only). In winter an outside ice-skating rink is available and equipment for cross-country skiing can be rented.

Activities: River rafting, hiking, bicycling, swimming, and evening programs. Winter activities include cross-country skiing and ice-skating. Badger Pass, 23 miles from Yosemite Valley, usually receives substantial snowfall and has four chair lifts and one cable tow to serve nine ski runs. Ninety miles of marked cross-country ski trails begin here.

HOUSEKEEPING CAMP

Yosemite National Park, CA 95389 • (209) 372-8338 • www.yosemitepark.com

Housekeeping Camp is a complex of 266 concrete and canvas guest rooms surrounding several larger wooden structures that provide support facilities, including a registration desk, a public laundry, a market, a shower building, and several common bathrooms. Rooms are built two to a unit, with the back of each room sharing a concrete wall with an identical room. The rooms are constructed of cement on three sides (each two-room unit has concrete walls constructed in an H pattern), with a canvas front and a canvas roof that extends over a concrete floor and a front concrete patio area that has a picnic table and a cooking shelf with a light and electrical outlet. A privacy fence surrounds the front of each patio. A large food storage box is next to each patio. The canvas entry door cannot be secured, which means that you should leave valuables locked in your vehicle.

Each room has one double bed and a bunk bed. The interior also has shelving, a mirror, an electric light, and an electrical outlet. None of the rooms has a private bathroom, so guests are required to use centrally located bathhouses. Guests must supply their own sheets, blankets, and pillows, although these can be rented at nominal cost at the registration building. Soap and towels are supplied without charge in the shower building. Most housekeeping units sit close together and offer little in the way of privacy or a view. Many are near a major park road or the crowded parking areas. Units on the bank of the Merced River offer the best views and are a superior choice.

Housekeeping Camp rooms represent national park lodging at its most basic. This area is best suited for groups or families with children, especially those who want to bring bicycles that can be ridden throughout this large complex. It is the only lodging facility in Yosemite Valley that allows cooking, a major advantage for many families. Actually, Housekeeping Camp is much like a large campground in which the tents are supplied. This is a stop on the free valley shuttle, allowing guests to ride to other locations for food, programs, or activities.

Rooms: The rooms are identical, with bedding for up to four persons. Two additional cots can be rented. None of the rooms has a private bath.

Wheelchair Accessibility: Four housekeeping units near a parking area have access to a wheelchair-accessible bathroom with a roll-in shower. A paved walkway is between the living units and the bathroom.

Rates: One to four persons pay the same price ($79.00); each additional person is $5.00 per night. Children four and under are an extra $4.00 per night.

Location: On the bank of the Merced River in the southeast section of Yosemite Valley, a short distance west of Curry Village.

Season: Spring to mid-October.

Food: No restaurant or snack bar is at Housekeeping Camp. A small market has limited groceries. A variety of restaurants and snack facilities can be reached via the free valley shuttle.

Facilities: Small market, shower, and laundry.

Activities: River rafting, swimming, and hiking.

YOSEMITE LODGE AT THE FALLS

Yosemite National Park, CA 95389 • (209) 372-1274 • www.yosemitepark.com

Yosemite Lodge at the Falls is a large complex of wooden buildings with two categories of overnight guest facilities, including one two-story motel unit and several one- and two-story lodge units. In all, the lodge provides a total of 245 rooms. The units are scattered about a service area that includes the registration building, located just south of Northside Drive in front of scenic Yosemite Falls. A variety of other stores and restaurants are near the registration building and within easy walking distance of any of the guest rooms. Registration parking is directly in front of the registration building, but overnight guest parking is a considerable distance from some of the rooms. Bellstaff are available to assist with luggage. Yosemite Lodge at the Falls is located in the northwest section of Yosemite Valley.

Nearly all of the 245 rooms at Yosemite Lodge at the Falls are in fourteen one- and two-story frame buildings constructed in the mid- to late-1960s. All of

A variety of tours are offered to Yosemite visitors. These include the two-hour Valley Floor Tour, the four-hour Glacier Point Tour, the Mariposa Grove Tour, the Big Trees Tram Tour, the Tuolumne Meadows Hikers' Bus, and the full-day Grand Tour, which combines the Glacier Point and Mariposa Grove Tours with a lunch at the Wawona Hotel. Most tours depart from Yosemite Lodge at the Falls. Tickets can be purchased at several locations in the valley. Call (209) 372-1240 for information.

these lodge rooms are virtually identical, with a dressing area, a hair dryer,, a television, a telephone, heat, a ceiling fan, and a full bathroom with a combination shower-tub. Beds are either a king or two doubles. Each room has a patio or balcony with a table and two chairs. These buildings do not have air-conditioning or elevators. Rooms in the two one-story buildings and top-floor rooms in the two-story buildings have vaulted beamed ceilings. Bottom-floor rooms have flat ceilings, making the rooms appear less spacious even though they are the same size. Lodge rooms are similar to large upscale motel rooms. Unfortunately, surrounding trees obstruct mountain and waterfall views from nearly all the rooms.

Yosemite Lodge at the Falls also offers nineteen smaller and less expensive standard rooms in a single two-story building constructed in the late 1950s adjacent to the registration building. All these rooms, which rent for about $35 less per night than the larger lodge rooms, have the same amenities as the lodge rooms. These rooms do not have a patio or balcony. Bedding in the standard rooms varies from one double bed to two queen beds. Four extra-large rooms on the second floor of this building are classified as "family" rooms that rent

for $16 more than standard rooms but are priced for four adults. These rooms each have a shower (no tub), a separate toilet, two sinks, and a double bed and from two to four single beds.

Our choice at Yosemite Lodge at the Falls is a second-floor lodge room on the back side of the Juniper or Laurel buildings. These rooms offer convenient parking but face away from the road and are relatively quiet. They also face away from Yosemite Falls, but few rooms in Yosemite Lodge at the Falls offer a view of this picturesque attraction. Our second choice would be any of the rooms in one-story Cottonwood. One disadvantage here is the distance from parking. Aspen, Dogwood, and Tamarack, three newer buildings with lodge rooms, are squeezed together on a corner between two parking lots. Rooms in these buildings are near parking but offer little privacy. With two or more children you will probably want to try for one of the four family rooms in the Cedar building.

Yosemite Lodge at the Falls is located in the center of facilities and activities. Food service includes a food court and an upscale restaurant. You will also find an ice

Yosemite Lodge at the Falls was a substantially larger complex prior to the disastrous flood of January 1997. Three days of rain flooded much of Yosemite Valley, including the Yosemite Lodge complex. The flood was actually similar in intensity to floods that occurred in Yosemite Valley during the previous one hundred years. The history of damaging floods caused the National Park Service to order the removal of more than 150 cabins and two lodge buildings that were in service prior to January 1997. In all, Yosemite Lodge lost approximately 200 rooms.

cream stand, an environmental shop, a gift shop, and a cocktail lounge with wireless Internet access. A tour desk is inside the registration building. The free shuttle stops across the street from the registration building and provides access to all the facilities and activities in the valley.

Rooms: Doubles, triples, and quads, with six persons in a limited number of rooms. All rooms have private baths.

Wheelchair Accessibility: Yosemite Lodge at the Falls has four rooms that are ADA compliant, which includes three lodge rooms and one standard room.

Rates: Standard rooms ($157); family rooms ($173), lodge rooms ($192). Rates quoted are for two adults. Each additional person is $13 per night for standard rooms, $11 for lodge rooms. Children twelve and under stay free. Prices are slightly lower from mid-November through mid-March, excluding holidays. Specials are offered during the off-season.

Location: In the northwest section of Yosemite Valley, near the double waterfall.

Season: Yosemite Lodge at the Falls is open year-round.

Food: A food court offers breakfast, lunch, and dinner at moderate prices. Breakfast includes pancakes, French toast, eggs, oatmeal, cold cereals, and bakery items. Lunch and dinner items include pizza, pasta, chicken, fish, salads, and desserts. Lunch and dinner prices range from $5.00 to $11.00. Beer and wine are available. In the same complex, the Mountain Room offers an excellent view of Yosemite Falls in a dining room that serves upscale dinners including steaks, seafood, and chicken ($16 to $30). Dinner reservations are recommended. Beer, wine, and other alcoholic beverages are available. The nearby Mountain Room Lounge serves sandwiches and salads from 4:30 p.m. (noon on weekends) to 10:30 p.m. A market behind the registration building sells limited groceries including beer, wine, and snacks.

Facilities: Gift shops, food court, restaurant, cocktail lounge, branch post office, bicycle rental, tour desk, swimming pool, outdoor amphitheater. Wireless Internet is available in the lounge, meeting spaces, and the outdoor amphitheater.

Activities: Evening programs, swimming, biking, hiking. Winter activities are listed under Curry Village.

Outside Yosemite Valley

Wawona Hotel

P.O. Box 2005 • Wawona, CA 95389 • (209) 375-6556 • www.yosemitepark.com

The Wawona (an Indian term meaning "big tree") Hotel is the grande dame of the national parks. While some would argue that Death Valley's Furnace Creek Inn and Yosemite's own Ahwahnee are more elegant, the Wawona is without a doubt one of the grandest. The Wawona Hotel is a complex of six white frame, shake-roofed buildings, the oldest of which was built in 1876. The newest of the buildings was constructed in 1918. The complex is similar in appearance to a late-1800s western military post. The Wawona Hotel is 4 miles inside the south entrance to Yosemite National Park and 25 miles south of popular Yosemite Valley. A free daily shuttle operates between the hotel and Yosemite Valley.

The six buildings at Wawona offer a total of 104 rooms. Each of the buildings contains overnight lodging rooms, although the size of the buildings and the rooms within them vary considerably. The main building, which houses registration, a large dining room, and an attractive lounge area, has twenty-nine rooms, all but one on the second floor. Each floor of this large, two-story building has an impressive wraparound veranda with white railings and posts. Wicker benches, chairs, and tables on the lower veranda offer a place for guests to relax while viewing the grassy front lawn that surrounds

■   ■   ■

President Teddy Roosevelt came to the Wawona Hotel on May 3, 1903. Assigned to room 215, the president dropped off his bags and went off to the Big Trees area to meet with conservationist John Muir. This meeting gave Muir an opportunity to convince Roosevelt to expand the park to include Yosemite Valley. Mariposa Grove and Yosemite Valley were at the time owned by the state of California.

■   ■   ■

a stone fountain. Beverages are served here during the late afternoon and early evening. The other five buildings are smaller but have a similar architectural style, including verandas with tables and chairs.

All of the rooms at Wawona have heat but no air-conditioning, telephone, or television. Although rooms vary by size, view, and building, only two price categories are used: with or without private bath. Fifty of the 104 rooms have a private bath and rent for about $70 per night more than rooms without a private bath. Guests in rooms without a private bath must use community shower and bathroom facilities. Community bathrooms, accessed from the outside porches, can require a walk past up to eight rooms, depending on the location of your room. All but two of the rooms in the main building are relatively small and without a private bathroom or in-room sink. Most have one queen bed. Rooms 223 and 224 each have a bathroom with a claw-foot tub. Views vary, with some rooms providing a scenic view toward the front lawn and others in an inside hallway having no view at all. Since the view is not considered in the rate, request a room in the front with a view of the lawn.

If staying in the main building isn't important (and it really shouldn't be because the rooms are quite small) and you want a private bath, request a room in one-story Clark Cottage or Washburn Cottage, but be aware that both cottages have a limit of two persons per room. Clark Cottage sits directly beside the main hotel building and offers attractive rooms. The four front rooms in Clark Cottage probably offer the best views. Corner rooms have an extra window that provides additional outside light. All rooms have a king-size bed, a ceiling fan, and a private bath. Two-story Washburn Cottage has a total of sixteen rooms, all with private baths. First-floor rooms are of nice size with a king bed. Upstairs rooms are smaller, have a queen bed, do not have a veranda, and require climbing a flight of stairs.

Moore Cottage with nine rooms sits on a hill directly behind the main hotel building and offers the most convenient parking at Wawona. Only two of the nine rooms, both on the first floor, offer a private bath. The four upstairs rooms are small, each with a single dormer window, and no veranda. In addition, guests with an upstairs room must use a long, steep stairway to carry luggage or use the community bath that is on the first floor. Try to avoid an upstairs room in Moore. Our two favorite rooms at Wawona are in Moore and include first-floor room 87, which is quite large and has a private bath, and corner room 89, which has a sink but not a private bath. Little White House is a small cottage with only three rooms, two of which have a private bath. The third room has connecting doorways to both the other rooms, and the entire building is an excellent choice for large family gatherings. The room without a bath (51) is large but requires guests to use bathroom facilities in another building if the room is not rented in conjunction with an adjoining room that has a bath. The two-story Annex has thirty-nine rooms, most of which have a double bed plus a single bed. Half the rooms each have a private bath with a claw-foot tub and shower. The other rooms, with in-room sinks only, have connecting doors for families that wish to rent two rooms. Room 137, with a private bathroom, is quite large and includes a double bed plus two single beds. All of the buildings are clustered closely together, so there should be no concern about the walking distance to the restaurant or lounge.

The Wawona Hotel is a peaceful alternative to lodging facilities in hectic Yosemite Valley. The free daily shuttle to Yosemite Valley allows the hotel to serve as a convenient base for a Yosemite vacation of several days. Why endure the hassle and expense of driving into the valley and searching for a parking place when you can hop a free shuttle and let someone else worry about the driving? The Wawona dining room retains its Victorian flavor, with tall windows offering views out the front and side of the main building. Outside tables are also available. Although named a hotel, the Wawona is actually more of a resort with a swimming

The Wawona Hotel has been in continuous operation for over 130 years, longer than any other lodging unit in the national park system. The Wawona had already served travelers for more than a decade before Yosemite National Park was established. In the early days guests enjoyed meals featuring vegetables gathered from a local garden and freshly prepared fish and venison from the nearby streams and woods. The hotel even had its own dairy so guests could enjoy fresh milk and cream. The Wawona, a National Historic Landmark, has its own golf course, which opened for business in June 1918 as the first course in the Sierra Nevada.

pool (the "tank"), a tennis court, and a nine-hole golf course. A practice putting green is on the hotel's front lawn. The hotel is adjacent to Pioneer Village, a collection of historic buildings that introduce visitors to some of the events shaping Yosemite's history. Included are a covered bridge, horse-drawn coaches, a homestead, and numerous other historic buildings. A free shuttle bus operates between the hotel and Mariposa Grove, the site of many giant sequoia trees.

Rooms: Mostly doubles, with a few triples and quads. About half the rooms have private baths. Rooms with private baths are often fully booked a year ahead during peak season. Previous guests often request particular rooms, so be as specific as possible about the type and location of the room you want.

Wheelchair Accessibility: Two first-floor rooms in the Annex have limited wheelchair accessibility, with a ramp and sidewalk from the main lodge building. The bathrooms have a combination shower-tub, and the hotel staff can install grab bars. The hotel dining room is wheelchair accessible from the back of the main lodge building.

Rates: Rooms with private bath ($199); rooms without private bath ($128). Rates quoted are for two adults and include a buffet breakfast. Each additional person is $13 per night without a bath and $21 per night with a bath. Only a few rooms can handle a rollaway that costs $11 per night. Children twelve and under stay free. Rates are slightly lower from mid-November to mid-March, excluding holidays. Several packages are offered for fall and winter.

Location: Twenty miles north of the town of Oakhurst and 4 miles north of the south entrance to Yosemite National Park. The hotel is approximately 25 miles from Yosemite Valley.

Season: Open mid-April through Thanksgiving and most weekends and holidays through the winter. Closed most of January.

Food: An attractive dining room, with a wall of windows to the west overlooking the front lawn and to the north providing a view of a wooded area, serves breakfast (free buffet or $8.00–$11.00 from the menu), lunch ($11.00–$17.00), and dinner ($21.00–$33.00). Reservations are accepted for dinner only for parties of six or more. A children's menu is available. Alcoholic beverages are served on the front porch, in the lobby, and in the dining room. During summer months an old-fashioned barbecue is served Saturday night on the front lawn. A snack shop at the golf shop in the bottom floor of the Annex offers sandwiches, chili, and beverages from spring to fall. A market with beer, wine, soft drinks, cold sandwiches, and limited groceries is a short walk from the hotel.

Facilities: Swimming pool, tennis court, nine-hole golf course, putting green, market, gift shop, post office, gas station, historic Pioneer Village.

Activities: Golf, tennis, horse rides, stagecoach rides, swimming, fishing, and hiking.

Tuolumne Meadows Lodge

Yosemite National Park, CA 95389 • (209) 372-8413 • www.yosemitepark.com

Tuolumne Meadows Lodge is a group of sixty-nine canvas tent cabins situated at 8,775 feet in the Sierras. The lodge offers stays of up to seven days and is an attractive location for visitors who plan to hike to other camps in the High Sierra Loop. Tuolumne Meadows also attracts people who enjoy the crisp air and open spaces of an alpine environment. The tents are on a hill to the east of a canvas lodge that houses the registration area and a dining room. The lodge is located about a mile off Tioga Road (California Highway 120), 9 miles from the Tioga Pass Entrance on the east side of Yosemite National Park. It is 52 miles from Yosemite Valley.

The sixty-nine tents at Tuolumne Meadows are virtually identical to those at Curry Village in the Yosemite Valley. Tents are on a cement slab, and each unit has an inside wood stove for heat. Each canvas tent is equipped with either four single beds or one double bed plus two single beds. Sheets, pillows, and blankets are provided. The lodge also has maid service. The tents have no electricity or plumbing, so guests must use a common bathhouse with showers. Guests are provided with candles for light, wood for the stove, and towels for the bathhouse. A large central parking lot is a moderate walk from many of the tent cabins. Tuolumne Meadows Lodge is in a lovely area of Yosemite National Park

■ ■ ■

Conservationist John Muir first visited Yosemite in 1868. Muir recruited Robert Underwood Johnson, editor of Century magazine, to use Johnson's influence to protect this area, especially in the high meadows that were being used to graze sheep. Muir and Johnson camped together in Tuolumne Meadows as they planned a strategy to gain national park status for the high country around Yosemite Valley.

■ ■ ■

At an elevation of 8,700 feet, Tuolumne Meadows is a center of summer activity in Yosemite National Park. It is also the main access point for the High Sierra camps—Merced Lake, Vogelsang, Glen Aulin, May Lake, and Sunrise Camp—that offer dormitory-style accommodations. These hike-in (or ride in on saddle) camps offer canvas cabins with concrete floors and single and double beds. Blankets are provided, but not linens. Breakfast and dinner at each camp are served in a central dining tent. The High Sierra camps are very popular, and reservations are made via lottery applications available by calling (559) 252-4848 or visiting www.yosemitepark.com. Applications are accepted November 1 to December 15, with the drawing held in mid-December.

■ ■ ■

and is appropriate for those who don't mind roughing it a little. The tent cabins are near the Tuolumne River's Dana Fork, which runs through the largest subalpine meadow in the Sierra Nevada. No cooking or picnicking is permitted in or near the tent cabins. The nearby restaurant serves regular breakfast items and five or six dinner entrees at reasonable prices. Beer and wine are available for purchase. Other facilities are at Tuolumne Meadows Store, about 2 miles away on Tioga Road.

Rooms: Doubles, triples, and quads. No rooms have private baths. There are no wheelchair-accessible cabins.

Rates: All tent cabins ($82). Rate quoted is for two adults. Each additional adult is $10.00; each additional child, $6.00.

Location: One mile south of Tioga Road, 9 miles west of the Tioga Pass entrance.

Season: Late spring to early fall. Season depends on the weather.

Food: A dining room in the registration/dining tent serves breakfast ($4.00–$8.00) and dinner ($8.00–$19.00). Reservations are required for dinner. Box lunches ($8.00) are available when ordered by 8:00 the previous evening. Fast food is available at Tuolumne Meadows Grill from 7:30 a.m. to 6:00 p.m. The grill is 2 miles away on Tioga Road.

Transportation: A hiker's bus runs between Yosemite Valley and Tuolumne Meadows Lodge (fee). A free shuttle operates between the lodge and the store.

Facilities: Minimal gifts and necessities are sold near the registration desk. Tuolumne Meadows Store has a post office, market, gas station, climbing school, and stable.

Activities: Hiking, fishing, horseback riding, and rock climbing.

WHITE WOLF LODGE

Yosemite National Park, CA 95389 • (209) 372-8416 • www.yosemitepark.com

Yosemite's mountain meadows were once used for sheep grazing. According to legend, a sheepherder in this area claimed he had seen a "white wolf"— thus, the name for this area. It's not certain that wolves ever inhabited this area of the Sierra Nevada, so the sheepherder may actually have spotted a coyote.

White Wolf Lodge comprises a wooden registration/dining building, four wood cabins, and twenty-four canvas tent cabins. A central bathhouse with showers is located near the tent cabins. White Wolf Lodge, at an altitude of 8,000 feet, is in an isolated part of the High Sierra, a short distance off Tioga Road via a paved road. The lodge is approximately 30 miles east of Yosemite Valley.

The lodge has four wood cabins, each with two double beds, propane heat, electricity, and a full bath. The cabins have a small front porch and are built as duplexes.

Tioga Road (California Highway 120), which accesses both White Wolf Lodge and Tuolumne Meadows Lodge, was originally built as a mining road in 1882–1883. It was modernized in 1961. The two-lane paved road climbs to an elevation of 9,945 feet as it winds 75 miles across the Sierra high country from Yosemite Valley to Lee Vining, California. The road closes in winter and, depending on the weather, generally reopens in May. Road and weather information is available from a National Park Service recording at (209) 372-0200.

The tent cabins at White Wolf Lodge are identical to the cabins described for Tuolumne Meadows Lodge. Each tent has a wood stove, with wood provided, candles for light, and either four single beds or one double and two single beds. Linens with maid service are provided. The tents have no electricity or plumbing. This area is known to have bears, so food must be stored in metal "bear boxes" located behind the tent cabins.

White Wolf Lodge provides solitude in an attractive outdoor environment. This is a place where it is easy to meet other guests, in part because of the type of people who choose to stay here, but also because there are not many activities to divert their attention. The cozy restaurant has a stone fireplace and serves breakfast and dinner in small inside and outside dining areas.

Rooms: Doubles, triples, and quads. Full bathrooms are only in the four wood cabins. A community bathhouse is available for guests in the tent cabins. No handicap-accessible rooms are available.

Rates: Tent cabins ($77). Rate quoted is for two adults. Each additional adult is $10.00 per night; each additional child, $6.00. Wood cabins with private bath ($105). Rate quoted is for one to four persons. No additional charge in the cabins for children twelve years and younger.

Location: A short distance north of Tioga Road, 30 miles east of Yosemite Valley.

Season: Late spring to early fall, depending on the weather.

Food: A small dining room serves regular breakfast items ($5.00–$8.50) and four to five dinner entrees ($7.00–$17.00). Reservations are advised for dinner.

Transportation: A hiker's bus that runs between Yosemite Valley and Tuolumne Meadows stops at White Wolf Lodge.

Facilities: Small store and restaurant; central bathhouse with showers.

Activities: Hiking.

COLORADO

Mesa Verde National Park

P.O. Box 8 • Mesa Verde, CO 81330 • (970) 529-4465 • www.nps.gov/meve

Mesa Verde (Spanish for "green table") is our country's outstanding archaeological national park that preserves sites built by ancient Native Americans who are claimed as ancestors by twenty-four current Native American nations. The park's magnificent cliff dwellings, abandoned in the late 1200s, represent the last 75 to 100 years of the 700 years of the Ancestral Puebloans who lived here on the mesa tops and sheltered alcoves of the canyon walls. Mesa Verde offers a variety of visitor activities, but most people come here to tour one or more of the park's impressive ruins. Tour tickets can be purchased 15 miles from the entrance station at Far View Visitor Center (open from mid-April to mid-October), which also has exhibits of prehistoric and historic Indian arts and crafts. Chapin Mesa Archeological Museum offers exhibits and a twenty-five-minute video presentation. The park's entrance road from U.S. Highway 160 is narrow with steep grades and sharp curves. Trailers must be dropped off 4 miles inside the entrance, near the campground. The 12-mile mountain road to Wetherill Mesa (open summer only) is not open to vehicles over 8,000 GVW and/or longer than 25 feet. Mesa Verde National Park is in the southwestern corner of Colorado, 36 miles west of Durango on US 160. **Park Entrance Fee:** $15 per vehicle/$8.00 per individual from late-May to September 1; $10.00 per vehicle/$5.00 per person the remainder of the year. Entrance fee is good for seven days.

Lodging in Mesa Verde National Park: Mesa Verde has a single lodging facility that provides a total of 150 rooms in seventeen older, motel-style buildings. Far View Lodge is 15 miles from the park entrance station, near Far View Visitor Center and Far View Terrace. None of the park ruins is within walking distance of the lodge.

FAR VIEW LODGE

P.O. Box 277 • Mancos, CO 81328 • (970) 529-4421 • www.visitmesaverde.com

Far View Lodge features an attractive adobe building housing the registration desk, a small lobby, a dining room, a gift shop, and a cocktail lounge, with seventeen separate but nearby motel-type wooden buildings, each with from four to twenty rooms that generally offer exceptional views. Paved roads near the lodge lead to the park ruins.

Far View Lodge is situated at an altitude of 8,250 feet on a shoulder of the Mesa Verde. It provides an outstanding view of up to 100 miles and three states: Colorado, New Mexico, and Arizona (hence the name). The lodge offers 150 rooms in two categories: standard and Kiva. All rooms have electric heat, a private bath with either a shower or a combination shower-tub, a coffeemaker, a hair dryer, a small refrigerator, and a telephone, but no television. Kiva rooms have been completely refurbished with wood or tile floors, new bathrooms, brass bowl sinks, superior mattresses, and authentic Native American and Southwestern artwork and handcrafted furnishings made by local artisans. Kiva rooms also have air conditioning and are available with either a king or two queen beds. Standard rooms are furnished with one king, one queen, two queens, or two double beds.

All of the seventeen lodge buildings are one-story except for two units on each side of the registration building, that are two-story. Each room has a large

■   ■   ■

Ranger-guided tours ($3.00 per person) at Cliff Palace (one hour), Balcony House (one hour), and Long House (ninety minutes) on Wetherill Mesa require tickets that are sold only at the Far View visitor center or at the Morefield Ranger Station. Tickets are not available at the sites. Tour spaces are limited, and tickets should be purchased upon arrival in the park. Commercial half-day and full-day guided bus tours ($50 per person for half-day tours) begin at Far View Lodge where tickets are sold. Self-guided tours at the Far View sites (³/₄-mile unpaved trail), Spruce Tree House (the park's best-preserved cliff dwelling), and Step House (³/₄-mile round-trip) do not require a ticket. Ladder climbing is required during each of the ticketed tours.

■   ■   ■

Mesa Verde National Park

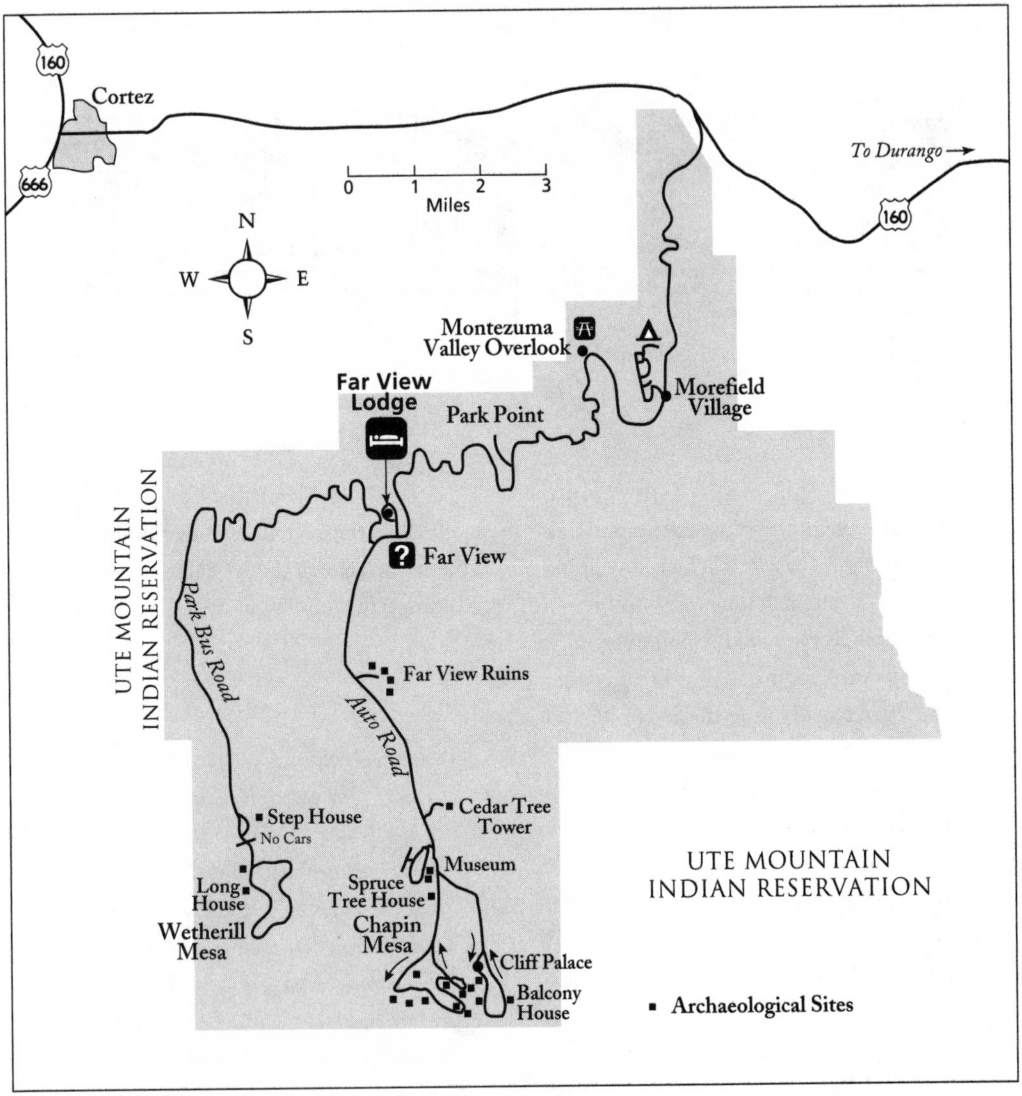

window and a private balcony with two chairs. The buildings are situated on a hillside so that all the rooms offer a view of mesas and canyons. The best views are in rooms 131 through 140 and 111 through 120. All are second-floor rooms of a two-story building with access that does not require climbing steps. Adequate parking is available directly outside each building.

Far View Lodge is ideally situated for an exploration of Mesa Verde National Park. It is a short distance off the main road to Wetherill and Chapin Mesas, a quiet but handy location because most guests visit both areas. The Metate Room, one of our favorite national park dining rooms, offers an attractive decor, scenic vistas, and excellent food. We have enjoyed fine dinners in the dining room during each of our five stays at the lodge. Alcoholic beverages including an extensive wine list are offered in the dining room and in a second-floor lounge with floor-to-ceiling windows and a large balcony. A quarter-mile paved trail from the lodge leads to the park's main visitor center, which has exhibits of both prehistoric and historic tribes of the region, including native jewelry and pottery. Tickets for ranger-guided tours of Cliff Palace, Balcony House, Long House, and other guided tours can be purchased in the visitor center. Another quarter mile along the same trail brings visitors to the Far View Terrace, which offers a cafeteria and a large gift shop. Guided bus tours of the park begin at the lodge, where reservations can be made and tickets purchased.

Rooms: Each room can accommodate one to four adults. Rates quoted are for two adults. All rooms have private baths with shower or a combination tub-shower.

Wheelchair Accessibility: Ten rooms, some in each category, have ramp access, wide doorways, grab bars, and a roll-in shower. Each of these rooms has one queen bed.

Reservations: Far View Lodge, P.O. Box 277, Mancos, CO 81328. Phone (800) 449-2288; fax (970) 533-7831. Deposit required for one night's lodging. Cancellation notice of seventy-two hours is required for refund of deposit.

Rates: Standard ($121); Kiva ($148). Rates quoted are for two adults. Each additional person is $10 per night. Children twelve and under stay free with adults. Special packages (room plus tour and/or food) are available. AAA and AARP discounts are offered, based on availability.

Location: Fifteen miles inside the entrance to Mesa Verde National Park. The nearest major town is Cortez, Colorado, 10 miles west of the park entrance.

Season: Far View Lodge is open from mid-April to late October.

Food: The registration building houses an attractive dining room with a unique combination of decorations, vistas, and menu items. Many of the tables are situated to take advantage of the outstanding views. Breakfast ($10) and dinner ($16–$30) are served. Alcoholic beverages are offered in the dining room and a lounge that also serves appetizers and sandwiches. A half-mile away, a cafeteria at Far View Terrace seasonally offers breakfast, lunch, and dinner ($6.00–$12.00). Beer and wine are available. Specialty coffees and ice cream are also offered in the cafeteria.

Transportation: Scheduled air service serves Cortez and Durango, where rental cars are available. The nearest train service is in Grand Junction, Colorado.

Facilities: Dining room, gift shop, cocktail lounge. Eleven miles away Morefield Village has laundry facilities, a gift shop, and a store with groceries, beer, wine, and camping supplies. A gift shop and cafeteria are at Far View Terrace and Spruce Tree Terrace.

Activities: Guided tours of Mesa Verde Puebloan ruins originate from Far View Lodge. Chapin Mesa Museum has exhibits on native tribes. Trails of from 1.5 to nearly 8 miles are available for hikers. Special events, such as Hopi dances and pottery demonstrations, are scheduled from May through October.

Pets: Small pets are permitted.

GEORGIA

■ **State Tourist Information**
(800) 847-4842 | www.georgia.org

Cumberland Island National Seashore

P.O. Box 806 • St. Marys, GA 31558-0806 • (912) 882-4336, ext. 224 • www.nps.gov/cuis

Cumberland Island National Seashore comprises more than 36,000 acres of freshwater lakes, magnificent beaches and dunes, and saltwater marshes on Georgia's southernmost coastal barrier island. The island is 18 miles long and, at its widest, 3 miles wide. The National Park Service limit of 300 visitors per day results in a visit to Cumberland Island National Seashore being one of life's great pleasures. The seashore is in southeast Georgia, approximately 30 miles north of Jacksonville, Florida, via Interstate 95 and Georgia Highway 40. Main access to the national seashore is only by a concessioner-operated boat (fee charged) from the small coastal town of St. Marys, Georgia. Access to the island's only public lodging facility is via an inn-operated boat from Fernandina Beach, Florida. No bridges provide vehicular access from the mainland to the island.

Lodging on Cumberland Island National Seashore: The only public accommodations are at Greyfield Inn, a privately owned and operated, turn-of-the-twentieth-century mansion situated in the southern portion of the island. Access to the inn is via a private ferry that makes three trips daily from Dock 3 at the waterfront in Fernandina Beach, Florida. Fernandina Beach is on Amelia Island, situated at the extreme northeast corner of Florida. No vehicular access is available to the island or the inn.

GREYFIELD INN

4 North Second Street • P.O. Box 900 • Fernandina Beach, FL 32035

(904) 261-6408 • www.greyfieldinn.com

Cumberland Island National Seashore

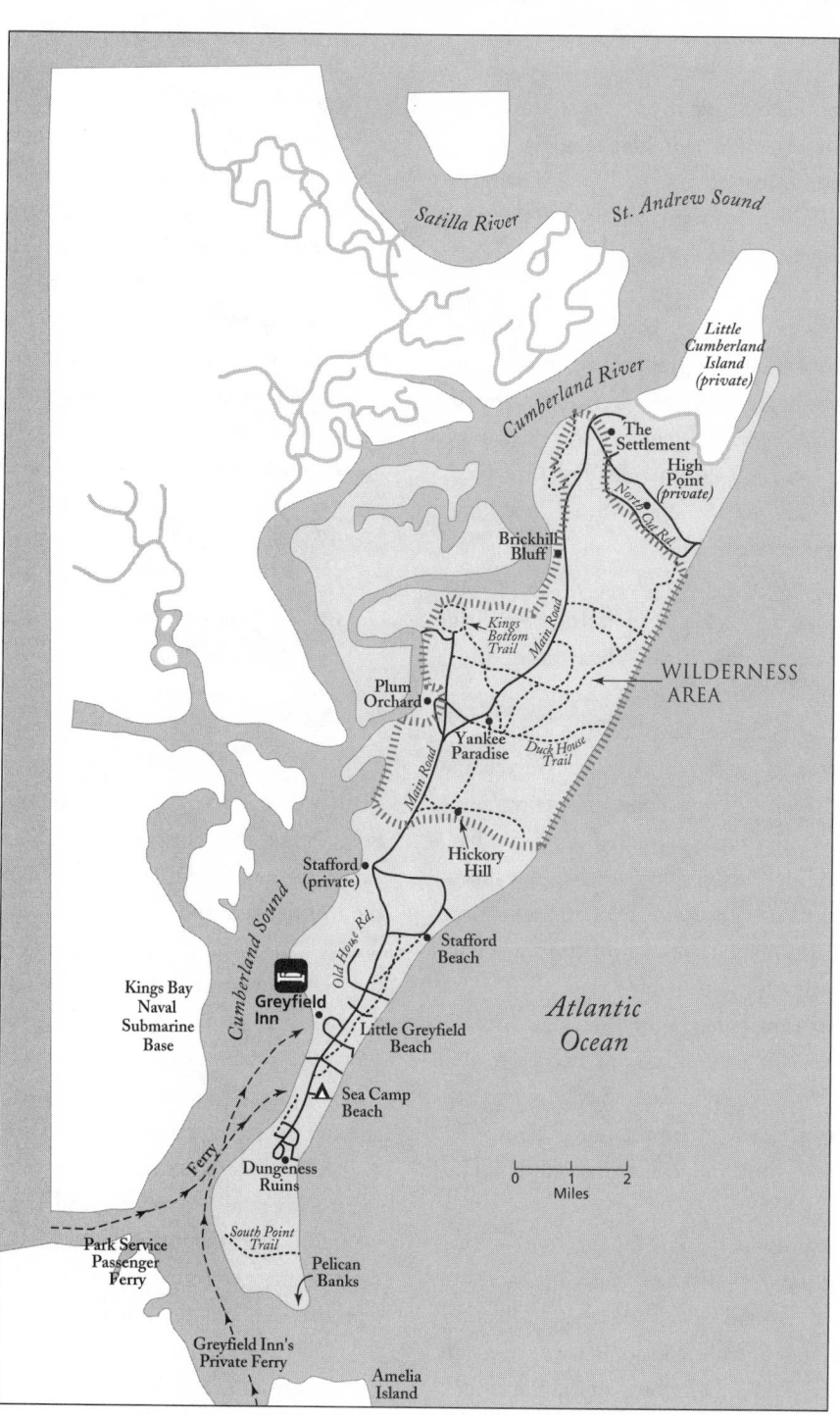

Satilla River

St. Andrew Sound

Cumberland River

Little Cumberland Island (private)

The Settlement

High Point (private)

North Cut Rd.

Brickhill Bluff

Kings Bottom Trail

Main Road

WILDERNESS AREA

Plum Orchard

Yankee Paradise

Duck House Trail

Main Road

Hickory Hill

Stafford (private)

Stafford Beach

Atlantic Ocean

Cumberland Sound

Old House Rd.

Kings Bay Naval Submarine Base

Greyfield Inn

Little Greyfield Beach

Sea Camp Beach

0   1   2
Miles

Ferry

Dungeness Ruins

South Point Trail

Pelican Banks

Park Service Passenger Ferry

Greyfield Inn's Private Ferry

Amelia Island

Greyfield Inn was constructed in 1901 for Margaret Ricketson, daughter of business tycoon Thomas Carnegie (brother to steel magnate Andrew). Margaret Ricketson's daughter, Lucy Ferguson, and her family opened the home to the public in 1962 as an inn. The inn provides ten rooms in the main house and six rooms in two separate but nearby cottage buildings. Both the main house and the two cottages are on the western side of the island near the dock area, where employees meet the ferry from Fernandina Beach. Other nearby buildings include a maintenance barn, where bicycles are stored, a bathhouse, and several private homes. The inn and its surrounding buildings sit in a large, cleared area surrounded by forests on three sides and the Intercoastal Waterway on the western side. The Greyfield Inn is accessible only via the inn's private boat that leaves from Fernandina Beach, Florida, and docks adjacent to the inn. Guests of the inn who arrive by private boat may also utilize the dock. Greyfield Inn offers day trips for $95 per person that include boat transportation, a picnic lunch, and use of the inn's facilities.

Entrance stairs on the south side of the inn lead to an impressive second-floor veranda with rocking chairs and a large porch swing. The second floor contains a large living room with fireplace, library, self-serve bar, and one bedroom. The dining room, kitchen, breakfast room, offices, and a small gift shop are on the first floor. Bedrooms and bathrooms occupy all of the third and fourth floors. No elevator is available.

Ten of the sixteen rooms at the Greyfield Inn are in the main house. Of these, only one bedroom, the Library Suite, is on the second floor. Seven rooms are on the third floor, and two are on the fourth floor. The rooms differ in size, furniture, and bath facilities. The bedrooms have either a double, a queen, a king, or two twin beds, depending on the size of the room. Price is determined by the size of the room and its accompanying bath facilities. All of the rooms have heating and air-conditioning, but not all rooms have a private bathroom. Six of the seven bedrooms on the third floor

■ ■ ■

Pittsburgh residents Thomas and Lucy Carnegie first came to Cumberland Island in 1881. After purchasing 4,000 acres on the island, the couple set about building an impressive plantation home, they named Dungeness, that would rival homes constructed by other millionaires on neighboring Jekyll Island. Thomas died in 1886, prior to completion of the home. Widow Lucy stayed on and expanded the family holdings until she had acquired nearly 90 percent of the island. The mansion that is now Greyfield Inn, given as a wedding gift to daughter Margaret and her husband Oliver Ricketson, is one of four homes that Lucy Carnegie had built on Cumberland Island for her children. The uninhabited Dungeness was destroyed by fire in 1959. The ruins at the south end of the island continue to attract tourists.

■ ■ ■

share two bathrooms. The seventh room, the two-room Porch Suite, accommodates three people and has a private bathroom. The Stafford and Dungeness Suites on the fourth floor and the Library Suite on the second floor each have a private bathroom. All bedrooms in the two one-story cottage units have private bathrooms. The larger cottage building has four bedrooms that share a common living area and a covered porch. The smaller cottage building has two bedrooms, with a common living area and a small, covered front porch.

All the bedrooms are comfortable and nicely decorated with family heirlooms and antiques. Our choice would be the Stafford Suite on the fourth floor of the main house, if you don't mind climbing stairs. If stairs are a problem, choose the Library Suite on the second floor.

Greyfield Inn is a place where you can relive the Old South, and do it in style. You don't need to cook, make the bed, or worry about meeting a deadline. There are no televisions to watch, cars to drive, or telephones to answer. In fact, the inn has just one telephone that it reserves for emergency use only. As a guest you will be treated to a full Southern breakfast with fresh-squeezed orange juice, a very nice picnic lunch, and a gourmet dinner at which guests are expected to dress appropriately (dinner jackets are available for those who left theirs behind). Your stay will include a half-day naturalist-guided tour to the north end of the island and a visit to the church where John Kennedy Jr. was married in 1996 to Carolyn Bessette. One of the country's most beautiful and uncrowded beaches is a short hike from the inn. Here you can jump in the waves, fish in the surf, or just stroll the pristine beach as far as you like. Perhaps you would like to hop on a bicycle and peddle down the dirt road to view the remains of Dungeness, Thomas Carnegie's burned mansion. A National Park Service visitor center is nearby. Stay alert and you may see some of the island wildlife, including the famous wild horses. Maybe you would prefer to curl up by the living room fireplace and read a book or sit in the porch swing on the veranda. Regardless, you should return home rested and ready for battle.

Rooms: All rooms except the Porch Suite accommodate only two people. The Porch Suite with a king and a daybed can accommodate three people. The six cottage rooms and four suites in the main house each have a private bathroom. A shower house (single shower) is located just behind the inn.

Wheelchair Accessibility: No rooms at Greyfield Inn are wheelchair accessible.

Reservations: Greyfield Inn, 4 North Second Street, P.O. Box 900, Fernandina Beach, Florida 32035-0900. Phone (866) 410-8051 or (904) 261-6408. A two-night minimum is required for all stays with the exception of holidays, which have a three-night minimum. A deposit equal to half the stay is required. A full refund requires thirty days' notice except for holidays, when no refunds are granted. Check-in is 1:00 p.m., and checkout is 11:00 a.m.

Rates: Rates range from $395 (marsh rooms and south porch) to $595 (Library and Porch Suites with private bath) per night. The majority of rooms are $495 per night. Taxes and gratuities add approximately 25 percent to the quoted room charge. Rates are for single or double occupancy and include three meals per day, plus unlimited snacks and non-alcoholic beverages; hors d'oeuvres at the evening cocktail hour; naturalist-led group nature tours; the boat trip to and from Fernandina Beach; and use of bicycles, beach equipment, and fishing gear. Mid-week rate reductions apply during the off-season. Check the Web site for special packages.

Location: The inn is located on Cumberland Island, the southernmost barrier island off the coast of Georgia. Access is from the boat dock in downtown Fernandina Beach, north of Jacksonville.

Season: Greyfield Inn is open all year.

Food: Three meals a day are included in the price of the room. Meals include a full breakfast, a picnic lunch, and a gourmet dinner of regional specialties. Hors d'oeuvres are served during the cocktail hour. Complimentary coffee, tea, soft drinks, and snacks are available throughout the day. A full cash bar and wine service are available to guests. With advance notice, special dietary needs can be met.

Transportation: Scheduled airlines and Amtrak serve Jacksonville, Florida, where rental vehicles are available. The inn offers free boat transportation from Dock 3 in downtown Fernandina Beach to the inn, three times a day, at 9:30 a.m., 12:15 p.m., and 5:30 p.m. The boat leaves Cumberland Island for Fernandina Beach at 8:00 a.m., 10:45 a.m., and 3:30 p.m. The boat ride takes about forty-five minutes.

Facilities: Dining room, bar, library, shower house, gift shop, bicycles, beach equipment, and fishing gear.

Activities: Guided nature tours, beach walking, hiking, swimming in the ocean, kayaking, bird-watching, bicycling, and fishing. Massage therapy and fishing charters (fee) with advance reservation.

HAWAII

■ State Tourist Information
(800) 464-2924 | www.gohawaii.com

Hawaii Volcanoes National Park

P.O. Box 52 • Hawaii Volcanoes National Park, HI 96718 • (808) 985-6000 • www.nps.gov/havo

Hawaii Volcanoes National Park comprises 333,000 acres of active volcanism, including 13,677-foot Mauna Loa and famous Kilauea, near where most of the park's activity is centered. An 11-mile paved road that circles the Kilauea Caldera provides access to scenic stops and nature walks. Hawaii Volcanoes National Park is located in the southeastern corner of the island of Hawaii. The visitor center and museum are approximately 29 miles southwest of Hilo, on Hawaii Highway 11, which bisects the park. **Park Entrance Fee:** $10.00 per vehicle or $5.00 per person, good for seven days.

Lodging in Hawaii Volcanoes National Park: Volcano House, with forty-two rooms, is the only hotel facility in the park. It is located just off Hawaii Highway 11 on the north end of Crater Rim Drive, which circles Kilauea Crater. Ten camper cabins operated by the same firm are at Namakani Paio Campground, 3 miles west of the park entrance, on HI 11. Additional lodging is available in nearby communities and in Hilo. Members of the military may find accommodations at Kilauea Military Camp, 1 mile west of Park Headquarters. Phone (800) 438-6707 from Oahu and (808) 967-7321 from out of state.

VOLCANO HOUSE

Crater Rim Drive • Hawaii Volcanoes National Park, HI 96718 • (808) 967-7321

www.volcanohousehotel.com

Hawaii Volcanoes National Park

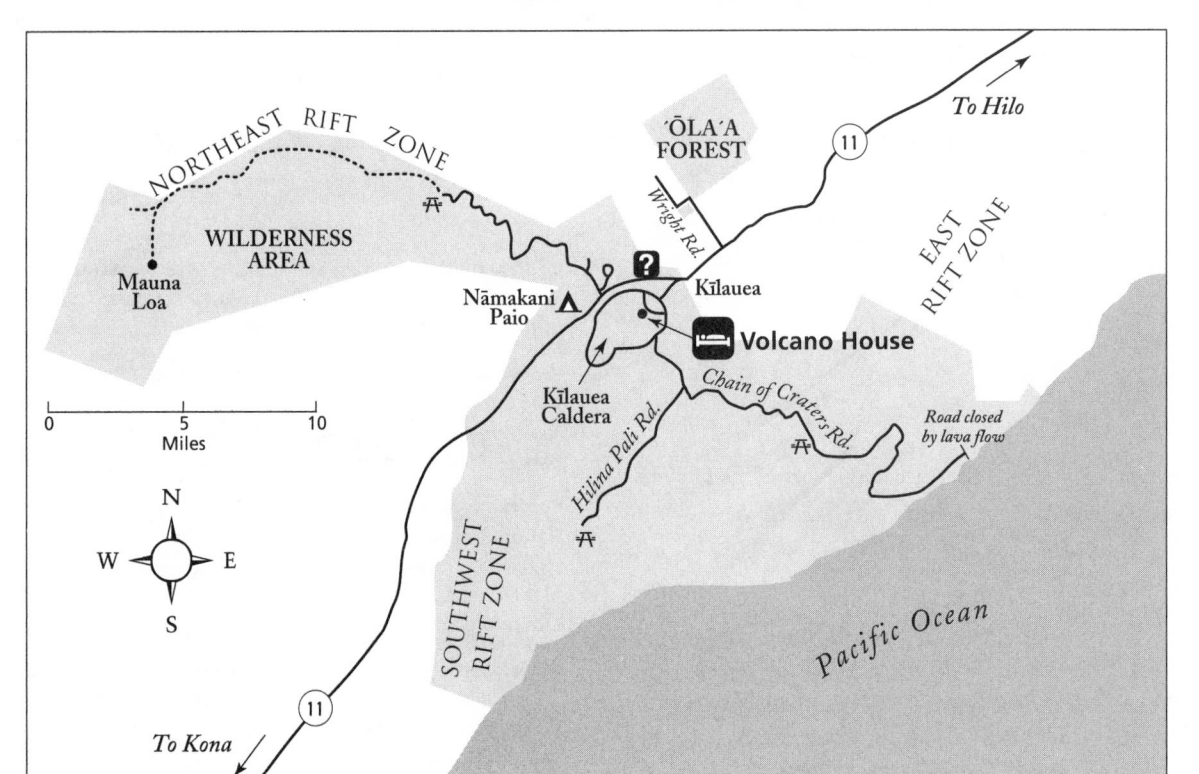

Volcano House is a rustic, two-story wood-and-stone hotel constructed in 1941 and expanded in 1962. The hotel has since been completely renovated. It is the oldest continuously operated hotel in Hawaii. The dining room, gift shops, cocktail lounge, snack bar, lobby, and most of the accommodations are all in a single building on the edge of Kilauea Crater. A separate two-story building, which was originally the rangers' station, houses ten rooms. Ten less expensive wood cabins without private baths are 3 miles from the hotel, in the Namakani Paio Campground. Volcano House is located just off HI 11, on Crater Rim Drive, which circles Kilauea Caldera.

The hotel offers a total of forty-two rooms, all of which have been refurbished with an island decor. Each room is furnished with koa wood furniture, carpeting, heat, telephone, and a private bath, most with a shower. Three hotel rooms have bathtubs. The rooms are divided into five classifications, distinguished primarily by size and view. Six crater-view deluxe rooms in the newer wing of the hotel are the largest offered. Five of these rooms have a king bed, and the other room has two doubles. Fourteen crater-view rooms in the original sections of the hotel have either a king, a queen with two twin beds, or two double beds. The twenty rooms in these first two classifications offer outstanding views of Kilauea Crater. The other twelve rooms in the original section of the hotel offer views of the ohia and fern forests and have either a king or two double beds.

Ten somewhat smaller rooms in a separate building called the Ohia Wing rent for substantially less than rooms in the main hotel. This former ranger station has

■　　■　　■

The original Volcano House was constructed in 1866 of grass and ohia poles. The first wooden hotel was built here eleven years later. This structure is across the road from the hotel and now serves as the Volcano Art Center. The main building of the hotel burned in 1940 and was replaced by the current Volcano House, which opened in November 1941. (Embers from the fireplace were saved in order to keep the fire burning.)

■　　■　　■

a small lobby with a fireplace and is surrounded by ohia trees. Eight of these rooms have garden views, while the remaining two are classified as standard rooms. Bedding in the Ohia Wing varies from two twins to a queen plus two twins.

The ten single-room wood cabins, which look like tiny A-frames, are located at Namakani Paio Campground, 3 miles from Volcano House. Each cabin has one double bed and one bunk bed, an electric light (no outlets), and an outdoor grill and picnic table. Linens, which include one pillow, sheets, a towel, and one blanket per bed, are provided when you check in at the Volcano House registration desk. You may wish to bring additional blankets, as the nights can be quite cold at that altitude and the cabins do not have heat. Cabin guests must use community bathroom facilities, which are situated among the cluster of cabins.

Volcano House is a convenient and interesting place to stay when you will be spending several days touring the Big Island, including a day in this unique national park. The location on the edge of the huge caldera is spectacular. The large lobby includes a famous fireplace that has been burning continuously for over 130 years. The Ka Ohelo Room serves a breakfast and lunch buffet, while the dinner menu includes entrees from Continental, American, and Pacific Rim cuisines.

A snack bar is open from 9:00 a.m. to 5:00 p.m. for a quick food stop. The historic Uncle George's Lounge is open from 4:30 to 9:00 p.m. for specialty drinks such as Pele's Fire. The hotel has two gift shops including one that specializes in Hawaiian arts and crafts created by local artisans. Many visitors like to experience this national park by hiking on over 150 miles of trails.

Rooms: Doubles, triples, and quads. All forty-two rooms in the hotel have a private bath. Cabins at Namakani Paio do not have private baths.

Wheelchair Accessibility: Two rooms are wheelchair accessible, one in the main hotel and one in the Ohia Wing. Both rooms have wide doorways, and the bathrooms have grab bars with a combination shower-tub.

Reservations: Volcano House, P.O. Box 53, Hawaii Volcanoes National Park, HI 96718. Phone (808) 967-7321; fax (808) 967-8429; or online at www.volcanohouse hotel.com. One night's deposit is required. Cancellation required seventy-two hours ahead of scheduled arrival.

Rates: Crater view deluxe ($230); crater view ($205); non-crater view ($175); Ohia garden view ($130); Ohia standard ($100). Namakani Paio cabins ($55). Rates quoted are for two adults. Each additional person is $20 per night in Volcano House and $10 in the cabins. Children twelve and under stay free with adults.

Location: Just off HI 11 on the north section of Crater Rim Drive. Volcano House is 30 miles from Hilo.

Season: Both Volcano House and Namakani Paio cabins are open year-round.

Food: Ka Ohelo Room serves daily breakfast ($12.50) and lunch buffets ($16.50). Dinner ($15–$38) is ordered from a menu. A less expensive snack bar serves chili, salads, sandwiches, and beverages. Limited groceries are available in nearby Volcano Village.

Transportation: The nearest scheduled airline service is in Hilo, where rental cars are available. A city bus operates between Hilo and the park's visitor center, which is across the road from the hotel.

Facilities: Restaurant, snack bar, cocktail lounge, gift shop, craft gallery, National Park Service visitor center, art center, golf course (1 mile away).

Activities: Hiking, biking, interpretive programs, golf.

KENTUCKY

■ **State Tourist Information**
(800) 225-8747 | Kentuckytourism.com

Mammoth Cave National Park

P.O. Box 7 • Mammoth Cave, KY 42259 • (270) 758-2180 • www.nps.gov/maca

Mammoth Cave National Park covers 52,830 acres, including the longest recorded cave system in the world. The park features rugged hillsides and beautiful rivers. A variety of guided cave tours are offered throughout the day. The park also has 70 miles of hiking trails and a gravel bicycle trail. Mammoth Cave National Park is located in central Kentucky, approximately 90 miles south of Louisville via Interstate 65. **Park Entrance Fee:** No charge.

Lodging in Mammoth Cave National Park: A single lodging complex in the park, managed by Forever Resorts, offers a wide variety of accommodations that are all close to the visitor center and ticket sales area for cave tours. Buses near the visitor center provide transportation to the cave entrance.

Mammoth Cave National Park

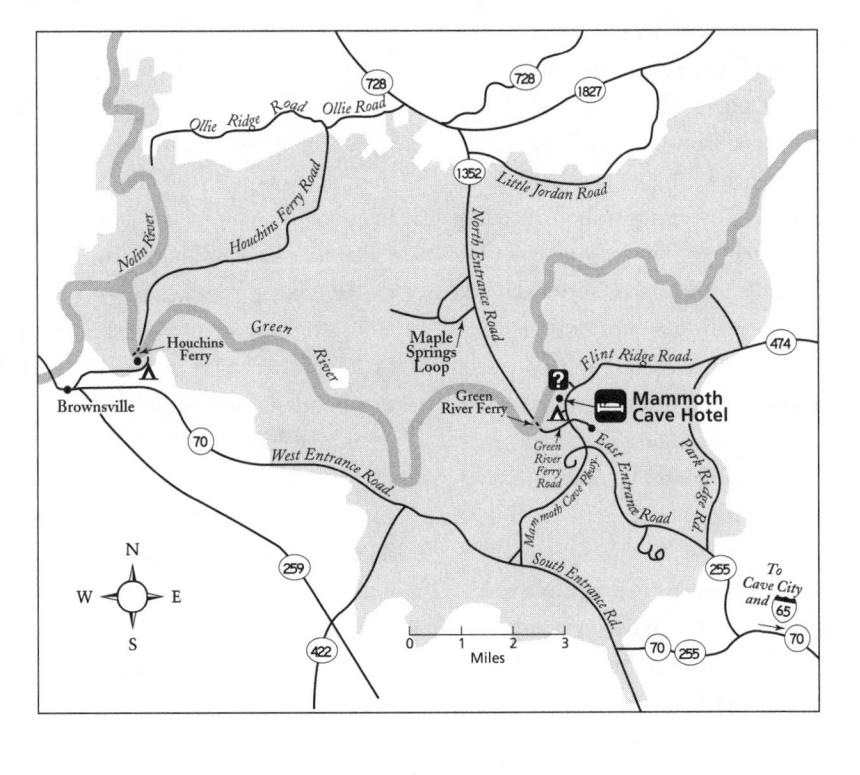

MAMMOTH CAVE HOTEL

P.O. Box 27 • Mammoth Cave, KY 42259-0027 • (270) 758-2225
www.mammothcavehotel.com

Mammoth Cave Hotel is actually much more than a hotel. It is a lodging complex consisting of thirty cottages, four one-story buildings, and a two-story brick hotel. In all, the complex provides ninety-two lodging units at reasonable rates. Registration for all lodging is just inside the front entrance to the main hotel, which also houses a wonderful craft store, a gift shop, meeting rooms, and three dining facilities. The lodging complex sits in expansive grassy areas near the National Park Service visitor center, where tickets are sold for tours of this world-famous cave. A paved walkway connects the hotel with the visitor center, where buses leave for scheduled cave tours. A large parking area is in front of the hotel. Mammoth Cave Hotel is located just off Kentucky Highway 70, in the southeastern section of Mammoth Cave National Park. The park is just off I-65 at either the Park City exit for northbound vehicles or the Cave City exit for those traveling south.

Four types of accommodations are available at Mammoth Cave Hotel. The least expensive lodging is the twenty Woodland Cottages, clustered on the north side of the visitor center. These rustic but pleasant wooden structures were constructed in the 1930s and are available mostly in two-bedroom units but also include four one-bedroom units, one three-bedroom unit, and one four-bedroom unit. Beds vary, but the four-bedroom unit can accommodate up to twenty individuals when rollaways are added. Each Woodland Cottage has hardwood floors, a vaulted ceiling, ceiling fans, a refrigerator, a coffeemaker, and a small private bath with hot water, a sink, a shower, and a toilet. The two-bedroom units also have a sink in each bedroom. The three-bedroom and four-bedroom units each have two bathrooms. None of these units has heat, air-conditioning, phones, or televisions. Windows and doors are screened to allow ventilation, but consider the lack of air-conditioning if you will be staying when the weather is likely to be hot and humid. These cottages are a nice size and offer more floor space than any of the other lodging choices at Mammoth Cave Hotel. Two-

The current Mammoth Cave Hotel is near the site of two earlier hotels, the first of which burned to the ground and a second that was torn down. The earliest hotel commenced operations in early 1837 when an entrepreneur connected several existing log cabins. This hotel, which was located just east of the current Mammoth Cave Hotel, was upgraded from 1839 to 1849 with a large two-story structure that included a second-floor ballroom. This early hotel was considered one of the state's finest and annually welcomed from 2,000 to 3,000 guests. It burned in 1916 and was replaced in 1925 by a second hotel situated across the parking lot from the current hotel building. The second hotel was expanded five years later to include thirty-eight rooms that could accommodate 200 guests plus a dining room that seated 125. This second hotel was near the current Hotel Cottages, hence their name. The hotel was torn down in 1979 after falling into disrepair and being removed from the National Register of Historic Places. A drawing of the first hotel is in the entrance to the current hotel's dining room and a painting of the second hotel is behind the front desk.

bedroom units 204/205, 206/207, and 208/209 are at the back of the complex next to a wooded area and offer the most privacy.

Ten Hotel Cottages across the parking lot from the main hotel sit in a semicircle in a large grassy area along the top of a wooded hillside. The small wood cabins, constructed in the 1930s, have electric heat, air-conditioning, a television, carpeting, a coffeemaker, and a small private bath with a shower but no tub. Each cottage has one double bed. The cottages face a wooded ravine, and two lawn chairs sit outside the front entrance to each cottage. The Hotel Cottages are situated some distance from the parking lot, so you should consider the required walk when booking a room.

The Sunset Terrace Units consist of four single-story buildings constructed in the 1960s. These fairly large units were refurbished in 2001 and are designed for families. Each unit offers electric heat, air-conditioning, a telephone, a television, and a full bath with a combination shower-tub. The units are identical, with two double beds, and each could easily accommodate a rollaway. Windows across the back side of each face out on a wooded area. Cement patios between the buildings have lawn chairs and tables. A large grassy area in front of the four buildings is a good place for kids to play.

The main hotel, constructed in 1964, has forty-two Heritage Trail Rooms in a two-story brick building adjacent to the registration/restaurant building. This building does not have an elevator, so access to second-floor rooms requires climbing a flight of stairs. Heritage Trail Rooms each have a full bath with a combination shower-tub, heat, air-conditioning, a small refrigerator, a telephone, a coffeemaker, and a television. Each room has a private balcony or patio with chairs and a small table. The rooms are small but nicely furnished and have either one king, one queen, or two double beds. Rooms on both floors are entered through an interior corridor that runs the length of the building. This building is the most convenient to the lobby and dining facilities. We suggest you choose a back room overlooking a wooded ravine.

Mammoth Cave National Park offers more than the cave tours for which it is so famous. In fact, this is one of our favorite parks, both for camping and overnight stays in the lodge. The area in which the lodging facilities are located is very pleasant, with lots of trees and open grassy spaces. Most park visitors have completed their cave tours by the late afternoon, so evenings are perfect for a quiet walk. Hiking trails and ranger-led walks are also available, and an amphitheater with evening programs is a short walk from any of the lodging facilities.

Cave tours are the most popular activity at Mammoth Cave National Park. Approximately a dozen different types of tours are offered, depending on the season and demand. Some tours are easy and last about an hour. Others are strenuous and last from three to six hours. A schedule of each day's cave tours is posted in the visitor center. Cave temperatures are in the fifties, and the paths can be slick, with many steps, so it is important to dress properly. Most tours fill rapidly, so, if possible, make a reservation prior to arrival by mail or phone (877-444-6777) or online at reservations.nps.gov. Reservations may be made up to five months in advance of the tour date you desire. If you arrive at the park without a reservation, be sure to head for the visitor center, where reservations can be made and tickets purchased. You will also be able to obtain information about the various tours that are offered.

If you plan to take a ranger-led cave tour, be certain to check in at the visitor center behind the hotel as soon as possible after your arrival so you that can reserve a tour time if you have not already done so prior to your arrival.

Rooms: Singles, doubles, triples, and quads. Some units can accommodate more than four persons. All rooms and cabins have private baths.

Wheelchair Accessibility: Four rooms near the lobby of the main hotel are fully wheelchair accessible with two rooms having roll-in showers and two with a combination shower-tub. These rooms are large, and each has two double beds. They enjoy all of the amenities of the other Heritage Trail Rooms, with the exception of a patio. Two fully wheelchair-accessible rooms are also available in Sunset Terrace Units.

Reservations: Mammoth Cave Hotel, P.O. Box 27, Mammoth Cave, KY 42259-0027. Phone (270) 758-2225; fax (270) 758-2301. One night's deposit required. Refund of deposit requires forty-eight-hour cancellation notice.

Rates: Woodland Cottages ($55–$99 depending on the number of guests and the number of rooms in the cottage). Hotel Cottages ($74 two persons). Sunset Terrace Units ($94 for up to three persons). Heritage Trail Rooms ($84 for two persons). Each extra adult is $7.00 per night in Woodland Cottages and $9.00 per night in the other Heritage Trail and Sunset Terrace Rooms. Rollaway beds are $9.00 per night. The hotel offers packages and seasonal discounts. Call for information.

Location: The lodging complex is near the National Park Service visitor center in the eastern section of Mammoth Cave National Park. From I-65, take exit 53 at Cave City when traveling south and exit 48 at Park City when traveling north. The hotel is approximately 7 miles inside the park entrance.

Season: The hotel and motel units are open all year. The Hotel Cottages are open from early spring to late fall, and the Woodland Cottages are open from late spring to early fall. Call for information on exact opening and closing dates.

Food: The Travertine Restaurant serves breakfast, lunch, and dinner ($6.00–$16.00). A breakfast buffet may be offered depending on the number of people staying at the hotel. The adjacent Crystal Lake Coffee Shop serves breakfast and lunch ($3.50–$8.00) and is open until 4:30 p.m. A fast-food restaurant is open from 10:30 a.m. to 5:00 p.m. from late spring to early fall. Mammoth Cave Hotel is in a dry county, and no alcoholic beverages are served. Limited groceries and snacks are available at the gas station.

Transportation: The nearest major airports are in Louisville, Kentucky, and Nashville, Tennessee, where rental vehicles are available. Scheduled bus service is in nearby Cave City, Kentucky.

Facilities: Gas station, pet kennels (free to hotel guests), restaurant, coffee shop, fast-food restaurant (summer only), gift shop, craft shop, nature trails, laundry, post office, canoe rentals.

Activities: Hiking, cave tours, horseback riding, fishing (no license required), canoeing, evening campfire programs (in season), ranger talks.

Pets: Pets are allowed only in the Woodland Cottages. A kennel is available without charge for hotel guests.

MICHIGAN

Isle Royale National Park

800 East Lakeshore Drive • Houghton, MI 49931 • (906) 482-0984 • www.nps.gov/isro

Isle Royale National Park comprises almost 572,000 acres, including the largest island in Lake Superior. Eighty percent of the park is under water. Isle Royale, approximately 45 miles long and 9 miles wide, is a roadless island of forests, lakes, and rugged shores. There are 166 miles of foot trails and numerous inland lakes on the island, where travel is via foot, boat, canoe, or kayak. Isle Royale has a rich history to share with present-day visitors. Native tribes mined copper here thousands of years before the French claimed possession of Isle Royale in 1671. The island became a possession of the United States in 1783 and was identified as Chippewa Territory until the mid-1800s. Copper mining continued during the latter half of the 1800s, when large areas were burned and logged.

Isle Royale is in northwestern Lake Superior, 22 miles southeast of Grand Portage, Minnesota. No roads or bridges provide access to the island. **Park Entrance Fee:** A user fee of $4.00 per person per day. National Park Service passes including the America the Beautiful Pass and senior pass are not applicable for the user fee. Staying one night in the lodge entails paying the user charge for two days—the day of arrival and the day of departure. Children eleven and under are exempt from the user fee.

Lodging in Isle Royale National Park: The only overnight accommodations inside the park are at Rock Harbor, on the south shore of the northeastern tip of the island. Rock Harbor Lodge features motel-type buildings and duplex housekeeping cabins, for a total of eighty rooms. Access to Rock Harbor is via seaplane or scheduled passenger boats from Houghton and Copper Harbor in Michigan's Upper Peninsula and from Grand Portage on Minnesota's north shore.

Isle Royale National Park

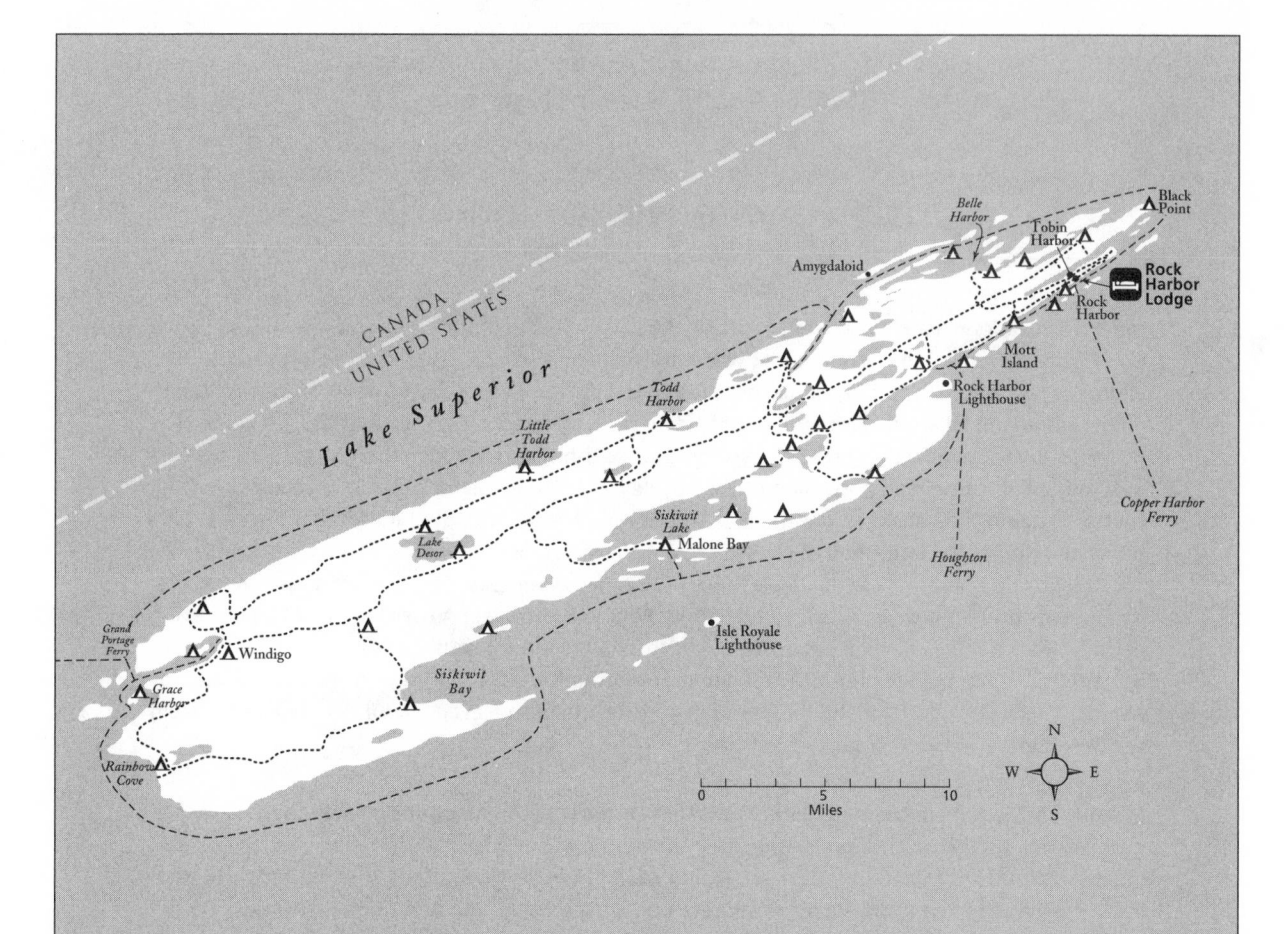

ROCK HARBOR LODGE

P.O. Box 605 • Houghton, MI 49931-0405 • (906) 337-4993 • www.isleroyaleresort.com

Rock Harbor Lodge is a relatively compact complex of four motel-type lodge buildings, twenty housekeeping cottages, and various support buildings nestled on a rocky shoreline of Lake Superior. Other buildings in the complex include a registration/administration building, a dining room/grill/gift shop, a small guest lounge, an auditorium, a store, a National Park Service visitor center, and a marina. The lodge buildings and cottages offer a total of eighty rooms. Paved walkways weave through the complex to connect all the buildings other than the auditorium, where access is via a gravel trail. Two of the four two-story lodge buildings sit side-by-side on each end of a small meeting room (actually an old lodge building) that serves as an occasional gathering place for guests. A nice deck with tables and chairs faces the lake behind the meeting room. All of the lodge buildings are directly on the shoreline of Lake Superior. The

housekeeping cottages are up a hill in a wooded area and are somewhat less convenient to the dining room. Luggage is picked up at the boat and delivered to each guest's assigned room. Luggage for departing guests is picked up in the rooms and delivered to the boat. Arriving guests receive a five-minute introduction from a park ranger before walking to the registration building to sign in and pick up room keys.

The four identical lodge buildings with stone-and-wood exteriors and paneled walls were constructed during the early 1960s. The paneling has since been removed, and the interior walls are now cement block and plasterboard. The sixty rooms in these buildings are carpeted and have a private bath with a combination shower-tub. The rooms each have heat and a coffeemaker, but no telephone, television, or air-conditioning. Bedding varies from a double bed, a double plus a twin, two twins, or a king. Rooms on the first floor enjoy a common wooden deck that runs the length of each building facing the lake. There are two chairs on the deck outside each room. Rooms on the second floor do not have a deck or balcony, but they offer a much larger window that provides an excellent view of the lake and some of its many islands. Second-floor rooms also offer the advantage of not having someone walking across the floor above you. Access to some of the lodge rooms requires climbing steps, so you should mention any mobility issues when making a reservation. Chippewa, with rooms 21 through 35, is the lodge building closest to the dining room, and first-floor rooms do not require climbing any steps.

Ten stone-and-wood duplex buildings offer twenty housekeeping cottages that sit in a wooded area on a bluff above Tobin Harbor. Each cottage has electric heat, an electric stove with oven, a microwave, a refrigerator, a coffeemaker, dishes, and utensils. Like the lodge units, there is no telephone, television, or air conditioning. These units have a double bed and one bunk bed (the wheelchair-accessible room has only one double bed) with linens and blankets but no maid service. The double bed slides into the wall and serves as a sofa during the day. Rollaways are available and easily fit into the large great room. The cottages are widely spaced to offer privacy and have large windows across the back side and one end, but only a few offer views of Tobin Harbor, and even these views are limited by trees. In addition, there is no deck or outside seating in which to relax and enjoy the outdoors.

Choosing a room at Rock Harbor Lodge depends on personal taste. The cottages offer more privacy and larger interior space and include cooking facilities. In all likelihood these appeal to families and individuals who plan a stay of several days. These units are nearly a quarter mile from the dining room, but this isn't an issue if you plan to cook most of your meals. The lodge buildings are closer to the dining room and offer excellent lake views. Choosing a lodge room means deciding whether

■　　■　　■

Although a number of national parks operate on a seasonal basis, Isle Royale is one of the few that completely shuts down. Every facility is closed and everybody, including all National Park Service personnel, departs the island prior to the harsh Lake Superior winter. The lodge closes to guests in early September when the manager and approximately a dozen employees (compared to about sixty-five employees during peak season) begin preparing the facilities for winter. Pipes are drained, and the heat is turned off. Canoes and kayaks are stored in the dining room, while benches are piled in the gift shop. Furniture remains in the rooms and cottages, but it is moved away from the windows where an errant tree limb might result in damage. The cycle is reversed in mid-May when the manager and about a dozen employees move into the cottages and begin preparing the facilities for an early June opening. This advance group prepares the plumbing and starts the boilers and refrigeration units. Rooms are cleaned and supplies ordered during the winter begin to arrive.

■　　■　　■

to ask for a first- or second-floor room. Second-floor rooms have some advantages, but we prefer a first-floor room that offers access to a deck. One of the pleasures of staying at Rock Harbor Lodge is sitting on the deck sipping a cup of hot coffee while listening to the wail of a loon and waiting for the sunrise.

Isle Royale is a special place that appeals to visitors desiring a different kind of vacation. There are no roads, no vehicles, and few people. You are unlikely to pass through the park on your way to somewhere else, and neither will anyone else. You can choose to pack in your food and select a cottage, or you can enjoy someone else doing the cooking in the grill or dining room. Be ready to hike or canoe, or spend time on one of the many guided tours. Although lodge rooms are available with the American plan (all meals included), the cost is about the same as if you purchased each meal separately. Take some food, even if you plan to frequent the dining room. Dining room food isn't inexpensive, so save money by eating a meal or two on your own—perhaps a bowl of cereal or muffins for breakfast or a sandwich for lunch. You might also think about eating a meal or two in the grill, which serves good sandwiches at a reasonable price. The grill also offers an outside deck for enjoying a pizza and beer on a nice day.

Rooms: Doubles, triples, and quads. Housekeeping cottages can accommodate up to six people. All rooms in the lodge buildings and housekeeping cottages have private baths.

Wheelchair Accessibility: Three lodge rooms and one housekeeping cottage are ADA compliant with a combination shower-tub that has a seat. (Note: No trails are wheelchair accessible.)

Reservations: From May through September, Rock Harbor Lodge, Isle Royale National Park, P.O. Box 605, Houghton, MI 49931. Phone (906) 337-4993. From October through April, Rock Harbor Lodge, P.O. Box 27, Mammoth Cave, KY 42259. Phone (866) 644-2003; or visit www.isleroyaleresort .com. A deposit of the first night's lodging is required to guarantee a reservation. A refund of 90 percent of the deposit is made for cancellations made at least five days prior to scheduled arrival.

Rates: All rates are quoted for two adults and include a complimentary half-day canoe rental. Peak season (early July to the end of the season)/low season (opening day to early July): lodge rooms on American plan ($386/$360), additional adult ($129/$123), additional child under twelve ($62/$60); American plan guests also get use of a canoe. Lodge rooms on European plan ($256/$230), additional adult ($60/$54), additional child under twelve ($18/$17). Cottages ($248/$223), additional adult or child ($53/$48). Rates include taxes and a 21 percent National Park Service utility pass-through fee.

Location: South shore on the northeastern tip of Isle Royale.

Season: The lodge is open from the second week in June through the first week in September. Housekeeping units are available from Memorial Day weekend through early September.

Food: The dining room offers a one-price menu for each of the three meals. Breakfast ($13.50) includes a variety of options including meat, eggs, potatoes, fruit, and French toast. Lunch ($16) includes about eight entrees that range from soup and salad to fish. Dinner entrees ($30.50) generally include fish, steak, chicken, pork chops, pasta, and an evening special. Children eat at a reduced price. A grill serves sandwiches (including a good hamburger), french fries, pizza, and very limited breakfast offerings from 7:00 a.m. to 7:30 p.m. Beer and wine are offered in the dining room and the grill. Limited grocery items including bread, milk, and ice-cream treats (no beer or wine) are sold at the marina store.

Transportation: Passenger boats to Rock Harbor Lodge depart from Houghton and Copper Harbor, Michigan, and Grand Portage, Minnesota. The Houghton trip takes six hours one-way and operates two days a week in each direction. Call (906) 482-0984. The trip from Copper Harbor takes three hours, and frequency varies depending on the season. Daily service is offered during high season from July 16 to August 15. Call (906) 289-4437. The boat from Grand Portage stops at Windigo and takes approximately seven and a half hours one-way to the lodge. Frequency of service varies with the season, although this boat generally operates three times per week from late May to early September. Call (651) 653-5872 for information. Check www.isleroyaleresort.com for the current schedule for each of the boats. Transportation information for Isle Royale is posted at www.nps.gov/isro/getthere.htm.

Seaplane service to Rock Harbor (thirty minutes one way) is offered from Houghton six days a week weather permitting. Call Royale Air Service at (877) 359-4753 or e-mail royaleairservice@aol.com for information. A lodge-operated water taxi will pick up hikers, campers, canoers, and kayakers at numerous places on the island. When planning a trip keep in mind the variable weather that can delay boat and seaplane departures to and from the island. Bad weather has sometimes kept lodge guests on the island an extra day or delayed guests with reservations from getting to the island.

Facilities: Dining room; grill; store with limited groceries, fishing equipment, and camping supplies; gift shop; and a marina with motorboat, kayak, and canoe rentals. The marina offers gasoline, diesel fuel, pumping services, and slips for boats up to 65 feet in length.

Activities: Hiking, guided walks, canoeing, kayaking, fishing, boat tours, evening National Park Service programs.

MINNESOTA

■ **State Tourist Information**
(800) 657-3700 | www.exploreminnesota.com

Voyageurs National Park

3131 Highway 53 South • International Falls, MN 56649-8904 • (218) 283-9821
www.nps.gov/voya

Voyageurs National Park preserves 218,000 acres of beautiful forested lake country that was once inhabited by French-Canadian fur traders, who used canoes to transport animal pelts and other trade goods through this area during the late eighteenth and early nineteenth centuries. A 1783 treaty established the U.S.–Canadian boundary along the waterway used by the voyageurs. The south side of the Kabetogama Peninsula is dotted with numerous islands, while the north shore is broken with many coves and small bays. One of the park's visitor centers is in its southwest corner, on Minnesota Country Road 123. Voyageurs National Park stretches 55 miles along the U.S.– Canadian border, east of International Falls in northern Minnesota. Summer travel within the park is confined to watercraft or floatplane. **Park Entrance Fee:** No charge.

Lodging in Voyageurs National Park: Overnight accommodations within Voyageurs National Park are available only at the Kettle Falls Hotel and Resort. Kettle Falls, in the northeast corner of the park, is reached via private boat or by private water taxi. Accommodations are available outside the park in Ash River, Crane Lake, Kabetogama Lake, and International Falls.

KETTLE FALLS HOTEL AND RESORT

12977 Chippewa Trail • Kabetogama, MN 56669 • (218) 240-1724 • www.kettlefallshotel.com

Voyageurs National Park

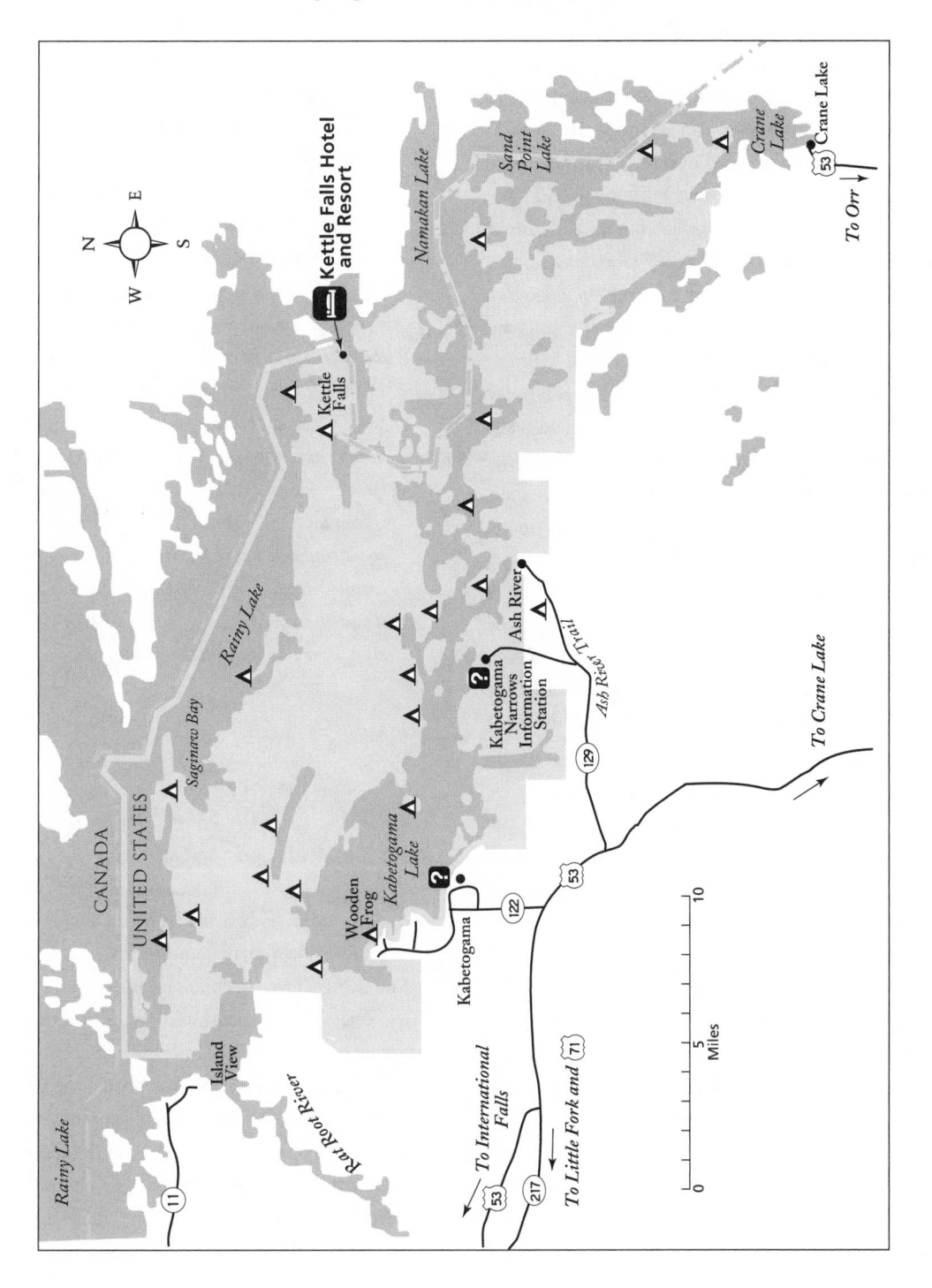

Kettle Falls Hotel and Resort is a relatively small lodging complex consisting of a historic two-story frame hotel plus three newer wooden villas that each contain from two to four lodging units, for a total of twenty-two rooms. The hotel is part of a National Register of Historic Places District that also includes the historic dam, a dam tenders cabin, and other sites and features. The first floor of the main building has a lobby, a dining room where they serve breakfast, lunch, and dinner including the best homemade rice soup we have eaten, and a saloon with a pool table, a working nickelodeon, and walls covered by antiques. Twelve guest rooms are on the second floor. The hotel sits in a small clearing surrounded by woods, and the villas overlook the rocky shore of Rainy Lake. A quarter-mile gravel road leads from the dock to the hotel. Transportation from dockside to the lodging complex is available. Kettle Falls Hotel and Resort is in the northeast corner of Voyageurs National Park and is reached only by boat or seaplane.

Transportation to the Kettle Falls via a hotel-operated boat is available (fee charged) on a daily basis from the Frontier Resort dock at the end of Ash River Trail (County Road 129). There is no charge for parking at the resort. Call the Kettle Falls Hotel and Resort for information. A free docking area is available for those who arrive via their own boats.

Three types of rooms are available. None of the rooms has a telephone or television, although a telephone is in the lobby and televisions are in the lobby and in the saloon. The least expensive rooms, all without private bath, are in the hotel, which was constructed from 1910 through 1913 to house construction workers who were building the nearby dam. The twelve hotel rooms are furnished with antiques and have either one double bed or two or three single beds. All these rooms are approximately the same size. The twelve hotel rooms and three modern community bathrooms with showers are on the second floor of the hotel. Coffee and rolls are served free to hotel guests in the dining room each morning.

Kettle Falls also offers ten villas in three separate

■　　　■　　　■

The building of Kettle Falls Hotel commenced in 1910, the same year construction began on the nearby dams. The original hotel included the lobby, kitchen, dining room, and ten bedrooms that span the front of the building. The north wing with additional bedrooms and the current saloon was added in 1915. The hotel initially served as a base for stonecutters and masons who worked on the dams, and later for lumberjacks and commercial fishermen. The original owner of the hotel, Ed Rose, sold the hotel in 1918 to Bob Williams, reputedly for $1,000 plus four barrels of whiskey. The Williams family owned the hotel until the National Park Service purchased it in 1977. In 1986 the National Park Service undertook an extensive rehabilitation of the building. Essentially, the building was taken apart and put back together after the foundation was stabilized. The Williams continued to manage the hotel as concessionaire into the 1990s, when the contract was sold to another individual.

■　　　■　　　■

buildings on the Rainy Lake side of the Kettle Falls Dam. These buildings, constructed in the early 1990s, are finished with a pine and oak decor. The villas have a screened porch, air-conditioning, and a private ceramic-tiled bathroom with a shower. Each villa also has a picnic table, lawn chairs, and an outdoor grill. Two of the buildings have two levels, while the other is a single story. The villas in each building are side-by-side with a connecting door that allows two adjacent units to be rented as a suite at a discounted price. One villa on each level has a full kitchen including a sink, stove, oven, microwave, coffeemaker, toaster, and full-size refrigerator. Pots, pans, dishes, and utensils are included. The connecting villa on the same level offers a refrigerator, microwave, and coffeemaker. The bedding in the villas includes either two bunk beds or a full bed plus a bunk bed. Villas in the one-story building and top-floor villas of the two-story buildings have a vaulted ceiling, include a table and four chairs, and are considerably larger than bottom-floor villas. They also have a large entryway with space available for storage and are at ground level requiring no steps. Villas on the bottom floor of the two-story buildings offer a larger screen porch and direct access to the lake. Access to the bottom-floor villas requires descending a series of steps. A three-night minimum stay is required when renting any of the villas. While the villas are newer and larger, you will save money and probably enjoy a more intimate lodging experience by choosing to stay in the hotel.

Although primarily geared to people who love to fish, even those with little interest in angling will enjoy the pleasant and relaxing atmosphere of this isolated resort. Spend the early morning on the screened porch sipping a cup of coffee. Take an afternoon stroll down the gravel road and stand where fur traders and trappers once portaged canoes around the falls. Walk to the dam overlook and you can actually view Canada, our neighbor to the north, while facing the south. In the late afternoon stroll into the bar with the sloping floor (resulting from a sinking building foundation) and knock back a cold one before sitting down to a walleye dinner. The hotel offers Internet access, satellite television, and long-distance telephone service (your own cell phone won't work here). One afternoon in late August we carried a picnic lunch to the dam overlook where, under cloudless blue skies, we looked up and saw a bald eagle circling overhead. Life doesn't get much better than this.

Rooms: Singles, doubles, triples, and quads. Villas with connecting doors can be converted to suites that accommodate up to eight people. All villas have private baths. Guests at the main hotel have access to community bathrooms.

Wheelchair Accessibility: Two villas, one with kitchen and one without, have wide doorways and a shower with grab bars and a seat. The toilet also has grab bars. The trail between the hotel and the villas is not paved, but a golf cart is available for transportation. The first floor of the hotel, with a dining room, saloon, and lobby, is wheelchair accessible.

Reservations: Kettle Falls Hotel and Resort, 12977 Chippewa Trail, Kabetogama, MN 56669. Phone (218) 240-1724 or (218) 240-1726 in the summer; (218) 875-2070 during the off-season. Reservations require a 30 percent deposit that is refundable (less a 15 percent fee) if canceled at least thirty days prior to scheduled arrival. Cancellation within thirty days of a scheduled arrival results in a deposit refund (less a 15-percent fee) only if the dates are filled by another party. Villa reservations require a 30 percent deposit and are refundable (less a 15-percent fee) only if the canceled dates are filled by another party.

Rates: Hotel rooms (single, $50; additional adult, $20; child, $15); villas per unit (night, $160; week, $750); villas with kitchenette per unit (night, $190; week $950); suite per unit (night, $290; week, $1,500). A three-night minimum stay is required in any of the villas. A rollaway is $15 per day.

Location: Kettle Falls Hotel and Resort is in the northeast corner of Voyageurs National Park.

Season: May through September.

Food: Meals are served daily in the dining room or on the screened porch. Breakfast ($4.00–$11.00) is served until 11:00 a.m., while dinner ($18.00–$23.00) begins at 4:00 p.m. Lunch selections ($5.00–$12) are also available at dinner. A limited children's menu is offered. Complimentary coffee and rolls are offered each morning for guests staying in the hotel.

Transportation: The nearest scheduled air service is 50 miles from Kettle Falls, in International Falls, Minnesota, where rental cars are available. With advance notice the hotel will arrange for pickup at the airport. Daily boat service, $42 per person, round-trip, is available to Kettle Falls from Ash River.

Facilities: Dining room, saloon, and a trading post with groceries, souvenirs, fishing tackle, live bait, and fishing licenses. Boat docks with fuel, portage service, and motorboat, canoe, and kayak rentals.

Activities: Hiking, bird-watching, boating, and fishing. Kettle Falls is the promised land for many fishers who travel long distances to have a shot at snagging a walleye. The kitchen staff will cook and serve your walleye for a nominal fee. Other frequent catches include northern pike, smallmouth bass, and crappie. Guide service is available when arrangements have been made ahead of time.

Pets: Pets are allowed in the villas at $10 per night, or $50 per week.

MISSOURI

Ozark National Scenic Riverways

P.O. Box 490 • Van Buren, MO 63965 • (573) 323-4236 • www.nps.gov/ozar

Ozark National Scenic Riverways covers 80,000 acres of forested hills and mountains along 134 miles of the beautiful Current and Jacks Fork Rivers. The rivers are especially popular for fishing and float trips in canoes, rafts, kayaks, and inner tubes, all of which can be rented. The park includes large freshwater springs and caverns. Ozark National Scenic Riverways is located in southeastern Missouri, 150 miles south of St. Louis. **Park Entrance Fee:** No charge.

Lodging in Ozark National Scenic Riverways: The riverways has a single lodging facility at Big Spring, 4 miles south of the town of Van Buren. Other accommodations are available outside park boundaries in Eminence, Mountain View, Salem, and Van Buren.

BIG SPRING LODGE AND CABINS

HCR 1, Box 169 • Van Buren, MO 63965 • (573) 323-4423

www.bigspringlodgeandcabins.com

Ozark National Scenic Riverways

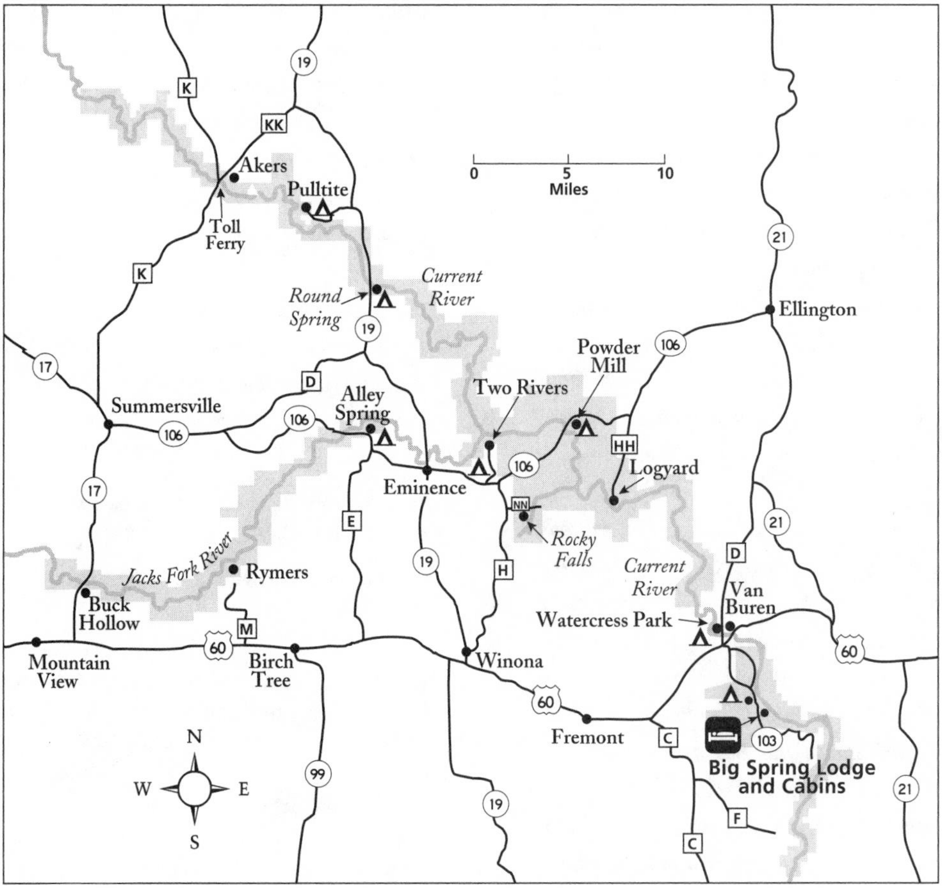

Map showing Ozark National Scenic Riverways with locations including Akers, Pulltite, Toll Ferry, Round Spring, Summersville, Alley Spring, Two Rivers, Powder Mill, Ellington, Eminence, Logyard, Rocky Falls, Jacks Fork River, Rymers, Buck Hollow, Mountain View, Birch Tree, Winona, Current River, Watercress Park, Van Buren, Fremont, and Big Spring Lodge and Cabins. Highways shown: 19, K, KK, 17, 106, D, E, M, 60, 99, H, NN, HH, 21, C, F, 103.

Big Spring Lodge and Cabins consists of a main lodge plus fourteen freestanding cabins. The timber-and-stone lodge building houses the registration desk, an attractive dining room, and a small gift area on a bluff overlooking the confluence of Big Spring and the Current River. The cozy dining room includes a small wing with windows that overlook the river. The rustic wood-and-stone and frame cabins on a hill above the main lodge building provide the only overnight accommodations at Big Spring. A paved road winds up the hill from the lodge to the cabins. Parking is available for each cabin, but access from parking to a cabin may involve climbing or descending numerous uneven steps.

The entire complex sits amid a thick forest of hardwood trees. Big Spring Lodge and Cabins is in southeastern Missouri, 4 miles south of the small town of Van Buren on Missouri Highway 103.

The fourteen cabins at Big Spring are available in four sizes that sleep two, four, six, or eight persons. The rate charged includes two, four, or six occupants depending upon the particular cabin that is rented. An additional fee is charged for guests that exceed the number included in the rate.

All the cabins have a private bath with shower but no tub. The cabins are roomy, with hardwood floors, stained wood walls, updated furniture, and a private

■   ■   ■

Big Spring Lodge and Cabins was built from 1934 to 1938, initially by the Civilian Conservation Corps (CCC) and, later, the Works Progress Administration (WPA), in what was then Big Spring State Park. The entrance station, lodge building, and initial cabins were constructed of local oak timbers and cut stone. Later cabins were of frame construction. Local employees started first on tourist cabin 403, classified as a Type A cabin. Next were cabin 402, similar in style to the first cabin, and the considerably larger Type B cabin 403, with two large stone chimneys and fireplaces. Nine additional Type E frame cabins with large stone chimneys were constructed, first by the CCC, and later by the WPA. Frame cabin 413, the only unit overlooking the Current River, was built as a residence for the fire-tower keeper. The main lodge building, on a hill overlooking the confluence of the Current River and Big Spring branch, and the entrance building were both completed in 1936. The Missouri State Parks Board signed over the state park to the National Park Service in 1969, and the Big Spring Historic District was placed on the National Register of Historic Places in 1976.

■   ■   ■

screened porch. They also have fans but no air-conditioning, telephone, or television. They each have kitchen facilities that include a two-burner cooktop, small refrigerator, microwave, toaster, and coffeemaker. They do not include an oven or utensils. Four cabins do not have a kitchen sink, and two cabins (413 and 414) do not have a fireplace. Be certain to discuss the size, bedding, and amenities of the cabin you will be renting when making a reservation. Outside each cabin is a grill and picnic table. The cabins are widely spaced along both sides of a paved road to provide relative privacy.

Big Spring Lodge and Cabins, a small lodging complex in a quiet rural area of Missouri, is a place where you can enjoy your own cabin in the woods at a relatively inexpensive price. Plan to read a few books, play some cards, and do a little hiking. Many of the visitors to Ozark National Scenic Riverways come to float on one or both of the Class II rivers that include 134 miles of clear, spring-fed streams. Nineteen National Park Service–authorized concessionaires rent canoes at or near Alley Spring, Big Spring, Paullotite, Round Spring, Two Rivers, and Watercress. Inner tubes are available for rent at several locations. A list of concessionaires is available from the National Park Service. On a rainy day you can sit in front of the stone fireplace in the small lobby area of the lodge building.

Rooms: From doubles to eight persons per unit. All cabins have a private bath with a shower but no tub.

Wheelchair Accessibility: No cabins are wheelchair accessible.

Reservations: Big Spring Lodge and Cabins, HCR 1, Box 169, Van Buren, MO 63965. Phone (573) 323-4423. A one-night deposit is required, and a two-night minimum stay is mandatory on weekends. Ten days' cancellation is necessary for a refund.

Rates: The three smallest cabins for two persons rent for $65 per night, while two large cabins for six guests rent for $120 per night. (There is an extra charge per person over six people.) Most of the remaining cabins that accommodate two to four persons rent for $80 per night. Each cabin rental includes a maximum number of occupants. Additional guests are $5.00 each per night.

Location: In southeast Missouri, 4 miles south of the town of Van Buren on MO 103.

Season: Mid-March through November.

Food: A cozy dining room serves breakfast, lunch, and dinner ($6.00–$25.00). Groceries are available in Van Buren.

Transportation: The nearest scheduled airline service is in St. Louis and Springfield, Missouri.

Facilities: Dining room.

Activities: Hiking, fishing, canoeing, tubing, swimming.

Pets: Pets incur a $10 per night charge.

MONTANA

Glacier National Park

P.O. Box 128 • West Glacier, MT 59936 • (406) 888-7800 • www.nps.gov/glac

Glacier National Park is among the most outstanding of America's national parks. Covering more than one million acres, it features towering mountains, glacial valleys, sparkling lakes, and more than two dozen glaciers. Visitor centers are on the west side at Apgar, on the east side at St. Mary, and in the high country at Logan Pass. The high country is best seen by driving or taking the free shuttle or Red Bus tour over the Going-to-the-Sun Road, a 50-mile winding two-lane road that bisects the park via the Continental Divide at 6,646-foot Logan Pass. If time permits, drive the Chief Mountain International Highway to Canada's Waterton Lakes National Park and the quaint town of Waterton. The 12-mile paved road from Babb to Many Glacier also offers outstanding scenery. The park is in northwestern Montana. The west entrance is 32 miles east of Kalispell, Montana. **Park Entrance Fee to Glacier National Park:** $25.00 per vehicle or $12.00 per person, good for seven days. A separate daily entrance fee of $20.00 per family ($7.80 per adult) is required to enter Canada's neighboring Waterton Lakes National Park, home of the Prince of Wales Hotel.

Lodging in Glacier National Park: Six lodging facilities are in four locations inside the borders of Glacier National Park. Two lodges sit just inside the park's west entrance from Kalispell in the village of Apgar. Apgar Village Lodge is privately owned and offers accommodations in historic cabins and two motel-type buildings. Nearby, Village Inn is directly on Lake McDonald and offers excellent lake and mountain views from each room of a two-story motel building. A short distance east on Going-to-the-Sun Road, Lake McDonald Lodge has numerous cabins and two two-story motel buildings in addition to rooms in what was once a private hunting lodge. On the east side of the mountain pass on Going-to-the-Sun Road, Rising Sun Motor Inn has motel units and numerous duplex cabins in an uncrowded area of the park's scenic high country. The picturesque Many Glacier area in the park's interior has two lodging facilities: historic Many Glacier Hotel, one of the great old national park lodges, and nearby Swift Current Motor Inn, with motel units and inexpensive rustic cabins. We have included two additional lodges that are located a short distance outside the park border but are closely associated with Glacier National Park. Glacier Park Lodge, in the small town of East Glacier on the east side of the park, is a classic lodge with a spectacular lobby. A short distance north of the border in Alberta, Canada, Glacier's sister national park of Waterton Lakes is the home of the Prince of Wales Hotel, one of North America's most picturesque national park lodges.

Reservations: All the lodges (except for Apgar Village Lodge) are operated by Glacier Park, Inc., P.O. Box 2025, 774 Railroad Street, Columbia Falls, MT 59912. Phone (406) 892-2525. A deposit of one night's stay is required. The deposit is forfeited for cancellations within three days of scheduled arrival. Cancellations prior to three days of arrival generally incur a $15 administrative fee. No administrative fee is charged for cancellations within thirty days from the date a reservation is made unless it is within thirty days of scheduled arrival. Apgar Village Lodge reservation information is listed separately in its write-up.

Glacier National Park

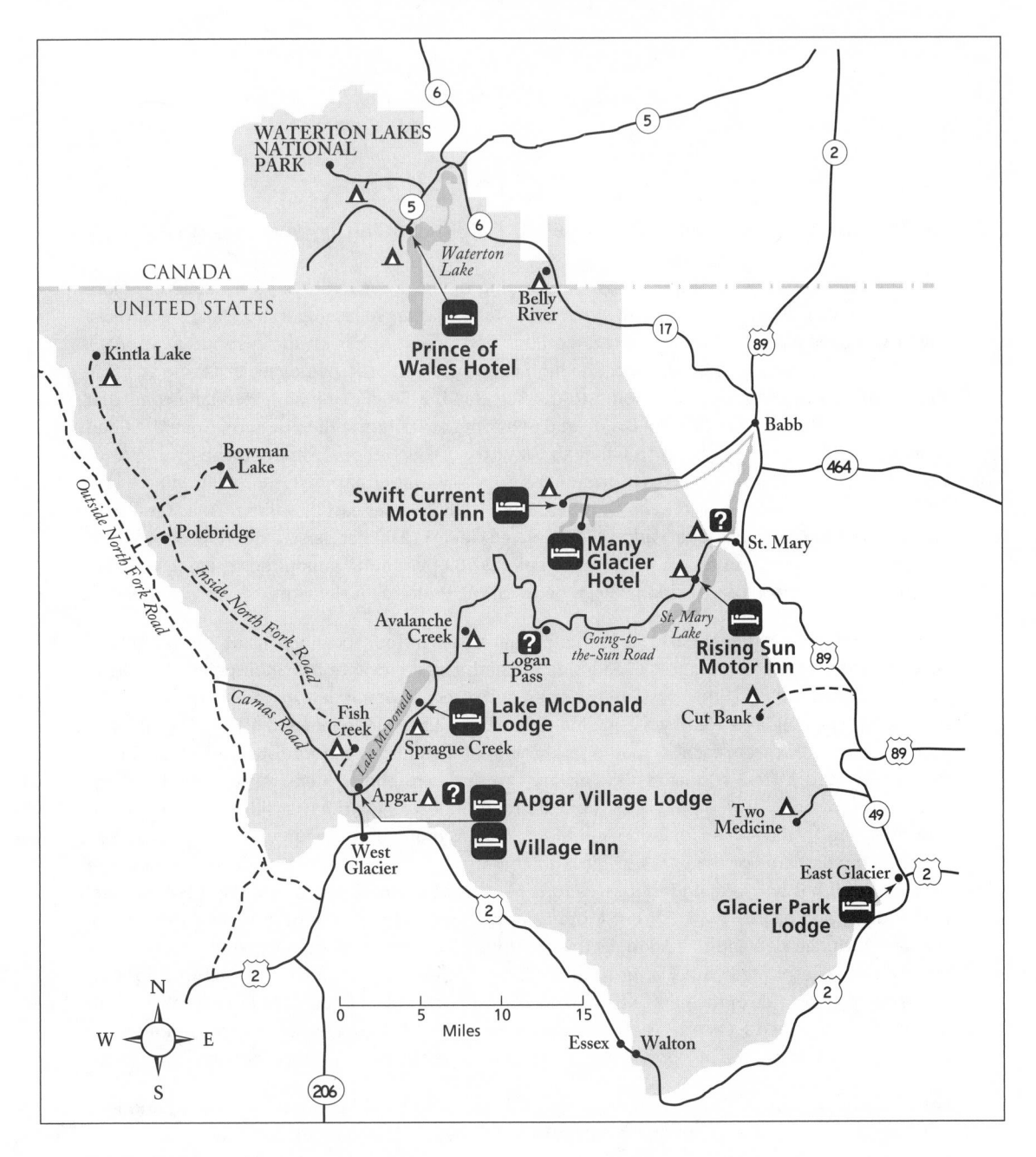

Transportation within the Park: Free shuttles that operate during July and August along the entire length of the Going-to-the-Sun Road offer the best way to see the most scenic parts of Glacier, especially when staying at one of the four lodges on or near the road. One shuttle route connects the Apgar Transportation Center (near Village Inn and Apgar Village Lodge) with points of interest (including Lake McDonald Lodge) up to the continental divide at Logan Pass. Another shuttle on the east side connects the St. Mary visitor center with Logan Pass. This shuttle stops at Rising Sun Motor Lodge. Riders can change shuttles at Logan Pass and traverse the entire Going-to-the-Sun Road and return the same day. The shuttles run every fifteen to thirty minutes depending on the route. A shuttle schedule or information about the shuttles is available at visitor centers. A separate hikers' shuttle (fee charged) operates within the park during July and August between St. Mary and Many Glacier Hotel. This connects at Many Glacier Hotel and the St. Mary visitor center with an east-side shuttle (fee charged) that operates between Glacier Park Lodge and the Prince of Wales Hotel. A variety of scenic interpretive tours in historic red "Jammer" buses are offered daily from each of the hotels except Prince of Wales. These tours are operated by the hotel concessionaire. Another tour company, Sun Tours, operated by the Blackfeet Indian Reservation, offers daily guided tours from East Glacier, St. Mary, West Glacier, and Browning. Call (800) 786-9220 or visit www.glaciersuntours.com for information.

Transportation to the Park: Commercial airline service and rental vehicles are available in Kalispell, Montana, on the park's west side and Great Falls, Montana on the east side. Amtrak stops on the park's east side directly across from Glacier Park Lodge and on the west side in the town of Belton/West Glacier, where a shuttle (892-2525) operates between West Glacier and Apgar Village and Lake McDonald Lodge.

Apgar Village Lodge

P.O. Box 410 • West Glacier, MT 59936 • (406) 888-5484 • www.westglacier.com

Apgar Village Lodge is a cluster of rustic wooden buildings including two small motel units, twenty-eight cabins, and a registration building . The entire complex is in a wooded area between McDonald Creek and the road through Apgar Village, a small commercial district on the west side of the park. The small registration building and one motel unit are on Apgar Road, and another motel unit and several cabins are on McDonald Creek. The majority of the cabins are in a wooded area between these two boundaries. None of the buildings sits directly on Lake McDonald, although the complex is no more than half a block from the shoreline of the lake. Apgar Village Lodge is near a restaurant and a National Park Service visitor center. The lodge is located in Apgar Village, 2 miles inside the west entrance to Glacier National Park.

Apgar Village Lodge offers a wide variety of accommodations. All the rooms have electric heat and private baths with showers but no air-conditioning, television, or telephone. Picnic tables are scattered about the complex. The least expensive rooms are in the motel building on the creek. These units do not have balconies, but the back window offers a good view of the creek. These small rooms have either one double bed, one queen-size bed, or one double bed plus a twin. The beds pretty much fill the room. The front motel building, with eleven rooms, is directly beside the registration building on Apgar Road. Each of the eleven units has two rooms, one with a queen bed and the other with a queen, a double, or two twins. Parking is directly in front of the building.

Most of the lodging at Apgar Village Lodge is in rustic cabins. The majority of the cabins are wood-frame, although several of the older units are of log construction. The cabins are fairly old but well maintained, with interiors that have carpeting and knotty pine walls and many with impressive beamed ceilings. The cabins do not have porches, although a picnic table is near each unit. Larger cabins have both front and back doors. Parking is directly in front of or beside each

Milo Apgar, an early homesteader in the area where Apgar Village now stands, arrived soon after the Great Northern Railway reached Belton (now called West Glacier) in the early 1890s. Unable to make it as a farmer, Apgar started offering overnight accommodations for miners and visitors to this beautiful area. Some of Apgar's original cabins are still standing as part of Apgar Village Lodge. Cabin 21 was part of Apgar's first home.

of the cabins. All but two of the twenty-eight cabins have a kitchen with a refrigerator, a stove, an oven, a sink, a toaster, a coffeemaker, and utensils including pots, pans, silverware, and glasses. Cabin sizes vary from a small unit with one double bed and no kitchen to a large unit that can sleep ten and has a bath and a half. The majority of the cabins have either one or two queen beds. Cabins 6, 7, and 8 have kitchens and are situated directly beside McDonald Creek. These three cabins offer the most desirable location in the complex, with cabin 6 being the most desirable of the three. Four other cabins with kitchens (cabins 10, 11, 12, and 22) face the creek from across a small parking area. Unfortunately parked cars directly in front of the cabins often block views of the creek. Each of the seven cabins noted above can sleep four adults.

Apgar Village Lodge offers rustic buildings in a relatively quiet setting. The complex tends to be quiet and is suited for people who like this type environment. Walks, wading in the lake, fishing, and kayaking are several of the activities available here. The National Park Service visitor center is about half a block away. Although the lodge doesn't have its own eating facility, a restaurant flanks the building. Gift shops and a grocery are a short walk away.

Rooms: Singles, doubles, triples, and quads. A few large cabins can hold six or more persons. All rooms have private baths with showers but no tubs. No rollaways or cots are available.

Wheelchair Accessibility: No rooms at Apgar Village Lodge are wheelchair accessible.

Reservations: Apgar Village Lodge, P.O. Box 410, West Glacier, MT 59936. Phone (406) 888-5484; fax (406) 888-5273. A deposit of one night's stay or 50 percent of the total cost, whichever is larger, is required. Reservations made prior to April 15 must be changed or canceled thirty days in advance of the arrival date for a deposit refund less a $15 cancellation fee. Cancellation for reservations made on or after April 15 requires seventy-two-hour notice for a refund. A $15 administration fee is charged for any cancellation.

Rates: McDonald Creek motel units ($89); front motel units ($109); one-bed cabin units ($94–$119); cabins with two or three beds ($133–$159); three-room cabin with five beds ($250). Rates for motel units and small cabins quoted are for two adults. Rates on medium and large cabins are for four adults. Rates are reduced from May 1 to mid-June and from mid-September to the end of the season.

Location: In the village of Apgar, Montana, 2 miles from the West Glacier entrance station.

Season: Early May through early October.

Food: A restaurant next to the motel on Apgar Road offers breakfast, lunch, and dinner from mid-May through most of September. Very limited groceries are sold at a gift shop next to the restaurant. The lodge is 2 1/2 miles from a full-service grocery store and several restaurants in the town of West Glacier.

Facilities: The village of Apgar has gift shops, a restaurant, an ice cream shop, boat rentals, and a National Park Service visitor center.

Activities: Nightly ranger/naturalist talks at the Apgar campground, boating, swimming (very cool water), fishing, hiking, sightseeing tours.

GLACIER PARK LODGE

East Glacier, MT 59434 • (406) 226-5600 • www.glacierparkinc.com • www.bigtreehotel.com

Glacier Park Lodge is one of the classic national park hotels built in the early 1900s by the transcontinental railroad companies in order to entice people to ride trains to the West. This majestic lodge was constructed in 1912 and 1913 by the Great Northern Railway, which was also responsible for building sister lodges Many Glacier and Prince of Wales. Freight and passenger trains continue to operate a little more than a stone's throw from the impressive hotel entry that is connected to the railway station by a corridor of beautiful flowers. The main lodge building was constructed in 1912, and the adjacent West Wing went up a year later. The

Glacier National Park is famous for the red "Jammer" motor coaches that transport people between the park hotels and sites. The coaches, built between 1933 and 1939 by the White Motor Company, have black canvas tops that can be rolled back for greater visibility by occupants. The coaches derive their name from the drivers who at one time had to "jam" the gears to get up the mountain roads of Glacier. Structural problems caused the Jammer fleet to be temporarily retired from service in August 1999. Following a collaborative effort among the National Park Service, Ford Motor Company, and the concessionaire, Glacier Park, Inc., the popular red buses returned to service in the summer of 2002 with propane-fueled engines and new chassis.

two buildings have a similar outside appearance and are connected by a covered walkway beginning at the south end of the giant lobby. The massive three-story lobby, with 40-inch-diameter fir and cedar pillars and surrounded by two interior balconies, consumes nearly all of the first floor of the main building. The West Wing is without a lobby and has more than twice as many guest rooms as the main building. A colorful swath of flowers separates a large front lawn. A parking area is near the hotel, but you will want to register and drop off luggage at the front door of whichever building you will be staying in. No elevators are in either building, but bell service is available. The lodge is at the intersection of U.S. Highway 2 and Montana Highway 49, just outside the southeast corner of Glacier National Park in East Glacier, Montana.

Glacier Park Lodge has 160 guest rooms plus a two-bedroom house. Rates for most of the rooms are the same regardless of size, location, or view. Rooms on the west side of both buildings have a view of the Rocky Mountains, while rooms on the east view the front lawn and distant rolling hills. All the rooms have heat, a telephone, and a private bath with a shower or shower-tub combination. None of the rooms have air-conditioning or a television. Bedding in nearly all the rooms varies from one double or one queen to two queen beds. Some of the rooms have balconies, although most of these are in the West Wing.

All fifty rooms in the main building are on the second and third floors behind wide balconies that surround the massive lobby. Rooms in the main building are all carpeted, but differ greatly in size. The hotel has a few value rooms that are quite small and rent for about $30 less than main lodge rooms. Some of the larger main lodge rooms include 263, 265, 267, and 269, which share a common balcony on the east (non-mountain) side of the building. Room 252 is also one of the larger main lodge rooms with two queen beds and a private balcony that offers a view of the mountains.

The adjoining West Wing has 110 rooms, most of which are classified as Great Northern Wing Rooms that are considerably larger than, but rent for the same price as, main lodge rooms. These rooms have hardwood floors, and the majority have two queen beds. Most West Wing rooms on the first and second floors have balconies. The lodge offers seven third-floor family rooms, four in the main lodge building and three in the West Wing. Each is a very large room with bedding that ranges from three doubles to four queens below a sloped ceiling. Family rooms rent for about $30 more and have well over twice the space of a Main Lodge room. They are also considerably larger than Great Northern Wing rooms. The windows in Main Lodge family rooms are low, so you must squat to gain any view. Family rooms in the West Wing have regular windows.

Five mini-suites, all in the West Wing, each have one king bed, overstuffed chairs, a decorative fireplace, and a balcony. The hotel has three suites, two on the second floor of the main lodge building and one on the first floor of the West Wing. All offer mountain views and large, upgraded bathrooms with a shower only. The two Main Lodge suites each have a king bed, a sofa bed, and lounge chairs. Suite 264 also has a table and four chairs, three very large windows, plus a private balcony. In this suite you can lie in bed and still have a good view of the mountains. The first-floor two-room West Wing suite with decorative fireplace, two bathrooms, and a private balcony has a king bed in the bedroom and a sofa bed and chairs in the living room. Situated on the ninth hole of the golf course is a one-story wooden house, renovated in 2005, called the Glacier Golf House. It has a living room, a dining area, a full kitchen (utensils and dishes supplied), two bathrooms with a combination tub-shower, and two bedrooms, each with two queen-size beds. A washer and dryer, telephone, and satellite television with a VCR/DVD player are included. The house has an outside deck with a gas grill, flower beds, and a rustic fence.

When choosing a room consider the ambience of walking out your doorway onto a wide balcony that overlooks the main lobby. This is part of the experience of staying in the main lodge building. On the other hand, no elevator is available, so you must climb at least one flight of stairs (twenty-four steps) each time you go to or leave your room. Rooms on the third floor require climbing two flights of stairs (another nineteen steps). In addition, rooms overlooking the lobby are sometimes a little noisy, especially during the early evening when the lobby is crowded with guests. One advantage of staying in the West Wing is that you can request a room on the first floor at lobby level. In other words, no climbing steps unless you leave the hotel. Another advantage is the larger size of West Wing rooms. If you desire a room in the main lodge, two good choices are 252 or 260, which are large and have balconies. Both rooms have a combination shower-tub. Main Lodge rooms on the ends of the building tend to offer marginal views, so you should shy away from these. In the West Wing, rooms 526 on the garden level (one flight down from the first floor; don't ask us why these rooms have 500 numbers) and 226 on the second floor are very large rooms

and have balconies on the mountain side of the building. Any of the even-numbered rooms on the first floor (104 through 124) of the West Wing offer a balcony and a mountain view. It is generally best to attempt to reserve a room with extra bedding in either building because these are likely to be the largest rooms in the hotel. For example, request a room with two queen beds even if you are reserving a room for two people.

Glacier Park Lodge is certainly a fun place to stay, if only to enjoy an evening reading a book and listing to music in the awe-inspiring lobby. It's a popular stop for train travelers who need walk only a relatively short distance along a flower-bordered path from the station to the hotel entrance. A complimentary hotel shuttle is waiting at the station to pick up luggage and guests who would rather ride. Glacier Park Lodge is a stop for the red Jammer buses that take travelers on narrated tours of the park. It is also a connecting point for the east side shuttle that offers service to St. Mary, where free National Park Service shuttles travel to Logan Pass on the Going-to-the-Sun Road. The hotel has a nine-hole golf course and a nine-hole pitch and putt. Unlike most other national park lodges, it has a swimming pool and a day spa. Horseback riding is also available. If you plan to stay several days and want variety in your meals, a short walk takes you to several restaurants, including an excellent Mexican restaurant, and a small grocery in the town of East Glacier.

Rooms: Singles, doubles, triples, and quads. Three family rooms accommodate up to eight persons. All rooms have a private bath.

Wheelchair Accessibility: Two rooms on the first floor of the West Wing each have a wide entry door and wide entry to a large bathroom with a raised toilet. One bathroom has a combination shower-tub with grab bars. A roll-in shower is in the second wheelchair-accessible room. A bathroom at the south end of the lobby and the lodge restaurant are both wheelchair accessible.

Rates: Value room ($140); main lodge ($170); Great Northern Wing room($170); family room ($199); mini-suite ($199); suite ($299); golf house ($449). Rates quoted are for two adults with the exception of the family room, which is quoted for four, and the golf house, which is a flat rate. Children eleven and under stay free. Each additional person is $15 per night. Rates are reduced from mid-May to mid-June.

Location: In East Glacier, Montana, at the intersection of US 2 and MT 49. The lodge is at the southeast corner of the park.

Season: Mid-May to mid-September.

Food: The dining rooms offer a buffet breakfast ($14.00), lunch ($9.00–$11.00), and dinner ($20.00–$30.00). Alcoholic beverages are served. The lounge serves snacks and sandwiches. A snack shop in the lobby sells breakfast muffins, cold sandwiches, ice cream, coffee, and cold drinks. Additional restaurants and a grocery are nearby in the town of East Glacier.

Facilities: Dining room, cocktail lounge, snack shop, gift shop, swimming pool, golf course. Restaurants, gas stations, and a grocery store are across the road in the town of East Glacier.

Activities: Hiking, horseback riding, shuffleboard, swimming, golf, evening entertainment, sightseeing tours.

LAKE MCDONALD LODGE

P.O. Box 210052 • Lake McDonald, MT 59921-0052 • (406) 888-5431
www.glacierparkinc.com • www.lakemcdonaldlodge.com

Lake McDonald Lodge is a complex consisting of a historic lodge building, fourteen structures with cabin accommodations, two two-story motel units, a dining room, an auditorium, several support buildings for employee housing, and a store. The main hotel is a rustic Swiss chalet–style lodge with a spacious, open lobby surrounded on three sides by upper-floor balconies. The lobby, dining room, gift shop, lounge, and two guest rooms are on the main floor, while the second and third floors are devoted to guest rooms. The lodge sits on a small hill facing Lake McDonald, which was used by visitors who arrived by boat until 1920, when the road was built. A huge fireplace with Indian designs in the masonry above the opening dominates the lobby with its large cedar columns in each corner. The balconies, supported by log beams and brackets, provide public areas with tables and chairs where guests can write letters, play cards, or read a book. A covered back patio has chairs and benches for relaxing while viewing Glacier National Park's largest lake.

Lake McDonald Lodge offers rooms of various sizes and bedding in the main lodge, cabins, and motel-type buildings. All the rooms have heat, a telephone, and a private bath with a shower (no tub) but no television or air-conditioning. The main lodge has thirty-two rooms, nearly all of which are on the second and third floors. Two wheelchair-accessible rooms are on the first floor. The building has no elevator. Bell service is available. Rooms in the lodge are priced the same regardless of size, bedding, and view. Bedding ranges from one to two double beds. Rooms 202, 212, 302, and 312 are desirable lakeside corner rooms with two windows. Rooms 201, 213, 301, and 313 are the largest in the lodge and have windows offering a view of the lake.

Fourteen buildings, some log and some frame, house a total of thirty-eight cabins that sit beside the main lodge and stretch along Lake McDonald. Most of these buildings comprise two, three, or four cabin rooms, although one particularly large building has six units. Parking is directly behind or in front of each cabin. Some of the cabins are entered from the lake side, while others are accessed from the side nearest the parking lot. All of the cabins have finished interiors and are on the lake, but views tend to be obscured by trees and bushes along the bank of the lake. Cabins are rented and priced in two classifications, small and large, even though units within each class vary in size and bedding. Twenty-two small cabins, which rent for about $45 less per day than the large cabins, have bedding ranging from two twin beds to two double beds. Sixteen large cabins have bedding ranging from a double plus a twin to two double beds plus a twin. Most of the large cabins offer significantly more floor space than the small, some of which are very small.

Lake McDonald Lodge is on the site of the earlier and smaller Glacier Hotel, which was built in 1895 by homesteader George Snyder. The property was sold in 1906 to land speculator John Lewis, who built cabins and operated a fishing and tourist camp. In 1913 Snyder hired Spokane, Washington, architect Kirkland Cutter to design a hotel that would compete with the hotels and backcountry chalets being constructed by the Great Northern Railroad. Concrete-and-stone foundations were completed just prior to the winter of 1913, and in June 1914 the hotel opened for business. In 1930 the hotel was acquired by a subsidiary of the Great Northern Railroad, and in 1957 the name was changed from Lewis Glacier Hotel to Lake McDonald Lodge. The lodge was included in the National Register of Historic Places in 1978 and partially renovated in 1988.

Two two-story wooden motel buildings near the store and some distance from the main lodge building offer a total of thirty rooms. Parking is between the two buildings that are parallel to one another. Neither building has an elevator. The relatively small rooms do not have balconies or offer a view. The larger motel building has twenty relatively small paneled rooms that are entered from outside walkways. The smaller motel building, with ten rooms, has interior hallways that can be entered from either end of the building. We prefer rooms in the larger unit (rooms 1 through 20) to rooms in the smaller unit.

Our first choice at Lake McDonald is one of the larger lakeside rooms (noted above) in the main lodge building. These rooms are off the sometimes noisy lobby area. Third-floor rooms are quieter than second-floor rooms but require climbing an additional flight of stairs. Freestanding cabin 8, with a large covered porch facing the lake, is our favorite large cabin. Cabin 12-B, with a nice covered porch facing the lake, is our favorite small cabin. Our least favorite lodging is the motel units, but if this is where you end up, ask for room 20 with two windows, one of which faces the lake.

Lake McDonald Lodge is the smallest and most intimate of the four historical lodges in Glacier National Park. Guests generally smile as they walk through the entrance doors and glance up at the large and colorful lamp shades that once hung in the Prince of Wales Hotel. Next their eyes scan across the balconies and huge log columns on which old hunting trophies continue to hang. A little farther in and to the left is the focal point of the lobby, a cavernous fireplace in which 5-foot logs burn. Lake McDonald Lodge offers a variety of activities besides sitting in a rocking chair enjoying the fireplace. The lake provides opportunities for boating and fishing, and although the water is a little cool for swimming, you might decide to take a refreshing dip down the hill from cabin 12. Boat tours of the lake leave from a small dock behind the lodge. A classic national park lodge dining room with a large fireplace and a wall of windows providing views of the lake offers evening specialties. An informal restaurant across the road serves Italian food in a casual atmosphere.

Rooms: Singles, doubles, triples, and quads. All rooms have a private bath with shower but no tub, with the exception of the two first-floor rooms.

Wheelchair Accessibility: The only two first-floor lodge rooms each have a wheelchair-accessible bathroom with a wide doorway and grab bars by the toilet and the combination shower-tub. Two cabins each have ramp access and a wheelchair-accessible bathroom with grab bars and a shower with a seat. The restaurant and lounge are also accessible.

Rates: Main lodge ($160); small cabins ($114); large cabins ($160); motor inn ($124). Room rates are quoted for two adults. Each additional person is $15 per night. Children eleven and under stay free.

Location: Ten miles inside the west entrance to Glacier National Park. The lodge is on Lake McDonald, just off the Going-to-the-Sun Road.

Season: End of May through September.

Food: A relatively small but attractive dining room in the main lodge serves a breakfast buffet ($14.00), lunch ($8.00–$13.00), and dinner ($17.00–$28.00). Alcoholic beverages are served here and in the adjacent lounge. No reservations are taken. The lounge offers food items from the restaurant's lunch menu all afternoon and evening. Across the road, a "Jammer-themed" pizzeria is open from 11:00 a.m. to 10:00 p.m. for pizza, pasta, hoagies, salads, and hamburgers ($8.00–$15.00). Beer, wine, and ice cream are sold, and takeout is available.

Facilities: Dining room, gift shop, cocktail lounge, restaurant, post office, general store, boat rental, riding stable.

Activities: Boating, hiking, fishing (no license required), boat tours of Lake McDonald, sightseeing tours, horseback riding, evening ranger programs. The Sperry Trailhead beginning near the lodge leads to Mt. Brown Lookout (5.3 miles), Snyder Lake (4.4 miles), and Sperry Chalet (6.4 miles).

MANY GLACIER HOTEL

P.O. Box 147 • East Glacier, MT 59434 • (406) 732-4411

www.glacierparkinc.com • www.manyglacierhotel.com

Many Glacier Hotel is one of America's classic national park lodges. The five-story Swiss-themed wooden structure with numerous gables and balconies is situated on the edge of Swiftcurrent Lake. Although it appears as a single structure, the hotel is actually two separate buildings connected by an enclosed walkway. The main floor is highlighted by an outstanding three-story lobby with log beams, interior balconies, and a huge conical metal fireplace suspended from the roof. Many guest rooms in both the main hotel and the annex offer outstanding views of Swiftcurrent Lake and the surrounding mountains. Parking is on a steep hill above the hotel, so stop at the hotel entrance to register and drop off luggage before parking your vehicle. A small elevator down the hallway near the lounge is temperamental, but bell service is available to assist with luggage. Many Glacier Hotel is in the northeastern section of Glacier National Park, 11 miles west of Babb on Many Glacier Road.

The hotel offers a total of 214 rooms of varying size, bedding, and view. All of the rooms have heat, a telephone, and a private bath but no television. All but ten rooms fall into three categories: lakeside, standard,

and value. Bedding in these rooms ranges from two twins to two doubles. The remaining rooms are two suites and eight family rooms. Lakeside rooms, the largest category, rent at a premium price and include all but a few of the rooms facing Swiftcurrent Lake. About half of these rooms have balconies, but room size and bedding vary, with the largest lakeside rooms being in the annex. Standard rooms are similar in size and bedding to lakeside rooms but do not offer a lake view, and fewer standard rooms have balconies. Value rooms are the least expensive rooms in the lodge and are generally quite small with two twins or one double bed. Rooms in this category may also offer an obscured view or be located on a main hallway in a heavy-traffic area. All rooms in a category rent for the same price regardless of size, view, or whether a balcony is available. Large lakeside rooms in the main lodge with excellent lake views and balconies are 158, 160, 362, and 364. Larger lakeside rooms without balconies in the main lodge include 222, 322, 332, 460, and 462. Larger lakeside rooms in the annex with balconies include rooms 102, 104, 112, 114, and corresponding rooms on the second

Construction on Many Glacier Hotel commenced in 1914, and the first guests were welcomed on July 4 of the following year. The annex next door was completed two years later. The Great Northern Railroad, which built the hotel, erected a sawmill and drying kiln near the site to process timber used in the construction. Trees for the lobby columns were harvested and shipped from Oregon and Washington. Even though most of the other timber and rocks came from the local area, the high cost of fixtures, glass, and boilers resulted in construction costs of $500,000. A swimming pool that sat beside the dining room and a stone fountain near the current gift shop have both been removed. The hotel once had its own hydro-electric plant at Swift Current Falls, but the unit was put permanently out of operation by a 1964 flood.

and third floors. Larger standard rooms in the annex include rooms 105, 205, and 305.

Six family rooms located on the fourth floor of the annex each consist of two bedrooms on each side of a bathroom. The family rooms have various bedding combinations that can sleep either five or six adults without use of a rollaway. Four of these rooms provide a lake view (rooms 400, 404, 408, and 414), and two do not, even though all six rooms rent for the same rate. Keep in mind that these are fourth-floor rooms and no elevator is available. In addition, a sloping roof results in reduced headroom. None of the family rooms has a balcony. Two mini–family rooms on the first floor each have two small bedrooms, one with a double bed plus a twin bed and the other with one twin bed. These units have one bathroom with a shower only and sit on the side of the building opposite Swiftcurrent Lake. Two suites on the second floor each consist of two bedrooms

and two bathrooms. One bedroom has a king bed and the other has a double bed. The suites are corner rooms, with balconies that provide excellent lake views.

If you request a room category, we think lakeside annex rooms are probably the best choice. These rooms are a nice size, offer an impressive view, and most enjoy a balcony. In addition, annex rooms are generally quieter than rooms in the main lodge, especially compared to those around the interior balconies, which are subject to lobby noise. The downside to staying in the annex is lack of an elevator, requiring guests on the upper floors to climb stairs. However, there are some excellent room choices in the main lodge. Our favorite room in the hotel is 268, a pie-shaped room near the elevator that has four windows offering views of the lake. Among the value category, basement rooms 62 and 64 each have an outside door that opens to a small grassy area that fronts the lake.

Many Glacier Hotel is a historic lodge in a scenic mountain setting that is identified by many experienced travelers as their favorite lodging facility in Glacier National Park. The large lobby, with its huge log columns and spectacular vistas, is a gathering place for guests, especially in the evening when its centerpiece, the huge conical fireplace, is lit. The attractive Ptarmigan Dining Room, with colorful flags draped from the ceiling and large windows overlooking Swiftcurrent Lake, is an enjoyable place to dine. You can listen to live music while trying the wild game sausage sampler that is offered as an appetizer. Take a few steps outside the hotel and you can begin a hike, kayak, fish, or enjoy a boat tour accompanied by a park naturalist. Or perhaps you would rather relax in one of the Adirondack chairs on the large porch that wraps around two sides of the first floor. A stable next to the parking area offers horseback riding. Evening natural history and musical programs are presented in the hotel basement.

Rooms: Singles, doubles, triples, and quads. Eight family rooms hold four to five persons. All the hotel rooms have private baths.

Wheelchair Accessibility: The lodge offers seven wheelchair-accessible rooms in various categories. Bathrooms vary from roll-in showers to tubs with grab bars.

Rates: Value rooms ($135); standard ($150); lakeside ($160); minifamily rooms ($160); family rooms ($212); suites ($255). Room rates quoted are for two adults with the exception of the family room, which is quoted for four adults. Each additional person is $15 per night. Rollaways are $15 per night. Children eleven and under stay free.

Location: In the northeast section of the park, at the end of Many Glacier Road, 11 miles east of Babb, Montana.

Season: Mid-June to mid-September.

Food: A restaurant offers a breakfast buffet ($14.00), lunch ($8.00–$13.00), and dinner ($17.00–$28.00). Alcoholic beverages are available in the dining room and in the Swiss or Interlaken Lounges that are just outside the dining room. Soup, salads, sandwiches, and appetizers are available in the lounges. A small store sells hot dogs, ice cream, yogurt, snacks, drinks, beer, and wine from 8:00 a.m. to 9:00 p.m. Limited groceries are available in a general store 1 mile up the road at Swiftcurrent Motor Inn. The motor inn also has a less expensive restaurant.

Facilities: Dining room; cocktail lounge; snack bar; gift shop; tour desk in lobby; horse stable; kayak, canoe, and rowboat rentals.

Activities: Hiking, fishing, boating, horseback riding, naturalist programs, evening entertainment, sightseeing tours, boat tours of Swiftcurrent Lake and Lake Josephine.

PRINCE OF WALES HOTEL

Box 33, Waterton, Alberta, Canada T0K 2M0 • (403) 859-2231
www.princeofwaleswaterton.com • www.glacierparkinc.com

The Prince of Wales Hotel, named after Prince Edward, who later became King Edward VIII, is a seven-story alpine chalet that may be the most picturesque of all the national park lodging facilities. The only Canadian park lodge constructed by the Great Northern Railroad, the hotel sits high on a bluff overlooking Waterton Lake and the charming town of Waterton. Built in 1927, the hotel features two-story windows across the south side of a six-story lobby. Interior balconies on each floor and huge timbers highlight the attractive lobby that is filled with chairs, tables, and sofas. The hotel is about 48 miles northwest of the town of St. Mary, Montana, via U.S. Highway 89 and the Chief Mountain International Highway, which turns off 4 miles north of Babb, Montana. The hotel may also be approached from the north on Canadian Highway 6 via Pincher Creek, Alberta. Visitors entering from the United States must pass through a Canadian port of entry. A Canadian park fee is required to enter Waterton Lakes National Park, in which the hotel is located.

Prince of Wales Hotel has eighty-six rooms on the five floors above the main floor lobby. Although an elevator stops at floors 1 through 4, it is ancient (the oldest in Alberta) and can only be operated by a hotel employee, who must be summoned. This means you will likely be climbing steps during your stay. Consider this when reserving a room because you may want to request a second- or third-floor room and save some steps. Also keep in mind that the elevator does not go to the fifth and sixth floors, where rooms are offered at a lower rate. Sixteen steps are between the fourth and fifth floors, and another sixteen steps are required to climb from the fifth to the sixth floor. Bell service is available to assist with luggage, but a room on the sixth floor will mean lots of steps.

Each of the hotel rooms has electric heat, a telephone, and a private bathroom but no television or air-conditioning. Most rooms fall into two classifications: lakeside or mountainside. Lakeside rooms offer a view of Waterton Lake and the surrounding mountains, while mountainside rooms, which rent for $55 less per night, do not offer as good a view. Rooms in both classifications are of nice size, with beds ranging from two twins to two doubles. Most of the bathrooms have a combination shower-tub, although a few have a shower only. Along with three suites, lakeside and mountainside rooms comprise all of the accommodations on the second, third, and fourth floors. All third-floor rooms, but only a few second- and fourth-floor rooms, have balconies. The wind is generally strong enough, especially on

While standing in the lobby near the registration desk, look up and try to spot a dark ceiling panel. This trap door hides a pulley that was once used to lower a rope to an employee who was hoisted to clean and change burned-out lightbulbs in the massive chandelier that hangs between the second and fourth floors. This was a prized job for one of the bellmen who was steered around the chandelier by means of ropes held by two of the bellman's colleagues. It is said that people came from miles around to witness the spectacle. Today, a crank is used to lower the chandelier.

the lake side of the hotel, that you won't want to spend much time on a balcony, so having one shouldn't be a major consideration in choosing a room. We especially like corner rooms with windows on two sides. Lakeside corner rooms include 201 and 225 on the second floor, and the corresponding numbered rooms on the third and fourth floors, plus 409 and 417 (mini-suite). Mountainside corner rooms include 200, 208, 214, and 222 on the second floor, and corresponding numbered rooms on the third and fourth floors.

The hotel offers twenty fifth-floor value rooms that are smaller, with variable views. About half face Waterton Lake. These rooms require climbing an additional flight of stairs, and the hotel's sloping roofline reduces headspace in some of these rooms, which rent for about $25 to $70 less than the mountainside and lakeside rooms, respectively. Value rooms have one double or two single beds. Bathrooms have a shower but no tub. Again, keep in mind that the lobby elevator does not provide access to the fifth floor. On the positive side, rooms on the fifth floor tend to be quieter, with the exception of 505, which is located near the elevator motor and can be noisy. Lakeside value rooms 509 and

517 each have one double bed and are slightly larger than most other value rooms.

The sixth floor (yet another flight of sixteen stairs to climb) has four rooms: two value rooms plus two two-room units. The two-room units have a double bed in each room and one bathroom with a shower but no tub. These two-room units have balconies and rent at the lakeside rate or the mountainside rate, depending on the side of the hotel on which the room is located.

The hotel has one fourth-floor lakeside mini-suite with a king-size bed and two wing-back chairs. This is the most requested room in the hotel. Two upscale suites on the third floor, the Prince and Princess, each have a living room, with a sofa bed, wet bar and refrigerator, coffeemaker, and separate bedroom with a king-size bed. The large bathroom in each suite has a bathtub and separate shower. These suites are expensive

▨   ▨   ▨

Great Northern Railroad president Louis Hill originally envisioned the Prince of Wales as a long three-story building similar to the hotel his firm had built a decade earlier at Many Glacier. Hill changed his mind several times and finally settled on the current seven-story rectangular building that was designed to resemble a Swiss chalet. Construction of the hotel was complicated by high winds and the need to bring all of the materials and supplies the last 25 miles by mules. The winds blew the building off center twice during construction and almost caused the project to be abandoned. The structure is anchored with large cables that run from the loft into the ground. The hotel opened during the summer of 1927, one year after construction commenced and fourteen years after the site was selected. It was closed for three years during the Depression and five years during World War II.

▨   ▨   ▨

and exquisite, with custom-designed furniture.

The Prince of Wales Hotel offers a touch of English tradition. High tea is served from 2:00 to 5:00 each afternoon in the lobby (Valerie's Tea Room), where you can relax and gaze at Waterton Lake. The hotel's striking lobby is flanked by the Royal Stewart Dining Room on one side and the Windsor Lounge on the other. Both provide an outstanding view of the lake and surrounding mountains. The lounge serves the dining room's full lunch and dinner menus and enjoys the hotel's only fireplace. A large gift shop is also on the main floor. The town of Waterton, with additional restaurants, clothing stores, and gift shops, is a short distance down the hill. Nearly all businesses accept credit cards and American dollars, although the latter are not always converted at a favorable rate.

Rooms: Singles, doubles, triples, and quads. All rooms have private baths.

Wheelchair Accessibility: The hotel has no wheelchair-accessible rooms. The dining room, lounge, and a first-floor bathroom are wheelchair accessible.

Rates: Value room with mountain view ($265); value room with lake view ($275); mountainside room ($290); lakeside room ($345); sixth-floor two room (mountainside–$290, lakeside–$345); mini-suite ($345); suite ($799). Rates quoted are in Canadian dollars for two adults. Each additional person is $15 per night. Rollaways are $15 per night. Children eleven and under stay free with an adult. Rates are 20 to 30 percent less during the weeks prior to mid-June.

Location: In Canada's Waterton Lakes National Park, about 48 miles northwest of St. Mary, Montana, and 30 miles south of Pincher Creek, Alberta.

Season: June to mid-September.

Food: An attractive dining room with a wall of windows offering a view of Waterton Lake serves three meals a day, including a continental breakfast ($9.00) and a hot breakfast buffet ($17.00), lunch ($10.00–$15.00), and dinner ($24.00–$36.00). The lounge serves the full lunch and dinner menus from the dining room. A traditional British tea with sandwiches, pastries, scones, cookies, and other sweets is served in the lobby each afternoon from 2:00 to 5:00 ($30). Several restaurants and a small grocery store are in the town of Waterton.

Facilities: Gift shop, dining room, cocktail lounge. Additional facilities are in the town of Waterton, a short distance away.

Activities: Hiking, golf, tennis, horseback riding, boat rentals, fishing, lake cruises, and national park programs are offered in Waterton.

RISING SUN MOTOR INN

P.O. Box 147 • East Glacier, MT 59434 • (406) 732-5523
www.glacierparkinc.com • www.risingsunmotorinn.com

Rising Sun Motor Inn, initially known as East Glacier Auto Camp, is a complex of wooden buildings, including a main registration/restaurant building, a general store with attached lodging rooms, nineteen duplex cabin buildings, and two motel-type structures. Rising Sun offers seventy-two rooms, approximately half of which are wooden cabins dating from 1941. Registration for all guest rooms is in the main building, which houses a restaurant and a small gift shop. The general store is across the parking lot, and the cabins and motel buildings are up a small hill but within walking distance of both the restaurant and the general store. The motor inn is in a scenic area overlooking St. Mary Lake and surrounded by tall mountains. It is located on the east side of the park on the Going-to-the-Sun Road, 6 miles from the park entrance at St. Mary.

Rising Sun Motor Inn offers three types of rooms, all of which rent for approximately the same price. Rooms in all three classifications have heat and a private bathroom with a shower but no tub. No television, telephone, or air-conditioning is in any of the rooms. The majority of the rooms are in thirty-five rustic cabins built as duplex units. The cabins are clustered on a hill behind the store with a few offering a view of the mountains to the south. Parking is directly in front of or beside each of the cabins. Interiors are finished with varnished plywood. The small bathroom has a toilet and shower; the sink is in the bedroom. The cabins have small windows, no porch, and beds that range from two twins to two doubles, although most of the units have a double plus a twin. Cabins 2 through 7 are larger in size and rent for the same price as the smaller cabins. We

■   ■   ■

The 52-mile Going-to-the-Sun Road, one of the country's most scenic drives, is the product of more than a decade of work that commenced in 1921. Although several routes were considered, 6,664-foot Logan Pass was chosen, partially because greater exposure to the sun would help clear the road of snow. It takes up to two months each spring to clear the road of snow, which can reach a depth of 80 feet in places. The road provides spectacular views of mountains, lakes, waterfalls, and glacial valleys in the heart of Glacier National Park. The road is winding and quite narrow. Vehicles longer than 21 feet or wider than 8 feet are prohibited from travel between Avalanche Campground and the Sun Point parking area.

■   ■   ■

would choose cabins 4, 5, or 6, all of which offer a good mountain view and receive morning sun.

The building housing the general store also includes nine lodging rooms that are accessed from an interior hallway entered from either the front or end of the building. A large covered porch with chairs and tables runs across the front of the building, which faces south toward the mountains. Plentiful parking is directly in front of the building in a large lot that separates the store from the restaurant. The rooms vary in size and bedding which ranges from one double to two doubles. Room 31, with two double beds, is very large. Room 37 on the corner of the building has windows on two sides and is the most desirable of the store motel rooms.

Two identical motor inn motel-type buildings are up the hill from the restaurant. Each building houses fourteen rooms, seven on each side. A covered walkway runs across each side of the two buildings. These rooms are all the same size with bedding that ranges from two

twins to two doubles. Rooms on the south side (rooms 8 through 14 in one building and rooms 22 through 28 in the other building) offer good views of the mountains and a fair view of St. Mary Lake. Corner rooms 8, 14, 22, and 28 have windows on two sides and offer a brighter interior. Parking is directly in front of each room.

Rising Sun Motor Inn is overlooked by many Glacier visitors, who know only about the park's four historical lodges. The inn enjoys a scenic location surrounded by towering mountains and up a small hill from the blue waters of St. Mary Lake. The lake is mostly out of direct view of the lodging units, and the surrounding mountains are only partially visible from some of the units. Still, this is a relaxing place to spend an evening. Walk a short distance from your room and gaze at some of the prettiest landscape in the United States. Rising Sun certainly isn't a busy or congested area, since most people on the Going-to-the-Sun Road drive right by. The restaurant, with a vaulted ceiling and large windows facing the lake and mountains, offers meals at reasonable prices. You can hike, fish, take a boat tour of St. Mary Lake, or just experience nature without bumping into hundreds of other vacationers.

Rooms: Singles, doubles, triples, and quads. All rooms have a private bath with a shower but no tub.

Wheelchair Accessibility: Four wheelchair-accessible rooms are in one of the two motor inn buildings. These rooms include ramp access and bathrooms with wide doorways and a grab bar for the toilet. The shower has a seat and an adjustable showerhead but does not have roll-in access. Two wheelchair-accessible rooms have two double beds, while the other two rooms have two twin beds. The restaurant, gift shop, and general store are also wheelchair accessible.

Rates: Cottages ($114); store motel rooms ($107); motor inn rooms ($124). Rates quoted are for two adults. Children eleven years and under stay free. Each additional person is $15 per night. Rollaways are $15 per night.

Location: East side of Glacier National Park, 6 miles west of the park entrance station at St. Mary.

Season: Mid-June to mid-September.

Food: A restaurant in the main building serves breakfast ($5.00–$10.00), lunch ($7.50–$12.00), and dinner ($7.50–$17.00). Lunch items are available for dinner. Beer and wine are served. Limited groceries, beer, and wine are sold in the general store.

Facilities: Restaurant, gift shop, general store with camping and fishing supplies and limited groceries.

Activities: Hiking, fishing, boating, boat tour of St. Mary Lake, sightseeing tours, National Park Service evening naturalist program in campground amphitheater. A trailhead near the camp store leads to Otokomi Lake (5.2 miles).

SWIFT CURRENT MOTOR INN

P.O. Box 147 • East Glacier Park, MT 59434 • (406) 732-5531

www.glacierparkinc.com • www.swiftcurrentmotorinn.com

Swift Current Motor Inn offers eighty-eight lodging rooms in a complex that has twenty-six cabins with a central bathhouse, four motel buildings, and a registration building that also houses a store and restaurant. The cabins and motel units sit behind the registration building, which offers a small lobby and a large covered porch with chairs. Plentiful parking is outside the registration building and directly beside the cabins and motel units.

Swift Current Motor Inn is in the northeast section of Glacier National Park, at the end of Many Glacier Road, 12 miles west of the town of Babb.

Both types of accommodations at Swift Current have electric heat but no air-conditioning, television, or telephone. The least expensive lodging is in cabins without a bathroom. A community bathroom has toilets and showers. The cabins, constructed in 1937, are rustic and plain, with painted wooden floors. They are nicely spaced, and all are single units (no duplex units, common among other lodges). Eighteen small one-bedroom cabins each have a double bed or a double bed plus a twin bed in one room and a sink (cold water only) and small picnic table in a separate room. Two one-bedroom cabins with a private bath rent for about

■   ■   ■

Swift Current Motor Inn is on the site of what was once a tepee camp established in 1911 by the Great Northern Railroad. Here guests slept on army cots in replicas of Blackfoot Indian tepees. By 1933 the tepees had been replaced by twenty-seven cabins and the area was called "Many Glacier Auto Tourist Camp." A year later the Civilian Conservation Corps constructed a campground and additional cabins. The current camp store was built in 1935. The following year a huge forest fire destroyed most of the cabins, which were rebuilt in 1937. In 1940 a central comfort station with showers was added. Three motel-type buildings and an employee dormitory (later converted to a fourth motel building) were constructed in 1955.

■   ■   ■

$25 per night more than the one-bedroom units without a bath. Six two-bedroom cabins have a small bedroom with a double bed on each side of a small room, with a sink and picnic table. These cabins do not have a private bathroom. The two-bedroom units rent for $10 per night more than the one-bedroom units without a bath. Cabins in Loop C are closest to the community bathhouse.

Four one-story wooden motel buildings house a total of sixty-two rooms in two price categories. Rooms in all four buildings have carpeted floors, a double bed plus a twin bed or two double beds, and a private bath with a shower but no tub. Three of the buildings near the back of the complex each have fourteen rooms, seven on a side, that are entered from walkways that run across both sides of each building. The rooms are average size, with walls that are partially paneled. The fourth motor inn unit, Pine Top, sits toward the front of the complex and has twenty rooms that are entered from an interior corridor. These rooms have no porch

or balcony and are smaller and a little less expensive than the rooms in the other three motel buildings.

Swift Current Motor Inn offers economical lodging in a scenic area of this magnificent national park. In fact, the one-bedroom cabins without bath are among the least expensive lodging offered in any national park. These are an excellent value and a good choice if use of a community bathroom is acceptable. Trees surround all of the lodging buildings, so you won't enjoy great vistas from your room, but good views are available near the registration building. The area is relatively quiet and a pleasant 1-mile walk from the fancier and more expensive Many Glacier Hotel. Swift Current is especially popular with hikers and serves as a trailhead for several popular hikes including those to Iceberg Lake, Swiftcurrent Pass, and Ptarmigan Tunnel, the latter of which guides hikers through an unusual 180-foot tunnel. A brochure and map of day hikes are available at the registration desk.

Rooms: Singles, doubles, triples, and quads. All the motel rooms have private baths. Most cabin guests must use a community bathroom.

Wheelchair Accessibility: Four wheelchair-accessible rooms in one of the motel buildings near the rear of the complex include ramp access and bathrooms with wide doorways and a grab bar for the toilet. The shower has a seat and an adjustable showerhead, but it does not have roll-in access. Two of the rooms have two double beds, while the other two rooms have two twin beds.

Rates: One-bedroom cabin without bath ($55); two-bedroom cabin without bath ($65); one-bedroom cabin with bath ($80); Pine Top ($107); Motor Inn ($124). Room rates quoted are for two adults. Each additional person is $15 per night. Children eleven and under stay free with an adult. A rollaway is $15 per night.

Location: In the northeast section of Glacier National Park at the end of Many Glacier Road, 12 miles east of Babb, Montana.

Season: Mid-June to mid-September.

Food: A restaurant in the registration building offers breakfast ($5.00–$10.50), lunch, and dinner ($7.50–$20.00). Lunch and dinner have the same menu featuring hamburgers, pasta, and pizza specialties. Beer and wine are served. Limited groceries, snacks, beer, and wine are available in the general store.

Facilities: Restaurant, laundry, and camp store with gifts, groceries, and supplies.

Activities: Hiking, sightseeing tours, evening campfire programs at the National Park Service campground. Fishing, horseback riding, and boat tours of Swiftcurrent Lake and Lake Josephine are available at nearby Many Glacier Hotel.

VILLAGE INN

1038 Apgar Street • Apgar, MT 59936 • (406) 888-5632 • www.glacierparkinc.com

www.villageinnatapgar.com

Village Inn is a two-story motel-style building constructed in 1956 with thirty-six rooms. The inn is at the end of the road, directly on the shore of scenic Lake McDonald. Each room enjoys an excellent view of the lake and the mountains beyond. A small registration area is located at the street end of the building. The inn has no food service, although a restaurant is a short walk up the street. Village Inn is located in the small village of Apgar, Montana, 3 miles inside the west entrance to Glacier National Park.

The inn offers four types of rooms. All the rooms are nicely furnished. They each have a coffeemaker,

heat, and a full bath but no air-conditioning, telephone, or television. All are wood paneled, and each room has a large window and an outside balcony or patio with excellent views of Lake McDonald. The rooms all have doors that open to the balcony or patio. Larger rooms on the first floor can also be entered from the parking lot behind the building. Unless you specifically desire one of the kitchen units, we recommend a second-floor room for increased privacy and a somewhat better view of the lake. The twelve least expensive rooms are small and sit at one end of the building, six on the second floor and six on the ground floor. Half the rooms have

Famous western artist Charles Russell had a home built beside Lake McDonald in 1908 by Dimon Apgar. Russell's studio, which still stands, was constructed eight years later.

one double bed, and the other half have two twin beds that nearly fill these rooms.

Ten two-bedroom family units, all on the second floor, have a double bed in one bedroom and either a double and twin bed or a double bed and a sofa bed in the second room. These rooms cost $30 more per night and are quite a bit larger than the least expensive rooms described above. On the first floor, eleven rooms have a bedroom with two double beds plus a separate kitchen area with a refrigerator, a sink, an oven, a stove, and all cooking and eating utensils. These are the same size as the two-bedroom units on the second floor, except they have a kitchen in place of the second bedroom. Village Inn has three suites. Two suites on the second floor each have a living room and two bedrooms, each with a double bed. A sofa bed is in the living room. One first-floor suite has two bedrooms and a kitchen and is wheelchair accessible.

Village Inn is a quiet place to spend a night on the west side of Glacier National Park. The inn doesn't enjoy the charm of the park's historical lodges, but the rooms are nice and the larger rooms with either two bedrooms or a kitchen are a good choice for families. The location at the end of a short road enables guests to avoid the crowds while enjoying a view of Lake McDonald and some of the park's scenic mountains. A gravel beach just outside the rooms leads to the cool waters of the lake. The inn is located less than a block from a restaurant that serves meals at reasonable prices. It is a short walk from a National Park Service visitor center where rangers are available to provide information about the park. You will also find three gift shops, an ice cream shop, and a nearby store offering limited groceries, beer and wine.

Rooms: Singles, doubles, triples, and quads. Some of the family units and two suites can hold up to six persons. All rooms have private baths.

Wheelchair Accessibility: A one-bedroom kitchen unit and the first-floor suite are wheelchair accessible, with a wide bathroom door and grab bars by the toilet and combination shower-tub.

Rates: One bedroom ($120); two bedroom ($150); one-bedroom kitchen units ($165); three-room suites ($165–$185). Rates quoted are for two adults with the exception of the suites, which are for four adults. Children eleven and under stay free with an adult. Additional adults are $15.

Location: In the village of Apgar, Montana, 3 miles from the West Glacier entrance station.

Season: May to October.

Food: A restaurant one block away on Apgar Road offers breakfast, lunch, and dinner from mid-May through most of September. Very limited groceries are sold at a gift shop next to the restaurant. The lodge is 2½ miles from a full-service grocery store and several restaurants in the town of West Glacier.

Facilities: The village of Apgar has gift shops; a restaurant; an ice cream shop; kayak, canoe, rowboat, and motorboat rentals; and a National Park Service visitor center.

Activities: Nightly ranger/naturalist talks at the nearby Apgar campground, boating, swimming (very cool water), fishing (no license required), sightseeing tours. Several hiking trails begin at Apgar.

NEVADA

Lake Mead National Recreation Area

601 Nevada Highway • Boulder City, NV 89005 • (702) 293-8906
www.nps.gov/lame

Lake Mead National Recreation Area comprises nearly 1.5 million acres of desert landscape surrounding Lake Mead and Lake Mohave. The 290 square miles of clear water in the two lakes is supplied by the Colorado River. Lake Mead is 110 miles long and results from the famous Hoover Dam near Boulder City, Nevada. Farther south, 67-mile-long Lake Mohave is formed by Davis Dam near Bullhead City, Arizona. The recreation area is particularly popular for water-related activities such as boating, fishing, and waterskiing. Areas near the lake are often five to ten degrees warmer than Las Vegas, which means that summer temperatures frequently rise to 110° Fahrenheit and above. The recreation area is located in southern Nevada and northwestern Arizona. Main access is via U.S. Highway 93, which connects Las Vegas, Nevada, and Kingman, Arizona. **Recreation Area Entrance Fee:** $5.00 per vehicle or $3.00 per person, good for five days.

Lodging in Lake Mead National Recreation Area: Five lodging facilities are scattered throughout Lake Mead National Recreation Area. Echo Bay Resort, Lake Mead Resort at Boulder Beach, and Temple Bar Resort are each on Lake Mead in the northern half of the recreation area. Cottonwood Cove Resort and Lake Mohave Resort at Katherine Landing are on Lake Mohave in the southern half of the recreation area. Echo Bay and Lake Mead Resort on Lake Mead, and Lake Mohave Resort on Lake Mohave are operated by Seven Crown Resorts of Irvine, California. Cottonwood Cove and Temple Bar are operated by Forever Resorts. All five facilities are geared to visitors interested in water-based activities, in particular boating and fishing.

Lake Mead National Recreation Area

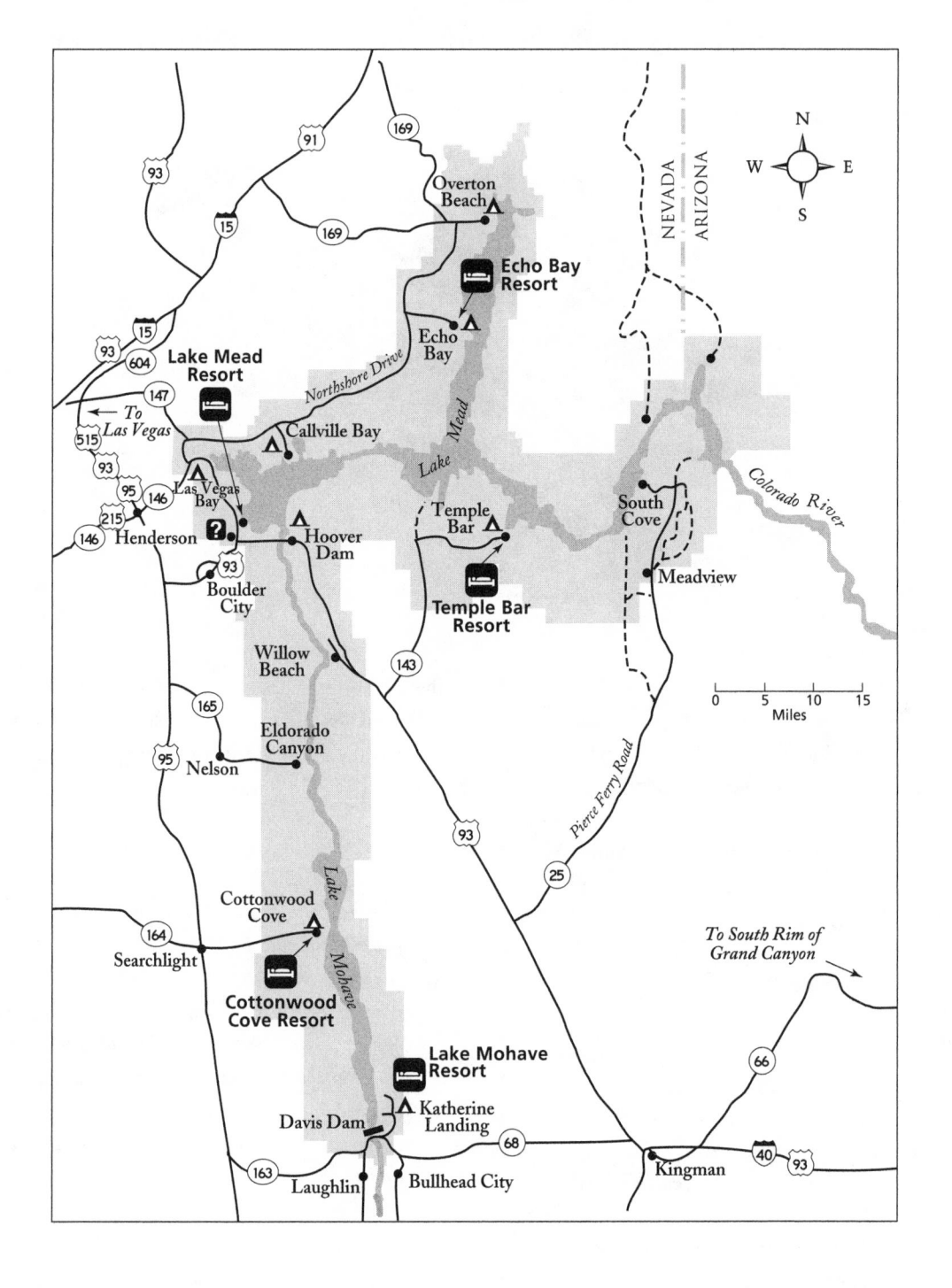

COTTONWOOD COVE RESORT

10000 Cottonwood Cove Road • Searchlight, NV 89046 • (702) 297-1464
www.cottonwoodcoveresort.com

Cottonwood Cove is a family resort with overnight accommodations, a cafe, and a large marina, all on the Nevada shoreline of Lake Mohave. The attractive single-story brick building with a red tile roof houses twenty-four guest rooms. Grass on both the front and back adds to the attractiveness of the building. A small restaurant is a short walk from all the rooms. Cottonwood Cove Resort is on the west side of Lake Mohave, 14 miles east of the intersection of Nevada Highway 164 and U.S. Highway 95. It is 70 miles southeast of Las Vegas, Nevada, via US 95.

Entry to the guest rooms is in the front, with sliding glass doors in the back. Parking is to the side and is a moderate distance from the end rooms. All of the rooms are the same size and are quite large. They each have heat, air-conditioning, carpet, cable TV, telephone, and a full bathroom with a combination shower-tub. Twenty-one of the rooms have two double beds, and the other three rooms have a king-size bed plus a queen-size sofa bed. Each guest room includes tables and chairs on a covered patio that overlooks the lake.

■ ■ ■

Cottonwood was the site of an automobile engine-powered aerial ferry that connected Chloride, Arizona, and Searchlight, Nevada. The aerial tramway, which operated until the 1930s, was located about 1 mile north of Cottonwood Cove. In 1946 the National Park Service issued a permit to Murl Emery to establish a landing at Cottonwood. He soon put in a dock and several tent cabins, one serving as a store.

■ ■ ■

Barbecue grills are in a grassy area that spreads across the back of the building.

The cafe serves three meals a day. A store/gift shop sells fishing licenses, bait, tackle, supplies, groceries, beer, and wine. A separate meeting room with a capacity of forty people is available for rent. The room includes a microwave, a sink, tables, and chairs.

Rooms: Doubles, triples, and quads. All rooms have a full bath.

Wheelchair Accessibility: One room is ADA compliant.

Reservations: Cottonwood Cove Marina, 10000 Cottonwood Cove Road, Searchlight, NV 89046. Phone (702) 297-1464. A deposit of one night's stay is required. A seventy-two-hour cancellation notice is required for a full refund.

Rates: All rooms ($115) from May through October; ($65) during Value Season, from November through April. Value Season rates not applicable during national holidays. Rates quoted are for two adults. Each additional person is $10 per night. Rollaway beds are $6.00 extra. Children five and under stay free. Check the Web site for special packages.

Location: Fourteen miles east of Searchlight, Nevada, on NV 164. The resort is approximately 70 miles southeast of Las Vegas, Nevada.

Season: The resort is open year-round.

Food: A cafe serves breakfast ($5.00–$10.00), lunch ($5.00–$10.00), and dinner ($5.00–$16.00). A store sells groceries, beer, wine, and supplies.

Transportation: No public transportation serves Cottonwood Cove. The nearest major airport is in Las Vegas, where rental cars are available. An airport is also in Laughlin, Nevada. The town of Searchlight has an airstrip where private planes may land.

Facilities: Cafe, convenience store/gift shop, meeting room, laundry in the nearby RV park, full-service marina that rents a variety of boats including houseboats, powerboats, fishing boats, and personal watercraft.

Activities: Volleyball, shuffleboard, horseshoes, fishing, boating, and waterskiing. Park ranger programs are offered in the nearby campground. Numerous casinos are about forty-five minutes south in Laughlin, Nevada, and one hour north in Las Vegas.

ECHO BAY RESORT

Overton, NV 89040 • (702) 394-4000 • www.sevencrown.com

A marina complex, Echo Bay Resort includes a 1970s two-story cement block motel that sits on a hill overlooking the west side of the Overton Arm of Lake Mead. Approximately half of the resort's fifty-two rooms face the water; a marina is in front. The motel, with several nearby palm trees, has an appearance similar to what you might expect near the Florida coast. A large wooden deck on the lake side is accessed from the second floor. Plentiful parking is directly behind the building and close to the main entrance to the registration area. The resort is 60 miles northeast of Las Vegas, Nevada, and the farthest north of the five lodging facilities in Lake Mead National Recreation Area. It is located at the end of a paved road, 5 miles east of Northshore Drive.

■　　■　　■

Many people who visit Lake Mead National Recreation Area are interested in houseboat rentals, which are available at the marinas. Most houseboats are about 14 feet wide, with lengths that range from 50 to 75 feet. The smaller units sleep six or eight persons, while the larger units can sleep a dozen or more. Be forewarned that houseboats aren't cheap to rent. Smaller houseboats often cost $350 to $500 per night for weeklong rentals and more for shorter rentals. Larger houseboats that hold up to ten or twelve persons rent for $500 to $700 per night for weeklong rentals and even more for two- or three-night rentals. Rental fees are often reduced during the off-season of mid-September to mid-June (excluding Memorial Day weekend). Houseboats are available at 7:00 a.m. on the first day and need to be returned by 4:00 p.m. on the last day. Reservations and deposits are required.

■　　■　　■

Echo Bay rooms each have a telephone, air-conditioning, heat, carpet, a television, a coffeemaker, and a hair dryer. Most also have two chairs on a private balcony or patio. Rooms on both sides of the building are accessed through a central corridor that is entered at either end of the building or near the main registration area. Three categories of rooms are offered. The least expensive have two double beds and face west, toward the parking lot. A few face a cement block wall and have no balcony or patio—try to avoid these. Twenty-five rooms face the water and have a single king-size bed; these cost $15 more than rooms on the opposite side of the building. Four extra-large rooms have two double beds, a sofa bed, and a small refrigerator.

Echo Bay is a water-based resort that appeals primarily to visitors who boat and fish. A National Park Service ranger station and campground are nearby, but most facilities are some distance away. A marina rents boats of all types, from personal watercraft to large houseboats. The main resort building has a 2,500-square-foot conference room on the second floor. The Tail O' The Whale restaurant with a nautical decor and adjacent cocktail lounge, has a wall of large windows offering a view of the lake. A snack bar/store with supplies and limited groceries is at the marina.

Rooms: Doubles, triples, and quads. All rooms have a full bath.

Wheelchair Accessibility: Two non-waterside rooms are wheelchair accessible. These are large rooms that have wide doorways, grab bars, and a low sink in the bathroom. Only one of the rooms has a roll-in-shower; the other shower has a lip.

Reservations: Seven Crown Resorts, P.O. Box 16247, Irvine, CA 92623-0068. Phone (800) 752-9669. A deposit of one night's stay is required. A seventy-two-hour cancellation notice is required for a full refund.

Rates: High season (April 1–October 31)/low season (November 1–March 31): Non-waterside ($100/$70); waterside ($115/$75); extra large room ($125/$85). Rates are quoted for two adults per room. Each extra person is $15. Children under five stay free. There is a one-time $10 fee for a rollaway bed.

Location: Sixty miles northeast of Las Vegas via Nevada Highway 147 and Northshore Drive. The resort is at the end of a paved road, 5 miles east of Northshore Drive.

Season: The resort is open year-round except Christmas Day. High season is during summer months, when the resort often fills on weekends.

Food: A full-service restaurant serves breakfast ($5.00–$10.00), lunch ($5.00–$10.00), and dinner ($8.00–$25.00), and a children's menu is available. Hours can change during the off-season. The cocktail lounge is open from 4:00 p.m. to midnight. A snack bar/store at the marina is open from 7:00 a.m. to 8:00 p.m.

Transportation: The nearest major airport is in Las Vegas, where rental cars are available. An asphalt landing strip 3 miles from Echo Bay provides access for private planes. The resort has a free pickup service when called ahead.

Facilities: A restaurant, cocktail lounge, and conference room are in the main building. An adjacent gas station sells gasoline, diesel fuel, and propane. A laundry facility is in the nearby RV park. A full-service marina rents a variety of boats, including houseboats, ski boats, patio boats, fishing boats, and personal watercraft.

Activities: Fishing, waterskiing, boating.

Pets: Pets are permitted with a $50 deposit and an additional daily charge of $10 per pet.

LAKE MEAD RESORT

322 Lake Shore Road • Boulder City, NV 89005 • (702) 293-2074 • www.sevencrown.com

Lake Mead Resort is a complex of four one-story cement block buildings overlooking the Boulder Basin section of Lake Mead, with a marina and floating restaurant and lounge situated a quarter mile down the road. The lodging buildings are in a grassy area a short distance back from the lakeshore. Lake Mead Resort is located at Boulder Beach, 6 miles north of Boulder City, Nevada. Of the five lodging facilities in Lake Mead National Recreation Area, this is the nearest to Las Vegas (30 miles).

Thirty-four of the resort's forty-four rooms are in two U-shaped block buildings positioned on each side

■   ■   ■

Lake Mead, with 550 miles of shoreline, is formed by famous Hoover Dam. The dam, completed in 1935, tamed this portion of the often wild Colorado River. The giant concrete structure required more than 5,000 men to work around the clock for five years. Downstream, Davis Dam was completed in 1953. Dam tours once offered have been discontinued indefinitely.

■   ■   ■

of the central registration building, which is parallel to the shoreline of Boulder Basin. All the rooms in both buildings are relatively small and have one queen-size bed. Each room has a small private bathroom with a combination shower-tub. The two corner rooms in each building have an extra window that allows for a brighter interior. A separate but nearby annex has eight larger rooms with two queen beds. The central registration building houses a conference room and two nice suites. Each suite has a living room, a bedroom with one queen bed, and a kitchenette with a stove, a microwave, a refrigerator, a coffeemaker, pots, pans, and eating utensils. The smaller of the two suites can sleep up to four with a twin sofa sleeper plus a rollaway in the living room. It has one television and one bathroom. The Super Suite can sleep a maximum of six with a queen sofa sleeper plus a rollaway in the living room. It has two televisions, two bathrooms, and a fireplace. All the rooms at Lake Mead Resort have air-conditioning, heat, and a television with cable.

Lake Mead Resort is in a good location for water-related activities punctuated with occasional trips to nearby Las Vegas. A swimming pool near the front of the lodge buildings has a large patio area with tables and lounge chairs. A marina near the restaurant rents boats, including houseboats, and sells fishing licenses.

Rooms: Mostly doubles, with some triples, and quads. The Super Suite will sleep six. All rooms have a private bath.

Wheelchair Accessibility: One room in the annex has a wide bathroom doorway and a combination shower-tub with grab bars.

Reservations: Seven Crown Resorts, P.O. Box 16247, Irvine, CA 92623-0068. Phone (800) 752-9669. Reservations require a deposit of one night's stay. A seventy-two-hour cancellation notice is required for a full refund.

Rates: High season (April 1–October 31)/low season (November 1–March 31): one queen ($85/$65); two queens ($95/$80); kitchen suite ($150/$120); kitchen Super Suite ($180/$140). Rates quoted are for two adults per room and four adults for the suite. Each additional person is $15. A one-time fee of $10 is charged for a rollaway bed. Children five and under stay free.

Location: Six miles north of Boulder City, Nevada, on Lakeshore Scenic Drive. The resort is 30 miles southeast of Las Vegas.

Season: The resort is open year-round except Christmas Day. High season is during summer months, when the resort often fills on weekends.

Food: A full-service restaurant, Tail O' The Whale, at the marina serves breakfast ($5.00–$10.00), lunch ($5.00–$10.00), and dinner ($8.00–$25.00). A children's menu is available. The cocktail lounge and store are also at the marina.

Transportation: The nearest major airport is in Las Vegas, where rental cars are available.

Facilities: Swimming pool. A restaurant, cocktail lounge, waterside store, and a tackle and bait shop are at the full-service marina. Ski boats, patio boats, fishing boats, and personal watercraft are available for rent (1–800–752–9669 or www.sevencrown.com).

Activities: Fishing, waterskiing, boating, and swimming. No lifeguards.

Pets: Pets are permitted with a $50 deposit and an additional daily charge of $10 per pet.

LAKE MOHAVE RESORT AT KATHERINE LANDING

Bullhead City, AZ 86430 • (520) 754-3245 • www.sevencrown.com

Lake Mohave Resort is a marina complex situated on a hill above Lake Mohave. The two motel buildings, constructed of cement block in the early 1970s, provide a total of fifty rooms in a large grassy area landscaped with palm trees. The resort is located at the south end of Lake Mohave, just off Nevada Highway 68, north of Davis Dam. It is the southernmost lodging facility in Lake Mead National Recreation Area. Lake Mohave Resort is 32 miles west of Kingman, Arizona.

The resort offers five types of accommodations. All of the rooms have air-conditioning, heat, a telephone, a television, and a bathroom. Six rooms have a private balcony or patio. Eleven of the resort's least expensive rooms have one king-size bed. Thirty-one rooms have two double beds. Six of these rooms include a kitchen and rent for an additional $10 per night. Eight rooms classified as kitchen suites have two queen-size beds. Each building has a covered walkway with chairs in front of each room. A single deluxe rental house, which sleeps up to ten persons, includes three bedrooms, two baths, and a full kitchen. The rental house is across the street from the main building.

Lake Mead and Lake Mohave offer excellent fishing and have open season on all species of fish year-round. Largemouth bass, rainbow trout, channel catfish, black crappie, and bluegill are in both lakes. Lake Mead is noted for an abundance of striped bass, some weighing fifty pounds and more. Rainbow trout are the most popular catch in Lake Mohave. Fishing from shore requires an appropriate state fishing license. Fishing from a boat requires a fishing license from either Nevada or Arizona and a special use stamp from the other state. Licenses and stamps are sold at most of the marinas.

Activities at Lake Mohave Resort primarily appeal to visitors who enjoy fishing, waterskiing, and boating. A full marina provides slips, moorage, a gas dock, and repair facilities. The marina has a full-service Tail O'

The Whale Restaurant and lounge. Laundry facilities are at the nearby RV park, and a convenience store and tackle shop are adjacent to the restaurant. The booming town of Laughlin, Nevada, and its many casinos are a short drive from the resort.

Rooms: Doubles, triples, and quads. All rooms have a bathroom. The house sleeps up to ten.

Wheelchair Accessibility: Two rooms are wheelchair accessible with wide bathroom doors and a combination shower-tub with an adjustable showerhead, a seat, and grab bars.

Reservations: Seven Crown Resorts, P.O. Box 16247, Irvine, CA 92623-0068. Phone (800) 752-9669. A deposit of one night's stay is required. A seventy-two-hour cancellation notice is required for a full refund.

Rates: High season (March 21–September 1)/low season (September 2–March 20): Room with one king bed ($95/$60); room with two double beds ($105/$70); kitchen with two double beds ($115/$80); kitchen suite with two queen-size beds ($125/$90); house ($250/$250). Rates for the regular rooms and the kitchen with two double beds are for two adults; rates for the kitchen suite are for three adults; rates for the house are for six people. Each additional person is $15.00, and a one-time fee of $7.50 is charged for a rollaway bed. Children five and under stay free.

Location: The resort is located on the shore of Lake Mohave, 32 miles west of Kingman, Arizona. It is 3 miles off NV 68.

Season: The resort is open year-round except for Christmas Day. High season is during summer, and the resort often fills on summer weekends.

Food: A full-service restaurant serves breakfast ($4.00–$8.00), lunch ($5.00–$9.00), and dinner ($8.00–$20.00). A children's menu is available. A snack bar is open during the summer with the same menu and take-out service. A store adjacent to the restaurant sells groceries and supplies.

Transportation: Kingman, Arizona, and Las Vegas both have airports with rental car service.

Facilities: A restaurant, cocktail lounge, store, and tackle shop are at the marina. Laundry facilities are at the nearby RV park. A full-service marina located in front of the lodge buildings rents houseboats, ski boats, patio boats, fishing boats, and personal watercraft (800-752-9669 or www.sevencrown.com).

Activities: Fishing, boating, swimming (no lifeguards), and waterskiing. Numerous casinos are a short distance away in Laughlin, Nevada.

Pets: Pets are permitted with a $50 deposit and an additional daily charge of $10 per pet.

TEMPLE BAR RESORT

Temple Bar Marina, AZ 86443 • (928) 767-3211 • www.templebarlakemead.com

Temple Bar Resort comprises two concrete-block motel-type buildings with eighteen rooms, four free-standing shake-sided cabins, a restaurant, an adjacent store, and a tackle and bait shop. The complex also includes a full-service marina. The resort is on the south shoreline of Lake Mead within view of a large monolith called The Temple. Temple Bar Resort is located on a paved road 28 miles northeast of U.S. Highway 93, which connects Las Vegas, Nevada, with Kingman, Arizona. It is 78 miles east of Las Vegas and 85 miles from Kingman.

All of the eighteen motel rooms at Temple Bar have heat, air-conditioning, a television, and a private bathroom. There are no telephones in the rooms; pay phones are available. The larger motel building houses twelve large rooms, six on each side. Each room has two double beds and a patio with table and chairs. Half of these units are desert-view rooms and the other half are lake-view rooms. A separate building has six rooms in three classes. Two traditional rooms offer a double bed and double sofa bed. Two kitchen units have one double bed and a sofa bed in one room. The kitchen area includes a stove with

an oven, a microwave oven, a full-size refrigerator, dishes, and basic cooking utensils. Two kitchen suites feature two double beds in a separate bedroom with a sofa bed in the living room/ kitchen. The four cabins have two double beds, a stove with an oven, a sink with hot water, and a refrigerator but no bath. The bathhouse is adjacent to the cabins. There are no dishes or cooking utensils provided in the cabins.

Rooms: Doubles, triples, and quads. Suites hold up to six adults. All rooms except cabins have a full bath.

Wheelchair Accessibility: One room is wheelchair accessible. It has ramp access and wide doorways; the bathroom has grab bars, and the tub has an adjustable showerhead and a seat.

Reservations: One Main Street, Temple Bar Marina, AZ 86443. Phone (928) 767-3211. A deposit of one night's stay is required. A seventy-two-hour cancellation notice is required for a full refund.

Rates: High season (April 1–October 31)/low season (November 1–March 31): Traditional rooms ($80/$65); desert-view rooms ($95/$85); lake-view rooms ($105/$80); kitchen units ($110/$90); kitchen suites $125/$100); cabins ($60/$50). Rates quoted are for two adults in regular units, three adults in kitchen suites, and four adults in cabins. Each additional person is $10. Children five and under stay free. A one-time $8.00 fee is charged for a rollaway bed.

Location: The resort is 78 miles east of Las Vegas, Nevada. It is at the end of a paved road 28 miles northeast of US 93.

Season: The resort is open year-round except for Christmas Day.

Food: A full-service restaurant serves breakfast ($4.00–$9.00), lunch ($5.00–$10.00), and dinner ($8.00–$20.00). A children's menu is available. A convenience store sells groceries and supplies.

Transportation: Kingman, Arizona, and Las Vegas have airports with rental car service.

Facilities: Restaurant, cocktail lounge, store, and tackle and bait shop. The Marina rents ski boats, deck cruisers, patio boats, fishing boats, and houseboats. Laundry facilities are at the nearby RV park.

Activities: Fishing, boating, swimming (no lifeguards), and waterskiing.

Pets: Pets are permitted with a $50 deposit and an additional daily charge of $10 per pet.

NORTH CAROLINA

■ **State Tourist Information**
(800) 847-4862 | www.visitnc.com

Blue Ridge Parkway

199 Hemphill Knob Road • Asheville, NC 28803 • (828) 271-4779• www.nps.gov/blri

The Blue Ridge Parkway comprises 93,000 acres in a narrow strip along 469 miles of winding road that follows the crest of the Blue Ridge Mountains. The parkway provides access to craft centers, campgrounds, scenic overlooks, log cabins, rail fences, and striking mountain vistas. Lodges, overlooks, restaurants, and other major points of interest along the parkway can be located according to milepost markers alongside the road. Mile marker 0 is at Rockfish Gap near Waynesboro, Virginia, the northern entrance to the parkway. Each mile is numbered progressively southward. Be certain to stop at a visitor center and acquire a free copy of the parkway folder that includes a map indicating the locations of points of interest. The parkway is in western North Carolina and western Virginia. The north end of the parkway connects with Shenandoah National Park, and the south end leads to Great Smoky Mountains National Park. **Parkway Entrance Fee:** No charge.

Lodging along the Blue Ridge Parkway: Four lodging facilities are within the boundaries of the Blue Ridge Parkway. Accommodations range from nice two-story lodges to very rustic cabins without a private bath. The facilities are scattered along the parkway from mile marker 86 in the north to very near the south entrance, near Great Smoky Mountains National Park.

BLUFFS LODGE

45356 Blue Ridge Parkway • Laurel Springs, NC 28644-9716 • (336) 372-4499

www.blueridgeresort.com

Blue Ridge Parkway

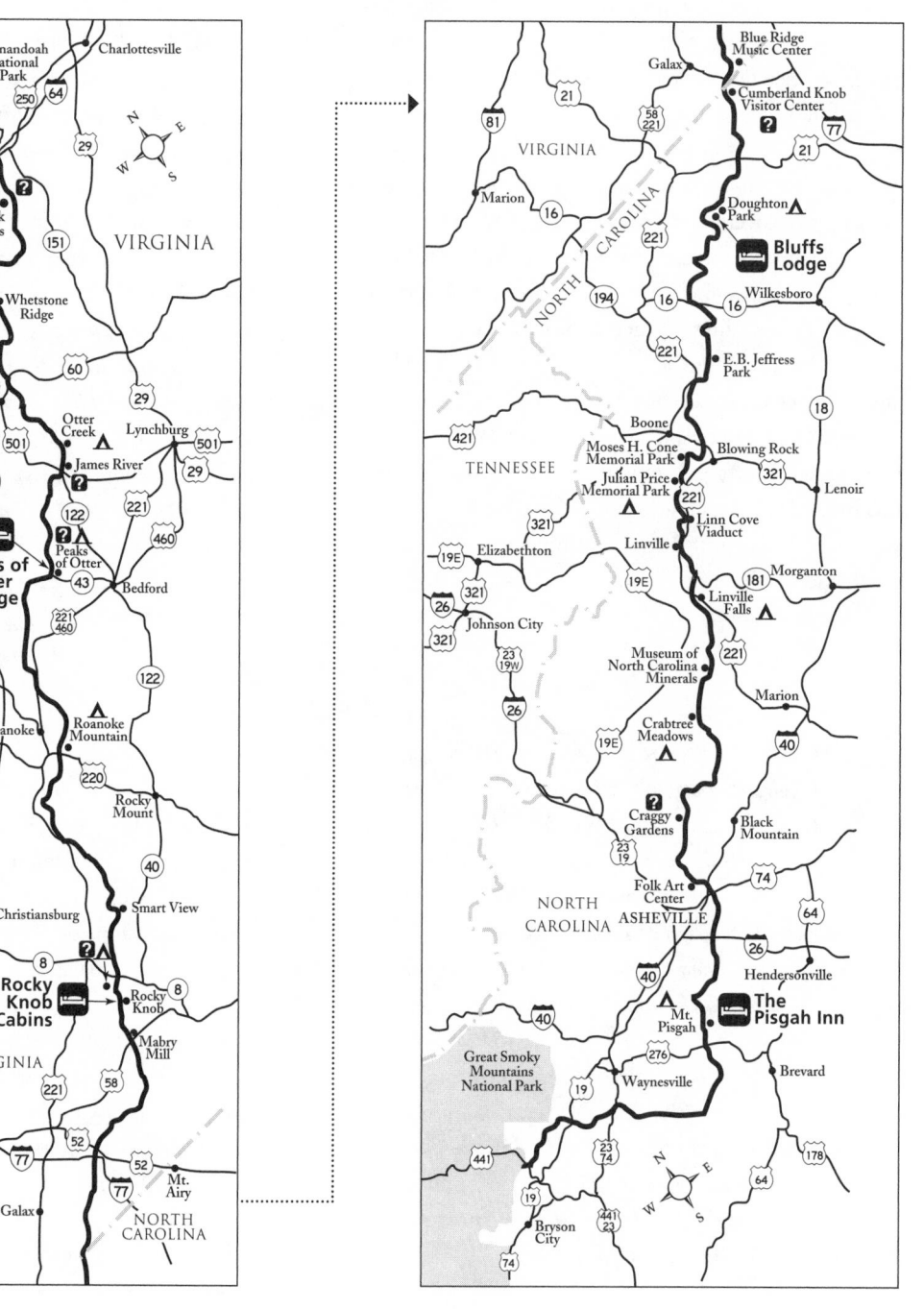

Bluffs Lodge consists of two identical two-story lodge buildings built into a grassy hillside overlooking a meadow and surrounding hills. No other buildings are connected to the lodge, although a coffee shop and gift shop are a quarter mile away on the parkway. Each lodge building contains twelve rooms, four on each floor of the back side facing the meadow and rolling hills and four rooms on the front facing the parking lot. A spacious, covered second-floor balcony runs across the back of each building. Chairs are on the balcony and on the rock walkways at ground level, as well as the front of the building. A nice rock patio area between the two buildings has a large outdoor stone fireplace and many chairs and tables for viewing the scenery or visiting. The buildings, which opened in 1949, are well maintained. Bluffs Lodge is in northern North Carolina in the Doughton Park area of the Blue Ridge Parkway. It is at milepost 241, about midway between the north and south entrances to the parkway.

■　■　■

Linn Cove Viaduct at mile marker 305 on the Blue Ridge Parkway is considered one of the most complicated concrete bridges ever built. It is one of America's most scenic bridges and has received half a dozen national design awards. The S-shaped viaduct was designed and constructed to minimize environmental damage. Skirting the perimeter of North Carolina's Grandfather Mountain, the viaduct is 1,243 feet long and contains 153 concrete segments, only one of which is straight. Although nearly all of the Blue Ridge Parkway had been completed and open to travelers by 1967, the viaduct was not finished until 1983. A trail leading underneath the viaduct begins at a visitor contact station at the south end of the viaduct.

■　■　■

■　■　■

Although the Blue Ridge Parkway was completed into the Doughton Park (then called Bluff Park) area in 1937, it was not until 1948 that construction commenced on a gasoline station and coffee shop. Doughton Park was also designated for the first of three inns to be constructed on the parkway. The National Park Service office drew up initial plans for the inn that, according to one person, looked "like a two story army barracks." The original plans were changed by new architects, who separated the structure with a patio and bent the two sections in the middle to conform to the contours of the land on which the lodge would be built. A gas station (currently a gift shop) across the road opened on May 28, 1949, and the first unit of Bluffs Lodge opened on September 1 of the same year. Excluding campgrounds, this was the first overnight lodging for visitors on the Blue Ridge Parkway.

■　■　■

All twenty-four rooms at Bluffs Lodge are nearly identical except for the views and bedding. Each room has heat, a ceiling fan, a coffeemaker, a hair dryer, and a tiled bathroom with a combination shower-tub, but no telephone, television, or air-conditioning. The rooms are not particularly spacious, but are clean and comfortable, and each has an amazingly large closet to store suitcases, coolers, clothes, and other gear you bring in. Several rooms have one queen bed, and two have a king bed, but the majority of rooms have two double beds. The best views are from rooms on the back side facing the southwest. Rooms in the front face the northeast, which can be an advantage on particularly hot days when you may not want to deal with the afternoon sun. Remember, there is no air-conditioning. We would choose a second-floor mountain-view room, preferably either 203A or 203B, which are end rooms with an added side window and brighter interior. In addition, other guests will not be walking by when they enter or exit their own rooms. The lodge is built on a hillside, so second-floor rooms do not require climbing stairs.

Bluffs Lodge is as peaceful a place to stay as you will find in any national park or, for that matter, anywhere at all. It is a quarter mile off the Blue Ridge Parkway, so you won't be bothered by traffic noise, and since no restaurant or visitor center is at the site, there is no congestion of people and vehicles. With only twenty-four rooms, you are likely to meet up with others who are seeking a similar experience. Without televisions to consume attention, you will almost surely find yourself striking up a conversation with other guests as you spend the late afternoon or early evening relaxing on the balcony or walkway outside your room. In the evening, guests often mingle in front of the large stone fireplace between the two buildings. A short walk up a nearby hillside provides an outstanding view of a valley and surrounding mountains. A unique experience when staying here is eating in the nearby old-fashioned coffee shop, which still offers counter service. Both the interior and exterior are virtually identical to when it opened in June 1949. Ellen, the server who waited on us during our August 2007 visit, had worked in the coffee shop for fifty-seven years! Who says employee loyalty has gone out of style? The coffee shop serves regional specialties including pinto beans and cornbread, biscuits and gravy, and country ham. Where else can you order barbecued pork with melted cheese served between two golden brown corn cakes topped with cole slaw?

Rooms: Doubles, triples, and quads. All rooms have a private bath with a combination shower-tub.

Wheelchair Accessibility: No rooms at Bluffs Lodge are specifically labeled as wheelchair accessible. Rooms can be accessed without steps, but the rooms do not have wide doorways or wheelchair-accessible bathrooms.

Reservations: Bluffs Lodge, 45356 Blue Ridge Parkway, Laurel Springs, NC 28644-9716. Phone (336) 372-4499. A deposit of one night's stay is required. A fee equal to one night's lodging is charged for cancellations made within forty-eight hours of scheduled arrival. A $15 fee is charged for cancellations of from two days to two weeks prior to scheduled arrival.

Rates: Mountain-view rooms ($95); front-view rooms ($85). Rates quoted are for two adults. Each additional person is $10 per night. Children twelve and under stay free with an adult. A rollaway is $10 per night. Rates are slightly higher on holidays and during October.

Location: In northern North Carolina, near the midpoint of the Blue Ridge Parkway at milepost 241. The lodge is a quarter mile off the parkway.

Season: The last weekend of April through the first weekend of November.

Food: A 1950s-era coffee shop a quarter mile from the lodge serves breakfast ($4.00–$9.00), lunch ($4.00–$11.00), and dinner ($6.00–$13.00). Regional specialties are offered. Hours are 7:30 a.m. to 7:30 p.m. daily. Snacks are sold at a gift shop next to the coffee shop.

Transportation: The nearest scheduled airline service is in Charlotte and Greensboro, North Carolina. Each city is about two hours from the lodge.

Facilities: No facilities are at the lodge. A coffee shop and gift shop are a quarter mile away on the Blue Ridge Parkway.

Activities: Hiking. Park Service rangers present weekend programs on the lodge patio.

PEAKS OF OTTER LODGE

85554 Blue Ridge Parkway • Bedford, VA 24523 • (540) 586-1081 • www.peaksofotter.com

Peaks of Otter Lodge consists of a main registration and dining building plus three adjacent two-story buildings that provide a total of sixty-three overnight rooms. All four of the attractive wood-and-cement block buildings were constructed in the mid-1960s and have a similar appearance. The buildings are on the grassy bank of Abbott Lake, and all the rooms provide an excellent view of this small but pretty body of water. Peaks of Otter Lodge is located about 25 miles north of Roanoke, Virginia, at mile marker 86 on the Blue Ridge Parkway. It is the farthest north of the four lodging facilities on the parkway.

All but three wheelchair-accessible rooms are in three two-story buildings connected end-to-end by covered walkways. Each of the three buildings sit on a grassy hillside below the parking lot. Because the buildings are built into a hillside, a half flight of stairs gains entry to a walkway that runs in front of the entry doors of either first- or second-floor rooms. Unit One, with rooms numbered in the 100s, is closest to the main lodge building, although the buildings are close together, so no room is far from the dining room and lounge. The rooms are bright and airy, with a large back window that offers a view of Abbott Lake backed by a wooded hillside. Scenic Sharp Top Mountain peeks over the southwest corner of the lake. All but two rooms have either a patio or balcony with two chairs. Each room has air-conditioning, electric heat, carpeting, and a tiled bathroom with a combination shower-tub, but no television or telephone. Two satellite televisions are in the main lodge, one in the lounge and the other in the ground-floor lobby, and pay telephones and ice machines are scattered about the complex. The majority of rooms have two double beds, while several have one king bed. We generally prefer second-floor rooms, but at this lodge you might want to choose a room on

A lodging facility served the Peaks of Otter area as early as 1834, when Polly Woods operated a combination tavern/lodge for nearly a decade. This was followed by several hotels built in this locale prior to the construction of the parkway through the Peaks of Otter area beginning in 1939. The initial development plan for the Peaks of Otter area envisioned a picnic area and aquatic center at the present lodge site in addition to twenty-two cabins on the hillside behind the current visitor center. Several proposals followed, including one that called for a lodge and a small lake to replace the aquatic center. The present lodge site was confirmed in 1951 with a plan calling for one large lodging structure. This plan underwent several changes, and construction of the present lodge got underway in 1962. Two years later work commenced on the lake. The lodge began operating year-round in 1973.

the first floor, where you can move your patio chairs onto a large grassy hillside leading to the nearby lake. In addition, you can use the lakeside doorway for a nice walk to the main lodge building.

Peaks of Otter Lodge is a favorite for many travelers on the Blue Ridge Parkway. The rooms are comfortable, and the view from a back balcony is similar to what an armchair traveler might see on a picture postcard. Plan to do a lot of hiking during your visit. A 1-mile paved trail behind the lodge is a pleasant place to stroll as it circles Abbott Lake. Other trails are nearby. Or perhaps you would rather walk down and fish in the lake (artificial lures only). Daily bus trips to Sharp Top Mountain (fee charged) leave hourly from the nearby camp store when weather permits. The country-style dining room, with its vaulted, beamed ceiling and large

windows overlooking Lake Abbott, serves three meals a day, including a Friday night seafood buffet and a Sunday country buffet. Beverages are served in an adjacent lounge with a large stone fireplace and great lake views.

Rooms: Singles, doubles, triples, and quads. All rooms have a private bath with a combination shower-tub.

Wheelchair Accessibility: Three rooms on the ground floor (one floor below the main entrance) of the main lodge building are ADA compliant. Access to the rooms is via an elevator from the main lobby. The rooms have either two doubles or a king bed plus a sofa bed. Depending on the room, the bathroom has either a roll-in shower or a combination shower-tub. Each room has a small refrigerator, a television, and telephone access to the front desk.

Reservations: Peaks of Otter Lodge, 85554 Blue Ridge Parkway, Bedford, VA 24523. Phone (800) 542-5927. One night's deposit is required. A twenty-four-hour cancellation notice is required for a full refund.

Rates: November–late May weekdays ($82), weekends ($92); late May–September weekdays ($109), weekends ($120); some holiday weekends and the month of October ($125–$130). Rates quoted are for singles or doubles. Each additional person is $8.00 per night. Children under twelve stay free. Rollaway beds are $8.00 per night. Call or check the Web site for special packages.

Location: Twenty-five miles north of Roanoke, Virginia, at mileposts 84/87 of the Blue Ridge Parkway.

Season: Open year-round.

Food: A dining room serves breakfast ($4.00–$8.00), lunch/dinner ($7.00–$27.00), including a special seafood buffet on Friday ($22.00) and a country buffet on Sunday ($16.00). A children's menu is available.

Transportation: Nearby Roanoke and Lynchburg, Virginia, each provide scheduled airline service. Rental cars are available in each town.

Facilities: Restaurant, cocktail lounge, gift shop, conference rooms, nature center, country store, National Park Service visitor center.

Activities: Hiking, fishing, interpretive programs, bus trip to Sharp Top Mountain, National Park Service campfire programs on weekend evenings.

THE PISGAH INN

P.O. Box 749 • Waynesville, NC 28786 • (828) 235-8228 • www.pisgahinn.com

The Pisgah Inn consists of three two-story buildings with a total of fifty-one rooms, a separate restaurant and gift shop, and a near by country store. Each building is of wood and masonry construction. All of the lodge rooms offer an excellent view of the distant mountains and are a short walk from the dining room. The three lodge buildings and the restaurant are situated at 5,000 feet on the side of 5,749-foot Mt. Pisgah. The inn, constructed in the mid-1960s, is in southwestern North Carolina, approximately 25 miles south of Asheville, North Carolina. It is the farthest south of the four lodging facilities on the Blue Ridge Parkway, at milepost 408.

Two types of rooms and one suite are offered. All of the rooms have heat, a tiled bathroom with a combination shower-tub, and a television, but no air-conditioning or telephone. Each room has a private balcony with rocking chairs. Most of the rooms have two double beds, and some have one queen-size bed. The back balcony and windows of each room generally offer excellent views of the distant mountains, although some of the first-floor "standard" rooms have views that are partially obstructed by nearby trees and plants. Choose a second-floor room if you don't mind climbing a flight of stairs. Adequate parking is close to each

■ ■ ■

The Biltmore Estate near Asheville, North Carolina, is one of this region's major visitor attractions. The 250-room mansion was constructed in the late 1800s by George Washington Vanderbilt, grandson of railroad tycoon Cornelius Vanderbilt. Allow at least a half-day for the full self-guided tour (fee charged) of the home, winery, gardens, and greenhouse. The Biltmore Estate is 3 blocks north of Interstate 40 (exit 50) on U.S. Highway 25.

■ ■ ■

The current Pisgah Inn is immediately adjacent to the location of an earlier inn on this same property that was donated by George Washington Vanderbilt, a grandson of railroad tycoon Cornelius Vanderbilt. The Pisgah Forest Inn was constructed of wormy chestnut in 1919 by landscape architect George Weston for the Biltmore estate. The inn had eleven rooms, a large dining room, and cabins that were added in the 1940s. Guests arrived via the narrow Buck Spring Trail that was restricted to arriving guests during the morning and departing guests during the afternoon and evening. Following the closure to overnight guests during the late 1960s, the lobby of the Pisgah Forest Inn continued to be used for special occasions such as speakers, wedding receptions, and get-togethers. The inn was torn down in 1991. The cabins were still used for several additional years as employee housing. Photographs of the old Pisgah Forest Inn are in the registration area of the Pisgah Inn.

building. Thirty rooms labeled "deluxe" are larger, have a coffeemaker and refrigerator and were remodeled in 2001. Twenty rooms rent as standard at a slightly reduced rate. The single suite located above the office is twice as large as a deluxe room. The suite is one large room with a king bed, two televisions, a sitting area with a sofa, a table and chairs, and the only fireplace (gas) in a room in the inn.

Pisgah Inn is a place to get away from the heat while enjoying mountain views and good food. Views from the rooms are the best of any lodging facility on the parkway. At an altitude of 5,000 feet, temperatures are generally cool, even during summer months when the surrounding valleys are hot and humid. Weekends

can be busy, so you might want to choose a weekday night or two if you have the flexibility. The restaurant, with its vaulted ceiling and ceiling-high windows on three walls, offers diners good views from nearly any table. Best of all, the restaurant has excellent food, with nearly a dozen daily specials for lunch and dinner. On the evening we dined, the menu included Walnut Crusted Trout with Raspberry Sauce and Apple Raisin Stuffed Pork Chop with Cider Glaze. The inn sits in an excellent area for hiking, and good fishing is about 10 miles away. National Park Service rangers conduct evening weekend programs across the road at the campground amphitheater.

Rooms: Singles, doubles, triples, and quads. All rooms have a private bath with a combination shower-tub.

Wheelchair Accessibility: Three first-floor deluxe rooms each have nearby parking and ramp access to the room. The bathroom has a wide doorway, a high toilet, and a combination shower-tub with grab bars.

Reservations: The Pisgah Inn, P.O. Box 749, Waynesville, NC 28786. Phone (828) 235-8228 or visit www.pisgahinn.com. One night's deposit is required. A fee of $15 is charged for cancellations made two weeks or less from the arrival date. One night's deposit is charged for cancellations made forty-eight hours or less from the arrival date.

Rates: Standard ($108); deluxe ($118); suite ($160). Rates quoted are for two adults. Each additional person is $9.00. Rollaways are $9.00 per night. Children twelve and under stay free. Rates are slightly higher during October and holidays.

Location: Southwest North Carolina, 25 miles south of Asheville on the Blue Ridge Parkway.

Season: April 1 through October 31.

Food: An attractive restaurant serves breakfast ($6.00–$12.00), lunch ($9.00–$16.00), and dinner ($17.00–$35.00). A nearby country store sells limited groceries.

Transportation: The nearest scheduled airline service is in Asheville, where rental cars are available. No public transportation services the inn.

Facilities: Restaurant, gift shop, laundry, country store.

Activities: Hiking, evening weekend programs at the nearby campground amphitheater.

ROCKY KNOB CABINS

266 Mabry Mill Road • Meadows of Dan, VA 24120-9603 • (540) 593-3503
www.blueridgeresort.com

Rocky Knob Cabins is a small complex consisting of one registration office/manager's cabin, a central bathhouse, and five older wooden buildings arranged in a semicircle behind the bathhouse. Two of the buildings are constructed as duplex units, for a total of seven rental cabins. The cabins are in a meadow surrounded by heavily wooded hills. The complex is in a very remote setting and has no lobby, dining room, or recreation hall. The buildings are from the 1930s, erected during construction of the parkway. Rocky Knob Cabins is in southern Virginia, at milepost 174 on the Blue Ridge Parkway. It is 54 miles south of Roanoke, Virginia.

The seven cabins at Rocky Knob Cabins are virtually identical except for the one wheelchair-accessible unit. Each cabin has a porch, a vaulted ceiling, two double beds, window fans, and a small electric heater. The kitchens have a table with four chairs, a full-size refrigerator, a two-burner stove top, and a sink with cold water only. Pots, pans, dishes, a coffeemaker, and utensils are provided. A patio table and two chairs, a grill, and two wooden rocking chairs are outside. One unit of each duplex cabin (unit 22 and wheelchair-accessible unit 18) has an indoor and outdoor fireplace. Firewood is available for purchase in the office. Except for the wheelchair-accessible unit, the cabins do not

■   ■   ■

Mabry Mill, at milepost 176, is a favorite stop for travelers on the Blue Ridge Parkway. The mill, operated by E. B. Mabry from 1910 to 1935, today serves country ham, barbecue, homemade biscuits, and corn and buckwheat pancakes. Native handicrafts, including pottery, woodcraft, and metalcraft, are available for purchase. A trail leads to the original gristmill, sawmill, blacksmith shop, and other outdoor exhibits. Demonstrations are presented in summer and fall.

■   ■   ■

The cabins at Rocky Knob were constructed in 1941 as the first of a planned series of "trail lodges" along the parkway. The complex was intended to accommodate Boy Scouts, Girl Scouts, and other youth groups. These were to be "rough-it" camps that would provide built-in bunks, benches, toilets, showers, and a picnic-type table. At the same time, authorities planned a conventional lodge, coffee shop, and gas station. The lodge and coffee shop were never built, and the gas station, completed in 1949, was converted to a visitor contact station in 1978. The cabins were never used as intended. Rather they were remodeled for use as family housekeeping units and made available to the public in 1950.

have a private bathroom, so guests must utilize a nearby central bathhouse that has sinks, toilets, and showers. The cabins also do not have air-conditioning, a telephone, or a television. If you don't care about having a fireplace, choose one of the three freestanding cabins. Our choice is cabin 21, which offers the best view from the front porch. If having a fireplace is important, request cabin 22, or, if available, wheelchair-accessible cabin 18, which has a fireplace plus a private bathroom with hot water.

Rocky Knob Cabins is certainly one of the more unusual lodging units in the national park system. Staying here is like returning to Appalachia in years past—many years past. The cabins are old but clean and comfortable. The deciding factor for many travelers is whether a community bath is acceptable. If you don't

mind this inconvenience and want to stay overnight in a very rural setting, Rocky Knob may be your place. Also, Rocky Knob has no planned activities or other facilities; you are on your own for things to do. You will also enjoy a sense of solitude that many seek in a vacation. If you don't want to cook, Mabry Mill, a famous stop 2 miles south on the Blue Ridge Parkway, serves meals from morning to early evening.

Rooms: Doubles, triples, and quads. Only the wheelchair-accessible cabin has a private bath.

Wheelchair Accessibility: One cabin in a duplex unit is ADA compliant with a roll-in shower.

Reservations: Rocky Knob Cabins, 266 Mabry Mill Road, Meadows of Dan, VA 24120-9603. Phone (540) 593-3503; during the off-season write Rocky Knob Cabins, P.O. Box 27, Mammoth Cave, KY 42259. Phone (270) 773-2191. One night's deposit is required. Cancellation notice of forty-eight hours is required for a full refund.

Rates: All cabins ($65). Rates quoted are for two adults. Each additional person is $8.00 per night. Rollaways are $8.00 per night. Cabins are $55 per night Sunday through Thursday when staying two or more nights, with the exception of October, November, and holidays.

Location: Southern Virginia, 1 mile off the Blue Ridge Parkway at milepost 174. The cabins are approximately 55 miles south of Roanoke, Virginia.

Season: May through the first weekend in November.

Food: No dining facilities are available. The Mabry Mill Restaurant, 2 miles south on the Blue Ridge Parkway, serves breakfast ($5.00–$9.00), lunch ($4.00–$8.00), and dinner ($4.00–$8.00).

Transportation: Scheduled airlines serve Roanoke, Virginia, where rental cars are available.

Facilities: Community bathhouse with showers.

Activities: Hiking, horseshoes, a swing (porch type).

Pets: Pets are permitted for $5.00 per night per pet, but they must be kept on a leash.

OHIO

Cuyahoga Valley National Park

15610 Vaughn Road • Brecksville, OH 44141 • (216) 524-1497
www.dayinthevalley.com • www.nps.gov/cuva

Cuyahoga Valley National Park encompasses 33,000 acres of a rural river valley that links the two urban centers of Cleveland and Akron. The national park offers a place to enjoy a stroll, hike, or bike along the 19-mile Ohio & Erie Canal Towpath Trail, a primary park attraction. Cuyahoga Valley National Park includes a restored 1800s farm and village, hiking and biking trails, several visitor centers, and the remnants of a company town built in 1906. Throughout the year, the Cuyahoga Valley Scenic Railroad operates the full length of the park and beyond. **Park Entrance Fee:** No charge. Fee for some special events.

Lodging in Cuyahoga Valley National Park: A bed-and-breakfast inn with six accommodations sits within the boundaries of the national park. The Inn at Brandywine Falls is midway between the north and south ends of the park, approximately 4 miles northeast of the crossing of Interstates 80 and 271. A large number and variety of accommodations are available just outside the border of the national park.

THE INN AT BRANDYWINE FALLS

8230 Brandywine Road • Sagamore Hills, OH 44067-2810 • (330) 467-1812
www.innatbrandywinefalls.com

Cuyahoga Valley National Park

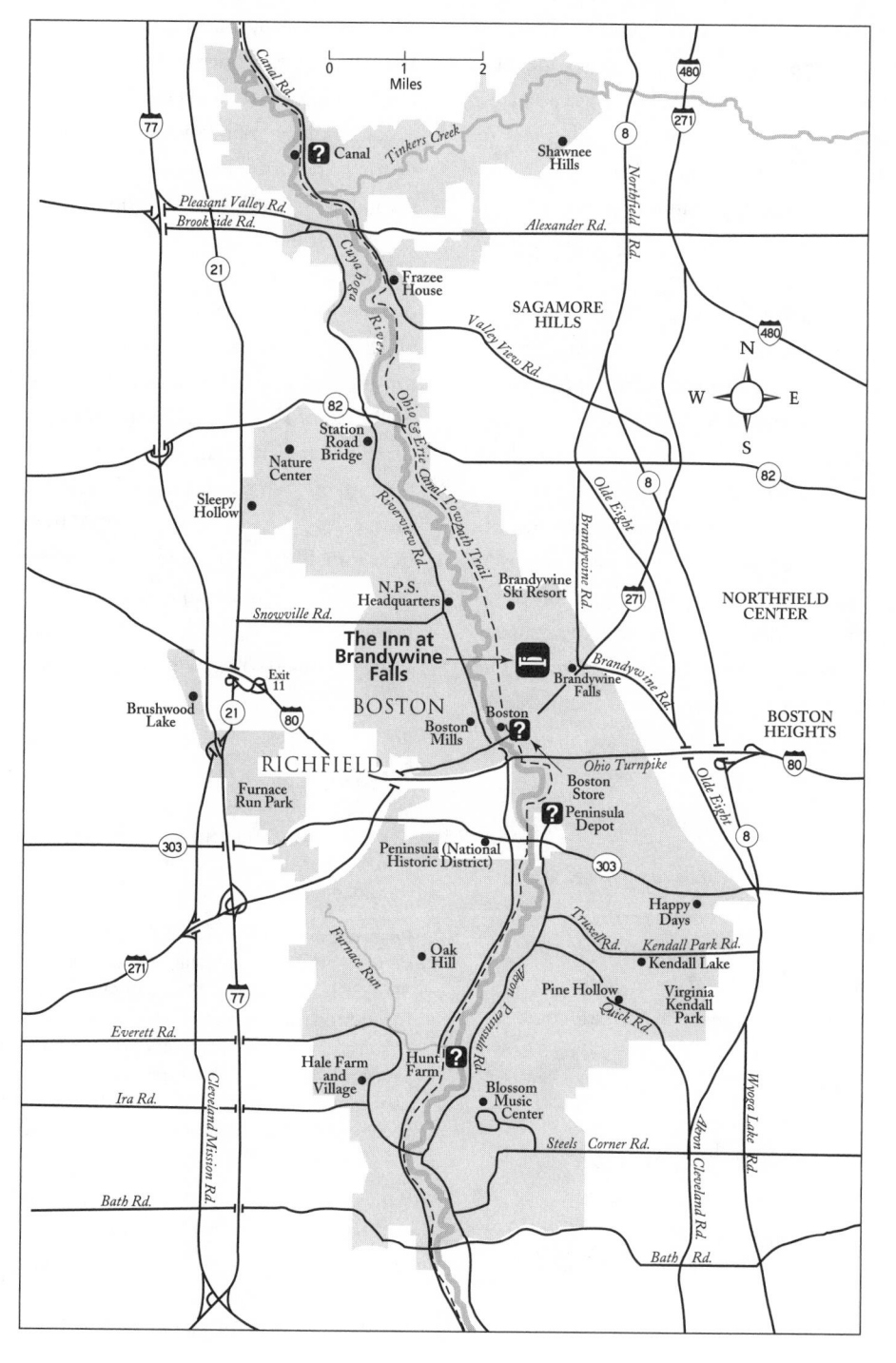

The Inn at Brandywine Falls is a pre–Civil War–era farmstead renovated in 1988 by an enterprising couple who operate it as a bed-and-breakfast under a fifty-year lease from the U.S. government. The property includes the main house, an adjacent carriage barn, and a nearby stable. Cats, chickens, goats, and an affable dog add to the country atmosphere of the inn, which is located on the east rim of the valley, approximately 3 miles north of I-80. From downtown Cleveland (forty minutes) take Interstate 77 south to Ohio Highway 82. Drive east about 6 miles to Brandywine Road, then 2.5 miles south.

The inn offers six overnight rooms, four in the main house and two in the carriage barn. All the rooms have heat, air-conditioning, a telephone, wireless Internet, and a private bathroom. The main house has three rooms on the second floor, one of which has one double bed. The other second-floor accommodations include the "Simon Perkins Room," with two double four-poster beds, and "Anna Hale's Garret Suite," which comprises a small bedroom with two double beds plus a small sitting room that can be used as a second bedroom. The single first-floor accommodation has a double sleigh

bed and is wheelchair accessible. The more expensive suites in the carriage house each have plank floors, a table and chairs, either a double futon or daybeds, a Franklin stove, a microwave, and a refrigerator, all on the first floor, plus a king bed in the loft. Each suite has a Jacuzzi plus a wall of windows that offers guests a feel of the outdoors. The bathroom in one suite is on the second floor, while the bathroom in the other suite is on the first floor.

Located in a rural area of Ohio, the Inn at Brandywine Falls is a place to relax and use as a base from which to explore this diverse national park. You can ride a train, drive to Cleveland and take in the Rock and Roll Hall of Fame, or sit on the front porch and sip tea. Sixty-seven-foot Brandywine Falls is a short walk from the inn, or you can hike the 1.7-mile-long Brandywine Gorge Trail. Guests are encouraged to use the inn's living room, library, dining room, and porch. A full breakfast of fresh-squeezed juice, fruit, fruit-filled oatmeal, homemade bread, and an entree is served each morning from 7:00 to 10:00 a.m. (from 8:45 a.m. on weekends).

■　　■　　■

The James Wallace family, who came to this area in the early 1800s, built the farmhouse that is now The Inn at Brandywine Falls. Although difficult to visualize from today's serene setting, this was once the thriving community of Brandywine Mills. Wallace built a mill powered by the nearby waterfall and used money earned from the business to purchase 600 acres and build a farmhouse. The farmhouse passed through five owners before being purchased by the National Park Service. The property was renovated by innkeepers Katie and George Hoy under an agreement with the NPS.

■　　■　　■

Rooms: Doubles, triples, and quads. All rooms have private baths.

Wheelchair Accessibility: One room on the first floor is barrier free, the bathroom has grab bars, and the combination shower-tub has a stool. A lift is available for the front entrance.

Reservations: The Inn at Brandywine Falls, 8230 Brandywine Road, Sagamore Hills, Ohio 44067-2810. Phone (888) 306-3381, (330) 467-1812 or 650-4965. A 65 percent deposit is required with a reservation. A two-week cancellation is required for a full refund unless the accommodation is subsequently booked by another party, or the guest purchases cancellation insurance for a modest fee. The innkeepers recommend that reservations be made at least two months in advance.

Arrival/Departure: Check-in between 4:01 and 6:45 p.m. and after 8:30 p.m. Checkout at 11:00 a.m.

Rates: Sunday through Thursday non-holiday prices: Main house rooms ($129); main house suite ($149); Carriage house suites ($215). Friday is $25 to $35 higher. Saturday and holidays are $50 to $100 higher. Prices are for two persons and include a full breakfast. Additional persons are $10 to $35 per night, depending on age. A 10 percent discount is offered for stays of three days or more, except holidays, and for two-day stays Sunday through Thursday from January 15 through May. Holidays are excluded.

Location: In northeast Ohio, midway between Cleveland and Akron.

Season: Open year-round.

Food: Breakfast is included. Fruit, homemade cookies, and hot beverages are provided at 4:30 p.m. and after 8:30 p.m. Alcoholic beverages may be brought by guests. Over a dozen restaurants are within 6 miles of the inn.

Transportation: Scheduled airline service is in Cleveland and Akron/Canton, where rental cars are available.

Facilities: Dining room for breakfast, library, wireless Internet.

Activities: Hiking and biking. Historic attractions, scenic railroad, museums, golf, and pond fishing nearby. Snow tubing, cross-country skiing, and downhill skiing during winter.

OREGON

Crater Lake National Park

P.O. Box 7 • Crater Lake, OR 97604 • (541) 594-2211 • www.nps.gov/crla

Crater Lake National Park encompasses 183,000 acres, including a deep blue lake that resulted from the collapse of Mt. Mazama, an ancient 12,000-foot volcano. A 33-mile paved road circles the lake, although heavy winter snowfall that averages 533 inches can keep portions of the Rim Road closed until July. Keep in mind that summer days can be cool and the nights quite chilly. Crater Lake is located in southern Oregon, 57 miles north of Klamath Falls. The major road into the park is Oregon Highway 62, which enters through the southwest corner. **Park Entrance Fee:** $10.00 per vehicle or $5.00 per person, good for seven days.

Lodging in Crater Lake National Park: The park has two very different facilities that provide overnight accommodations. Crater Lake Lodge offers seventy-one rooms in a historic but completely rebuilt four-story wooden lodge on the rim of Crater Lake. Mazama Village Motor Inn offers forty basic and less expensive rooms 7 miles south of the rim. While Crater Lake Lodge is one of the classic national park lodges, with a back patio, a large lobby, a cozy dining room, and two fireplaces, Mazama Village Motor Inn is more of a motel unit. Both locations have eating facilities.

CRATER LAKE LODGE

Crater Lake National Park, OR 97604 • (541) 830-8700 • www.craterlakelodges.com

Crater Lake National Park

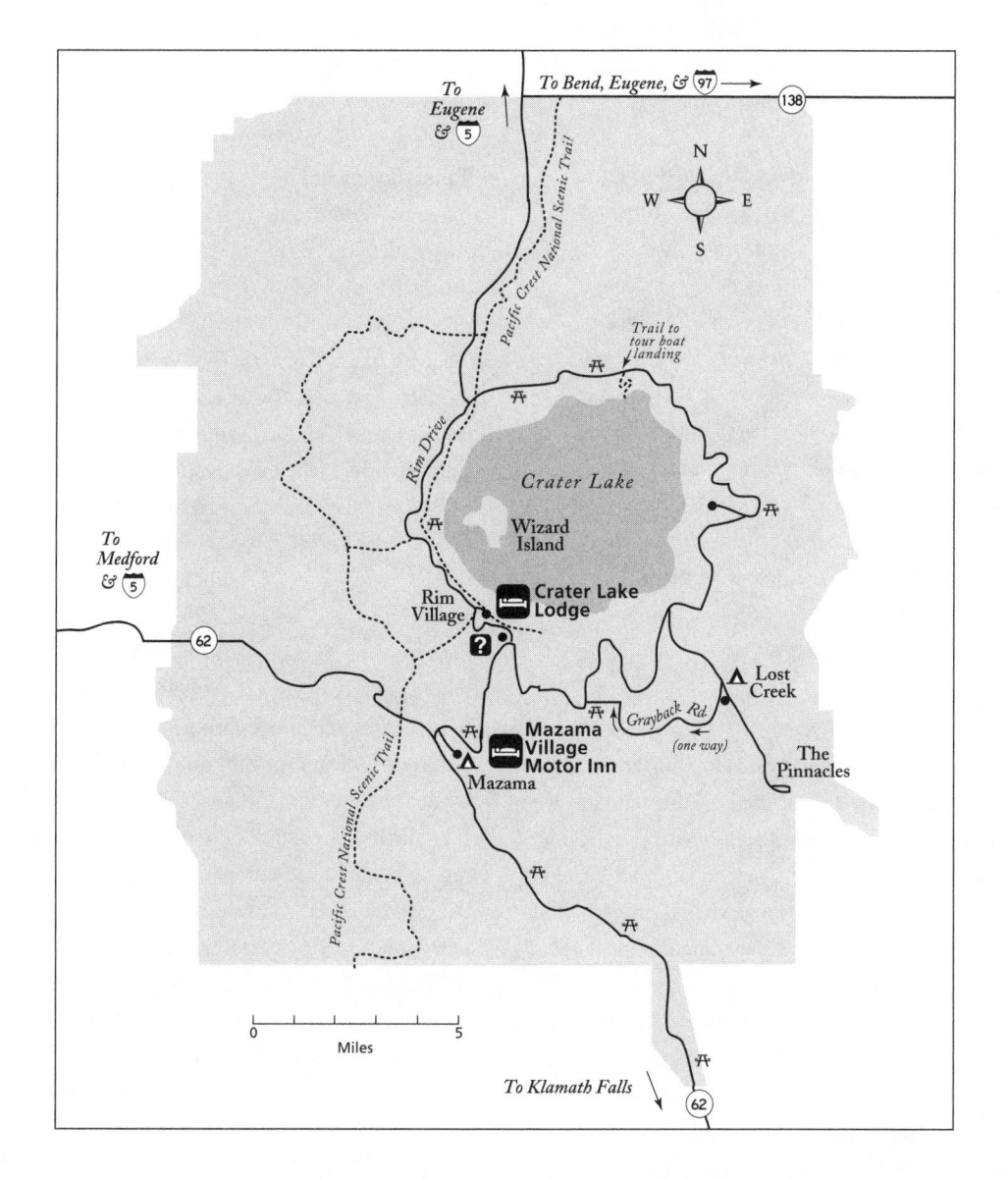

Crater Lake Lodge offers a total of seventy-one rooms in a restored national park hotel. The four-story stone-and-wood building was originally completed in 1915 and reopened in 1995 after a six-year renovation. The building is on the rim of Crater Lake, allowing guests to view from the windows of some rooms what many consider to be America's most beautiful lake. The lodge building has a cozy dining room on the first floor, which also encompasses the registration desk, lobby, and Great Hall with its massive stone fireplace. Another stone fireplace is in the registration lobby. Two elevators are near the registration area. Parking may involve a short walk,

Construction on Crater Lake Lodge commenced about a decade after Crater Lake became a national park in 1902. The building, while impressive from the outside, suffered from many structural faults. Over the years major maintenance, including the installation of columns to support the ceiling and walls in the Great Hall, was required to keep the lodge in operation. The National Park Service assumed ownership of the lodge in 1967 and in the early 1980s started considering its demolition. The lodge was closed to visitors in 1989, but public and political pressure resulted in congressional support for a $15 million rehabilitation that included everything from a new foundation to a new roof frame. Essentially, the lodge was torn down and completely rebuilt from the ground up for a reopening in May 1995.

so it is best to unload luggage from a loading zone at the front entrance or at the end of the building, then move your vehicle to a parking spot. Bell service is available. Crater Lake Lodge is at the east end of Rim Village. The lodge is 15 miles from the north entrance to the park and 7 miles from the south entrance.

Rooms at Crater Lake Lodge are grouped into five price classifications depending on size, view, and bedding. Four smaller first-floor rooms without a view are cheapest, and four two-story loft rooms on floors three and four are most expensive. The remaining sixty-three rooms offer lake views, excellent lake views, or valley views. The remodeled rooms look much newer than the exterior of the lodge would lead you to expect. All are nicely furnished and have heat but no air-conditioning, telephone, or television. The rooms do not have coffeemakers, although complimentary coffee is available each morning in the Great Hall. Most rooms have full bathrooms with a combination shower-tub. A few rooms have bathtubs only. Bedding varies from one to two queen-size beds. Rooms at the back look out on the lake; those at the front look across the parking lot toward the mountains. Second-floor rooms have the largest windows and may be the best choice on the lake side. Third-floor windows in most rooms are high (your chin may rest on the windowsill), and fourth-floor windows are smaller but have window seats. The few first-floor rooms have virtually no view. Corner room 401, with one queen-size bed, offers a great lake view including Wizard Island from the claw-foot bathtub. Rooms 301 and 201 also offer this same lake view, just not from the tub. Room 410 is quite large and has two window seats that provide a lake view. Room 213 allows guests to lie in bed and look out the window at Crater Lake. Room 221, a large corner room with two queen-size beds, offers good views of both Crater Lake and Garfield Peak. The four two-level loft rooms have a queen bed on each floor. Loft rooms are entered from the third floor, where guests can view the valley. Lake views are available from the fourth-floor bedroom. Two loft rooms have the bathroom (claw-foot tub) on the third-floor entry level, while the other two loft rooms require guests to climb to the fourth-floor bedroom to reach the bathroom. Rooms on both floors are comparatively large. The lodge has two second-floor rooms directly above the kitchen that are rented on-site unless specifically requested when a reservation is made. Access requires several steps, and the rooms do not offer a lake view. The Peyton Room is large and in most hotels would be classified as a suite. It has a separate bedroom plus a large living area that can easily accommodate one or two rollaways. The Garfield Room is smaller with one queen bed.

Crater Lake Lodge is one of our favorite national park lodges. Situated in a breathtaking location, the lodge provides travelers with a modern facility that radiates the rustic charm appropriate for one of our country's oldest national parks. Rocking chairs on the large back porch that spans the length of the original hotel offer a relaxing (and, often, chilly) place to sit and view Crater Lake's deep blue water. Guests often spend much of their time in the Great Hall talking, playing cards and board games, reading, or just sitting in rocking chairs enjoying the flames and warmth of the huge gas log fireplace. Here is a place to make new friends on a lazy afternoon or after a meal in the cozy dining room. The dining room is quite small, and it is wise to make dinner reservations at the same time you book a lodge room.

Rooms: Doubles, triples, and quads. All rooms have a private bath, most with a shower-tub combination.

Wheelchair Accessibility: Six rooms on the first floor are ADA compliant. The front door to the lodge has ramp access, and the side door nearest the wheelchair-accessible rooms is at ground level.

Reservations: Crater Lake Lodge, Crater Lake National Park, 1211 Avenue C, White City, OR 97503. Phone (541) 830-8700. A deposit of one night's stay is required. A cancellation notice of forty-eight hours is required for a full refund less a $10 fee.

Rates: Ground floor ($136—four rooms only); most rooms ($170–$190); two-level loft rooms ($260). Rates quoted are for two adults except the loft rooms, which are for four adults. Children eleven and under stay free in the same room with an adult. Each additional person is $25. Weekend packages are offered in early spring and late fall.

Location: On the south rim of Crater Lake, 15 miles from the north entrance and 7 miles from the south entrance to Crater Lake National Park.

Season: Late May to mid-October. The lodge generally sells out from mid-June to the end of September.

Food: A dining room offers breakfast ($8.00–$11.00), lunch ($9.00–$14.00), and dinner ($24.00–$32.00). A children's menu is available. Alcoholic beverages are served. Reservations are required only for the dinner meal. A snack bar at Rim Village serves soups, salads, and sandwiches. A family-style restaurant at Mazama Village offers pizza, pasta, soup, and salads.

Transportation: Scheduled airline service is available to Klamath Falls, Medford, and Eugene, Oregon, where rental cars are available.

Facilities: A dining room. Rim Village, a short walk from the lodge, has a gift shop, snack bar, and small National Park Service visitor center.

Activities: Boat tours of Crater Lake, hiking, fishing, and ranger-guided walks.

Mazama Village Motor Inn

Crater Lake National Park, OR 97604 • (541) 594-2255 • www.craterlakelodges.com

Mazama Village Motor Inn offers a total of forty rooms in ten modern chalet-style wooden buildings that are clustered side-by-side in two groups of five. The one-story buildings, constructed in 1983, each contain four guest rooms and are situated in a heavily wooded area. Ample parking is directly in front of each building, making it convenient to unload and load luggage. The lodging complex is a short walk from facilities in Mazama Village that include the registration desk, a small market, and an attractive family-style restaurant. Mazama Village Motor Inn is in the southern section of the park, at the intersection of Highway 62 and the road to Rim Drive. It is 7 miles from the rim and 22 miles from the north entrance of Crater Lake National Park. At an altitude of 6,000 feet, the complex offers warmer conditions than at the higher rim area where Rim Village and the more famous Crater Lake Lodge are located.

All of the rooms at Mazama Village Motor Inn are identical in size, bedding, and layout except for two that are wheelchair accessible. This is basic motel-style lodging with two queen-size beds and a small table

■　　■　　■

Mazama Village derives its name from the ancient volcano that formed what is now Crater Lake. This dormant volcano is a member of the Cascade Range, a string of volcanoes that extend from Lassen Peak east of Redding, California, to Mt. Garibaldi near Vancouver, British Columbia. Mt. Mazama may once have towered to 12,000 feet above sea level before a violent eruption occurred about 7,700 years ago. After the chamber inside the mountain was emptied, the walls of the volcano collapsed to form a caldera that filled with water from rain and snow and resulted in the nation's deepest lake, at 1,932 feet.

■　　■　　■

and two chairs that basically fill the room. The rooms have heat and a coffeemaker, but no air conditioning or television. The bath has a shower but no tub. Each room has a large sliding window, although there are no particularly good views, so no one room or building is preferable to any other. Each building has a picnic table near the entrance that makes it handy to eat a picnic lunch or cook a meal on a propane stove (if you carry one). The wheelchair-accessible rooms have one queen-size bed and a somewhat larger bathroom.

The motor inn is a lower-cost alternative to the more upscale Crater Lake Lodge, and the ease of moving luggage between your vehicle and a room at Mazama is a real plus. The location is convenient to laundry facilities, a market, and a family-style restaurant. It is also within walking distance of the National Park Service campground where evening programs are presented. An easy 7-mile drive takes you to the rim, where you should spend part of a day exploring Rim Village and Crater Lake Lodge. The main National Park Service visitor center is between Mazama Village and Rim Village. We prefer the least expensive ground-floor rooms at Crater Lake Lodge that cost about $20 per night more than rooms at the motor inn. Although these lodge rooms are somewhat smaller than rooms at Mazama, the ambiance and location of the lodge are worth the relatively small difference in cost. If these four rooms at the lodge are unavailable, the cost difference between the two lodging facilities is much greater, which may make you more likely to tilt toward choosing a room at the motor inn.

Rooms: Doubles, triples, and quads. Each room has a full bath with a shower but no tub.

Wheelchair Accessibility: Two rooms are ADA compliant. The restaurant is wheelchair accessible.

Reservations: Crater Lake National Park, 1211 Avenue C, White City, OR 97503. Phone (541) 830-8700. A deposit of one night's stay is required. A cancellation notice of forty-eight hours is required for a full refund less a $10 fee.

Rates: All rooms ($115). Rate quoted is for two adults. Each additional person is $9.00 per night. Children eleven and under stay free with an adult. Rollaway or crib is $9.00 per night.

Location: On the south side of Crater Lake National Park, 8 miles from the west entrance.

Season: Early June to early October.

Food: A family-style restaurant a short distance from the inn offers pizza, pasta, soup, and salads. A snack bar with soups, salads, and sandwiches is at Rim Village. Crater Lake Lodge has an upscale restaurant.

Transportation: Scheduled airline service is available to Medford, Klamath Falls, and Eugene, Oregon, where rental cars are available.

Facilities: Restaurant, gift shop, market, laundry, public showers, self-service gas pump.

Activities: Hiking and evening naturalist programs, depending on snowmelt.

Oregon Caves National Monument

19000 Caves Highway • Cave Junction, OR 97523 • (541) 592-2100
www.nps.gov/orca

Oregon Caves National Monument was established in 1909 to protect eleven small caves plus a 3-mile-long cave that is home to endangered bats and includes all of the earth's six main types of rock. The area covers 480 acres of old-growth forest, including part of the most diverse conifer forest in the world. The monument is located in southwestern Oregon, 20 miles east of the town of Cave Junction via Oregon Highway 46. Although OR 46 is paved, the last 8 miles are crooked and steep. Drivers should be cautious due to icy conditions in late fall or early spring. Parking at the monument is limited, especially for motor homes and vehicles pulling trailers. Trailers can be dropped off at the Illinois Valley Visitor Center in the town of Cave Junction or on the entry road to the monument at Grayback Campground .

Guided cave tours operate daily from mid-March through late November. Tour times and frequency vary by season, with summer tours beginning at 10:00 a.m. and ending at 6:00 p.m. Tours last approximately ninety minutes and cover a little over half a mile. The tours are moderately strenuous and include over 500 mostly steep and uneven steps. Frequent bending is required through low and narrow passageways. The last tour of the day during summer weekends is a flashlight or candle tour. The cave temperature is 44° Fahrenheit year-round, so be sure to dress properly and wear shoes suitable for walking and hiking. Jackets are generally available to borrow in the visitor center where cave tour tickets are sold. Children must be at least 42 inches tall and pass a step test to qualify for a tour, but special tours are offered for families with children who are too small to be eligible for regular tours. Canes, staffs, walking aids, tripods, and backpacks are not permitted in the cave. **Monument Entrance Fee:** No charge for entrance to the monument, but a fee is charged for cave tours.

Lodging in Oregon Caves National Monument: A classic six-story chateau with twenty-three guest rooms is the only lodging facility in this relatively small national monument. The chateau is at the end of the road near the entrance to the main cave. Motels and restaurants are in the town of Cave Junction.

THE CHATEAU AT THE OREGON CAVES

P.O. Box 1824 • Cave Junction, OR 97523 • (877) 245-9022 • www.oregoncavesoutfitters.com

The Chateau at the Oregon Caves remains an undiscovered national park lodge for many seasoned travelers. Unlike numerous facilities that call themselves a lodge, but are not, at least in the traditional sense, the chateau is a classic lodging facility. The registration area, lobby, dining room, coffee shop, gift shop, and all the overnight rooms are in the same alpine-style wooden building that was constructed in 1934 and became a National Historic Landmark in 1987. The lobby is entered on the building's fourth floor (which the chateau classifies as the first floor), and overnight rooms are on that floor and the two floors above. A restaurant and 1930s-style coffee shop are one floor below. The Chateau at the Oregon Caves is located at the end of OR 46, 20 miles east of Cave Junction, Oregon.

The six-story chateau retains a coziness and warmth that modern hotels lack. It has the feel and look you expect in a national park lodge. The exterior is covered with cedar bark sheathing, and wood shakes top the roof with its many gables. The large lobby area, with huge log supports and giant ceiling beams, is dominated by a double-hearth marble fireplace that burns real wood, not gas. Some of the original furnishings, including, chairs, card tables, writing desks, and a piano, remain in the lobby. Original furnishings are also in a few guest rooms. Luggage can be unloaded directly in front of the lodge entrance, and parking is a short distance away. The chateau often fills on summer weekends, but rooms are likely to be available on most weekdays.

All twenty-three guest rooms offer steam heat and a private bathroom, but no air-conditioning, telephone, or television. Rooms on the first floor have ceiling fans and electric baseboard heat to supplement the steam heat that is generally operated only during the evening and early morning when needed. The rooms differ with respect to size, layout, view, and bedding, which ranges from one double in a very small room (classified as an "economy" room) to a queen plus two doubles in the family suites. Most rooms are classified as "standard" or "deluxe" with either one queen or two double beds. Some rooms offer a view of a tree-covered ravine, while

Oregon Caves National Monument

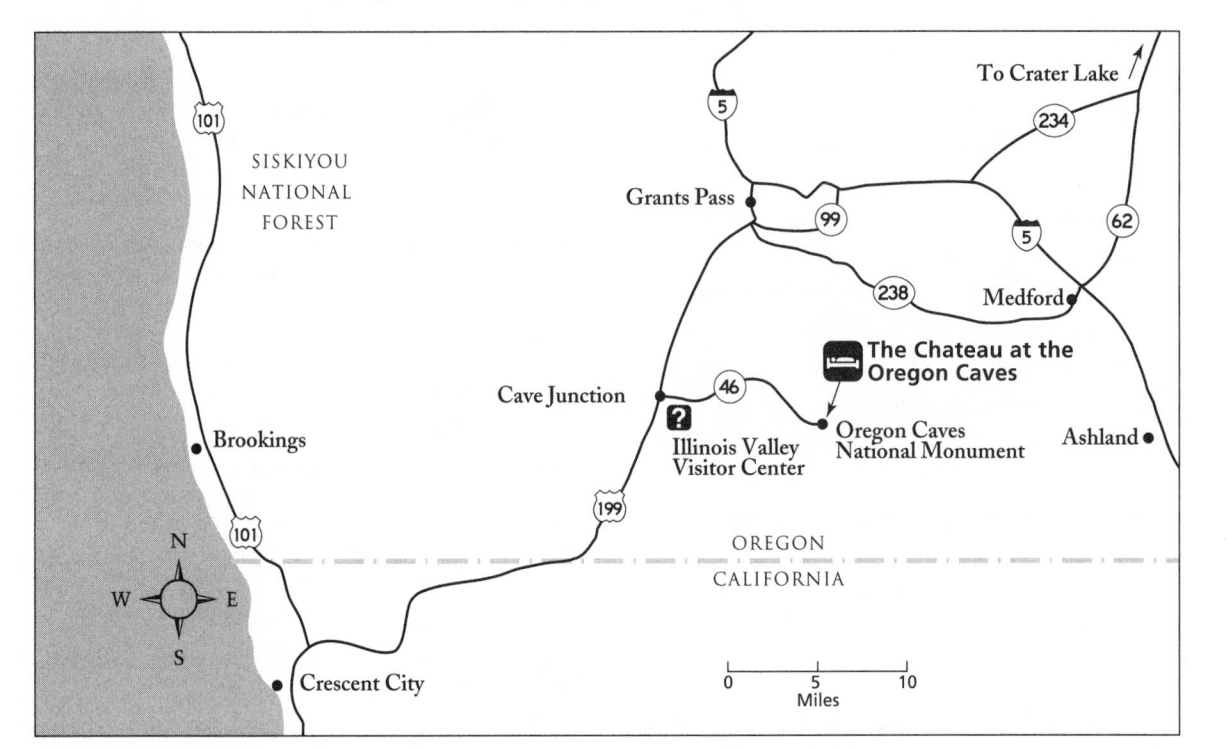

others overlook the parking lot or entrance road. Several rooms on the top floor are snuggled under gables. Five suites on the second and third floors each have two large bedrooms and one bath. The chateau has no elevator. Second-floor rooms require climbing twenty-three steps, while third-floor rooms require an additional fifteen steps. Top-floor rooms are the quietest, in part because the floors squeak. We like first-floor deluxe corner room 105 with two double beds, which is convenient to the lobby and offers a good view of the ravine. Deluxe room 205 directly above offers the same good view. Room 201 is quite large, has one queen bed, and offers a view and the pleasant sound of the waterfall. Room 312 has a unique toilet location. When arriving we suggest you ask to view several available rooms. You may find a room that is larger and/or offers a better view than your assigned room. If you plan to visit in the spring or fall when temperatures are cool, remember that first-floor rooms have electric baseboard heating to supplement the steam heat.

■   ■   ■

The first wooden buildings, including the original chalet, were constructed here in 1923 by a group of businessmen who hoped to profit from curious tourists attracted to the caves. The current Chateau at the Oregon Caves was completed at a total cost of $50,000 in 1934 and remains relatively unchanged since its construction. A local nonprofit organization, Oregon Cave Outfitters, assumed management of the chateau in 2002.

■   ■   ■

■   ■   ■

The Chateau at the Oregon Caves served as the meeting place for two men, who together would alter the way people viewed nature . . . and other things. Harold Graves, a businessman and photographer from Portland, Oregon, was taking photographs in the park one day when he encountered another visitor, William Gruber. Gruber was carrying a tripod on which he had mounted two cameras side by side. The two men met later that evening in Graves's room at the chateau, where Gruber described his idea for a viewing device that would place the viewer in the middle of the scene. That meeting led to the development of the ViewMaster, a viewing device familiar to nearly every child.

■   ■   ■

The Chateau at the Oregon Caves is one of the most unique lodges in any national park. It is relatively small and yet generally uncrowded, because most travelers have yet to discover it. That is their misfortune. The area offers good hiking and a tranquil setting that is ideal for individuals searching for peace and quiet. What a great place for a honeymoon! When is the last time you stayed in a lodge that had a small stream running through the dining room? The chateau does, and you can hear the water ripple through as you enjoy a meal. Our last visit included an excellent dinner of stuffed trout before we spent the remainder of the evening sitting in front of the glowing fireplace while reading and talking with other guests. Depending on your arrival time, spend the first afternoon taking a cave tour

and the next day hiking one or more of the monument's several trails. Enjoy an evening reading a good mystery in front of the large fireplace.

Rooms: Doubles, triples, and quads. One family suite can accommodate up to seven persons. All rooms have a private bath, although some on the third floor have only a tub or a shower. There are no wheelchair-accessible rooms.

Reservations: Oregon Caves Outfitters, P.O. Box 1824, Cave Junction, OR 97523. Phone (541) 592-3400 or (877) 245-9022. A credit card guarantee for one night's stay is required. Cancellation within forty-eight hours of scheduled arrival results in a charge of one night's stay. A cancellation notice of more than two days, but within thirty days, results in a $10 fee.

Rates: Economy ($90); standard ($105); deluxe ($125); suite ($140–$160). Rates are for two adults except in suites, where rates are for four adults. Children twelve and under stay free with an adult. Each additional person is $15 each per night. A full breakfast is included in the price of the room. Special packages are offered throughout the season.

Location: Twenty miles south of Cave Junction, Oregon, at the end of OR46.

Season: The lodge is open from May through mid-October. Cave tours are offered mid-March through late November.

Food: An attractive dining room with large windows offering views of the ravine is open for dinner only ($17–$25). Reservations are recommended but not required. A retro coffee shop on the same floor serves guests a complimentary full breakfast, lunch ($6.00–$9.00), ice cream, and real milk shakes. The gift shop sells ice cream and beverages.

Transportation: The nearest scheduled air service is in Medford, Oregon, about 50 miles away.

Facilities: Gift shop with crafts made by local artisans, restaurant, and coffee shop. A National Park Service visitor center is a short walk from the lodge.

Activities: Cave tours, ranger programs and nature walks, and hiking. Several hiking trails begin at the lodge.

SOUTH DAKOTA

Badlands National Park

P.O. Box 6 • Interior, SD 57750 • (605) 433-5361 • www.nps.gov/badl

Badlands National Park comprises 244,000 acres of prairie grasslands and scenic eroded landscape created millions of years ago by slow-moving streams. An ancient sea once covered this region, which contains a variety of fossilized remains including crabs, clams, and snails. When traveling east on Interstate 90, use exit 110 at Wall to access the Badlands Loop Road and its numerous exhibits, scenic overlooks, and self-guiding trails. Travelers driving west on I-90 access this road by using exit 131. The Ben Reifel Visitor Center in the park's eastern section has exhibits and a video presentation that help interpret the history and geology of the Badlands. Three other National Park Service units—Jewel Cave National Monument, Wind Cave National Park, and world-famous Mount Rushmore National Memorial—are a short distance west of Badlands National Park. Information on these and other nearby attractions is available at the visitor center in Badlands National Park. **Park Entrance Fee:** $15.00 per vehicle or $7.00 per person, good for seven days.

Lodging in Badlands National Park: Cedar Pass Lodge, with twenty-one small cabins and a large cottage, provides the only overnight accommodations in Badlands National Park. The lodge has a dining room and nice gift shop selling specialized items related to the plains and America's westward expansion. Additional accommodations are along the interstate. A two-story motel is just outside the park's boundary and within sight of Cedar Pass Lodge. Cedar Pass Lodge is 8 miles south of I-90 on Badlands Loop Road.

CEDAR PASS LODGE

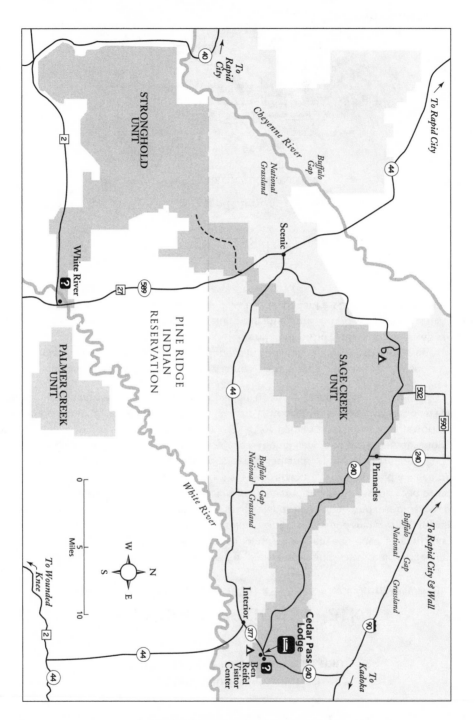

Badlands National Park

Cedar Pass Lodge is a complex of small, mostly free-standing stucco cabins situated on each side of a U-shaped drive in a grassy area behind a wood-and-stucco registration building that houses a restaurant and large gift shop. All the cabins are a short walk from the registration desk and restaurant. Adequate parking is directly beside or in front of each cabin. Cedar Pass Lodge sits in an area of grass and small trees at the east end of Badlands National Park, within view of the Badlands. It is 8 miles south of I-90 and just south of the park's main visitor center.

The lodge offers twenty-one cabins plus a large cottage unit. The cabins are similar, but each is a little different. They are small but nicely spaced and well maintained both inside and out. Each cabin has carpeting, wood-paneled walls, and a private bathroom. Three one-bedroom cabins (3, 14, and 15), the three two-bedroom cabins (1, 2, and 16), and the cottage each have a combination shower-tub. The remaining cottages have showers only. The dark wall paneling and small windows result in relatively dark interiors, although adequate lighting is provided by a combination of lamps and ceiling lights. Picnic tables are scattered about the complex, and each cabin has a small front porch with a bench or two chairs. The cabins vary in size, but most are freestanding one-bedroom units with two double beds or a double bed plus a single bed. Three two-room cabins have two doubles plus one queen or three doubles plus a single bed. Cabins 10, 11, and 12, each with one bedroom and two double beds, are fairly large and can accommodate a rollaway. These are at the end of a row of cabins and have front doors and porches that face east, away from the afternoon sun. On the same side of the road, cabin 3 has two double beds and an attractive exterior style. Across the road with no other unit nearby, cabin 33 with one queen bed has a similar exterior and is sometimes called "The Dollhouse." This is the smallest cabin at Cedar Pass Lodge. One large cottage (actually, a complete house with a fenced back yard) near the registration building has two bedrooms, one with a queen

Cedar Pass Camp was opened here in 1928 to provide refreshments to the growing number of sightseers to this area. By the 1930s the facility had become an important stop for Badlands travelers. The owner, Ben Millard, died here in 1956, and Cedar Pass Lodge was purchased by the National Park Service in 1964. Cedar Pass Lodge was operated by the Oglala Sioux Tribe of the Pine Ridge Indian Reservation from 1971 to 2002.

and the other with two doubles. It also has a living room/dining room and a full-size kitchen with a refrigerator, gas range, and washer and dryer. Pots, pans, and eating utensils are included. Try for the cottage if your party includes four or more people. The lodge concessionaire also operates Badlands Inn, an 18-room facility a short distance outside the park.

Cedar Pass Lodge is a convenient location from which to explore Badlands National Park. It is also a quiet and restful place to stay the night before or after a visit to nearby attractions Mount Rushmore National Memorial, Jewel Cave National Monument, Wind Cave National Park, and Custer State Park. The lodge is a short walk from the park's Ben Reifel Visitor Center, which includes exhibits to explain the geology and history of this rugged section of South Dakota. It is also near the park campground, where evening programs are presented in summer by National Park Service rangers. Guided walks and other programs are scheduled daily from various points in the park. An 80-mile loop drive through the park to the small town of Scenic and back through Buffalo Gap National Grassland on South Dakota Highway 44 offers an interesting day of sightseeing and hiking. Take a side trip to the town of Wall (north of the Pinnacles entrance to the park), where famous Wall Drug gives away ice water and sells coffee for a nickel.

Rooms: Singles, doubles, triples, and quads. Three cabins with two bedrooms and the cottage hold up to six adults. All units have a private bathroom, some with a shower and others with a combination shower-tub.

Wheelchair Accessibility: None of the cabins at Cedar Pass Lodge is ADA compliant. Cabin 1 is "wheelchair friendly."

Reservations: Cedar Pass Lodge, Box 5, Interior, SD 57750. Phone (605) 433-5460; fax (605) 433-5560. A credit card guarantee is required. Cancellation requires twenty-four hours' notice.

Rates: One-bedroom cabin ($75); two-bedroom cabin ($90); cottage ($105). Rates quoted are for two people. Additional persons are $10. Children ten and under stay free. Prices are reduced from early to mid-May and from mid-September to closing in mid-October. AAA and AARP members receive a 10 percent discount.

Location: At the eastern end of Badlands National Park, 8 miles south of I-90 at exit 131. Guests who will be approaching on I-90 from Rapid City should take exit 110 and drive the Badlands Loop Road (South Dakota Highway 240), which passes by the lodge.

Season: Mid-April to mid-October.

Food: A cafe-type restaurant serves breakfast ($4.00–$8.50), lunch ($5.00–$7.00), and dinner ($7.50–$16.00). Menu items include buffalo burgers, trout, and Sioux Indian tacos. A children's menu is available.

Transportation: The nearest commercial airport is in Rapid City, South Dakota, where rental vehicles are available.

Facilities: Restaurant, gift shop with a large selection of silver jewelry and crafts made by local artisans, National Park Service visitor center.

Activities: Hiking, evening interpretive programs.

Pets: Pets are permitted for an extra charge of $10 per pet, per night.

TEXAS

Big Bend National Park

P.O. Box 129 • Big Bend N.P., TX 79834 • (432) 477-2251 • www.nps.gov/bibe

Big Bend National Park covers 801,000 acres of wild and scenic desert, mountain ranges, steep-walled canyons, and ribbons of green plant life along the fabled Rio Grande. Because of its remote location, the park is not as crowded as some of the other national parks. Popular activities at Big Bend include bird-watching, hiking, and rafting on the Rio Grande. The park is located on the Mexican border in southwestern Texas. **Park Entrance Fee:** $20.00 per vehicle or $5.00 per person, good for seven days.

Lodging in Big Bend National Park: Chisos Mountains Lodge in the park's Basin area offers the only lodging in Big Bend National Park. The road to the Basin is not recommended for trailers exceeding 20 feet and RVs exceeding 24 feet. A trailer village at Rio Grande Village is available for visitors with trailers and motor homes.

CHISOS MOUNTAINS LODGE

Basin Rural Branch • Big Bend National Park, TX 79834-9999

(432) 477-2291 • www.bigbendresorts.com

Big Bend National Park

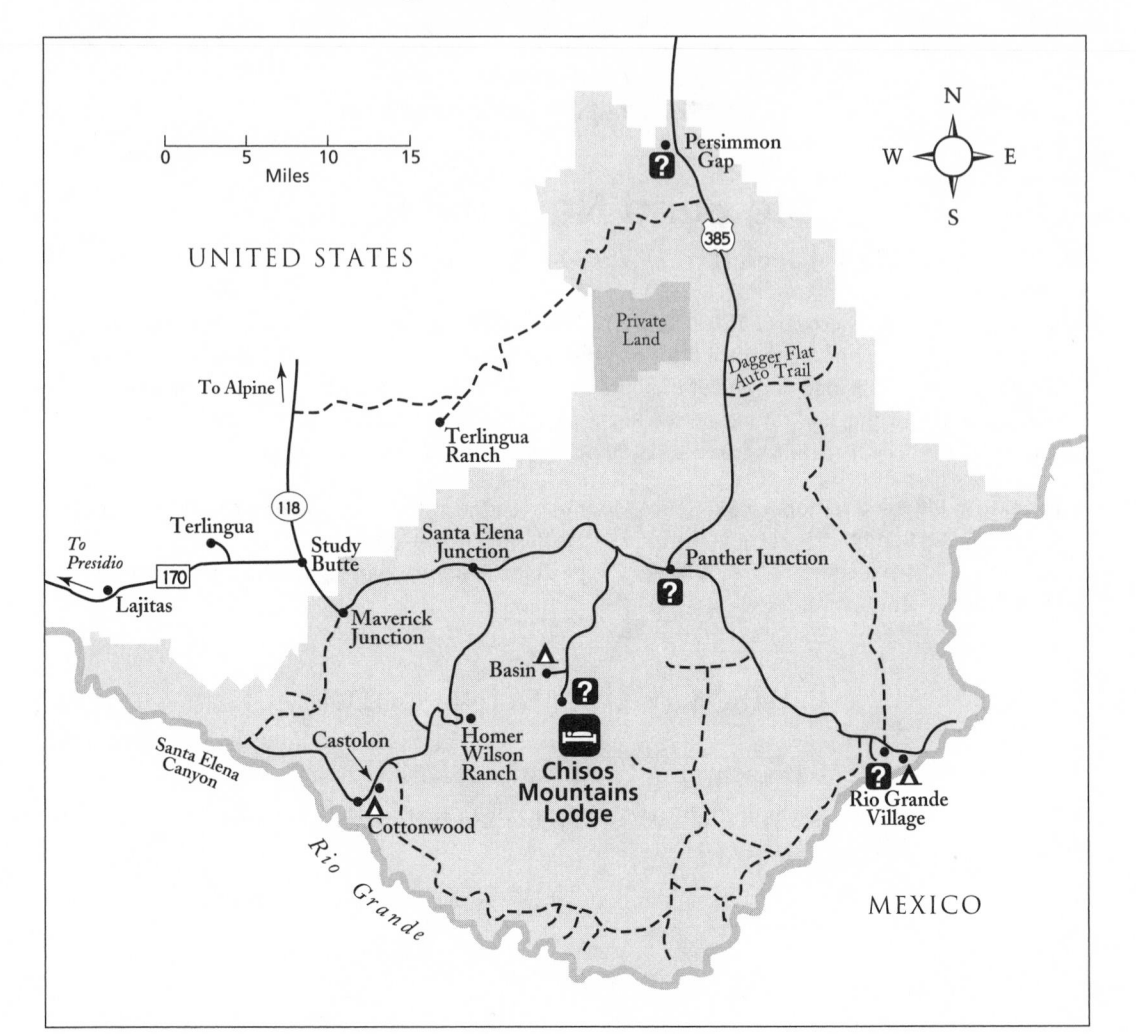

Chisos Mountains Lodge is a group of modern motel-type units and older stone and adobe cabins and lodge units in the scenic Basin area of Big Bend National Park. All the lodging units rent for about the same price and are open year-round. The Basin area of Big Bend is approximately 40 miles inside the north park entrance, which itself is 40 miles south of U.S. Highway 90. In other words, this is a pretty remote lodge in a very remote national park. The good news is the Basin area

of the park provides breathtaking scenery along with the outdoor experience you are probably seeking in a national park visit. The lodge is at an altitude of 5,400 feet, which results in moderate summer temperatures when much of the rest of the park swelters in the desert heat. Scenery is provided by the Chisos Mountains, which surround and tower 2,000 to 3,000 feet above the Basin and are fully contained within Big Bend's boundary.

Bird-watching is a major activity in Big Bend National Park, where more than 450 species have been identified. Although most are migrants that pass through after wintering in Latin America, occasional rare species end up in Big Bend after wandering off-course. The Chisos Mountains of Big Bend are the only location in the United States where the rare Colima warbler can be observed. Multiday birding seminars are regularly sponsored by the Big Bend Natural History Association.

Chisos Mountains Lodge is actually a combination of a main registration and food-service building and four types of separate lodging units for a total of seventy-two rooms. All rooms have heat, a small refrigerator, a microwave, a hair dryer, and a coffeemaker. About half the rooms are in three two-story motor-lodge–type Casa Grande units that offer semi-private rear balconies with a view of the surrounding mountains. These units, built in 1989, each have two double beds except for four wheelchair-accessible rooms that have one double bed. Each room has a full tiled bath and air-conditioning.

The Rio Grande Motel consists of two one-story motel-type buildings constructed in the late 1970s, each with ten rooms, five on a side. Chairs are outside each room along a covered walkway. Rooms on the west side of the two buildings (even-numbered rooms) offer better views than rooms on the backside. Rooms have two double beds, a full tiled bath, and air-conditioning. They are quite a bit smaller and offer inferior views compared to rooms in Casa Grande units.

The Emory Peak Lodge and the Roosevelt Stone Cottages offer a quieter setting a short distance away from the other lodging units. One duplex and four freestanding stone cottages were constructed in the late

1930s by the Civilian Conservation Corps. Five cottages each have three double beds and a bath with a shower but no tub. They also lack air-conditioning but do have ceiling fans. The thick construction, stone floors, vaulted ceilings, and cross-ventilation generally result in a comfortable inside temperature. Most popular with frequent visitors to Big Bend is cottage103, which has a full covered porch and offers the best mountain views of any of the park's lodging facilities. Cottage 100 is isolated, has air conditioning and a covered porch, and offers a king bed, love seat, television, telephone, and table with four chairs, making it a nice honeymoon cottage. Eight 1950s-era Emory Peak Lodge units situated near the cottages each have one single and one double bed (one unit has a king bed), a full tiled bath, and a vaulted beamed ceiling with a ceiling fan. These units are in two buildings, each with four rooms. Access to one of the buildings involves climbing thirty-five steps along a gradual slope.

With the exception of cottage 100, none of the rooms have a television or telephone. Unless you splurge for either cottage 100 or 103, we recommend the Casa Grande units in buildings A, B, and C. Rooms in all

Although the Rio Grande is one of the major natural features of Big Bend National Park, by the time the river forms the southern boundary of the park, most of the water is supplied by the Rio Conchos, which flows out of Mexico, rather than the headwaters of the Rio Grande. Much of the water of the Rio Grande has evaporated or been diverted for irrigation by the time the river reaches the western border of the park. Abrasive particles carried in the water give the river its impressive power to carve the canyons that have formed along its path.

three buildings are large, offer good views, and cost the same as rooms in the smaller motel units. Second-floor rooms offer better views and more privacy.

Other than the Roosevelt Stone Cottages and Emory Peak Lodge units that are located a short distance from the main Basin area, the units are arranged in a circular fashion near the building that houses registration, a gift shop, and a dining room. Adequate parking is available near each of the buildings, although a couple of the Casa Grande units require a climb of approximately thirty steps to reach the second floor. If stairs are a problem, you should note this in your reservation request. The cottages and Emory Peak units are about a quarter mile away from the other units, but everything in the Basin is within walking distance. Also in the Basin is a small store, with a limited selection of groceries and camping supplies, and a post office substation. A National Park Service visitor center is next to the store. A variety of hikes and nature programs are offered in season. A self-guided trail and access to several other trails originate near the lodge.

The Chisos Mountains Basin is only a small part of a very large national park that offers much to attract visitors, especially during the spring and fall, when temperatures are mild. The main National Park Service visitor facilities are at Panther Junction. Here you will find the visitor center and a host of facilities, including a post office and gas station. Other major activity areas of the park center on Rio Grande Village, 20 miles southeast of park headquarters, which offers hiking, camping, a trailer park, a coin laundry, showers, groceries, general merchandise, gasoline, propane, and a visitor center. Castolon, a historic district 35 miles southwest of the visitor center, offers a campground, a ranger station, historic exhibits, and a frontier store that sells picnic supplies, groceries, and general merchandise.

Rooms: Doubles, triples, and quads. A few units sleep up to six. All rooms have private baths.

Wheelchair Accessibility: Four Casa Grande units are equipped with wheelchair-accessible features including a larger bathroom with a combination shower-tub and grab bars.

Reservations: Forever Resorts, Chisos Mountains Lodge, Basin Rural Branch, Big Bend National Park, TX 79834-9999. Phone (432) 477-2291; fax (432) 477-2352. A deposit of one night's stay is required. A cancellation notice of forty-eight hours is required for a refund; a $10 cancellation fee applies to all canceled reservations. Failure to arrive on the designated date means automatic forfeit of the deposit and cancels the reservation. Reservations in any calendar year may be made at the beginning of the previous year.

Rates: Casa Grande ($115); Rio Grande ($115); cottage ($143); lodge unit ($112). Rates quoted include tax and are for two adults. Each additional person is $10 per night. Children under twelve stay free with two paying adults.

Location: About 40 miles south of the north park entrance station and 30 miles east of the west entrance station.

Season: All lodging units are open year-round. Heaviest season is in the spring up to Memorial Day and in the fall following Labor Day. The lodge is heavily booked during Thanksgiving and Christmas holidays.

Food: A full-service restaurant serves a daily breakfast buffet ($8.25), lunch ($5.00–$10.00), and dinner ($6.00–$20.00). The restaurant is located in the main lodge building and within walking distance of all rooms.

Transportation: No public transportation is available to or through the park. Train and bus service is provided to the town of Alpine, about 110 miles north of the park, where rental cars are available. Airlines serve Del Rio, Midland-Odessa, and El Paso, Texas, where rental cars are available.

Facilities: The Chisos Basin has a store, post office substation, visitor center, restaurant, gift shop, and washer and dryer. A visitor center, gas station, post office, and small grocery are at Panther Junction. A variety of supplies and services are at Rio Grande Village, 20 miles southeast of Panther Junction. A frontier store at Castolon sells picnic supplies, groceries, and general merchandise

Activities: Hiking, bird-watching, guided walks, and National Park Service programs. Float trips on the Rio Grande are available with your own equipment (permit required) or through one of four local services approved by the Park Service.

Pets: Pets are permitted only in the Roosevelt Stone Cottages.

U.S. VIRGIN ISLANDS

■ **State Tourist Information**
(800) 372-8784 | USVI-info.com

Virgin Islands National Park

1300 Cruz Bay Creek • St. Thomas, VI 00830 • (340) 776-6201 • www.nps.gov/viis

Virgin Islands National Park, encompassing nearly 14,700 acres, features quiet coves, blue green waters, and white sandy beaches fringed by lush green hills. The park is located on St. John Island and can be reached via hourly ferry service across Pillsbury Sound from Red Hook, St. Thomas. Ferry service also operates from Charlotte Amalie. Major airlines fly from the U.S. mainland to St. Thomas and St. Croix. **Park Entrance Fee:** No charge.

Lodging in Virgin Islands National Park: Although a variety of lodging is available on the island, Cinnamon Bay Campground, with tents and cottages, offers the only accommodations within the national park. Cinnamon Bay is on St. John Island's north shore, midway across the island via North Shore Road. The campground is a fifteen-minute taxi ride from the town of Cruz Bay, where the ferries dock.

CINNAMON BAY CAMPGROUND

P.O. Box 720 • Cruz Bay, St. John • U.S. Virgin Islands 00831 • (340) 776-6330

www.cinnamonbay.com

Virgin Islands National Park

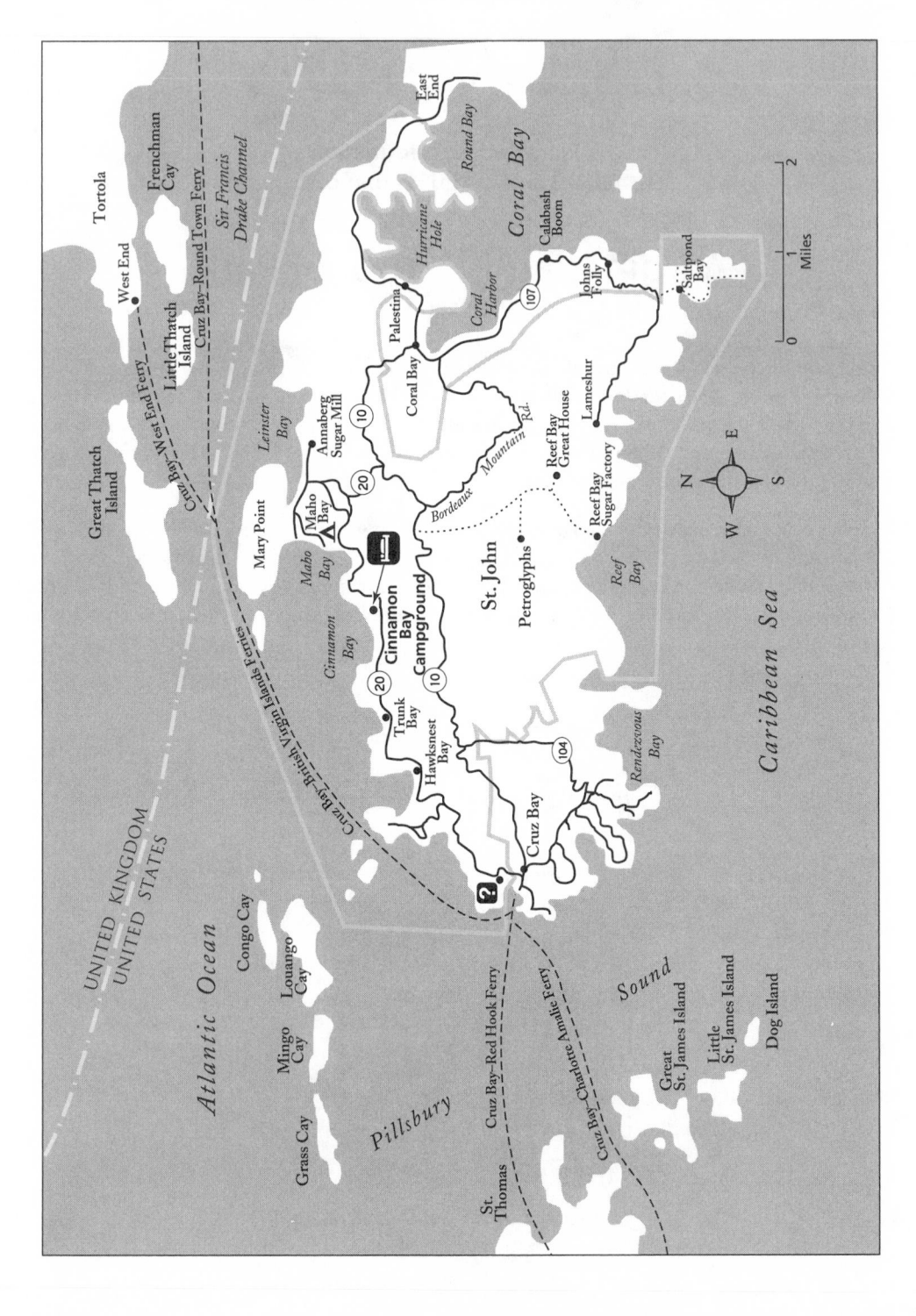

■   ■   ■

Rosewood Hotels & Resorts, the firm that manages Cinnamon Bay Campground, also operates exclusive Caneel Bay on the same island. Although separated by two bays and only a few miles, in cost and accommodations these two facilities are a world apart. For example, rooms at Caneel Bay run from $350 to $1200 daily, depending on season and type of accommodation. The 171 rooms include wall safes, personal bars, and handcrafted furniture. Three restaurants provide a choice of formal, eclectic, and casual dining.

■   ■   ■

Cinnamon Bay Campground is a complex of cottages, tents, separate bathhouses, plus a main building that houses a registration area, restaurant, and general store. The cottages and tents are grouped separately, with bathhouses in each grouping. All the buildings are located in a natural area of trees a short walk from half-mile-long Cinnamon Bay Beach.

The forty cottages are 15 by 15 feet and constructed of cement sides and floor with front and back screening to allow breezes from the trade winds. Each cottage has an outside terrace and is equipped with electric lights, a table and chairs, a ceiling fan, a picnic table, a charcoal grill, a propane stove, an ice chest, a water container, and eating and cooking utensils. The concessionaire provides linens for four twin beds in each cottage that are made by the guest on the day of arrival. Additional linens can be obtained twice a week at the front desk. The central bathhouse has cool-water showers. The cost of the cottages varies, with those closer to the beach being more expensive.

Forty-four tents have a wood floor and are 10 by 14 feet. Each tent includes four cots with a 3-inch mattress, a propane stove, a charcoal grill, a gas lantern, an

ice chest, a water container, and utensils. A picnic table is under a large canvas flap that extends from the front roof. As with the cottages, beds are made on the day of arrival, and fresh linens are available at the front desk twice a week. Three bathhouses scattered throughout the tenting area also have cool-water showers.

Cinnamon Bay Campground offers the ultimate national park experience in which the accommodations permit a full appreciation of the natural surroundings. Both the cottages and tents are a short walk from Cinnamon Bay Beach. Phones, safe-deposit boxes, and storage lockers are near the lodging facilities. A general store carries a wide range of personal items plus grocery items if you are interested in cooking some of your own meals. A restaurant is available when you choose to eat out. No laundry facilities are in the campground. Not surprisingly, water-based activities such as snorkeling are popular, and sailboards, sea kayaks, and sailboats are available for rent at a water sports center. Park rangers offer daily activities, which include walks, talks, and snorkeling. Reservations are required for most of the activities with park rangers (340-776-6201).

Rooms: Doubles, triples, and quads. None of the cottages or tents have a private bathroom.

Wheelchair Accessibility: One cottage and one tent are wheelchair accessible. The community bathrooms have facilities that are wheelchair-accessible.

Reservations: Cinnamon Bay Campground, P.O. Box 720, Cruz Bay, St. John, U.S. Virgin Islands 00831. Phone (800) 539-9998; (340) 776-6330. Reservations can be guaranteed with a credit card. A 50 percent deposit is required. Payment must be made in full at the time of check-in (personal checks are not accepted). Cancellations are required at least thirty days prior to arrival for a full refund. Later cancellations will be charged the equivalent of a three-night stay. Reservations for the winter months should be made at least four to six months in advance.

Rates: Cottages ($77–$100) from May 1 through December 14, ($120–$155) from December 15 through April 30; tents ($64) from May 1 through December 14, ($88) from December 15 through April 30. Rates quoted are for two adults. Children under three stay free with an adult. Each additional person is $19 per night. Maximum occupancy of four persons is permitted. Meal packages are available.

Location: On the north shore of St. John Island, approximately 4 miles (fifteen minutes) from the town of Cruz Bay on the island's west end.

Season: Open year-round. Peak season is January through June.

Food: A Caribbean/American bar and grill serves breakfast ($6.00–$10.00), lunch ($6.00–$10.00), and dinner ($11.00–$22.00). Groceries are available at a general store.

Transportation: Ferries for Cruz Bay, St. John, leave from Red Hook ($3.00 per person) and Charlotte Amalie ($7.00 per person) on St. Thomas. Taxis (about $3.00 per person) provide transportation from Cruz Bay to the campground. For more information check the Web site at www.cinnamon bay.com or call (800) 539-9998.

Facilities: Restaurant, general store, beach shop, water sports center with boat rentals.

Activities: Swimming, snorkeling, fishing, hiking, National Park Service activities, and commercial guided tours.

UTAH

◼ State Tourist Information
(800) 200-1160 | www.utah.com

Bryce Canyon National Park

P.O. Box 170001 • Bryce Canyon, UT 84717 • (435) 834-5322 • www.nps.gov/brca

Bryce Canyon National Park comprises nearly 36,000 acres highlighted by numerous alcoves cut into cliffs along the eastern edge of the Paunsaugunt Plateau. The cliffs are bordered by badlands of vivid colors and strange shapes called hoodoos for which this park is most famous. A paved road with numerous scenic pullouts leads 18 miles south from the entrance to Rainbow Point. Trailers are not permitted beyond Sunrise Point, which lies about 3 miles inside the park entrance. The park is in southwestern Utah and most easily reached via U.S. Highway 89 to Utah Highways 12 and 63.

A free shuttle service that begins outside the park serves the lodge and the northern portion of the park. Lodge guests and other park visitors can hop on and off the shuttle at the lodge and ten additional stops including the NPS visitor center, Inspiration Point, and Bryce Point. The shuttle operates from late May until early September. **Park Entrance Fee:** $25 per vehicle, good for seven days.

Lodging in Bryce Canyon: Bryce Canyon Lodge, with several types of accommodations, offers the only lodging in Bryce Canyon National Park. All rooms are comfortable and within easy walking distance of both the main lodge and spectacular Bryce Canyon. The lodge is in the northern section of the park, about 1.5 miles south of the park entrance and visitor center. Privately operated motels are just outside the park entrance.

BRYCE CANYON LODGE

1 Bryce Canyon Lodge • Bryce Canyon National Park, UT 84717 • (435) 834-5361
www.brycecanyonlodge.com

Bryce Canyon National Park

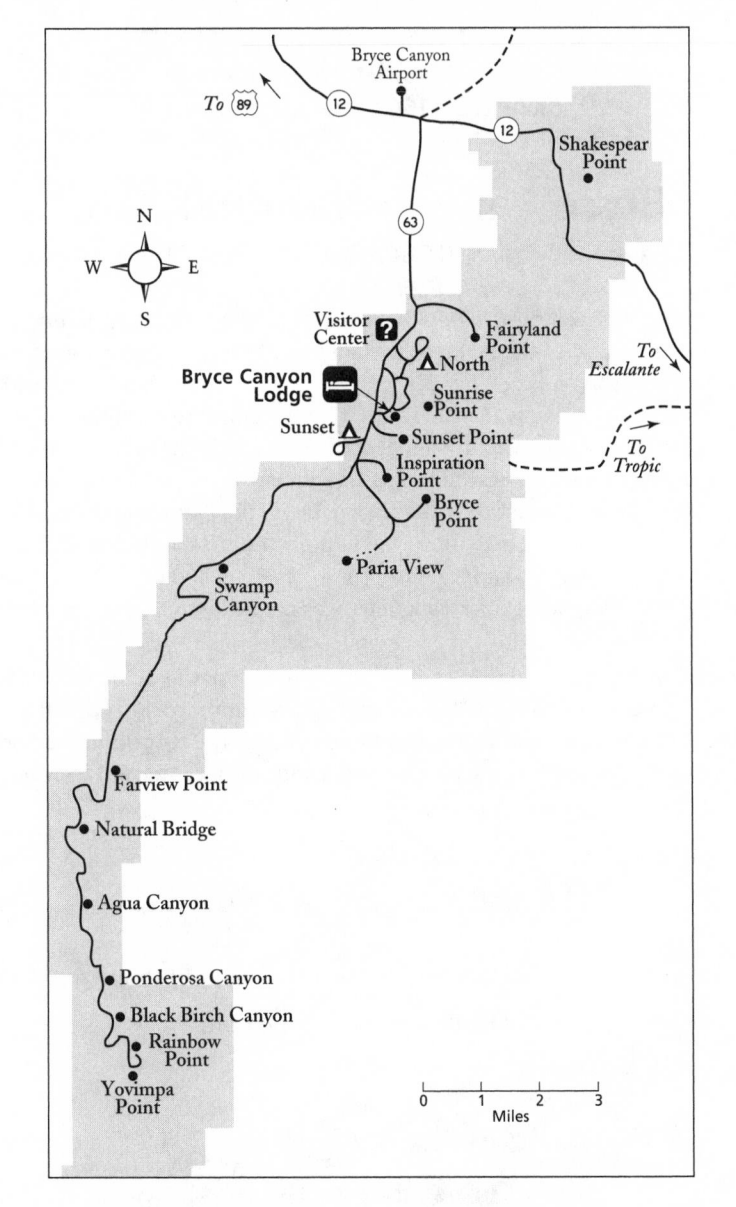

Bryce Canyon Lodge offers a total of 114 rooms in a complex of two motor lodge units, fifteen multiunit log buildings with forty cabins, and an impressive wood-and-stone main lodge building that houses the restaurant, registration area, and three suites plus a studio.

The main lodge was constructed in the 1920s and has been completely renovated. The lodge was designed by Gilbert Stanley Underwood, the same architect who designed the Ahwahnee in Yosemite, Zion Lodge, and Grand Canyon Lodge on the North Rim. The attractive lobby area has a huge stone fireplace surrounded by chairs. A large brick porch with chairs and benches stretches across the entire front of the building and offers guests a pleasant place to spend idle time. The porch faces a wooded area that separates the lodge from the canyon rim. Bryce Canyon Lodge is located near the rim of the canyon, about 1.5 miles south of the park visitor center and entrance station.

Each of the three types of lodging facilities at Bryce Canyon Lodge is attractive. All of the rooms have heat, carpeting, a fan, and a telephone, but no air-conditioning or television. Forty Western Cabins are built from two to four to a building. Most of these

Construction on Bryce Canyon Lodge began in 1923, and the foundation and skeletal work were completed the following year. The original building, with upstairs accommodations and an office, lobby, dining room, kitchen, showers, and toilets on the main floor, was completed by May 1925. Wings and a rock facade were added the following year, when the lodge was opened for operation. In September 1927, the recreation hall was added, and sixty-seven standard and economy cabins were grouped around the lodge. The few original cabins that remain are currently used by the National Park Service. The other economy cabins were sold and moved. By September 1927, five deluxe cabins (the current Western Cabins) had been constructed. The remaining ten deluxe cabins were completed by 1929. These cabins remain in use. The wavy pattern of shingles on both the lodge and the cabins was designed to conform to the swaying motion of the surrounding pine limbs. The pattern also facilitated snow to slide off the roofs.

cabins have two queen-size beds, a gas fireplace, and a dressing room with a sink. The full tiled bathrooms were totally refurbished in 2004–2005. The log and limestone cabins, constructed in the 1920s, are roomy and nicely finished. Half of the Western Cabins have log-beamed vaulted ceilings. These are the cabins constructed two to a building with bark remaining on the logs. Each cabin has a private covered front porch with a bench. Cabins 506, 517, 525, 533, and 537 have windows and porches that face a large wooded area but are a longer walk from the parking area. Two nearly identical two-story motor lodge buildings were brought into the park and assembled in 1985. These buildings have a total of seventy rooms that were renovated in 2004. Each room has two queen-size beds (a few have one queen) and a full tiled bath. These units each have a private covered balcony with a table and two chairs. Rooms on both sides of the building are entered through a central hallway that can be accessed at either end or in the middle. These are attractive units that resemble upscale two-story lodge buildings. Rooms on the second floor and rim side of each building provide the most privacy and best views. The Sunrise building is closest to the lodge.

Three second-floor suites and one studio are the only sleeping rooms in the main lodge building. The suites each have a bedroom with one queen-size bed and a separate sitting room; both rooms have ceiling fans. The suites also have a full tiled bath but no balcony. These rooms are nice and roomy, and it is convenient to stay in the main lodge, where the restaurant and lobby are located. The single studio is identical to the suites but without a separate sitting room.

Bryce Canyon Lodge is a relaxing place to spend several days while you explore this colorful and uncrowded national park. It sits in a heavily treed area with attractive vistas and numerous outdoor activities including hiking and horseback riding. A short walking trail from the front porch of the lodge leads to spectacular overlooks along the canyon rim. An information

■   ■   ■

Bryce Canyon Lodge is the only remaining lodging facility constructed in this region in the 1920s by the Utah Parks Company, a subsidiary of the Union Pacific Railroad. The Union Pacific was interested in stimulating tourism to the region and competing against other railroads that were building similar facilities in Glacier National Park, Yellowstone National Park, and the South Rim of the Grand Canyon. The "U.P. loop" consisted of lodges at Zion National Park, the North Rim of the Grand Canyon, Bryce Canyon, and Cedar City, where a spur line connected to the Union Pacific main line in Lund. Unable to sell the operation, the Union Pacific in 1972 donated all of the Utah Parks Company's property, including lodges, cabins, curio shops, and service stations, to the National Park Service, which soon signed TWA Services, a subsidiary of Trans World Airlines, as concessionaire.

■   ■   ■

desk in the hotel lobby provides information about the area and several tours that originate near the lodge. With only four rooms in the main lodge building, your choice will generally be between the Western Cabins and motel units. We have always liked the cabins in this park and suggest them as your choice, especially if you plan to stay two or more nights. The cost difference is small, and the cabins provide an atmosphere that isn't matched by a stay in the motor lodge units. Don't fret if there are no cabin vacancies, however, because rooms in the motor lodge units are quite nice.

Rooms: Doubles, triples, and quads. All rooms have a full bath.

Wheelchair Accessibility: Each of the two motel units offers two first-floor end rooms with wheelchair accessibility. The buildings have ramp access, but the rooms are some distance from parking. A large bathroom has an extra-wide door and grab bars by the toilet. One room in each building has a roll-in shower, while the other has a tub-shower combination. The main lodge, with the registration area, restaurant, and gift shop, has ramp access from the parking lot in the back. None of the Western Cabins or suites is wheelchair accessible.

Reservations: Xanterra Parks and Resorts, 6312 S. Fiddlers Green Circle, Suite 600N, Greenwood Village, CO 80111. Phone (888) 297-2757; fax (303) 297-3175; www.brycecanyon lodge.com. Reservations may be made up to thirteen months in advance. A deposit of one night's stay is required. Cancellation notice of forty-eight hours is required for a refund.

Rates: Western Cabins ($166); motel units ($156); suites ($170); studio ($126). Children sixteen and under stay free with an adult. Each additional person is $10 per night. Rollaways are $12.00 and cribs are $5.00 per night.

Location: The lodge is near the north end of Bryce Canyon National Park, about 1.5 miles south of the visitor center that is located near the park entrance station. The lodge is within walking distance of the rim of the canyon.

Season: Bryce Canyon Lodge is open from April 1 through November 1. The park is open year-round.

Food: A full-service restaurant serves breakfast ($5.00–$10.00), lunch ($8.00–$11.00), and dinner ($14.00–$24.00). Beer and wine are available. A children's menu is available. Reservations are recommended for dinner. Groceries and snacks are available at a general store at Sunrise Point, about 1 mile from the lodge.

Transportation: Airlines serve Cedar City, St. George, and Salt Lake City, Utah, and Las Vegas, Nevada. Rental cars are available at each of these airports. Greyhound/Trailways serves St. George and Cedar City. Amtrak serves Salt Lake City.

Facilities: A full-service dining room and gift shop are in the main lodge building. A general store 1 mile north of the lodge near Sunrise Point has snacks and groceries.

Activities: The National Park Service conducts a variety of lectures, nature walks and talks, and slide presentations. A schedule with times is posted at the lodge and the visitor center. Two-hour and half-day mule and horse trips into the canyon are offered daily. Information and reservations are available by calling (435) 679-8665 or visiting www.canyon rides.com. Information on these and other activities is available at the tour desk located in the lobby.

Zion National Park

S.R. 9 • Springdale, UT 84767 • (435) 722-3256 • www.nps.gov/zion

Zion National Park comprises approximately 147,000 acres of colorful canyons and mesas that create phenomenal shapes and landscapes. Scenic drives and trails provide access to canyons, sculpted rocks, cliffs, and rivers in one of the most beautiful areas operated by the National Park Service. Zion is in southwestern Utah, with the southwest entrance approximately 150 miles northeast of Las Vegas, Nevada.

The park entry fee includes unlimited access to the free National Park Service shuttle system, which comprises two loops. The Springdale loop connects the town of Springdale with the visitor center and transportation center just inside the park entrance. The second loop operates from the visitor center to the end of Zion Canyon Scenic Drive. Zion Canyon Lodge is one of several stops on the Zion Canyon Scenic Drive shuttle. The Mount Carmel area on the park's east side remains accessible by vehicle. The drive is beautiful, but exceedingly slow. **Park Entrance Fee:** $25 per vehicle or $12 per person, good for seven days.

Lodging in Zion National Park: Zion has only one lodging facility inside the park. Zion Lodge is located on Zion Canyon Scenic Drive, 3 miles north of Utah Highway 9, which crosses the southeastern section of the park. Driving Zion Canyon Scenic Road to the Zion Lodge requires a permit that must be obtained at the visitor center and displayed on the vehicle windshield. The visitor center keeps a listing of lodge guests. Additional lodging is available in the town of Springdale, just outside the park's southwest entrance.

ZION LODGE

Zion National Park • Springdale, UT 84767 • (435) 772-3213 • www.zionlodge.com

Zion National Park

Zion Lodge comprises a central lodge building that houses registration and dining facilities, plus seventeen separate but nearby buildings that provide a total of 122 rooms for overnight accommodations. No overnight rooms are in the main lodge building. The lodge is fronted by a large grassy area with cottonwood trees and surrounded front and back by the beautiful red sandstone cliffs that make this such a scenic national park. The North Fork of the Virgin River is across the road from the lodge. The wood and Navajo sandstone main lodge building is a one- and two-story, V-shaped, ranch-style structure that was constructed in 1966 on the site of the original lodge, which burned earlier the

same year. The new lodge is attractive but does not have the majestic appearance of its older sister lodges at Bryce Canyon and the North Rim of the Grand Canyon. Zion Lodge is located on Zion Canyon Scenic Drive, 3 miles north of the main park road. The lodge is approximately 4.5 miles north of the National Park Service visitor center.

Two major types of accommodations plus six suites are available at Zion Lodge. All of the lodging is separate from but near the main lodge building. All rooms have heat, air-conditioning, carpeted floors, a telephone, and a hair dryer but no television. Forty Western Cabins each offer two double beds, a gas fireplace, and a full

A camp of wood-framed tents opened in 1916 on the site of Zion Lodge. The original lodge, designed by Gilbert Stanley Underwood (1890–1961), was constructed in 1925 for the Union Pacific Railroad, which wanted to promote tourism in southern Utah. The current Western Cabins were constructed in the late 1920s. Fire destroyed the main lodge during renovations in the winter of 1966. The present building, which underwent a major renovation in 1989–1990, was completed only three months after the fire.

tiled bath. The cabins were constructed in the 1930s two or four units to a building, and the interiors were remodeled in 1997–1998. These wood-framed cabins with vaulted ceilings and a small porch are somewhat smaller but similar in design to the western log cabins in both Bryce Canyon and the North Rim of the Grand Canyon. The cabins are closely clustered in the front and at the end of one of the motel buildings south of the main lodge. Cabins that face west are closer to parking and offer a better view of the red cliffs across the river. These include cabins 505, 509, 516, 517, 518, 520, 522, 523, 528, and 529.

Seventy-six motel-type rooms are in two large, two-story motor lodge buildings, which were remodeled in 2006–2007. A stone fireplace is in the central lobby area of the larger of the two buildings. Rooms have either two queen beds or one king bed and a full tiled bath. Each room has a private balcony with a table and two chairs or a bench. The rooms are accessed from an interior corridor that runs the length of each building. The best rooms for privacy and quiet are on the rear side of the second floor of each building. These are all odd-numbered rooms. Rooms on the front face the

parking area but generally offer good views of red cliffs to the west. Six two-room suites on the second floor of the motor lodge buildings offer a bedroom with a king bed and a sitting room with a queen sofa bed, chairs, and a refrigerator. Each suite includes two sinks and a bathroom with a shower-tub. Each suite has a large covered balcony with table and chairs.

The choice between a Western Cabin and a room in one of the two motor lodge buildings is pretty much a toss-up. Motor lodge rooms are nice and offer quite a bit more interior space than the Western Cabins. If the nights will be cool and you enjoy a gas fireplace, then paying a few extra dollars for a Western Cabin is probably money well spent. Keep in mind, however, that the cabins are closely spaced and have relatively small front porches. The choice between the Western Cabins and other lodging is not nearly as clear-cut in Zion as at its sister parks, Bryce Canyon and the North Rim of the Grand Canyon.

Zion Lodge's scenic setting along Zion Canyon Scenic Drive is convenient to hiking trails. The lodge

Navajo sandstone, which forms the canyon walls in Zion National Park, is a porous rock that absorbs rainfall. The moisture percolates through the rock and may require many decades (some say centuries) to reach the base of a large cliff. Perhaps the best example in Zion of this phenomenon is 2,000-foot Weeping Rock, where you can walk under the rock and feel the water dripping. Moisture seeping from the rock results in hanging gardens and spring wildflowers. Weeping Rock is accessed via a quarter-mile trail from Zion Canyon Scenic Drive north of Zion Lodge. This is a stop on the shuttle.

is a stop on the free shuttle that provides service along Zion Canyon Scenic Drive and to the visitor center and nearby town of Springdale. [Be aware that summer months generally bring hot days to Zion, where daytime temperatures often reach 100° Fahrenheit. In fact, the *average* high temperature in July is 100 degrees.] A large grassy area in front of the lodge is a pleasant place to read a book, eat a picnic lunch, or lie on a blanket under a cottonwood tree. A lobby in front of the registration desk has chairs and sofas for relaxing. A spacious, wood-paneled restaurant on the second floor has large front windows that offer an outstanding view of the front grounds and colorful canyon walls surrounding the lodge. A large balcony is available for outside dining when weather and temperature permit. The lodge also has a lounge, cafe, coffee bar, auditorium, and gift shop. A 0.6-mile paved trail to Lower Emerald Pools begins opposite Zion Lodge. The longer, 2-mile walk leads to Middle Emerald Pools.

Rooms: Doubles, triples, and quads. All rooms have a full bath.

Wheelchair Accessibility: Four first-floor wheelchair-accessible rooms are in the motel building nearest the lodge registration building. These rooms have either one or two queen beds, and two of the rooms have bathrooms with roll-in showers. The other two rooms have a combination shower-tub with grab bars. Two Western Cabins offer partial wheelchair accessibility with ramp access, but the exterior and bathroom doorways are too small for wheelchair access. One of these Western Cabins has an extra large bathroom with grab bars. An elevator in the main lodge building provides wheelchair access to the restaurant on the second floor. Shuttle buses serving the lodge are equipped for wheelchair access.

Reservations: Xanterra Parks and Resorts, 6312 S. Fiddlers Green Circle, Suite 600N, Greenwood Village, CO 80111.

Phone (888) 297-2757; fax (303) 297-3175. A deposit of one night's stay is required. A cancellation notice of forty-eight hours is required for a full refund.

Rates: Western Cabins ($167); motor lodge ($154); suites ($177). All rates quoted are for two adults. Children sixteen and under stay free. Each additional person is $10. Rollaways are $12.00 and cribs are $5.00 per night. Discount rates are offered December to mid-March, and special packages are also available in the off-season.

Location: Three miles north of the main park highway on Zion Canyon Scenic Drive.

Season: All of the units of Zion Lodge are open year-round. The lodge is often full from early April through October.

Food: An attractive restaurant on the second floor of the main lodge building serves breakfast ($5.50–$9.00), lunch ($7.00–$10.00), and dinner ($15.00–$20.00). Dinner reservations are required and should be made prior to or immediately upon arrival; otherwise you are likely to end up with a very early or very late dinner. Alcoholic beverages are served. A children's menu is available. A coffee bar in the lobby is open from 6:00 a.m. to 1:00 p.m. A cafe at the north end of the main lodge building offers outside dining with pizza, sandwiches, salads, ice cream, soft drinks, and beer from 11:00 a.m. to 7:00 p.m. in season. Groceries and restaurants are in the town of Springdale and can be reached via the free shuttle that stops at the lodge.

Transportation: Scheduled airlines serve Cedar City, St. George, and Salt Lake City, Utah, and Las Vegas, Nevada, where rental cars are available. Scheduled bus service is available to St. George and Cedar City. Amtrak serves Salt Lake City.

Facilities: Post office, gift shop, restaurant, lounge, coffee bar, and cafe.

Activities: Horseback rides begin at the corral across the road from the lodge. For information and reservation call (435) 679-8665 or visit www.canyonrides.com. Naturalist programs are offered throughout the park by National Park Service personnel. Schedules are posted at the front desk of the lodge and in the visitor center. Hiking is the most popular activity in Zion National Park

VIRGINIA

■ **State Tourist Information**
(800) 847-4882 | www.virginia.org

Shenandoah National Park

3655 U.S. Highway 211 East • Luray, VA 22835 • (540) 999-3500
www.nps.gov/shen

Shenandoah National Park comprises 199,000 acres of forested mountains through an 80-mile stretch of the Blue Ridge Mountains. Most of the park's features lie alongside 105-mile Skyline Drive, a slow but scenic two-lane road that wanders along much of the crest of the mountain range. The road accesses lodges, campgrounds, and overlooks from the north entrance at Front Royal to the south entrance near Waynesboro, Virginia. The park brochure provided at entry stations identifies places of interest and park facilities according to mile markers alongside the west side of the road. The park has more than 500 miles of hiking trails, including a 101-mile stretch of the Appalachian Trail. Shenandoah National Park is located in northern Virginia, with the northern entrance some 60 miles west of Washington, D.C. The south entrance connects with the north end of the Blue Ridge Parkway. The northern half of the park tends to be the most crowded. Shenandoah National Park is the northern terminus for the Blue Ridge Parkway, which meanders through Virginia and North Carolina. The parkway is listed in the North Carolina section of this book. **Park Entrance Fee:** $10.00 per vehicle or $5.00 per person, good for seven days.

Lodging in Shenandoah National Park: Three locations in Shenandoah National Park provide lodging facilities, all of which are in the central section between mile markers 40 and 60. Big Meadows Lodge and Skyland Resort are relatively large complexes with a historic lodge and cabins and modern lodging units. Lewis Mountain Cabins is a very small facility with cabins only. All three facilities are operated by the same concessionaire, ARAMARK.

Reservations for All Lodging Facilities: ARAMARK Convention and Tourism Services, P. O. Box 727, Luray, VA 22835. Phone (888) 896-3833; www.visitshenandoah.com. The first night's deposit is required. Refund of deposit less a $15 fee requires a seventy-two-hour advance cancellation.

Transportation: Scheduled airline service is available to several towns surrounding Shenandoah National Park, including Washington, D.C. (use Dulles), and Charlottesville and Harrisonburg, Virginia. Bus service is available to Waynesboro, just outside the south entrance to the park, and Amtrak (800-872-7245) provides passenger rail service to Charlottesville, Virginia. No public transportation is available in the park.

Shenandoah National Park

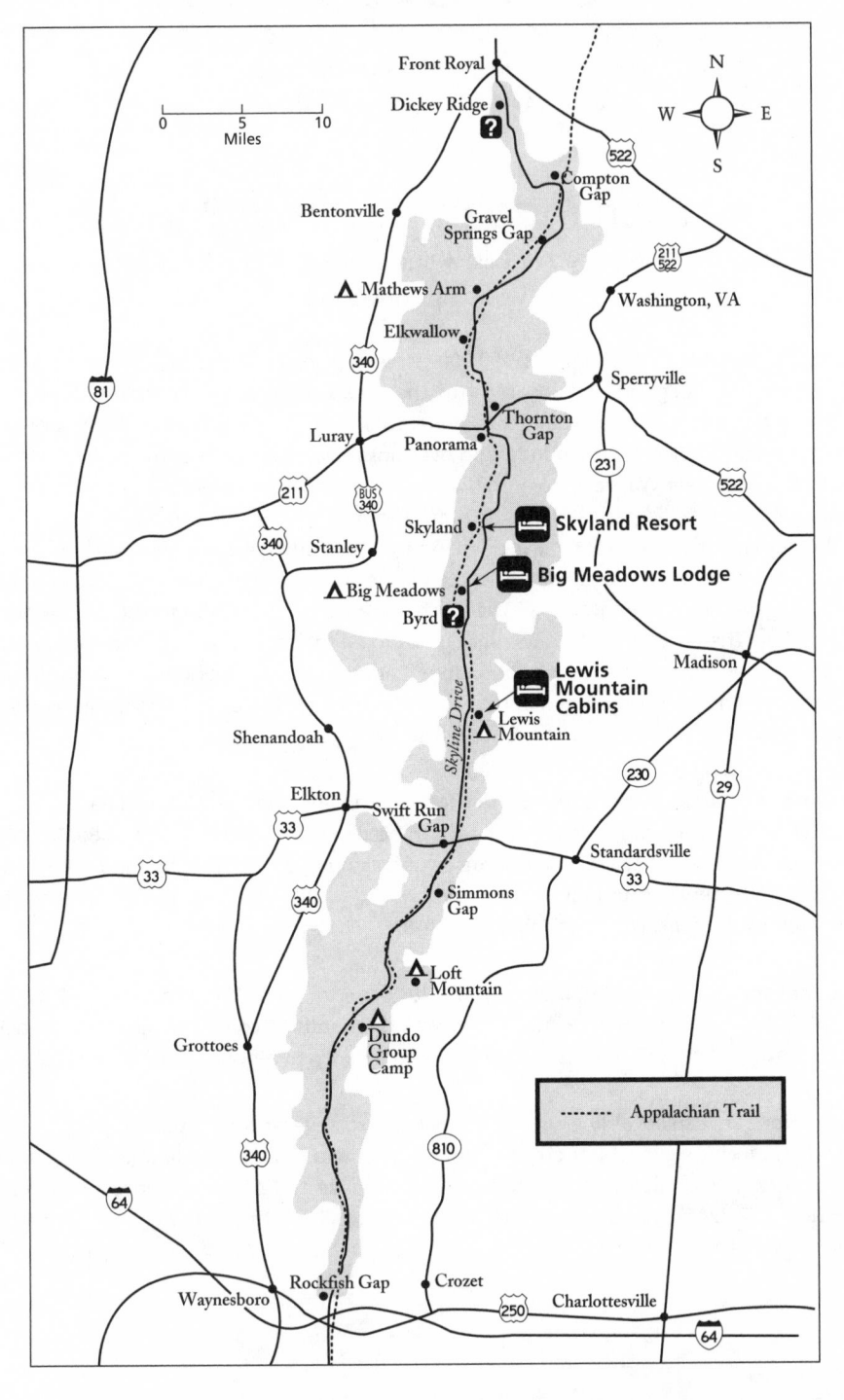

BIG MEADOWS LODGE

P.O. Box 727 • Luray, VA 22835 • (540) 999-2221 • www.visitshenandoah.com

Big Meadows Lodge is a complex consisting of a historic main lodge building plus five cabins, all of which were constructed in 1939, and six one- and two-story lodge buildings that together offer a total of ninety-seven rooms. All of the buildings are in close proximity so that guests have an easy walk from any of the rooms to the main lodge, which houses an attractive dining room, a large great room, a downstairs TV room and taproom, or tavern. Excellent views of the Shenandoah Valley are available from the dining room, the great room, and a large stone porch that runs across the backside of the main lodge. The main lodge also has overnight rooms on three floors. Registration parking is just outside the building, and adequate parking is a short walk from most of the lodging units. Big Meadows is in a heavily forested area at an altitude of 3,510 feet and is located at milepost 51, about midway between the north and south entrances to Shenandoah National Park. The northern entry point to Big Meadows is via U.S. Highway 211 from Luray, Virginia. The lodge is 15 miles north of Swift Run Gap Entrance and U.S. Highway 33.

Big Meadows Lodge offers six categories of accommodations. In ascending order of price, they include main lodge rooms (rooms in the main building), lodge units, cabins, deluxe units, mini-suites, and suites. All rooms have a private bathroom, wood paneling, heat, and a coffeemaker. None has a telephone. Only the mini-suites and deluxe rooms have a television, and only the deluxe rooms have air-conditioning. The suites, mini-suites, and cabins each have a fireplace with wood provided

The main lodge has twenty-five relatively small rooms on three floors. Most of these rooms have one double bed or two twin beds and will accommodate two persons only. Two larger rooms have two double beds and one room has a queen-size bed. Each room in the main lodge has a private bathroom with a tub, a shower, or both. Rooms 1 through 6 on the main floor provide good valley views. Rooms on the upper floor have dormers and are entered from an interior hallway that is accessed from a stairway in the lobby of the main lodge and also from an outside doorway. An elevator in the great room provides access to the bottom floor and the taproom but not to second-floor rooms. As in many older hotels and lodging buildings, the main lodge at Big Meadows has some quirky and interesting rooms. One of these is 13 and 14, which has two separate bedrooms and two separate bathrooms. It can only be rented as one room because of the single fire escape. Room 23 on the second floor has a good valley view but is above the kitchen and its associated noises.

Six one- and two-story lodge buildings house sixty-two rooms in a combination of suites, mini-suites, deluxe units, and standard lodge rooms. Rooms in each category have a balcony or patio with a table and chairs. Four one-story lodge buildings sit end to end on a wooded hillside. Three of these buildings (Piedmont, Blackrock, and Hawksbill) were constructed in the 1940s, while the other (Crescent Rock) offers only mini-suites and was built in 1986. The standard lodge rooms in these one-story buildings have two double beds and are relatively small. The rooms each have a private bathroom, most with a combination shower-tub, although a few have a shower only. Two rooms in Piedmont have two bedrooms while most of the rest of the standard lodge rooms have connecting doors. The newest units at Big Meadows, Doubletop and Rapidan, were remodeled in 2007 with new furniture, including two queen beds, simulated wood floors, air conditioning, and ceiling fans. These deluxe units sit on a hillside overlooking the valley and have rooms that are larger, brighter, and nicer than rooms in the one-story units. They each have a private balcony or patio that offers good valley views, especially from the second floor, where rooms also have a vaulted ceiling.

Ten mini-suites in the Crescent Rock building each have one large room with a vaulted ceiling, stone fireplace, television, and nice balcony with table and chairs. Eight of the mini-suites have a king-size bed and a sofa bed, while the other two, which are wheelchair

Big Meadows Lodge, named for a nearby grassy meadow, is constructed of stones cut from the Massanutten Mountains across the Shenandoah Valley. Built by Civilian Conservation Corps and mountain labor, the lodge was completed in 1939 and is listed on the National Register of Historic Places. Paneling in the bedrooms and the dining room came from the native chestnut trees that once grew here on the Blue Ridge but were virtually wiped out by the 1930s blight. Beams in the lounge and dining room are native oak. Heavy cement shingles protect the building from the harsh mountain winters.

accessible, have one double bed and chairs. The six suites each have two rooms, a small bedroom with either two double beds or one king, plus a large living room with a stone fireplace, chairs, a sofa bed, a small refrigerator, and a private balcony. The suites are situated at the ends of three one-story lodge buildings and connecting doors allow the addition of another bedroom (at an extra charge) to make a two-bedroom suite.

Five wooden duplex buildings house ten cabin rooms near the main lodge. The cabins sit in a grassy area surrounded by trees and offer no particularly good views. Each cabin has paneled walls, carpeting, a stone fireplace, and connecting doors, so both cabins in a building can be rented as a single unit. Each has a small bathroom with a shower only. All except one cabin have one bedroom, most with a double bed, although a few have two twin beds. One cabin has two bedrooms, one with a double bed and the other with two twins. This unit has a bath and a half but rents for only $3.00 per night more than the one-bedroom units. The cabins are quite small and only one (120) has a large screened front porch. The other cabins have chairs on the lawn near the front steps. Cabin units 110 and 111 are next to the playground, a convenient location if you have children, but not a particularly desirable choice if you don't.

With all the lodging options at Big Meadows, which should you choose? All things equal, we like the two newest and remodeled units of Doubletop and Rapidan. These are more expensive than the one-story lodge units, but they offer a brighter interior and excellent views from the balconies and patios. In addition, they have air-conditioning and ceiling fans, desirable amenities during warm afternoons. Choose a second-floor room at Doubletop and you will only have to climb half a flight of stairs. The disadvantage of these two connected units is that neither is directly next to a parking area. If the season is right and you enjoy a fireplace, choose one of the cabins. These are relatively small but nicely spaced and close to the main lodge. If you want to splurge and desire a fireplace, choose one of the ten mini-suites in Crescent Rock. We like these better than the suites.

Big Meadows Lodge is a place to relax, especially during the fall when the morning air is crisp and trees display their parade of brilliant colors. The great room in the main lodge retains its original 1930s appearance, with a large stone fireplace, a row of rocking chairs, handcrafted furniture including sofas and chairs, and outstanding vistas from large picture windows. Here you can enjoy a good book, play a board game, or just sit and enjoy the scenery. Walk out back and you can enjoy the view from a chair on the stone patio. The attractive dining room, with a beamed vaulted ceiling and wall of windows overlooking the valley, is a pleasant place to linger over a morning cup of coffee or an evening trout dinner. Activities include numerous special events such as Virginia wine tasting weekends and craft demonstrations. The large National Park Service visitor center near the entrance to Big Meadows offers exhibits, information, and an excellent presentation on the history of Shenandoah National Park. A nearby general store sells camping equipment, limited groceries, and fast-food items.

Rooms: Doubles, triples, and quads. Suites will accommodate up to six adults. Connecting rooms are available in the main lodge, the lodge units, and the deluxe units. All rooms have a private bath, although some have only a shower or a tub.

Wheelchair Accessibility: Two mini-suites and one room in the main lodge are ADA compliant. The mini-suites in Crescent Rock have a combination shower-tub, and the main lodge room has a roll-in shower. The dining room and taproom are wheelchair accessible.

Rates: Main lodge ($78–$123); cabins ($100–$103); lodge units ($93); deluxe units($131); mini-suites ($138); suite ($140). Higher rates are charged for weekends and during October. Rates quoted are for two adults. Each additional adult in a lodge room is $11. Rollaways are $11 per night. Discounts are available Sunday through Thursday nights for AAA, AARP, and Shenandoah National Park Association members and for active military personnel. Children under sixteen stay free with an adult. Check the Web site for special packages offered seasonally.

Location: At milepost 51.2, about midway on Skyline Drive between the north and south entrances to Shenandoah National Park.

Season: Last week in April to the first weekend in November.

Food: A full-service dining room serves breakfast ($6.00–$12.00), lunch ($8.00–$18.00), and dinner ($16.00–$32.00). Beer and wine are available. A children's menu is available. A taproom opens each afternoon to serve appetizers, sandwiches, and chili. A convenience store at the entrance to Big Meadows has limited groceries and a coffee shop that serves breakfast and fast-food items including burgers and fries from 9:00 a.m. to 8:00 p.m.

Facilities: Restaurant, gift and craft shop, taproom, TV room, conference room, and a nice playground area for children. A gas station, coffee shop, convenience store, and National Park Service visitor center are at the nearby Big Meadows Wayside.

Activities: Hiking and fishing. Nightly entertainment is presented in the taproom. The National Park Service gives frequent programs at the visitor center, the lodge, and throughout the park. Park concessionaire ARAMARK offers a variety of guided hikes (fees charged) including one from Skyland Resort to Big Meadows Lodge with a night's stay at each lodge. ARAMARK also offers special events throughout the season. Call (888) 896-3833 or visit the Web site for details.

LEWIS MOUNTAIN CABINS

P.O. Box 727 • Luray, VA 22835 • (540) 999-2255 • www.visitshenandoah.com

Lewis Mountain is one of the smallest lodging units in all the national parks. The entire complex consists of one building with a registration desk and a small store, seven one-story structures that provide a total of nine overnight rooms, and a hikers' cabin. Lewis Mountain Cabins has no lobby, dining room, swimming pool, or cocktail lounge. A small parking lot sits beside the registration building, and all the cabins are a short walk away. The entire complex is in a heavily forested area with no particularly good views. Lewis Mountain Cabins is at mile marker 57.5, in the central section of Shenandoah National Park. It is about 6 miles south of Big Meadows.

The nine cabins at Lewis Mountain date from the 1930s but are well maintained both inside and out. Each has wood paneling, hardwood floors, electric heat, and private baths with a shower, with the exception of one two-bedroom wheelchair-accessible cabin that has an extra-large bathroom with a combination shower-tub. The cabins do not have air-conditioning, telephone, or television. Each cabin has a small front porch with two chairs plus a covered picnic pavilion with a table, barbecue pit, electric light, and electrical outlets. Wood is

■   ■   ■

In the early 1940s, Virginia still had "separate but equal" facilities for African Americans. The Lewis Mountain area was originally designated for blacks and called Lewis Mountain Negro Area. The National Park Service was responsible for caring for the campground, picnic area, and utilities, while the concessionaire constructed the original five cabins. An additional two cabins were brought in later. In 1945 National Park Service concessionaires were told by the U.S. government to move to full integration, and Lewis Mountain Cabins was integrated a year later.

■   ■   ■

not provided but is available for purchase at the store. Two of the buildings are constructed as duplexes, with two cabin rooms per unit. These four cabin rooms each have one double bed. Five of the buildings have two bedrooms, one on each side of a bathroom. The two-bedroom units, which cost about $30 per night more than the one-bedroom cabins, have a double bed in each bedroom. The single hikers' cabin with two bunk beds has a potbellied stove but no bath or running water. Public bathrooms are located in the store and the nearby campground. Bunk beds have mattresses, but guests must supply their own linens for the hikers' cabin.

Lewis Mountain Cabins is the smallest and one of the least expensive lodging options in Shenandoah National Park. This is an especially inviting place where you can take an evening stroll through the adjacent picnic area or along a stretch of the Appalachian Trail that runs beside the nearby campground. Sitting on the front porch of cabin 8 early one morning, we watched a young bear come out of the woods, scamper up a tree, look around, climb down, and then search the complex for something to eat. What a great way to start the morning! During another stay, this time in cabin 10, we ate dinner at the picnic table while being closely observed by a large owl perched on the dead branch of nearby tree.

Because all your food and cooking utensils must be carried to the cabin, this lodging facility is most appropriate for a multiday stay. The small store has ice and some of the things you may forget. The cabins provide adequate interior space, and the separate covered picnic area in back of or beside each cabin is a great place to grill steaks or roast some hot dogs. A restaurant at Big Meadows Lodge and a grill at the wayside beside the National Park Service visitor center are only 6 miles north on Skyline Drive.

Our favorite single cabin is 10 because of its location away from the road. Its picnic area is also probably in the best location of any of the cabins. Cabin 1 and 2 (for whatever reason, each two-bedroom cabin is assigned two numbers) is probably the best choice for a two-bedroom unit because it has only a single neighboring cabin. If you anticipate good weather and want to save money, you might consider choosing the hikers' cabin that rents for about a third of the cost of a one-bedroom cabin. The unit is small but has a nearby parking space and a nice covered patio with a picnic table. Remember, however, that occupants must use the bathroom in the campground or at the store.

Rooms: Doubles, triples, and quads. Each cabin, with the exception of the hikers' cabin, has a private bathroom.

Wheelchair Accessibility: One two-bedroom cabin is ADA compliant with a combination shower-tub. The store, showers, and laundry are wheelchair accessible.

Rates: Single-bedroom cabins ($83); two-bedroom cabins ($111); hikers' cabin ($29). Higher prices are charged on weekend nights and during October. Special packages are available seasonally.

Location: Between mile marker 57 and 58, near the midpoint of Skyline Drive. Lewis Mountain is about 6 miles south of Big Meadows.

Season: First week in May to the last weekend in October. The cabins tend to be full on all weekends and during July, August, and the first part of October.

Food: No restaurant or other dining facilities are at Lewis Mountain. A small store with limited groceries is in the registration building.

Facilities: Small store, pay showers, and laundry facility.

Activities: Hiking.

SKYLAND RESORT

P.O. Box 727 • Luray, VA 22835 • (540) 999-2211 • www.visitshenandoah.com

Skyland Resort is a wide-ranging complex of approximately three dozen one- and two-story structures, including twenty-six buildings and cabins that provide overnight accommodations. Lodging buildings range from freestanding rustic cabins constructed in the early 1900s to a modern two-story motel-type building with twenty rooms. Some of the buildings sit on a bluff, others are along a wooded hillside, but most are on a plateau overlooking the beautiful Shenandoah Valley. The registration building at the top of the hill has a small, comfortable lobby with chairs, tables, a television, and a wall of windows offering an outstanding view of the Shenandoah Valley. An adjacent building has a craft and gift shop, a taproom, a small lounge area, and a nice dining room with windows that provide a valley view. Chairs on a patio area between the two buildings offer a pleasant place to sit and view the valley. Lodging structures are scattered about a wide area, although three lodge buildings on the top of the hill are near the registration and dining buildings. Many of the remaining buildings and cabins are down a hill and some distance from the dining room. Many, but not all, of the

178 rooms offer good views of the valley. Some have great views from private balconies, while views from other rooms are blocked by trees or nearby buildings. Skyland Resort is at mile marker 42, 10 miles north of Big Meadows in the central section of Shenandoah National Park. Situated at 3,680 feet, it is at the highest point on Skyline Drive.

The lodging complex offers five classes of accommodations: lodge rooms, deluxe rooms, cabins, family cabins, and suites. A wide price range applies to each category depending on size, view, and bedding. All the rooms have wood paneling, a private bathroom, a coffeemaker, and heat, but no telephone. The six suites and about half the lodge rooms each have a television. Most rooms at Skyland Resort are in a series of fifteen one- and two-story lodge buildings that sit on a bluff overlooking the valley.

Lodge buildings vary in size and age, but most have a television, ceiling fan, and a hair dryer. Bedding available in lodge rooms is two doubles, two queens, or one king. Two of the lodge buildings, Laurel and Franklin, are newer and larger, with rooms that rent as deluxe units. Each of the lodge rooms has a balcony or patio, but views vary depending on the building location and whether there are trees between the building and the valley.

Our favorite lodge building is Shenandoah, which has five rooms, including one suite, that each offer excellent views of the Shenandoah Valley. Corner room 73 is particularly desirable and less expensive than the suite that is directly above. Staying in the Shenandoah building requires walking an uphill grade from the parking lot, but this is a small price to pay for staying in this building. Pinnacles offers a good choice if you want to be close to the restaurant and registration building. This building sits on a hillside, so entry is easier to a second-floor room than a first-floor room.

The least expensive accommodations at Skyland Resort are cabins in nine historic buildings constructed between 1906 and 1922. Most of the cabins have a bathroom with a shower only and a small porch with chairs. The cabins tend to have small windows and dark, paneled interiors. None has a television. The units are scattered among trees, and most do not offer a view of the valley. In addition, most are not close to the registration building or dining room. Cabins differ in both

■   ■   ■

The Skyland area was originally developed in the 1850s to mine copper. Surrounding timber was used to make charcoal for a copper smelter. It was not until 1886 that the son of one of the original mine owners considered the possibility of developing the area as a resort. By the early 1900s Skyland had a dining hall, a recreation hall, bathhouses, and bungalows, all paid for by the sale of cabin sites and loans. The developer operated Skyland as a concessionaire for the National Park Service until 1937.

■   ■   ■

size and bedding, ranging from six small units with one double bed to a large freestanding unit with a separate bedroom, a gas fireplace, and a large front porch. The latter, cabin 68, called Byrd's Nest, is our pick of the cabins, although it doesn't offer a valley view. Cabin 59, with two double beds plus a twin bed, sits across from the playground. It has a large front porch and is a good choice for families with children. Adjoining cabin 60, with identical bedding, can be combined with cabin 59. Three cabin rooms in Fell can be rented individually or as a unit, the latter being a popular option for large families. Cabin 173 in Fell has a queen bed and a separate living room fronted by a large picture window offering a commanding view of the valley. This unit does not have a balcony, but a large grassy area with chairs and a picnic table in front of the building offers a pleasant place to relax while enjoying the view.

Three cabins were restored and converted in 2005 from multiple units back to their original status as freestanding cabins. Now classified as family cabins, these units have either one or two separate bedrooms and each features a living room, a large porch with a picnic table, and a kitchenette with a sink, a microwave, a small refrigerator, and eating utensils. One of the family cabins can sleep six adults, while the other two sleep four. Two of these units have a gas fireplace.

Six suites each comprise two rooms on the end of four lodge buildings. Four of the suites are in buildings near the dining room, and two are in buildings down the hill on a plateau. Each suite offers a living room with a sofa bed and a wood-burning fireplace (wood provided), plus a separate bedroom. An adjoining room with a connecting door can be added at additional cost to provide a second bedroom.

Beds vary from a double plus a twin to two queens. The two suites down the hill offer a view of the valley, but the four suites nearer the registration building each have a balcony with valley views blocked by trees.

Skyland Resort, the largest lodging facility in Shenandoah National Park, offers accommodations for a wide range of tastes, from historic cabins for visitors who want to experience the rich history of this region to modern lodge rooms for people who want to enjoy the natural beauty of the Blue Ridge Mountains, but in style. This is a place where people come for weddings, family reunions, honeymoons, and weekend rest periods. A conference hall convenient to many of the cabins and lodge rooms can be reserved (fee charged) for planned gatherings. Your main decisions in choosing a room will be lodge room or cabin, valley view or nature view, and double beds, queen beds, or king bed. Lodging units are spread over a fairly wide area, so if location and/or view is an important consideration, be certain this is stated when making a reservation. Activities at Skyland and nearby locations include horseback riding, pony rides, guided hikes, ranger programs, and special events such as craft displays, workshops, and festivals sponsored by the concessionaire. The resort includes an attractive dining room that serves three meals a day and has a wide range of menu options. A large taproom serves appetizers beginning in the early afternoon. Nightly entertainment is offered here.

Rooms: Doubles, triples, and quads. Some suites sleep up to five, and one family cabin accommodates up to six adults. Some rooms, including the suites, can connect with adjacent rooms. All rooms have a private bath with a shower or a combination shower-tub.

Wheelchair Accessibility: Two rooms in Pinnacles (nearest the dining room) and two in Laurel (the newest building at Skyland) are ADA compliant with a combination shower-tub. One family cabin has ramp access, wide doorways, and a bathroom with grab bars and a roll-in shower. The restaurant and craft/gift shop each have ramp access.

Rates: Lodge units ($93–$112); deluxe units ($120–$131); cabins ($72–$122); suites ($131–$174); family cabins ($233–$243). Higher rates are charged on weekends and in October. Lodge rooms, cabins, and four suites are priced for two adults; family cabins and two suites are priced for four adults. Each additional adult in a lodge room is $11. Rollaways are $11 per night. Discounts are available Sunday through Thursday nights for AAA, AARP, and Shenandoah National Park Association members and for active military personnel. Children under sixteen stay free with an adult. Check the Web site for special packages that are offered seasonally.

Location: At milepost 42, about midway on Skyline Drive between the north and south entrances to Shenandoah National Park. Skyland is the northernmost lodging facility in the park.

Season: End of March to the end of November.

Food: An attractive dining room serves breakfast ($4.00–$12.00), lunch ($7.00–$18.00), and dinner ($17.00–$32.00). Beer and wine are available. A children's menu is available. An adjacent taproom serves appetizers beginning in the early afternoon.

Facilities: Restaurant, taproom, craft and gift shop, conference hall (fee), large children's playground, stables, trails.

Activities: Hiking, horseback riding, pony rides, National Park Service ranger-led programs, nightly entertainment. Park concessionaire ARAMARK offers a variety of guided hikes (fees charged) including one from Skyland Resort to Big Meadows Lodge that includes a night's stay at each lodge. ARAMARK also offers special events throughout the season. Call (888) 896-3833, or visit the Web site for details.

Pets: Pets are permitted only in Canyon units at an extra charge of $25 per night.

WASHINGTON

■ **State Tourist Information**
(800) 544-1800 | www.experiencewa.com

Mount Rainier National Park

Tahoma Woods, Star Route • Ashford, WA 98304 • (360) 569-2211 • www.nps.gov/mora

Mount Rainier National Park encompasses 235,625 acres, including the greatest single-peak glacial system and one of the most popular mountain-climbing areas in the continental United States. Mount Rainier, the ancient volcano at the center of the park, is surrounded by snow, forests, and subalpine flowered meadows. Visitor centers are at Sunrise, Ohanapecosh, Paradise, and Longmire, the latter being the park's oldest developed area. The road from the Nisqually Entrance in the park's southwest corner to Longmire is considered one of the world's most beautiful forest roads. Mount Rainier National Park is in southwestern Washington, 89 miles south of Seattle. It is 64 miles west of the town of Yakima, Washington. **Park Entrance Fee:** $15.00 per vehicle or $5.00 per person, good for seven days.

Lodging in Mount Rainier National Park: Mount Rainier has two inns that offer very different lodging experiences. National Park Inn is a small, cozy lodge in a heavily forested area with a view of Mount Rainier. The much larger and busier Paradise Inn is at a higher altitude that offers better mountain views in an alpine environment. Despite the different environments, the two lodges are both in the southern end of the park and only about 13 miles apart.

NATIONAL PARK INN

Mount Rainier National Park • Longmire, WA 98397 • (360) 569-2275

www.rainier.guestservices.com

Mount Rainier National Park

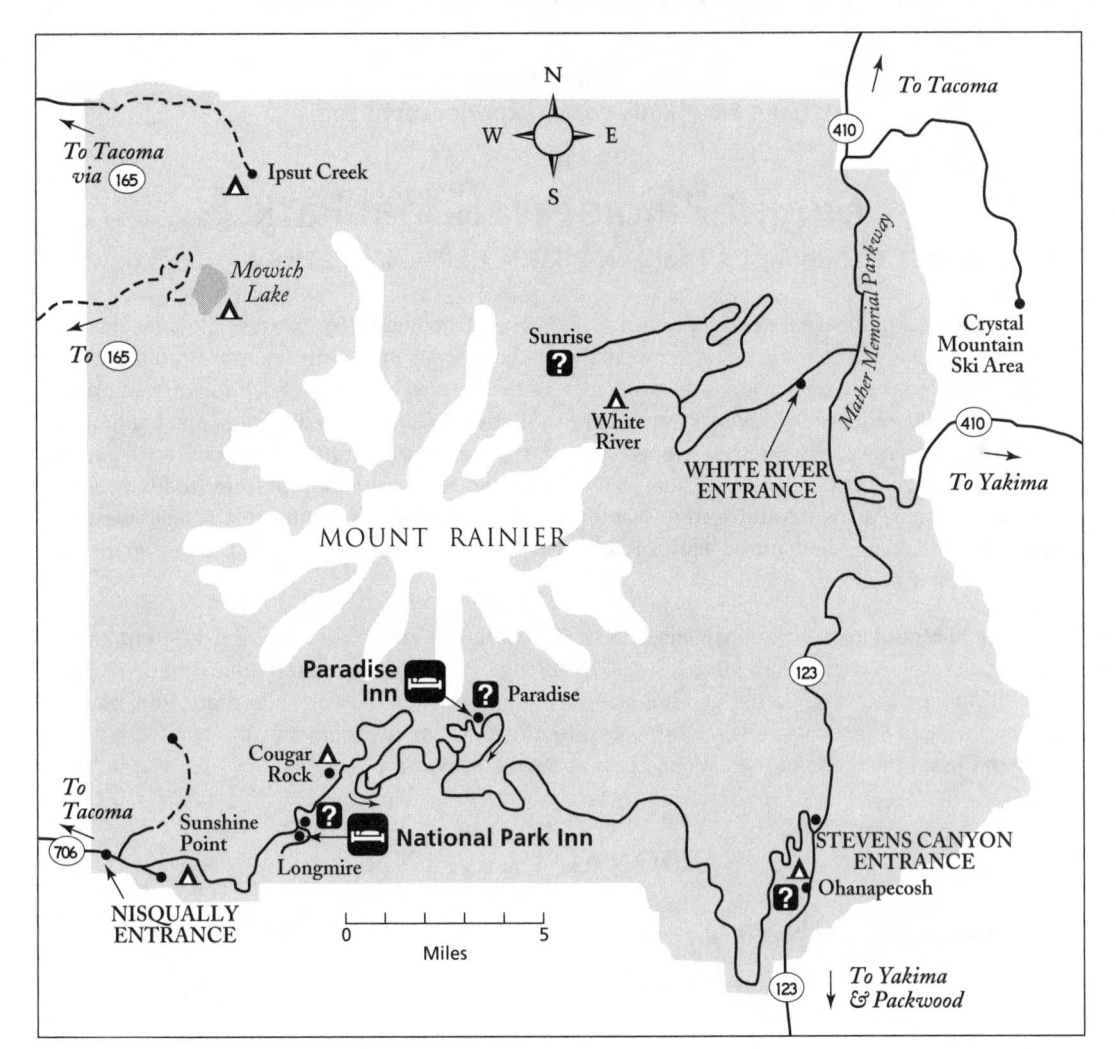

National Park Inn is a small but pleasant two-story wooden lodge with twenty-five overnight rooms, all but two of which are on the second floor. The inn is at an altitude of 2,700 feet, surrounded by an old-growth forest of Douglas fir, western red cedar, and western hemlock. National Park Inn retains the character of an early 1900s lodge even though the building has been completely modernized. The inn is entered from a large parking area in back of the building. The lodge is on Washington Highway 706, 6 miles from the southwest entrance to Mount Rainier National Park. It is 13 winding miles from the much larger inn at Paradise.

The twenty-five rooms at National Park Inn are different in terms of size, bedding, and bathrooms. In general, the rooms are comfortable but small. Two suites each have two rooms, one with a double bed and the other with two twin beds. All of the rooms have heat, a window fan, a coffeemaker, a hair dryer, and bathrobes, but no air-conditioning, telephone, or television. All but seven rooms have private baths with a tub, a shower, or both. Rooms without a private bathroom have an in-room sink and access to two community showers and baths on the second floor. Most rooms have two twins, one double, or one queen bed, although two rooms have two double beds. Although the rooms can be quite dissimilar, with the exception of the two suites, the cost for two adults depends only on whether or not a room has a private bath. Rooms with a bath cost about $35 per night more than rooms without a private bath.

Room 7, with a private bath, is much larger than average and has one queen bed and two twin beds. Rooms 6, 8, and 10, with a bath, and 12, 14, and 16, without a bath, which are along the front of the building, have a good view of Mount Rainier when it isn't shrouded in clouds. We suggest you request larger room 16 if using a community bathroom is acceptable.

■　　■　　■

The current National Park Inn was constructed as an annex of the original three-story, sixty-room National Park Inn, most of which burned in 1926. Fortunately the Annex had previously been moved to the opposite side of the road and was spared by the fire. The Annex was subsequently reopened as the National Park Inn and underwent a major remodeling in 1936. Another extensive renovation occurred in 1989, when the inn was essentially rebuilt from the ground up for reopening in May 1990. The adjacent building currently housing the gift shop was constructed in 1911 as a clubhouse for the first lodge and is the only structure at this location that remains on its original site.

■　　■　　■

All rooms are entered from an inside corridor that is accessed via a stairway from the lobby area. No elevator is available. Two handicap-accessible rooms are on the first floor.

National Park Inn is much smaller and cozier than the lodge at Paradise. There aren't a lot of people here and activities in the immediate vicinity are minimal, but if you desire a comfortable and quiet place to read a book, get to know your spouse and kids, or just recharge your batteries, the National Park Inn is a good choice for an overnight stay. A large covered porch with numerous chairs runs the length of the building. A guest lounge just off the check-in area has a large stone fireplace, sofas, tables, chairs, games, and puzzles. Complimentary tea and cookies or scones are served here each afternoon. The general store next door sells gifts, limited groceries, beer, and wine. A National Park Service visitor center and a museum with exhibits on geology and wildlife are a short walk from the inn.

Rooms: Doubles, triples, and quads. Eighteen of the twenty-five rooms have private baths. Community baths are on the second floor.

Wheelchair Accessibility: The inn has two ADA-compliant rooms on the first floor, where the registration desk, guest lounge, and dining room are located.

Reservations: Mount Rainier Guest Services, P.O. Box 108, Ashford, WA 98304-0108. Phone (360) 569-2275; www.rainier.guestservices.com. Credit card guarantee is required when the reservation is made. Cancellation requires seven days' notice plus a $15 handling fee. Less than seven days' notice results in a charge of one night's room rate plus tax.

Rates: Rooms with baths ($143); rooms without baths ($107) two-room unit with bath ($197). Rates quoted are for two adults, except for the two-room unit, which is for three adults. Each additonal person is $15. Children under two stay free with an adult, using existing bedding in the room. Special winter packages are available October through April.

Location: Six miles from the southwest entrance to Mount Rainier National Park on WA 706. The inn is 13 miles from Paradise, the park's other lodge.

Season: Open all year.

Food: An informal dining room on the main floor is open for breakfast ($6.00–11.50), lunch ($7.00–$14.00), and dinner ($13.00–$21.00). A children's menu is available. Snacks and drinks may be purchased at the gift shop/store next door.

Transportation: The nearest major airport is SeaTac, located between Seattle and Tacoma, Washington, where rental cars are available. Amtrak also serves these cities.

Facilities: Dining room, post office, general store that sells gifts and some food items, museum, National Park Service visitor center, hiker information center. The store rents cross-country ski equipment during winter months. Lessons are available. Gasoline is not available in the park but may be purchased at Ashford and Elbe.

Activities: Hiking, fishing, ranger-guided walks, snowshoeing, cross-country skiing.

Paradise Inn

Mount Rainier National Park • Paradise, WA 98398 • (360) 569-2275

www.rainier.guestservices.com

Paradise Inn is a large wooden two-story lodge building with an attached four-story annex that offers some of the most striking views of the park's snow-covered peaks, including Mount Rainier. The inn has 117 rooms, most of which are in the annex that is reached via an enclosed walkway from the lobby of the main building. The primary structure was completed in 1917, and the annex was added in the 1920s. Paradise Inn is located at the base of Mount Rainier at an altitude of 5,400 feet, in the southern end of Mount Rainier National Park, 19 miles from the park's southwest entrance station.

The inn is on a hill such that the outside entry to the lobby is the hotel's third floor. An immense stone fireplace is at each end of the huge two-story lobby, which has a vaulted ceiling and runs most of the length of the building. The lobby is filled with tables, benches, sofas, and stuffed chairs. Massive log beams frame a mezzanine that wraps around the inside of the floor above. The parking lot is often crowded, so it is best to temporarily park beside the entrance to unload and load luggage. Assistance with luggage can be requested at the registration desk. There are no elevators, so access to all guest rooms other than those on the third floor requires climbing stairs.

Paradise Inn has several categories of rooms, all of which have heat but no air-conditioning, telephone, or television. The thirty-two least expensive rooms without private bath are all in the main lodge building. Most are very small rooms (approximately 8 feet by 12 feet, including a small open closet area) with a sink and bedding that ranges from two twin beds to one double bed, to one double plus a single. Room 467 does not have a private bath and is quite large, with three double beds. It is the only room in the hotel that can hold six people without adding a rollaway. Room 446, also without a private bathroom, is somewhat larger than average and has two double beds. It is next to the stairway, which is sometimes noisy. The thirty-two rooms without a bath share four showers, one men's restroom, and one women's restroom. The restrooms were redone in 2006 and 2007 and are quite nice. Additional restrooms are on the floor below near the stairway. The next room classification includes seventy-seven rooms with bathrooms, nearly all of which are in the annex. Bathrooms have a tub, a shower, or both. Rooms have two twin beds, a double plus a twin bed, two double beds, or one queen-size bed.

Ten rooms have two bedrooms and one bath. One bedroom has a double bed, a queen, or a double plus a twin, and the other has two twins. These rooms have the added amenity of a coffeemaker and rent for about $60 per night more than the one bedroom with a bath, so you might consider one of these if you are traveling with children. Paradise also offers two suites, each with a bedroom with a queen-size bed, a separate sitting room with a futon, a coffeemaker, and a private bath.

Rooms in both the main lodge building and the annex offer varying views, but none have a particularly good view of Mount Rainier. When making a reservation you should consider that rooms in the annex are on four floors, and there is no elevator. Thus, you may be required to climb two flights of stairs each time you

The original structure of Paradise Inn, including the existing lobby, dining room, kitchen, three storerooms, and guest rooms above the dining room, was constructed in 1917 of Alaskan cedar salvaged from standing dead timber resulting from a nearby fire in 1885. The huge logs were hauled by horse-drawn wagons from an area near Narada Falls and Canyon Rim to the present site. The ceiling-high cedar logs and attached bracing were added later to support the roof under the heavy snowfalls in the Paradise area. The original inn offered thirty-three rooms, and the attached annex was added in the 1920s. Most of the lobby's woodwork was done by a German carpenter, who used only an adze in his work. He also built an unusual piano and a huge grandfather clock, which remain in the lobby.

go to or from your room. Ask for a room on the third floor (the hotel entry level) if you want to avoid climbing stairs.

Choosing a room without a bath will save $50 per night and put you nearer the lobby (and the morning coffee). These rooms are small but relatively comfortable and were repainted and recarpeted in 2007. If you require a private bathroom, try for a room in the annex with two double beds or a double bed plus a single bed. These are larger but rent for the same price as a room with two twin beds. Rooms 317 and 319, each with two double beds, enjoy a large window area that offers good views of the Tattoosh Mountain Range. Room 411 allows guests to look out the window while taking a bath.

Paradise Inn is a classic national park lodge. At an altitude of 5,400 feet, this area can be quite cool and foggy, even during summer. On the plus side, Paradise

The need for major structural work resulted in the closure of Paradise Inn during the 2006 and 2007 seasons. Concrete replaced the old frame walls, and a new concrete foundation stabilized the building that was originally constructed on a bed of large rocks. The three giant fireplaces, two in the lobby and one in the dining room, were photographed, taken apart, and rebuilt stone by stone after a concrete base and concrete inner structure had been poured. Parquet flooring was replaced with fir (the original flooring) in the lobby, dining room, gift shop, and cafe, while hall carpeting was replaced, rooms were repainted, and two guest showers were added in the inn's older section. Public bathrooms on the first and second floors were redone. The former bar on the main floor was converted to additional handicap-accessible rooms that now line the walkway between the main building and the Annex. The contractor brought in 180 Alaska cedar logs that were used as replacement and additional support beams. Additional renovations planned for the Annex were delayed due to a shortage of funds. Overall, the two-year renovation cost approximately $22 million.

Inn is noted for many varieties of subalpine flowers that bloom during July and August. Paradise Inn is a heavily visited area of the park, and lots of people, both guests and visitors, browse through the lobby area. Tables and chairs on the mezzanine offer a more relaxing place to read, play cards, or just people watch in the lobby below. Complimentary coffee and tea are offered each morning. Complimentary coffee, tea, and cookies are served for guests here each afternoon. The attractive 200-seat dining room with a beamed ceiling offers a few entrees

such as Buffalo Meatloaf with Jack Daniel's Sauce that are not found on most menus. A small cafe with inside and outside seating serves beer, wine, and less expensive food.

Rooms: Singles, doubles, triples, and quads. Not all rooms have private baths.

Wheelchair Accessibility: Seven rooms in the passageway between the main lodge and the annex are ADA compliant. Disabled parking spaces are near the front door of the inn.

Reservations: Mount Rainier Guest Services, P.O. Box 108, Ashford, WA 98304-0108. Phone (360) 569-2275; www.rainier.guestservices.com. A credit card is required to reserve a room. A minimum of seven days' notice must be given for a full refund less a $15 handling fee. Less than seven days' notice results in a charge for one night's room rate plus tax.

Rates: Rooms without a bath ($99); rooms with a bath ($149); two-room units with a bath ($210); suites with a sitting room ($228). Rates for two-room units and suites are for three adults. Each additional person is $15. Children under two stay free with an adult, utilizing existing bedding in the room.

Location: Paradise Inn is on Highway 706, 19 miles from the southwest entrance to Mount Rainier National Park.

Season: The lodge is open from mid-May through the first part of October, depending on weather.

Food: An attractive dining room with seating for 200 offers breakfast ($7.00–$13.00), lunch ($9.00–$13.00), and dinner ($18.00–$29.00) daily, with a special Sunday brunch. Alcoholic beverages are available. Dinner reservations are not accepted. A children's menu is available. A cafe off the lobby serves soups, salads, sandwiches, beer, and wine. A grill in the nearby National Park Service visitor center serves sandwiches, hamburgers, soups, and beverages.

Transportation: The nearest major airport is SeaTac, located between Seattle and Tacoma, Washington, where rental cars are available. Amtrak also serves these cities.

Facilities: Restaurant, cafe, gift shop, post office, hiker information center, nearby National Park Service visitor center. Gasoline is not available in the park but may be purchased at Ashford and Elbe.

Activities: Hiking, guided walks, evening programs in the lobby, fishing, mountain climbing, snowshoeing, cross-country skiing, and tubing.

North Cascades National Park
Lake Chelan National Recreation Area
Ross Lake National Recreation Area

810 State Route 20 • Sedro-Woolley, WA 98284 • (360) 856-5700 • www.nps.gov/noca

The North Cascades National Park complex, covering 1,069 square miles, offers magnificent alpine scenery that is unmatched in the continental United States. Heavy precipitation has produced alpine lakes, waterfalls, ice caps, more than 300 glaciers, and glacier-carved canyons such as Stehekin (Native American for "the way through") that sits at the head of 55-mile long Lake Chelan. Compared to many other national parks, this scenic park is relatively wild and uncrowded. The park complex is located in northern Washington (the north boundary borders on Canada). Primary access to the area is via Washington State Route 20, which bisects the park through a portion of the Ross Lake section. **Park Entrance Fee:** No charge.

Lodging in North Cascades National Park Service Complex: Three major lodging facilities are in the North Cascades National Park Complex. Two of the three are in or near the village of Stehekin at the north end of Lake Chelan in Lake Chelan National Recreation Area. The other is at the south end of Ross Lake in Ross Lake National Recreation Area. Stehekin Valley Ranch is a privately owned facility surrounded by the North Cascades National Park Complex but is unregulated by the National Park Service. In addition, a smaller lodging facility (Silver Bay Inn Resort with two cabins, a house, and one room; phone 509-687-3142; or email stehekin@silverbayinn.com) and several privately owned cabins, often with vehicles, are also available for rent near Stehekin. For information on the area, call Lake Chelan Chamber of Commerce at (800) 4-CHELAN. When traveling to Stehekin, keep in mind that no ATMs are available, and not all businesses accept credit cards.

The lodging facilities at Stehekin are reached only via commercial boats or floatplanes that leave from the town of Chelan or Field's Point Landing. The largest and least expensive boat (approximately $39 round-trip) takes four hours one way and leaves Chelan each morning at 8:30. A faster and more expensive boat ($59 round-trip) takes two and a half hours and leaves at the same time. Both boats are operated by the same company, Lake Chelan Boat Company. Reservations are recommended. For information call (509) 682-4584, or visit the Web site at www.ladyofthelake .com. You will save money and see more by selecting the slower boat, Lady of the Lake II. This is probably the best choice on your first trip to Stehekin. The scenery between Chelan and Stehekin is beautiful, and the captain sometimes approaches the shoreline when wild animals are spotted. For those in a hurry, floatplanes are available for round-trips ($165) or one way ($120), with flights taking approximately thirty minutes. Chelan Airways offers several transportation options, including fly/boat trips that allow flying one way and taking a chartered boat the other way ($165). The charter boat trip takes approximately two hours. For information about air transportation contact Chelan Airways at (877) 682-5556 or (509) 682-5555. You can also check the firm's Web site at www .chelanairways.com.

The only other national park lodging facility in the North Cascades Complex is Ross Lake Resort in Ross Lake National Recreation Area. This resort consists of floating cabins, and guests must carry in all food because no food service of any kind is available at or near the resort. Ross Lake Resort is reached via State Route 20, which bisects the North Cascades Complex. Most guests choose to take the combination ferry/truck/speedboat route from near Diablo Dam, 65 miles east of Burlington on State Route 20. To get to the free parking area, cross Diablo Dam and turn right to park in the resort parking lot. A sign on State Route 20 indicates the turnoff. The ferry, operated by Seattle City Light and departing each day at 8:30 a.m. and 3:00 p.m., takes you to the end of Diablo Lake. The charge is $20 per person roundtrip, payable in cash. A maximum of three carry-ons per person is permitted. You will then be met by the resort truck, which will carry you and your luggage on a winding gravel road to Ross Lake ($7.00 round-trip, payable at the resort). From there you will transfer to a speedboat that quickly crosses the lake and delivers you directly to your assigned cabin. No reservations are necessary for either the ferry or the truck. Guests interested in hiking to the resort can park their vehicle on State Route 20 at milepost 134 (the Ross Lake/Ross Dam trailhead). It is a 1-mile hike down the trail to the gravel road and another mile to the boat docking area across the lake from the resort. The last power pole beside the road has a telephone that can be used to call the resort for pickup (dial 18-31974; $2.00 charge per person).

STEHEKIN LANDING RESORT

P.O. Box 3 • Stehekin, WA 98852 • (509) 682-4494 • www.stehekinlanding.com

Stehekin Landing Resort comprises seven wooden buildings, five of which have a total of twenty-seven overnight units. The registration desk is inside the store across a small parking area and up a flight of stairs from the boat dock. The store and restaurant are fronted by a wooden deck with chairs and picnic tables. A registration sign is above the entrance. The lodge is on the east bank near the north terminus of Lake Chelan, across the road from the boat dock. There are also a laundry, a post office, a few stores, and a large National Park Service visitor center. Shuttle service and tours for the Stehekin Valley begin near the dock.

A total of twenty-seven units of various sizes and configurations are available at the lodge. All of the rooms have a private bath with a shower or a combination shower-tub, heat, and electricity but no telephone,

North Cascades National Park/Lake Chelan National Recreation Area/ Ross Lake National Recreation Area

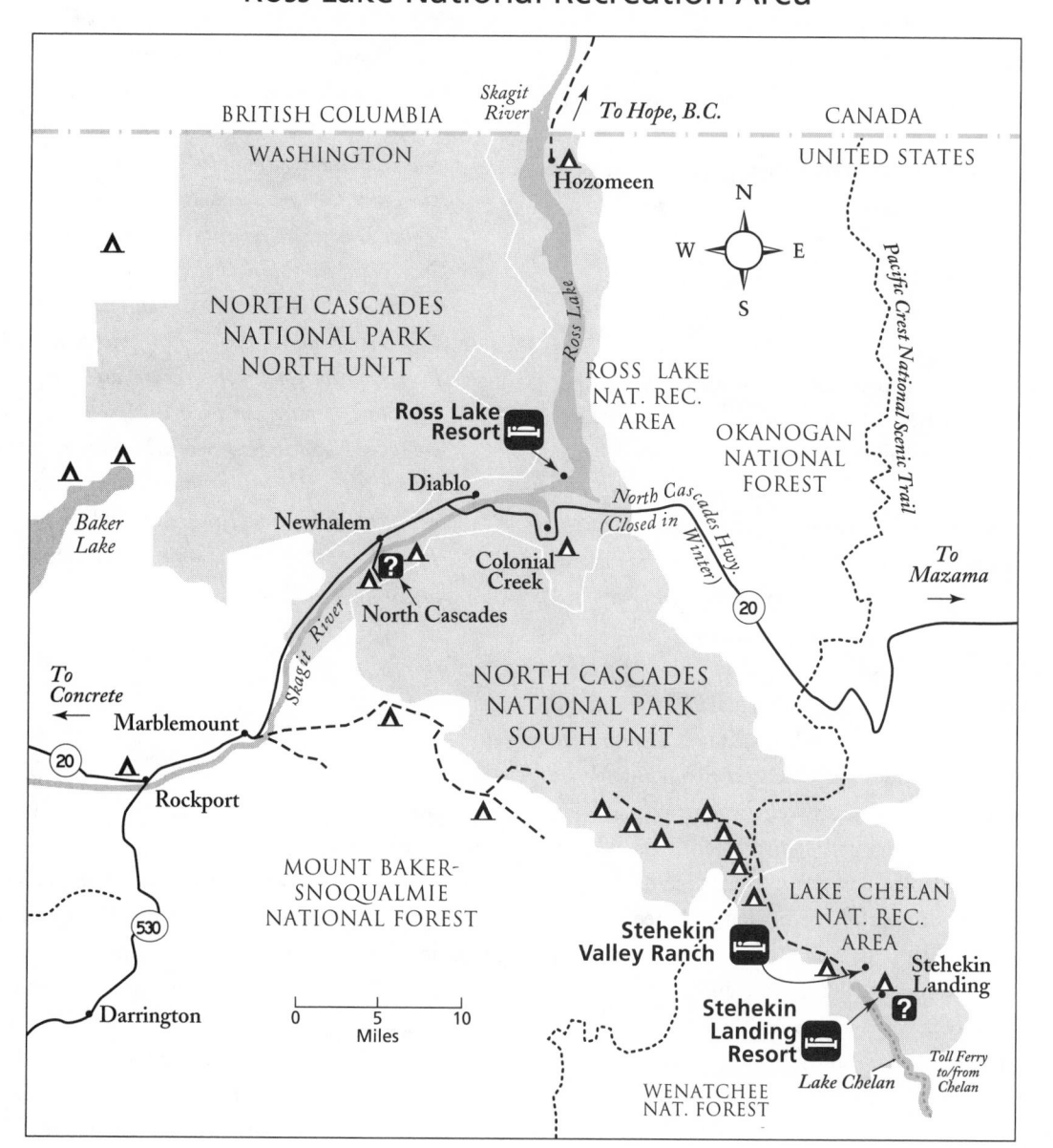

television, or air-conditioning. Ten standard rooms, eight of which are above the store, are the least expensive. These small rooms do not have a balcony or offer a view of the lake, but a sitting area with books, games, and puzzles at the end of the hallway has a good view of the lake. Standard rooms have either one queen-size or two twin beds. Standard rooms 5 and 6 on the lower floor of an A-frame building have nice interiors and are preferable to rooms above the store.

Eleven lakeview rooms in a two-story motel-style building next to the restaurant are larger than standard rooms. Each lakeview room has at least one large window and a balcony facing Lake Chelan. Three of these rooms are larger and rent for approximately $25 per night more than the other eight rooms. The five first-floor rooms, 9 through 13, have a significantly larger balcony than the upstairs units. The eight regular-size lakeview rooms each have either a king bed or a queen bed plus a twin sofa bed. Beds in the three large lakeview rooms range from one queen plus a queen sofa bed to two queen beds plus a queen sofa bed.

Six kitchen units have a kitchen with a stove, an oven, a refrigerator/freezer, a coffeemaker, a toaster, and all utensils including pots and pans. These six units are in four different buildings. One unit two flights above the store (no elevator) has two bedrooms plus a living room and sleeps seven with the sofa bed. This unit has large windows facing the lake and can become uncomfortably warm during July and August. A freestanding building with a large deck and wheelchair accessibility has two bedrooms and a living room and can sleep seven with two futons. An A-frame building sleeps six, with a bedroom and living room plus a loft bedroom. The A-frame has a large deck facing the lake on the main floor, which is one flight above ground level. Views from the deck are somewhat obstructed by buildings. The three other kitchen units are in a triplex building with a large deck. Smaller units 2 and 3 each sleep three people with a king bed and a twin sofa bed. Unit 4 is larger and can sleep six in one bedroom and a separate

■   ■   ■

Stehekin Landing Resort is not the only lodging facility to have served the public at Stehekin. The small Argonaut Hotel with several rooms and a store was under construction, when in 1892 it was sold to Merritt Field, who built a three-story hotel that could house one hundred guests in fifty rooms. Faced with flooding as a result of the proposed Lake Chelan Dam, Field sold the hotel in 1915 to the Great Northern Railroad, which continued operations until 1927, when the building was demolished. Timber and beams from the hotel were used to construct the Golden West Lodge farther up the hill, which operated here until 1971, when it was sold to the National Park Service, which currently utilizes the building as a visitor center. The current Stehekin Landing Resort is a conglomeration of two hotels that were acquired by the National Park Service in 1968.

■   ■   ■

living area. All three units have a deck facing the lake.

One unit, "Lake House," is a full-size home that can accommodate up to twelve people. This has three bedrooms, a full kitchen, a washer and dryer, a fireplace, and a hot tub. The Lake House sits directly on Lake Chelan a short distance from Stehekin Landing.

We believe the lakeview rooms are the best choice for two adults not interested in cooking. They offer a good view of Lake Chelan and are worth the nominal price difference compared to the smaller standard rooms. For families, kitchen unit 1 with two bedrooms, a living room, and kitchen is best, although some people might prefer the ambience of the A-frame unit. Keep in mind that few grocery items are available for sale at Stehekin, so you must bring food if you plan to use a kitchen. The Safeway store in Chelan will box and deliver groceries to the boat for customers who purchase goods the day before they are to depart for Stehekin.

Stehekin Landing Resort is a remote and interesting place to stay after a scenic boat trip up the lake. Settle into your room and then spend part of the afternoon exploring this small village that could well be in Alaska. After dinner at the restaurant, walk out to the dock or up the road and enjoy nature at its finest. A shuttle service is available to Stehekin Valley Ranch, which offers an alternative for dinner. One building at the landing houses a recreation room with a fireplace, a satellite television, a pool table, and exercise equipment. This is available as a conference room for retreats.

Stehekin Landing Resort serves as the center for Stehekin activities, including boat and bicycle rentals, snowshoe rental in the winter, bus tours, and hikes. Buses for tours of the valley leave from the resort.

Rooms: Doubles, triples, quads, with a few kitchen units sleeping up to seven. The Lake House can accommodate up to twelve.

Wheelchair Accessibility: Two units at the lodge are wheelchair accessible. One lakeview room has a large bathroom with a wide doorway. The room has one queen, and the bathroom has grab bars by the toilet and in the combination shower-tub. The freestanding kitchen unit has ramp access and an extra-wide doorway to both the cabin and the large bathroom, which has grab bars by the toilet and in the combination shower-tub. An electric lift on the dock provides wheelchair access to the store, restaurant, and rooms.

Reservations: Stehekin Landing Resort, P.O. Box 3, Stehekin, WA 98852. Call (509) 682-4494. Payment in full is required to book a reservation. Cancellation of sleeping units requires fourteen days' notice. Cancellation of the kitchen units and the Lake House requires thirty days' notice.

Rates: Standard rooms ($119); lakeview rooms ($134–$159); kitchen units ($159–$179); Lake House ($329). Rates quoted are for two persons with the exception of the Lake House, for which the rate is for four persons. Each additional adult is $10 per night. Rates for children six through eleven are an additional $5.00 per night. Children under six stay free. Kitchen units and the Lake House require a two-night minimum. For stays of three or four nights, rates are reduced by 10 percent; for stays of five or more nights, rates are reduced by 20 percent. Reduced rates of $30–$40 per room and $80 for the Lake House per night are offered from October 16 to June 14, excluding all major holidays. Special fall, winter, and spring packages are offered along with a Hiker's Special. Check the Web site at www.stehekinlanding.com for more information.

Location: The north end of Lake Chelan next to the Stehekin boat dock.

Season: The resort is open all year, although services, lodging, and facilities are fully operational only from mid-May to mid-October. Only the six kitchen units and Lake House are open year-round. Restaurant hours are reduced, or the restaurant is closed, at various times during fall, winter, and spring. Check with the resort about specific dates.

Food: An adjacent restaurant offers breakfast ($7.00–$10.00), lunch ($10.00–$15.00), and dinner ($20.00–$25.00). Dinner reservations are required. Beer and wine are served. A children's menu is available. A small store sells milk, chips, beer, and wine. The Valley Shuttle offers transportation to Stehekin Valley Ranch, which is open for dinner.

Transportation: Major airports are in Seattle and Spokane, Washington, where rental cars are available. The resort is reached from Chelan only via boat or floatplane.

Facilities: Dining room, recreation room, convenience store, craft store, post office, laundry, National Park Service visitor center, marina, boat and bicycle rentals. Snowshoe rentals in winter.

Activities: Hiking, fishing, boating, cycling.

Stehekin Valley Ranch

P.O. Box 36 • Stehekin, WA 98852 • (800) 536-0745 • www.courtneycountry.com

Stehekin Valley Ranch is an isolated lodging complex that includes a two-story dining hall, fourteen wooden cabins, a corral, and a small sporting goods shop. The buildings sit in a grove of maple trees next to a large pasture and are surrounded by mountains. The cabins are a short walk from the dining hall, which includes a small registration/gift shop area, a loft reading room, separate men's and women's bathhouses, and an attractive log-beamed dining area with three massive picnic tables and a wood stove. The location offers outstanding views and access to excellent hiking, rafting, and fishing in a restful and friendly atmosphere. Three meals a day, including an excellent dinner, are included in the price of a room, with the exception of the two kitchenette cabins. There are no televisions or telephones, and cell phones do not work at the ranch. Stehekin Valley Ranch is 9 miles north of the public boat dock at Stehekin and is reached via a free shuttle from the dock.

Lodging at the ranch is in three types of cabins. Seven older cabins, constructed in 1983, are wood sided with heavy canvas roofs. These tent cabins have cement floors, screens, and canvas shades (no glass) as window coverings, unfinished interiors, and no heat, electricity, or running water. The seven differ in size, with cabin 5 with one double bed being smallest and cabins 1 and 2 being largest and each having a double bed plus three twin beds. The other four canvas-covered cabins each have either a double plus two twins or a queen plus one twin. Community bathroom facilities including shower rooms are on the first floor of the main building, a short walk from all the cabins. A kerosene lantern in each cabin provides the only artificial source of light, so bring a flashlight if you will be staying in one of these cabins. Despite the rustic appearance, these units are clean and comfortable, and the choice of many regular guests. Five of the seven cabins (cabins 1 though 5) are directly beside the pasture and provide excellent mountain views. Cabins 11 and 12 are higher on the hill with views obstructed by other cabins.

Five larger wooden cabins with metal roofs were constructed in the mid-1990s. Each of these cabins has a painted cement floor, an unfinished interior, and a large front porch with chairs. Sliding windows with screens are on the front and two sides of the buildings. These cabins also have electric lights, an electrical outlet in the bathroom, and a private bathroom with a shower, but they do not have heat. Three of these cabins have one queen-size plus two twin beds. Cabins 9 and 10 are newer and larger with a loft bedroom that has two twin beds, while the downstairs has a futon and queen-size bed. The five newer metal-roofed cabins are larger, brighter, and more comfortable than the older canvas-covered cabins. However, they are situatedbehind five of the canvas-roofed cabins, which block their view of the pasture and mountains.

Two kitchenette cabins built in 2006 allow guests the option of preparing their own meals. These units, similar in size to the smaller metal-roofed cabins, have finished interiors, one queen bed, a futon, a private bathroom, and a kitchenette with a sink, propane stove, a small refrigerator, cookware, and tableware. A vehicle is provided for guests (pay only for fuel used). Meals are not included in the price of these two cabins, although guests can pay extra and eat in the dining hall. Remember: If you plan to cook, you will need to bring your own food, as there is no grocery store in Stehekin.

The choice of a cabin depends in large part on whether you want a private bathroom. The five metal-roofed cabins cost about $10 per person more per day but offer more interior space and a private bathroom and are likely to be more comfortable in cool or rainy weather. On the other hand, the canvas-covered cabins may offer more of the ambience you seek from this type of vacation. The dining hall and loft reading room are always open to play cards, converse with other guests, or read. If you want to cook for yourself and prefer the

Hugh Courtney, grandfather of the current owners of Stehekin Valley Ranch, homesteaded fifty-two acres in the Stehekin area in 1916. One of his sons, Ray, purchased the twenty-acre dairy farm where the ranch is currently located and started a successful pack trip business. Six of Ray's children are currently involved in a variety of businesses, including the operation of the ranch. The present lodging operation commenced in 1983 with the construction of the main building and canvas-roofed cabins. Stehekin Valley Ranch is on private land that is surrounded by Lake Chelan National Recreation Area.

convenience of your own transportation, select a kitchenette cabin.

Stehekin Valley Ranch is a place with lots of outdoor activities, including river rafting, kayaking, horseback riding, mountain biking, fishing, and hiking. Three-hour trail rides leave each morning and afternoon from the nearby corral. Riding lessons are offered to anyone six years and older. Mountain bikes are available for rent. Guests at Stehekin Valley Ranch enjoy free use of the shuttle that connects Stehekin Landing with the ranch. The shuttle also stops at the bakery and Rainbow Falls. Hiking trails begin at High Bridge, which is on the route of the Pacific Crest Trail.

The dining room, with three large dining tables, provides a great atmosphere for talking with other guests as you enjoy exceptional meals of fish, chicken, and steak. Best of all are the homemade pies served each evening. After dinner relax on the porch outside the dining room or walk up the stairs to a small loft reading room. Guests sometimes linger in the dining room to chat, read, or play board games.

Rooms: Fourteen individual cabins, most of which sleep up to four people. Two larger cabins can sleep up to six. Seven canvas-roofed cabins have no private bath. Seven cabins, two with a kitchenette, have a private bath with shower.

Wheelchair Accessibility: None of the cabins is wheelchair accessible.

Reservations: Write P.O. Box 36, Stehekin, WA 98852. Call (800) 536-0745. A deposit of 50 percent of the total is required at the time the reservation is made. Cancellation must be made in writing at least twenty-one days prior to reservation date in order to receive a 75 percent refund. No refunds for later cancellations.

Rates: Canvas-covered cabins ($85 per adult, $65 per child ages four to twelve, $25 per child ages one to three); cabins with bath (two adult minimum, $95 per adult, $75 per child age four to twelve, $30 per child age one to three); cabins with bath and kitchenette ($150 per night for one or two persons). Discounts are available for stays of three or more nights. Meals are included for all cabins except the two with kitchenettes. Packages that include a variety of activities such as rafting and horseback riding are available.

Location: Nine miles north of Stehekin Landing. A free shuttle for guests of the ranch operates four round-trips daily between Stehekin Landing and the ranch.

Season: Mid-June to early October.

Food: Three meals a day are included in the price of the room. Breakfast includes meat, eggs, pancakes, French toast, oatmeal, and fruit, among other items. Lunch choices include hamburgers, soup, and the makings for cold-meat sandwiches. Guests can make sack lunches after breakfast. The dinner is outstanding, with a choice of steak, chicken, fish, and a daily special. The homemade pie for dessert is world class. Vegetarian meals are available. Alcoholic beverages are not available, but guests may bring their own. For those with a kitchenette, groceries purchased at the Chelan Safeway store the day before your Stehekin departure will be boxed and delivered to the appropriate boat.

Transportation: Major airports are in Seattle and Spokane, Washington, where rental cars are available. Scheduled boat service is available to Stehekin Landing from Chelan. Floatplanes are available at Chelan. A valley shuttle system operates every three hours beginning at 8:15 a.m. between Stehekin Landing and Stehekin Valley Ranch. The shuttle also stops at the bakery and other points along the road.

Facilities: Dining room, small gift shop, outdoor store, reading room, bicycle rental.

Activities: Fishing, hiking, river rafting, kayaking, trail rides, riding lessons, ultralight backpacking and gear classes, mountain trips, bicycling, volleyball, horseshoes.

Ross Lake Resort

503 Diablo Street • Rockport, WA 98283 • (206) 386-4437 • www.rosslakeresort.com

Ross Lake Resort, one of the most unusual lodging facilities in a national park, consists of a row of floating cabins, bunkhouses, and support buildings along the shoreline of 22-mile-long Ross Lake. The rustic looking, shake-sided cabins and bunkhouses are constructed on wooden docks attached to huge cedar logs that float on the water and are cabled to shore. The floating base allows the cabins to rise and fall with the water level of the lake.

Ross Lake Resort caters to people who love to fish, boat, hike, and just relax. The resort also includes an office, small marina area, and associated outbuildings. It is located in a wild and beautiful area, so don't be surprised if the resort owner scares off an inquisitive black bear that has walked out of the woods behind the cabins. Guests do not have access to television, radio, or the Internet, and even your cell phone will be out of range. The isolation alone makes the resort a refreshing place to visit. The lake and mountain views from large windows along the front of each cabin make it even better.

The resort is located at the base of Ross Lake, a short distance up from Ross Dam. Access is via Washington Highway 20, which bisects North Cascades National Park Complex. Guests must either hike 2 miles to a boat-pick-up point across from the resort or utilize scheduled transportation by ferry/flatbed truck / speedboat to reach the resort. Keep in mind that guests MUST BRING ALL THEIR OWN FOOD BECAUSE NO FOOD SERVICE OF ANY KIND IS AVAILABLE AT OR NEAR THE RESORT.

Four classes of accommodations are offered at Ross Lake Resort: Private Bunkhouse rooms, Little Cabins, Modern Cabins, and Peak Cabins. All have woodstove or electric heat, private bathrooms, and kitchens with pots, pans, plates, utensils, a microwave, a coffeemaker, and a toaster. The cabins with woodstoves have plenty of firewood and an axe. Two Adirondack chairs in which to relax and enjoy the fantastic view of the lake and mountains are in front of or beside each cabin. Several gas grills are near the cabins.

Ross Lake Resort evolved from numerous floating cabins that were built on the lake to house workers engaged in logging and the construction of nearby Ross Dam. The dam was completed in 1949, and the power station was added several years later. Although the current cabins are modern, an adventurous atmosphere remains for resort guests.

The three Private Bunkhouse rooms were built in 1982 and are reproductions of the bunkhouses used by the dam construction crews. Each unit consists of one large room with four bunk beds (eight total beds), a large table with chairs, and a woodstove. The kitchen area includes an electric stove and oven and a full-size refrigerator. These are typically rented to large families or groups of six or more who come to fish.

The two Little Cabins, constructed as a duplex, both have a bunk bed plus a queen bed in an area separate from the kitchen that includes a stove, oven, small refrigerator, woodstove, and table with chairs. These are nicely done and the smallest and least expensive of the three types of cabins.

The eight Modern Cabins were constructed over a ten-year period, with the last unit completed in 1971. All have since been remodeled. Each cabin has an open front room with a kitchen area that includes a stove, oven, a full-size refrigerator, and a large table with six padded chairs. Six of the eight Modern Cabins have two single beds and a woodstove in the front room, while the other two have electric heat (rather than a woodstove) and three single beds. (Remember to specify your wishes when making reservations if a woodstove is an important part of your vacation enjoyment.) There is a bunk bed in a very small bedroom between the front room and the bathroom. This area is handy luggage storage for couples who sleep in the front room.

The most expensive accommodations are the two Peak Cabins constructed in 1996. These large, two-story cabins have electric heat plus a woodstove. They are the only accommodations with a complete kitchen, including a dishwasher, and a full-size bathroom with a combination shower-tub. The front room has a sofa bed, a cushioned chair, and a large table with chairs. A small bedroom off the front room includes a single bed and a bunk bed. The loft area, a major attraction for many guests, includes a queen bed, two single beds, and a cushioned chair.

Ross Lake Resort is in as beautiful a setting as you will find in any national park. Guests typically spend most of their stay boating, fishing, hiking, and reading. There are few distractions to keep you from enjoying a relaxing lifestyle. Sit in front of your cabin sipping a desired beverage, reading a book by your favorite author, and taking in mountain views across the lake. It is best to visit when you can stay for several days, because transportation to and from the resort is limited to twice a day in each direction. You are unlikely to enjoy much relaxation if you arrive at 4:00 p.m. one afternoon and leave at 8:30 a.m. the next morning. Even choosing the 2:30 p.m. departure doesn't allow sufficient time to appreciate this beautiful part of Washington.

Choosing among the four classes of accommodations is mostly determined by the number of people who will be included in your group. All of the accommodations, except the Bunkhouses, have large front windows that provide an outstanding view of the lake and mountains. The two Peak Cabins offer considerably more room and are situated at the far end of the row so that few other guests will be traipsing in front of your cabin. On the other hand, two people are easily accommodated in one of the Little Cabins, which are not only less expensive, but situated so that other guests must walk behind, rather than in front of, your cabin.

Rooms: The least expensive accommodations, the Little Cabins, offer bedding for up to four guests but are better suited

for a couple or a couple with one or two small children. The Modern Cabins can accommodate up to six people with the use of a rollaway bed but are more comfortable for two to four people. The Peak Cabins can accommodate up to nine people but are better suited for two couples or a couple with three or four children. Each Bunkhouse holds up to eight people, but they had better be good friends.

Wheelchair Accessibility: Each of the two Peak Cabins has a small ramp by the entry door, a large bathroom with a wide doorway, and grab bars in the bathtub. A tub-shower stool is available.

Reservations: Ross Lake Resort, 503 Diablo Street, Rockport, WA 98283. Phone (206) 386-4437. A required deposit is based on the cabin classification and number of nights requested. A cancellation notice of thirty days is required for a refund, less a $10 fee. A boat rental is required during weekends.

Rates: Private Bunkhouse ($188.00 for up to six people; $8.00 each additional person); Little Cabin ($122.00 for two people; $10.00 each additional person); Modern Cabin ($148.00 for two people; $10.00 each additional person); Peak Cabin ($261.00 for up to four people; $15.00 each additional person). Children three years and under stay free. Rates are reduced Sunday through Thursday during October with a boat rental.

Location: Approximately 130 miles northeast of Seattle, Washington, via Interstate 5 and WA 20. The resort sits directly on Ross Lake just above Ross Dam.

Season: Mid-June through the end of October.

Food: No stores or restaurants of any kind are at or near the resort. Visitors must carry in their own food and beverages. Candy, soft drinks, and ice are sold in the office.

Transportation: The nearest major airport is in Seattle, where rental cars are available. The resort is not accessible by road. Seattle City Light provides ferry service (fee) from near Diablo Dam just off WA 20 to a dock at the end of Diablo Lake. From there Ross Lake Resort operates a truck (fee) to the resort's speedboat that delivers guests to the appropriate cabins.

Facilities: Canoes, single and double kayaks, and 14-foot motorboats are available for rent. A fuel barge and limited repair facilities are at the marina. A small paperback lending library is in the office.

Activities: Hiking, fishing, boating. Fishing licenses are sold at the office. Fishing gear is available for rent.

Olympic National Park

600 East Park Avenue • Port Angeles, WA 98362 • (360) 565-3130
www.nps.gov/olym/home.htm

Olympic National Park covers 1,442 square miles of mountain wilderness and includes active glaciers, 57 miles of scenic ocean shore, and the finest remnant of Pacific Northwest rain forest. The strip of the park along the Pacific Ocean includes some of the most primitive coastline in the continental United States. Olympic National Park is composed of two sections, located in the northwest corner of Washington. Main access is via U.S. Highway 101, although roads penetrate only the perimeter of the park. **Park Entrance Fee:** $15.00 per vehicle or $5.00 per person, good for seven days.

Lodging in Olympic National Park: The park has four facilities with overnight accommodations. Kalaloch Lodge is located directly on the coast and perfect for beach walkers. Sol Duc Hot Springs Resort is an inviting destination for those who want to spend time relaxing in a hot mineral pool. Lake Crescent Lodge and Log Cabin Resort are situated on the northern edge of the park in heavily wooded areas on opposite sides of beautiful Lake Crescent. We have also included charming Lake Quinault Lodge, which is across Lake Quinault from the park's southern boundary.

KALALOCH LODGE

157151 Washington Highway 101 • Forks, WA 98331 • (360) 962-2271 or (866) 525-2562
www.visitkalaloch.com

Kalaloch Lodge is a complex of wooden buildings that includes a main lodge, numerous cabins, a motel-style unit, and a store, all situated on a bluff overlooking the Pacific Ocean. Only a few overnight rooms are in the main lodge building, whose gift shop includes the registration desk for all rooms in the complex. This building also houses the restaurant. All of the cabins and other lodging units are adjacent to and within easy walking

Olympic National Park

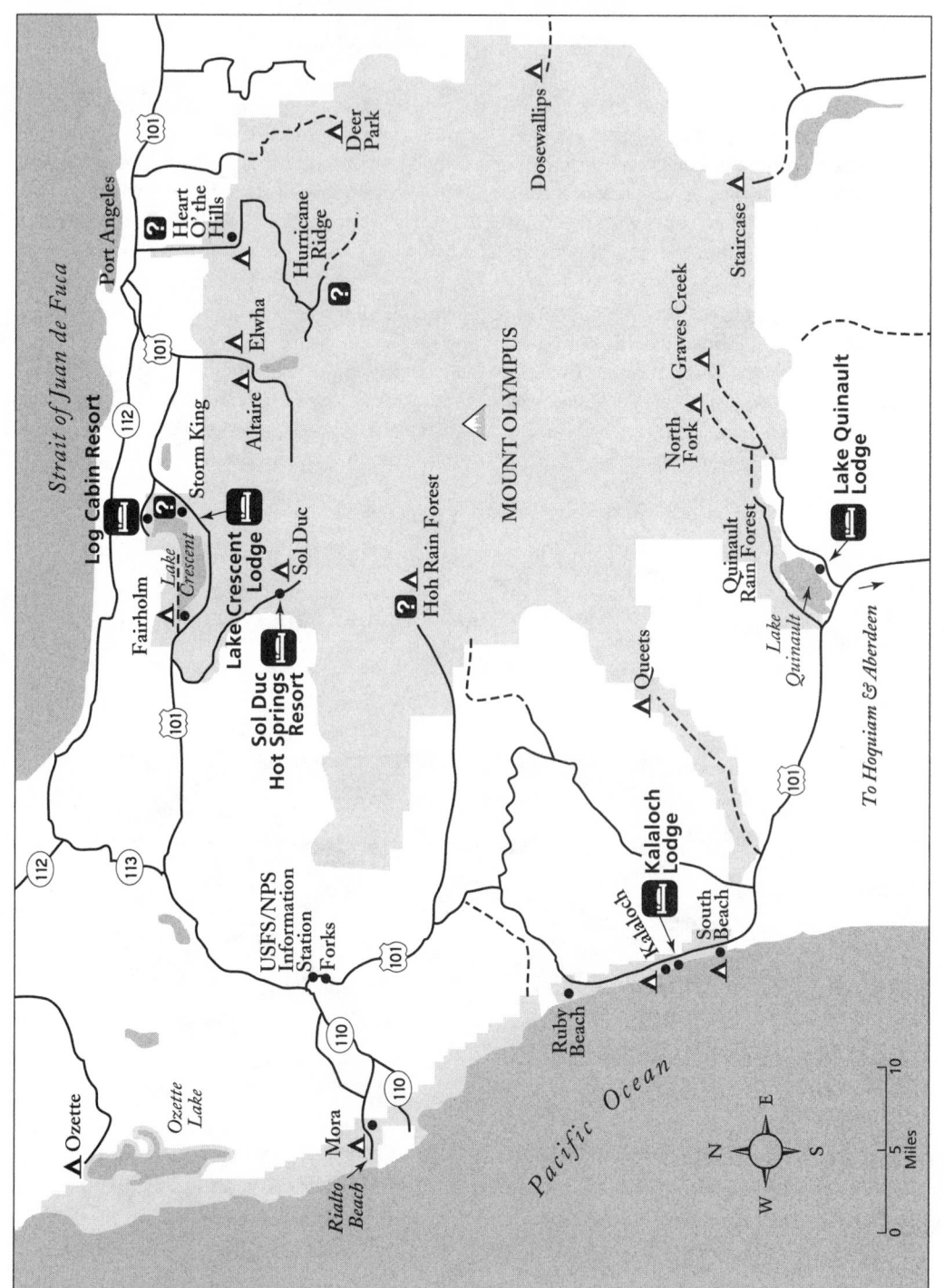

distance of the main lodge. Kalaloch Lodge is located on US 101, 35 miles south of Forks, Washington. The lodge is 95 miles southwest of Port Angeles, Washington.

The lodge offers a total of sixty-four guest rooms in four categories, all of which have a coffeemaker, hair dryer, electric heat, and private bath, but no telephone, air-conditioning, or television (except for suites in the main lodge). The main lodge building has ten guest rooms, including two suites. All but one of the rooms are on the second floor and accessed from a central hallway reached from the lobby stairway. There is no elevator. These rooms each have a bath with a shower but no tub. Room size varies, with five rooms having one queen-size bed and other rooms having up to one queen plus one double and two single beds. Each of the suites has a combination living room–bedroom with one king-size bed and a sofa bed. Becker's Suite, which has a fireplace, is only rented as a suite during the summer months; during the remainder of the year, it becomes a library/reading room for lodge guests. Rooms 1 (on the first floor), 6, 7, and 8 and the suites provide an ocean view. Rooms 5 and 9, with one queen, one double, and two single beds each, are quite large but located above the kitchen and can be noisy. Five rooms, including 5 and 9, can only be rented on-site.

The two-story Seacrest House has six regular rooms, plus four suites. This building sits behind two bluff cabins. The six regular motel-style rooms are very spacious with two queen-size beds and a private bath that includes a shower but no tub. Each room enjoys its own covered patio or balcony and large windows that face the ocean but do not provide an ocean view. Three suites have a sitting room with a fireplace (wood provided) and two separate bedrooms with one double and one queen-size bed plus a sofa bed. One bedroom and the sitting room have large windows. The fourth suite is one large room with a fireplace, a queen bed, and a futon.

Twenty Bluff cabins, each with cedar siding, vaulted ceilings, and tile floors, have covered back porches

The current Kalaloch Lodge sits on the site of an earlier lodging facility constructed in the late 1920s by Charles Becker, who had acquired forty acres just south of Kalaloch Creek. Becker's operation included a home, lodge, and several frame cabins constructed on the bluff overlooking the ocean. Additional cabins were constructed between 1934 and 1936 following completion of US 101. The owner added more cabins and relocated some of the existing cabins back from the bluff following World War II, during which the resort was occupied by the U.S. Coast Guard. Between 1950 and 1954 Becker erected a new main lodge building that remains in use today. In 1978 the National Park Service purchased the Becker operation and renamed it Kalaloch Lodge. Within four years a new concessionaire had completed construction of twenty-two log cabins that have become a major part of the current operation. ARAMARK Corporation won the contract to manage Kalaloch Lodge in 1989.

offering an excellent ocean view. Approximately half these cabins have a single room with two queen beds or one queen bed plus a futon. The remainder each have either one or two separate bedrooms with bedding that can sleep from six to eight persons. All but six of the Bluff cabins have kitchens with a sink, a stove, a refrigerator, an oven, pots, pans, and utensils. When reserving a Bluff cabin keep in mind that some have a woodstove or fireplace, some have a kitchen, and the larger units have both.

Sitting directly behind the bluff cabins are twenty-four log cabins with exteriors that have been sided with cedar and interiors that retain exposed log walls. These are comfortable cabins with tiled floors, vaulted ceilings, a woodstove (small bundle of wood provided), and a kitchen with a refrigerator, stove, sink, and table with four chairs. The kitchens were totally renovated in 2008. Most of these cabins have one bedroom with a queen bed plus another queen bed in a separate living area that also has a futon. One large log cabin has two bedrooms, each with a queen bed plus a living room with a sofa bed. . Although these cabins sit back from the bluff, cabins 24 through 27 provide an ocean view when standing by the front windows. Parking is directly in front of or beside each cabin.

Kalaloch Lodge is for people who want to experience the sounds, smell, and wildness of the Pacific Ocean. Guests can enjoy the roar of the sea as they walk the beach or read a book. A wide sandy beach just below the bluff is reached via a set of steps that begins near the Bluff cabins. The ocean water is relatively cold with potentially dangerous riptides, so you probably won't want to swim, but strolls along the beach are one of the pleasures of staying at Kalaloch. Consider bringing a kite because the ocean breeze makes this a perfect place to hone a skill you probably last used many years ago. National Park Service rangers lead daily walks along the beach and to various points in the park during the summer months. The lodge restaurant has large windows that allow diners to gaze at the ocean. Keep in mind that this coastal area is generally breezy and can become quite foggy, so be prepared for the likelihood of winds, mist, and chilly weather that are all part of the experience of a visit to the Pacific Northwest.

Rooms: Doubles, triples, and quads. Several cabins can hold more than four persons. All accommodations have a private bath, most with a shower but no tub.

Wheelchair Accessibility: Two Bluff cabins and one log cabin are ADA compliant. A ramp at the main lodge building provides wheelchair access to the restaurant.

Reservations: Kalaloch Lodge, 157151 U.S. Highway 101, Forks, WA 98331-9396. Phone (866) 525-2562 or (360) 962-2271; www.visitkalaloch.com. A deposit of one night's stay is required. A cancellation notice of seventy-two hours is required for a refund less a $15 fee.

Rates: Two sets of rates apply to all rooms; peak rates are from late May through early October, plus all weekends and holidays. Off-peak rates are 25 to 50 percent less, but not applicable to Bluff cabins. Lodge rooms ($164); lodge suites ($296); Seacrest House regular rooms ($165); Seacrest suites ($186); Bluff cabins ($205–$299, depending on size); log cabins ($181–$202, depending on size). Rates quoted are for two persons. Each additional person is $15 per night. Rollaways are $10 per night. Children five years old and under stay free.

Location: Directly on the Pacific Ocean, 35 miles south of Forks, Washington, on US 101.

Season: Kalaloch Lodge is open year-round.

Food: A restaurant serves breakfast ($5.00–$15.00), lunch ($9.00–$13.00), and dinner ($12.00–$26.00). Dinner reservations are required. Alcoholic beverages are served. A children's menu is available. Limited groceries including beer and wine can be purchased at the store adjacent to the main lodge building.

Transportation: The nearest major city with scheduled air and train service is Olympia, Washington, where rental cars are available.

Facilities: Restaurant, gift shop, gas station, and small store. A National Park Service visitor center is a short distance down US101.

Activities: Hiking, beachcombing, whale watching, kite flying, surf fishing. Ranger-guided walks are offered each day during summer months.

Pets: Pets are allowed in cabins only for $15 per pet, pet night.

LAKE CRESCENT LODGE

416 Lake Crescent Road • Port Angeles, WA 98363 • (360) 928-3211
www.lakecrescentlodge.com

Lake Crescent Lodge comprises a classic lodge building flanked at each end by cottages and one- and two-story motel structures. The main lodge, constructed in 1916 as the Singer Tavern, has only five overnight rooms, all upstairs and without a private bath. All other accommodations are separate but near the main lodge. The entire complex is situated on the south shore of scenic Lake Crescent among giant hemlock and fir trees in the shadow of Mount Storm King. Registration for all lodging at Lake Crescent Lodge is just inside the door of the main building in the lobby area highlighted by a huge stone fireplace. A gift shop, a restaurant, a lobby bar, and an inviting sunroom are also on the main floor of the same building. Virtually all the accommodations, including the cottages, offer a view of Lake Crescent. Lake Crescent Lodge is located 21 miles west of Port Angeles, Washington, just off US 101.

The lodge offers several types of accommodations, including lodge rooms, cottages, and motel-type units.

All rooms have a hair dryer, a coffeemaker, and heat but no air-conditioning, television, or telephone. All rooms except those in the main lodge have a private bath. Pets are permitted only in the Roosevelt Fireplace Cottages and the Singer Tavern Cottages. Parking is convenient to all the rooms. The least expensive accommodations are the five relatively small but attractive rooms on the second floor of the main lodge building. These rooms are entered from an interior hallway via a lobby stairway. All have a double bed and an in-room sink, but no private bathroom. Two shower rooms and two small bathrooms are in the hallway. All five rooms are on the west side of the building and offer a terrific view of Lake Crescent and the mountains on the opposite shore.

Four Roosevelt Fireplace Cottages, two with one room and the other two with a living room plus a bedroom, were constructed from 1945 to 1947. These units are quite nice, with hardwood floors, wood interiors, a small refrigerator, a microwave, and a stone

Lake Crescent Lodge was completed in 1916 and initially called Singer's Lake Crescent Tavern after owner Avery Singer. The current enclosed porch facing the lake was originally part of a long veranda that wrapped around the north and west faces of the building. The gift shop occupies the former dining room. Singer built a row of sixteen cabins the same year and subsequently added a row of frame tents that were later converted to cabins. Lodge guests arrived via boat until 1922, when the road from Port Angeles was extended along the south shore of the lake. The sunroom has a photo of the original lodge, which Singer sold in 1927. Lake Crescent Lodge has hosted luminaries such as Henry Ford, Frank Sinatra, William O. Douglas, Robert Kennedy, and, of course, President Franklin D. Roosevelt.

fireplace (wood provided). All four cottages are on the shore of Lake Crescent and at the opposite end of the main lodge building from the other cabins and motor lodge buildings, a location that provides more privacy and quiet than other accommodations in the complex. These are the most expensive and by far the most desirable accommodations at Lake Crescent. With only four units available, they are also difficult to reserve and often booked several years in advance. The two one-room Roosevelt Fireplace units are in a duplex wood-frame building. They each have two queen beds. The two cottages with two rooms are freestanding and have one queen in the living area and two double beds in the bedroom.

Thirteen one- and two-bedroom Singer Tavern Cottages are constructed two or three units to a building. The cottages retain the scale and historic character

of the original cabins that were torn down in the 1980s. Each shake-sided cottage has a covered porch with chairs, and all but one (cottage 19) offer a good porch view of Lake Crescent. The cottages sit side-by-side in a large grassy area adjacent to the main lodge building. These cottages have large interiors with hardwood floors. The bathrooms, with a combination shower-tub, are quite nice. Ten of the cottages are one-bedroom units with either one or two queen beds. The three two-bedroom cottages with one bathroom have two queen beds in one room and a queen plus a twin bed in the other room. The two-bedroom units provide double the space but don't cost a great deal more than those with one bedroom. Singer Tavern Cottages 20 and 21 sit closest to the lake and to the parking lot but can suffer from the noise of substantial pedestrian traffic as guests walk between the lodge and parking lot or hiking trails. Cottage 5 is nearest to the main lodge but backs up to a parking area.

Three separate buildings house motor lodge rooms. The Marymere Lodge is a one-story motel-type, cement-block-and-wood-frame building with ten rooms that each have large front and back windows. This building was constructed in 1959 and has direct access to the lake and provides excellent lake views. A covered porch with chairs runs across the lake side of the building. Each room is relatively large and has two queen beds and a tiled bath with a combination shower-tub.

The two-story wood-frame Storm King Motor Lodge, built in 1962, is situated among trees back from the lake, but its ten rooms each provide relatively good lake views. The rooms are fairly small, and each has a queen bed, balcony or patio with chairs, and private bath with a tiled shower. Two-story Pyramid Mountain Lodge, constructed in 1991, offers the newest accommodations in the complex. This attractive wooden building sits among trees back from the lake. Each of its ten rooms has a covered balcony or patio that looks out over a grassy area leading to Lake Crescent. The rooms each have two queen beds and a tiled bathroom with a combination shower-tub. Rooms on the top floor have vaulted ceilings. A railing across second-floor balconies obscures views when sitting, so try for a ground-floor room if you choose this building.

The five second-floor rooms in the main lodge offer the best value if you don't mind using a community bathroom. The two community bathrooms and showers are certainly adequate for guests staying in the five rooms, which have no more than two occupants each. Lodge rooms are relatively small, but the front windows offer picture-postcard views of one of the country's most beautiful lakes. Plus, there seems to be a more intimate park experience when staying in the main building of a national park lodge. The Roosevelt Fireplace Cottages are by far the nicest accommodations and worth the extra cost per night compared to the Singer Tavern Cottages. Among the motor lodge units we would choose Marymere, where you can view the lake from your bed.

A visit to Lake Crescent Lodge will almost certainly be an enjoyable experience no matter which accommodation you choose. The lodge offers a laid-back atmosphere in a picturesque setting and is one of our favorite places to stay. Arrive early in the afternoon so that you can spend time relaxing in an Adirondack chair on the grassy lawn beside the lake. Here you can read a book or visit with friends or other guests while stealing glances at boaters on the lake. If you need to expend some energy, rent a rowboat and view the lodge and surrounding mountains from a different perspective. Or perhaps you would rather hike one of the nearby trails and stand in awe of giant Douglas firs that grow in the old-growth forest.

Rooms: Doubles, triples, and quads in most units. Some units hold up to seven persons. All rooms outside the main lodge building have private bathrooms.

Wheelchair Accessibility: One first-floor room at Pyramid Mountain Lodge is the only handicap-accessible room at Lake Crescent Lodge. This room has one queen bed and a large bathroom with a wide doorway and a combination shower-tub with grab bars. A paved path leads to the room from wheelchair parking that is some distance away.

Reservations: Lake Crescent Lodge, 416 Lake Crescent Road, Port Angeles, WA 98363-8672. Phone (360) 928-3211, ext. 10. A deposit of one night's stay is required. Cancellation at least seven days prior to scheduled arrival is required for a refund less a $15 fee. Reservation modifications also incur a $15 fee.

Rates: Summer season (late May through late September plus all weekends and holidays)/value season (remainder of the year): Historic lodge rooms ($99/$68); Singer Tavern Cottages: one-room ($180/$132); two-room ($213/$156); Roosevelt Fireplace Cottages: one-room ($222/$163); two-room ($231/$169); Pyramid Motor Lodge ($158/$116); Storm King Motor Lodge ($145/$106); Marymere ($150/$110). Rates quoted are for two persons. Rollaways, cribs, and additional persons are $15 extra per night. Children under six years of age stay free.

Location: Twenty-one miles west of Port Angeles, Washington, on US 101.

Season: The lodge is open year-round. Only Roosevelt Fireplace Cottages and Singer Tavern Cottages are open from late September to early May.

Food: An attractive dining room on the main floor serves breakfast ($7.00–$11.00), lunch ($9.00–$19.00), and dinner ($13.00– $34.00) from late May through late September. The lounge serves soups, salads, burgers, and fish and chips. Alcoholic beverages are available in both the lounge and dining room.

Transportation: Scheduled airline service is in Port Angeles, Washington, where rental cars are available. A Port Angeles bus provides daily service to the lodge during the summer.

Facilities: Boat rental, restaurant, lobby bar, swimming beach, dock, gift shop.

Activities: Swimming, hiking, boating, fishing.

Pets: Pets are allowed only in the cottages for $15 per pet, per night.

LAKE QUINAULT LODGE

P.O. Box 7 • Quinault, WA 98575 • (360) 288-2900 • www.visitlakequinault.com

Lake Quinault Lodge is a complex of six shake-covered buildings, including a picturesque two-story main lodge that houses the registration desk/gift shop, dining room, lobby area, indoor heated swimming pool, and men's and women's dry saunas. The main lodge has guest rooms on both floors, but most rooms are in five buildings on either side of the main lodge building. The lodge is in the middle of a rain forest, on a hill overlooking the south shore of Lake Quinault. The beautiful setting includes attractive landscaping, eighty-year-old redwood trees, and a wide lawn that flows from the back of the lodge to the lake. Lake Quinault Lodge is on South Shore Road, 2 miles east of US 101. The turnoff from US 101 is 40 miles north of the town of Hoquiam. The lodge is in Olympic National Forest, across the lake from Olympic National Park. We have included this lodge because of its proximity to the park and the fact that the same concessionaire operates two nearby lodges in Olympic National Park.

Lake Quinault Lodge offers a total of ninety-one rooms in four classifications. All rooms have a coffeemaker, a hair dryer, heat, and a private bathroom, but no air-conditioning or telephone. Televisions are only in the Lakeside and Fireplace units. None of the buildings has an elevator. The main lodge was constructed in 1926 and has thirty guest rooms. Rooms in the main lodge differ in view and configuration but are generally smaller than rooms in the five other buildings. Lodge rooms have ceiling fans and beds that vary from one queen to one king to two double beds. About half the rooms offer a lake view and rent for approximately $20 extra per night compared to rooms on the opposite side that face the road and front drive. Rooms 102, 104, and 106 on the front side have windows that face a nearby roof and offer absolutely no views. You may also want to avoid room 206, which is above the kitchen and can be noisy. This room is generally rented only to walk-ins, who are informed of the potential problem. Many returning guests request corner rooms 107 or 223, with two windows and a lake view.. Several other rooms in the main lodge, all of which were totally refurbished in 2008 to 2009, offer excellent views of the lake.

Adjacent to the main lodge, the Boathouse, constructed in 1923 and the only remaining original building, offers nine rooms that vary in size and view. Rooms in the Boathouse are paneled in pine and were refurbished in 2002. Beds vary from one queen to two queens plus a twin-size futon. This rectangular wooden building with rooms on all four sides has a large covered porch around three sides and is reminiscent of a western bunkhouse. Each room has a private bathroom with a shower but no tub. Room 304, with a lake view, is particularly large, with two queen beds, a twin futon, and a table with four chairs. Room 308, on the back side, has a partition that separates a bedroom from the sitting area that has a queen sofa sleeper. One suite (room 309) on the second floor of the Boathouse has a large sitting room with a kitchen area that includes a small refrigerator and a sink along with a dining table and four chairs. A separate bedroom has a king bed, and two rollaways are available. A large bathroom has a shower but no tub. The Boathouse is the only building at Lake Quinault Lodge in which pets are permitted. This is a positive if you have a pet, but can be a negative if your neighbor has a barking dog.

At the other end of the main lodge building and connected by a covered walkway are two side-by-side wooden buildings that house sixteen Fireplace units. These attractive two-story buildings were constructed in 1972 and refurbished in 2007– to 2008. The Fireplace units are the most expensive and considered by most guests to be the nicest rooms at Lake Quinault Lodge. The rooms are quite large, and each contains a gas fireplace, a television, one king bed, and a full bath with a combination shower-tub. Fireplace units each have a large private balcony or patio facing the lake, but views from the first floor of both buildings tend to be obstructed by trees and bushes, giving guests the

The first log structure to accommodate travelers to Quinault was built in the 1890s. Another facility, Lakeside Inn, was constructed here in 1923. The inn eventually changed its name to The Annex (now the Boathouse) following the construction of Lake Quinault Lodge in 1926. Even though lumber, glass, fixtures, and furniture had to be hauled over 50 miles of dirt road, the lodge was completed at a cost of $90,000 in only fifty-three days. Guests can still view original stenciled designs on the beamed ceiling of the lobby. Lake Quinault Lodge's most famous guest was President Franklin D. Roosevelt, who visited here in 1937, one year before signing legislation that created Olympic National Park. He did not stay overnight at the lodge.

feeling of being in a private garden. Second-floor rooms 226 through 230 offer outstanding lake views. Parking is directly in front of the two buildings with Fireplace rooms. Try for a second-floor room if you don't mind climbing a flight of stairs. Among the ground floor Fireplace rooms, we like corner room 111, which offers a reasonably good lake view combined with some privacy provided by nearby bushes. Patio chairs can be pulled out to the surrounding grassy area.

On the far side of the Boathouse are two shake-sided modern-style buildings that house thirty-six Lakeside units. These three-story buildings were constructed in 1990, and the rooms were refurbished in 2006. The rooms are nicely furnished and spacious, although not quite as large as the Fireplace units. Most rooms have either two queen beds or a king bed plus a sofa bed, television, and small private balcony that faces the lake. These units are closest to the lake, although lake views from the windows and balconies are mostly blocked by nearby cedar and fir trees. Some Lakeside rooms have connecting doors. Noise can filter through the closed doors, however, so you may want to avoid rooms with connecting doors if you only require one room. Lakeside rooms are entered from an outside walkway on each floor, reached from either a stairway or a series of ramps. No elevator is in either Lakeside building, so a room on the third floor will require climbing two flights of stairs or toting luggage up an extended ramp system.

Lake Quinault Lodge offers a variety of activities in a scenic lake setting. The rustic lobby with its hardwood floor, large brick fireplace, comfortable furniture, and windows that overlook the lake is the focal point of the lodge. It is perfect for reading, playing board games or completing jigsaw puzzles, conversing with friends, or just enjoying the fireplace on a rainy day. When the weather clears, move out to a chair on the spacious back porch or lawn. Activities range from games such as badminton and bocce ball, to swimming in the lake or indoor pool, to kayaking. Sporting equipment can be borrowed from the lodge. The dining room has two walls of large windows that offer excellent lake views. A lobby bar sells coffee, espresso, beer, wine, cocktails, and other beverages. Across the road from the lodge, a country store sells general merchandise, sandwiches, and groceries. Next door is the Quinault Historical Society Museum. The thirty-minute loop drive around Lake Quinault offers excellent views of the rain forest and the possibility of an elk sighting.

Rooms: Doubles, triples, and quads. A few rooms sleep more than four. Each room has a private bath, with the majority having a combination shower-tub, although some rooms have either a bathtub or a shower, but not both.

Wheelchair Accessibility: Two first-floor lakeside rooms with one queen bed are ADA compliant. Ramp access at the front of the main lodge building provides wheelchair access to the registration area, restaurant, and lobby area.

Reservations: Lake Quinault Lodge, P.O. Box 7, Quinault, WA 98575-0007. Phone (800) 562-6672 or (360) 288-2900; www .visitlakequinault.com. First night's payment is required. A seventy-two-hour cancellation notice is required for full refund less a $15 cancellation fee.

Rates: Rates vary depending on day, season, and occupancy. Lakeside rooms ($130 –$175); Main Lodge lake view ($130–$174); Main Lodge woodside ($109–$158); Fireplace units ($150–$235); Boathouse lake view ($120–$160); Boathouse woodside ($90–$154); Boathouse suite ($195–$275). Rates quoted are for two adults; each additional person is $13. Children under five stay free. Check the Web site for special packages offered throughout the year.

Location: On the south shore of Lake Quinault, 2 miles east of US 101 on South Shore Road.

Season: The lodge is open year-round.

Food: The dining room serves breakfast ($8.00–$15.00), lunch ($7.00–$19.00), and dinner ($17.00–$42.00). Reservations are required for dinner. A service bar in the lobby offers drinks and appetizers during the afternoon. A general store across the road serves hamburgers, pizza, sandwiches, ice cream, and beverages including espresso and milk shakes. It also sells groceries, beer, and wine.

Transportation: The nearest scheduled air and rail service is in Seattle, where rental cars are available.

Facilities: Heated indoor pool; men's and women's dry saunas; recreation room; canoe, kayak, seacycle, and boat rentals; swimming beach; auditorium; dining room; service bar; gift shop; gas station; museum; general store. A U.S. Forest Service visitor center is next door.

Activities: Guided walks, canoeing, kayaking, seacycling, boating, badminton, bocce ball, croquet, horseshoes, and evening programs are popular during summer. Fishing, hiking, swimming, Ping-Pong, and board games are available year-round.

Pets: Pets are allowed only in the Boathouse at $25 per night, per pet.

Log Cabin Resort

3183 East Beach Road • Port Angeles, WA 98363 • (360) 928-3325 • www.logcabinresort.net

Log Cabin Resort is a complex of freestanding cabins and linked A-frame chalets scattered in front of and alongside a main lodge building that houses motel-type rooms. The one-story wooden main lodge, constructed in the 1950s, houses the registration desk, a restaurant, a cafe, a small store, and a lobby with lots of antiques. A parking lot is immediately in front of the lodge; other parking is near the chalets and cabins. Virtually all of the cabins and rooms offer excellent views of beautiful Lake Crescent and the mountains on the southern shore. Log Cabin Resort is located in the far northern section of Olympic National Park, on the north shore of Lake Crescent. It is 21 miles west of Port Angeles, Washington, 3.5 miles off US 101 on East Beach Road.

The resort offers four types of accommodations. All of the rooms have electric heat, but no air-conditioning, television, or telephone. No cooking or eating utensils are provided in any of the units with kitchens. The main lodge building has four attached motel-type

Log Cabin Resort is on the site of the former Log Hotel (also known as Log Cabin Hotel or Hotel Piedmont), the first hotel built on Lake Crescent. The two-story Log Hotel was constructed of peeled cedar logs and had an attached observation tower that was also built of logs. The hotel burned in 1932, and the present Log Cabin Resort was built in the early 1950s on the same site. A large photo of the old hotel is in the lobby of the resort.

rooms that each have one queen-size bed, one queen-size futon, a private bath with a shower but no tub, and a kitchen area with a sink, coffeemaker, microwave, and small refrigerator. The rooms are paneled and have a large back window that provides a view of Lake Crescent. A table and two chairs are beside the window and a back door that opens to a private patio with table and chairs. The rooms are entered through an outside door directly beside the parking lot.

Alongside the lodge along the shoreline are two buildings that each have six attached A-frame rooms with small lofts. The first floor of these rooms has a bathroom with a shower, double bed, futon, kitchen sink, coffeemaker, microwave, and refrigerator. A second double bed is in the loft reached via a stairway. Windows across the back allow good lake views. A cement patio across the back of both buildings has a picnic table and grill for each room.

Eight rustic cabins constructed in 1928, three with kitchens, are available in a variety of sizes, with several types of bedding that range upward from a double and a single bed. The cabins each have a private bath with either a shower or a tub. Each cabin has a covered front porch with chairs that allow guests a good view of the lake and mountains. The three cabins with kitchens each have a stove, oven, sink, coffeemaker, microwave, and refrigerator. Six of the cabins are arranged in a semicircle on a grassy hillside overlooking the lake. A picnic table is in front of each cabin. The least expensive accommodation at Log Cabin Resort is one of four camping log cabins with electricity but no plumbing. Each cabin has two double beds, but guests are required to provide their own bedding or it can be rented. Outside each cabin are a picnic table and fire barrel. A community bathroom with showers is located just behind the cabins.

Log Cabin Resort is a good choice for families who enjoy water-based activities in a magnificent mountain and lake setting. Guests have plenty to do, with a roped lake swimming area just beside the lodge, boat rentals (canoes, paddleboats, kayaks, and rowboats), and fishing. Guests can often be seen reading a book in the grassy area beside the lake. A 4-mile-long trail along an old railroad bed beside the lake passes by the resort. A nicely decorated restaurant has a wall of windows that offers diners excellent views of the lake. A patio area directly behind the main lodge is available for outside dining.

Rooms: Singles, doubles, triples, and quads. The A-frame chalets and some of the cabins can hold up to six persons.

Wheelchair Accessibility: No wheelchair-accessible rooms are available at the resort.

Reservations: 3183 East Beach Road, Port Angeles, WA 98363. Phone (360) 928-3325; fax (360) 928-2088. A deposit of one night's stay is required. A cancellation notice of seven days is required for a full refund less a $10 fee.

Rates: Lodge rooms ($114); A-frame chalet ($145); cabins ($89–$103); camping log cabins ($55). Rates quoted are for two adults. Each additional person is $12.50 per night in all lodging, with the exception of the camping cabins, where each additional person is $5.00. Children three years and under stay free.

Location: The resort is 18 miles west of Port Angeles, Washington, on US 101, 3.5 miles on East Beach Road on the north shore of Lake Crescent.

Season: Late March to September 30.

Food: An attractive restaurant in the main lodge serves a breakfast buffet ($13.00) and dinner ($9.00–$28.00). Take-out pizza is available for lunch. Alcoholic beverages are served. A cafe serves hot dogs, burgers, fish and chips, espresso, other beverages, and ice cream from 8:00 a.m. to 8:00 p.m.; microwaveable foods are sold in the store and a microwave is available for use.

Transportation: The nearest scheduled air service is in Port Angeles, where rental cars are available.

Facilities: Swimming beach, boat rental, boat launch, gift shop, limited groceries, laundry, fishing supplies.

Activities: Fishing, hiking, boating, swimming.

Pets: Pets are allowed in the cabins only. There is a $12.50 fee per pet, per day.

SOL DUC HOT SPRINGS RESORT

P.O. 2169 • Port Angeles, WA 98362 • (866) 476-5382 • www.visitsolduc.com

Sol Duc (a Native American term meaning "sparkling water") Hot Springs Resort includes a single two-story wooden lodge building constructed in the 1980s and twenty-nine modern wooden buildings, for a total of thirty-two rooms. The former owner's home (the River Suite) is also available for group rental. There are no overnight accommodations in the main lodge building, which houses the registration desk, a small lobby area, a gift shop, a small convenience store, a restaurant, and restrooms. The resort is known primarily for more than twenty hot mineral springs that feed three pools located immediately behind the lodge. A large swimming pool is in the same complex. The resort is situated in the Sol Duc River Valley, surrounded by the heavily treed mountains of Olympic National Park. Sol Duc Hot Springs Resort is 42 miles west of Port Angeles, Washington, in the northwest corner of Olympic National Park. The resort is near the end of a paved road, 12 miles southeast of US 101.

Sol Duc Hot Springs Resort offers thirty-two modern wood-frame cabins plus one house, all of which were constructed in the early 1980s. Twenty-six cabins are freestanding units, while six cabins are in three duplex buildings immediately beside the lodge. The freestanding cabins sit in a large grassy lawn that also includes porch swings and picnic tables. The cabins are in two categories; those with a kitchen and those without. Except for kitchens and bedding that ranges from one king to two queens plus a twin-size sofa bed, all the cabins are virtually identical, with finished interior walls, carpeted floors, electric heat, a table and chairs, a full bathroom with a combination shower-tub, a hair dryer, and a coffee maker. None of the cabins have a telephone, air-conditioning, or a television. Cabins without a kitchen include a twin-size sofa bed. The interiors of the cabins are similar to, but perhaps a little larger than, most motel rooms. The three duplex units and five freestanding cabins with a kitchen area are each

The first hotel at Sol Duc Springs was opened in 1912. The elaborate hotel, constructed by a man who claimed the mineral springs had cured him of a fatal illness, included tennis courts, bowling alleys, golf links, a theater, and a three-story sanatorium with beds for one hundred patients. Unfortunately, sparks from the fireplace ignited the shingle roof and burned down the hotel only four years after its completion. According to legend, the fire short-circuited the hotel's wiring, causing the organ to begin playing Beethoven's "Funeral March" while the building was burning.

furnished with a sink, a microwave, a full-size refrigerator, a stove, an oven, a toaster, pans, dishes, and eating utensils These units rent for about $30 per night more than cabins without a kitchen. Parking is available near each of the cabins, so handling luggage isn't a problem. The River Suite, a three-bedroom house with two baths, a full kitchen, a living room, a dining room, a family room, a sunroom, and a deck overlooking the river, is available for group rental. All of the living space is on the second floor.

People generally visit Sol Duc to enjoy the natural hot springs that have made this area a popular tourist destination for nearly a hundred years. The resort has three circular pools of hot mineral water and a regular heated swimming pool, all located immediately behind the main lodge building. The largest hot-water pool and a small shallow pool for children each have mineral water at a temperature of 99° to 101° Fahrenheit. Another small pool has mineral water at a temperature of 104° Fahrenheit. These pools are relatively shallow and designed for sitting, not swimming. A larger

swimming pool in the same complex has heated regular water, rather than mineral water. The larger mineral water pool and the swimming pool have ramps for wheelchair access. Guests have free use of the pools; other visitors can use the facilities for a fee.

Sol Duc Hot Springs Resort is a place to unwind. You can hike in the morning, soak in a mineral water pool after lunch, get a professional massage in the late afternoon, take a nap in your cabin, then walk to the lodge for supper. If your cabin includes a kitchen, you may prefer to fix a meal and eat on your front porch or at one of several picnic tables scattered about the lawn. After that it's time for a good night's sleep so you can start all over again the next morning. A restaurant in the main lodge serves breakfast and dinner, while lunch is available at a deli beside the pool. Plenty of hiking trails near the resort lead into the rain forest and to the beautiful Sol Duc Falls. Evening programs on natural history are occasionally offered by rangers at the nearby National Park Service campground.

According to Quileute Indian legend, dragon tears are the source of the hot springs at Sol Duc. Whether dragon tears or natural phenomena, the hot springs have drawn people to this area for many years. In the early 1900s the springs were claimed by Theodore Moritz, who said the hot mineral water helped him recuperate from an injury in the woods. In the early 1920s the third owner of this property built two pools, a 50-by-150-foot freshwater pool without heat and a 50-by-60-foot hot springs pool. The sides of these pools were knocked out in 1984 and replaced by the four pools currently in use.

Rooms: Doubles, triples, and quads. The River Suite with two full bathrooms can sleep a maximum of fourteen people.

Wheelchair Accessibility: Three freestanding cabins, one with a kitchen, are ADA compliant with a combination shower-tub. No grab bars are by the toilet. A ramp allows entry to the main lodge building and restaurant. Wheelchair access is available to one hot mineral pool and the freshwater pool. Wheelchairs are available for loan.

Reservations: Sol Duc Hot Springs Resort, P.O. Box 2169, Port Angeles, WA 98362. Phone (866) 476-5382. A deposit of one-night's stay is required. A cancellation notice of seventy-two hours is required for a full refund less a $15.00 fee.

Rates: Cabin without kitchen ($141); cabins with kitchen ($172). Rates quoted are for two persons. Each additional person is $22 per night. Children under four stay free.

Location: Twelve miles southeast of US 101. The resort is in the northern part of Olympic National Park, 42 miles from Port Angeles, Washington.

Season: The lodge is open to overnight guests from April 1 to October 31.

Food: A restaurant in the main lodge building serves a breakfast buffet ($8.00) and dinner ($10.00–$29.00). Beer and wine are available. Sandwiches and beverages are available at the poolside deli from 11:00 a.m. to 4:00 p.m. during the summer. A few groceries, beer, and wine are sold near the registration desk.

Transportation: Port Angeles, Washington, is the nearest city with scheduled air service and rental vehicles.

Facilities: Heated swimming pool, heated mineral pools, restaurant , deli, gift shop, convenience store, and licensed massage practitioners.

Activities: Swimming, hiking, fishing, and soaking in mineral baths. Occasional evening National Park Service campfire programs.

Pets: Pets are allowed in the cabins for $15 per pet, per night. They are not allowed in the pool area or on the trails.

WYOMING

Grand Teton National Park/
John D. Rockefeller Jr. Memorial Parkway

P.O. Drawer 170 • Moose, WY 83012 • (307) 739-3300
www.nps/gov/grte/ • www.nps.gov/jodr/

Grand Teton National Park, which covers nearly 310,000 acres, includes the famous Teton Range, considered by many as the most beautiful mountain range in the United States. The park's three visitor centers are at Moose, Jenny Lake, and Colter Bay. A visitor center jointly operated by the U.S. Forest Service and the City of Jackson is at the north end of Jackson. The 24,000-acre John D. Rockefeller Jr. Memorial Parkway is a 7 1/2 -mile corridor that links the south entrance of Yellowstone National Park with the north entrance to Grand Teton National Park. The Snake River, which flows through both parks, offers excellent float trips. The two parks are in northwestern Wyoming, directly south of the West Thumb area of Yellowstone National Park. **Park Entrance Fee:** $25 per vehicle, $20 per motorcycle, or $12 per person, good for seven days. This entrance fee also covers Yellowstone National Park.

Lodging in Grand Teton National Park: Grand Teton National Park and the John D. Rockefeller Jr. Memorial Parkway together provide a total of seven lodging facilities. Flagg Ranch Village is the only one of the seven that is located in the parkway, which lies between Grand Teton and Yellowstone. Triangle X Ranch, the only working dude ranch in a national park, is the most unusual lodging facility in the park— maybe in any park. The least expensive facilities are at Colter Bay. The view rooms at Jackson Lake Lodge are some of the most upscale accommodations. Jenny Lake Lodge, with a four-diamond rating, is a quaint facility but is relatively expensive, even considering that horseback riding, bicycles, breakfast, and a five-course dinner are included in the price.

COLTER BAY VILLAGE

P.O. Box 240 • Moran, WY 83013 • (307) 543-3100 • www.gtlc.com

Colter Bay Village, a major recreation center for Grand Teton National Park, includes a grocery store, gift and tackle shop, laundromat, two restaurants, a National Park Service visitor center, a marina, and a gas station. The lodging facility at Colter Bay consists of 166 rooms in log cabins plus sixty-six tent cabins. A small cabin rental office handles registration for the log cabins, while a separate office farther down the road takes care of registration for the tent cabins. The two types of accommodations are in separate areas, but both are near the restaurants and other facilities.. Colter Bay Village is located on the shore of Jackson Lake, about 15 miles south of the north entrance to Grand Teton National Park.

Colter Bay has two very different types of accommodations. The least expensive lodging is in sixty-six tent cabins. This lodging is about as basic as you will find outside your own tent. The tent cabins are constructed of two canvas walls and a canvas roof connected to two log walls. The cabins each contain a woodstove (wood is not provided but can be purchased), electric lighting, and two sets of bunk beds with thin vinyl-covered mattresses. A picnic table is on a canvas-covered porch just outside the front door. Guests are responsible for everything else, including sheets, blankets, pillows, and utensils. Sleeping bags, cots, blankets, and pillows can be rented at the registration office. Two restroom facilities without showers are in the immediate area. Showers (fee) are available at a nearby laundry facility. The tent cabins are on a hill and offer views of pine trees, and a few sites have limited views of the Tetons.

Colter Bay also has 166 log cabins clustered on a hillside of pine trees, grass, wildflowers, and weeds along paved roads behind the commercial center. All cabins have electric heat and, other than two semiprivate dorm units, a private bath with a shower. They do not have a telephone, a television, or air-conditioning. The well-maintained cabins are of varying sizes and

Grand Teton National Park/
John D. Rockefeller Jr. Memorial Parkway

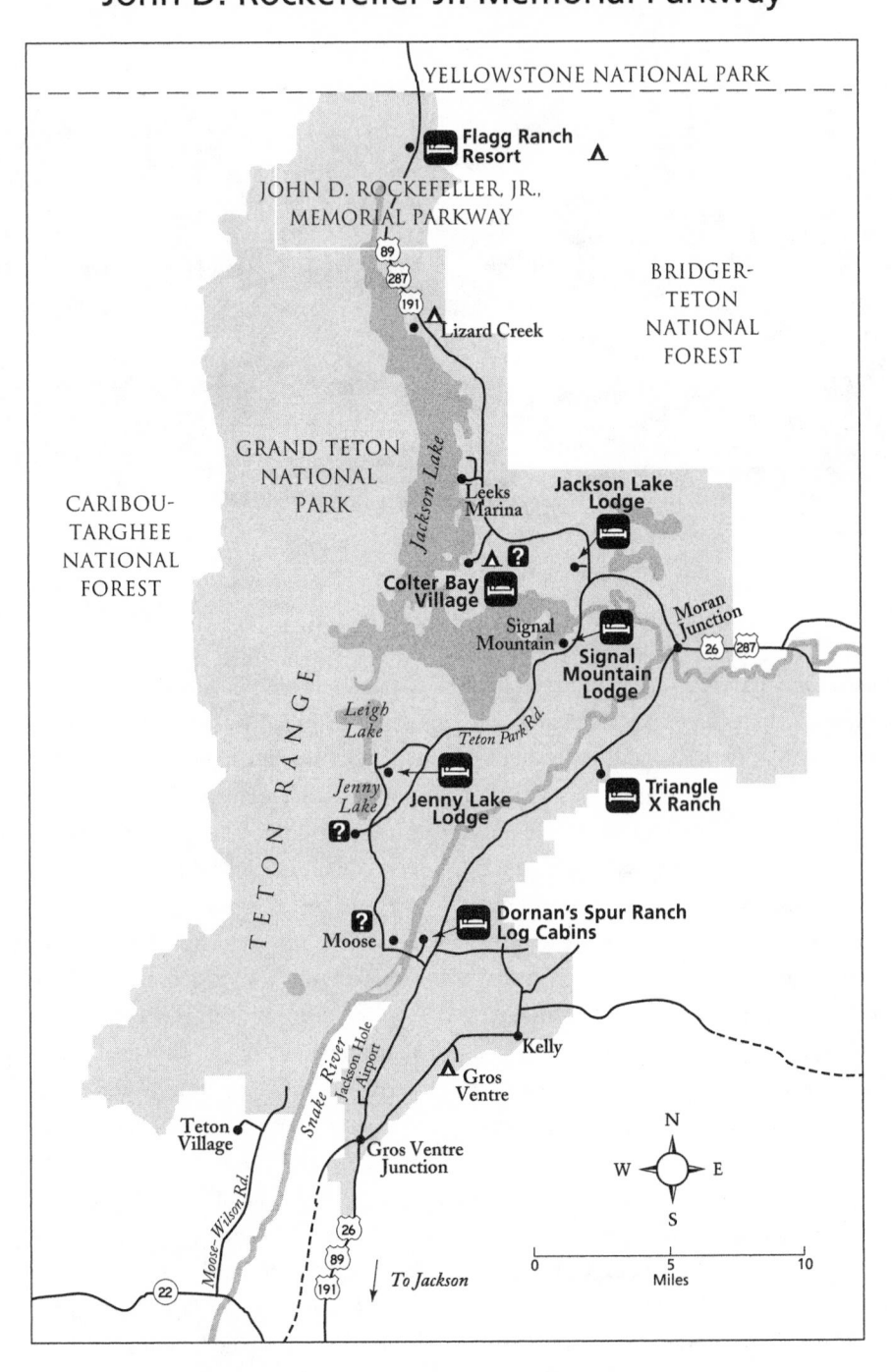

ages, with vaulted log-beamed ceilings, attractive log or wood interiors, and linoleum floors (only one-room cabins 401 and 403 and two-room cabin 405 have carpeting). Parking is in front of each unit.

Most of the one-room cabins are constructed as duplex units, although a few are freestanding, and one particularly long building includes six cabins. Only a few of these cabins have a front porch. Bedding ranges from one double to two doubles plus a single. Cabins 637 and 639 are each freestanding with a nice porch overhang. Cabin 212, with floor to ceiling windows on one wall, was once an artist's studio and is the most unusual cabin at Colter Bay. One-room cabin 471 was constructed more than one hundred years ago and is the oldest cabin in the Colter Bay complex.

Forty-two cabins each have two rooms, most with a bedroom on each side of a common bathroom. Most two-room cabins are freestanding with a very small front porch. About half of these cabins have a double bed in one room and two twin beds in the other room. Units 617 and 810 in this group sit on a hill and offer more privacy than most other cabins, although staying in either unit will involve some climbing. The other two-room cabins are a little larger, have two double beds in each room, and are priced somewhat higher, but the price includes up to four adults. Cabins 1031, 1035, 1039, 1043, and 1055 in this group are particularly desirable because they are on a dead-end road and back up to a wooded area.

Two log buildings in the cabin area offer a total of nine rooms without private bath. These semiprivate dorm rooms are nice, but occupants must use a community bathroom. Four units in one building each have two twin beds and two hallway bathrooms. Five units in a nearby building behind the restaurant are smaller, with one double bed. Bathrooms here must be entered from outside the building. The building with twin-bed units is far more desirable because the rooms are bigger (especially rooms 460 and 466), the bathroom is inside, and the location is quieter. A guest lounge with couches,

■   ■   ■

Most of the buildings at Colter Bay Village were moved here from other locations around the Jackson Hole area. At one time Jackson Hole had many small dude ranches and tourist resorts, typically consisting of a central lodge building and five to thirty log cabins. After Grand Teton National Park was expanded in 1950 with a gift of 34,000 acres from John D. Rockefeller Jr., most of the old lodges were closed and many of the cabins were moved via flatbed truck to Colter Bay, where the cabins were modernized with new roofs, electricity, and plumbing. In fact the existing Colter Bay cabin office was once the old store at Square G Ranch located just north of Jenny Lake. The ranch also supplied many of Colter Bay's cabins. Other cabins came from the old Teton Lodge at Moran, the old Jackson Lake Lodge, and the Circle H Guest Ranch. Cabins from several other old resorts were moved to Colter Bay during the 1960s. A written history of each cabin is framed and posted inside the cabin. Guests may ask the front desk for a keepsake history of the cabin in which they stayed.

■   ■   ■

chairs, and game tables is next door. The major drawback is that these buildings have no insulation between rooms, so guests are likely to hear conversations in adjacent rooms.

Colter Bay Village offers some of least expensive lodging in Grand Teton National Park. Although the main village area, with a marina, restaurants, gift shops, grocery store, laundry facility with showers (fee), and the National Park Service visitor center, is generally bustling with people and vehicles, the lodging is far enough away to escape most of the noise and congestion. At the same time, it is close enough that guests can easily avail themselves of the facilities. If you don't mind a room without a private bath, the semiprivate dorm rooms are by far the best value, at about half the price you will pay for the smallest cabin and a few dollars more than a tent cabin, where you have to supply your own bedding and pay for a shower that is some distance away. Colter Bay Village offers a variety of activities, including horseback riding, raft trips, fishing, lake cruises, and boating. Walking down to the lakeshore in the early evening is one of the pleasurable experiences of staying here. A pool at Jackson Lake Lodge is available to Colter Bay guests, and a free shuttle connects Colter Bay with Jackson Lake Lodge and the town of Jackson.

Rooms: Doubles, triples, and quads. A few two-bedroom units can accommodate up to eight persons. All but the semiprivate dorm cabins have a private bath. None of the tent cabins has a private bath.

Wheelchair Accessibility: Three wheelchair-accessible cabins with asphalt paths to the doorway are ADA compliant. The bathrooms each have a shower with a slight lip and a fold-down seat. These rooms are on each side of the guest lounge. Both restaurants and the accompanying bathrooms are wheelchair accessible, as are the grocery store and convenience store at the gas station.

Reservations: Grand Teton Lodge Company, P.O. Box 240, Moran, WY 83013. Phone (800) 628-9988, (307) 543-3100. A deposit of one-night's stay is required. A cancellation notice of three days is required for a refund less a $15 fee.

Rates: Tent cabins ($43); semiprivate dorm cabins ($49); one-room cabins ($89–$135); two-room cabins ($149–$179). Rates quoted are for two persons with the exception of the larger two-room cabins, where rates are quoted for four adults. Each additional person is $6.00 per night in tent cabins, $10.00 per night in log cabins. Children eleven and under stay free with an adult.

Location: North section of Grand Teton National Park, 40 miles north of Jackson, Wyoming.

Season: Late May to late September for log cabins. Early June to early September for tent cabins.

Food: Colter Bay has two eating establishments. The Chuckwagon Restaurant serves a continental breakfast buffet ($8.00) and a full breakfast buffet ($11.00), lunch ($8.50–$12.00), and dinner ($12.00–$21.00). The John Colter Café Court serves soups, salads, sandwiches, and Mexican dishes ($6.00–$10.00). A grocery store in the village sells bakery items, deli sandwiches, and ice cream in addition to a fairly extensive line of groceries, beer, and wine.

Transportation: The nearest scheduled air service is in Jackson, Wyoming, where rental cars are available. With advance notice, a lodge shuttle (fee charged) will meet flights. A free lodge shuttle operates between Colter Bay, Jackson Lake Lodge, and the town of Jackson.

Facilities: Restaurant, food court, grocery store, gift shop, tackle shop, stables, marina, boat rental, service station, laundromat, National Park Service visitor center with museum and gift shop.

Activities: Hiking, fishing, guided fly-fishing, boating, boat cruises, horseback riding, float trips, bus tours to Yellowstone National Park and through Grand Teton National Park, ranger/naturalist talks and walks during the day, evening campfire programs. The swimming pool at Jackson Lake Lodge is available to registered guests from Colter Bay Village.

Pets: Pets are allowed in some cabins.

DORNAN'S SPUR RANCH LOG CABINS

P.O. Box 39 • Moose, WY 83012 • (307) 733-2522 • www.dornans.com

Dornan's Spur Ranch is a lodging complex of twelve modern cabins constructed in six log duplex buildings that are clustered in a courtyard of grass and wildflowers. The cabins and log registration building are down a hill from a small commercial center that includes a grocery, bar and pasta restaurant, gift shop, sporting goods store, wine shop, and chuckwagon restaurant. The entire complex rests in a scenic basin next to the Snake River. Parking is beside the registration building and a short distance from the cabins. Two-wheel carts are kept near the registration building for guests to use in transporting luggage along walkways leading to each of the cabins. The cabins sit on a portion of a little less than ten acres of Dornan family land surrounded by Grand Teton National Park. Dornan's is located near the south end of the park, at Moose Junction.

The twelve modern log cabins, constructed in 1992, are well maintained both inside and out. Each cabin has a combination living room–kitchen area, a full bathroom with a combination shower-tub, and either one or two bedrooms. The kitchen has a table and four chairs. The bedrooms have one queen-size bed with a down comforter, and the living room includes a sofa bed. A door off the living room leads to a small covered wooden deck with table and chairs. A charcoal grill (but not charcoal) is beside each porch. The cabins sit near the famous Snake River and have been sited so that most of the decks offer a view of the Tetons. One duplex unit houses Cascade and Garnet, two one-bedroom cabins that are next to the river and provide excellent mountain views. Larkspur, a two-bedroom unit, has a patio that faces the river.

Although the cabins are duplex units, we experienced minimal noise from our neighbors. The cabins are roomy with hardwood floors in the living room–kitchen, nice tile in the bathroom, and fully carpeted bedrooms. Voice mail service and Internet access are available in all units. The kitchen is equipped with a

■   ■   ■

The land on which Dornan's now welcomes travelers is a little less than half the twenty acres Evelyn Dornan homesteaded in the early 1920s. Evelyn, a divorcee who was born and raised in Philadelphia, first visited Jackson Hole in 1918 with her sixteen-year-old son, Jack. In the 1930s, Jack developed a portion of the property into a dude ranch that was deeded to him in 1941 by his mother. Evelyn, who lived to be eighty-three, sold her remaining ten acres to the National Park Service in 1952. Although the park service attempted to purchase the remaining acreage, Evelyn's strong-willed son stood his ground and, with wife Ellen, continued to operate Dornan's until their retirement in 1972, when the business passed to their sons.

■   ■   ■

full-size refrigerator, a stove, an oven, a coffeemaker, a toaster, dishes, and all utensils. All you need to bring is the food, or you can stroll up the hill to the grocery and purchase some nice sirloins and that special bottle of wine. All this makes for a very pleasant stay.

Dornan's log cabins are among this area's nicest accommodations. The food is good, the people are nice, and the scenery is magnificent. Enjoy breakfast while sipping a cup of coffee and taking in the mountain views from your cabin deck. If you are around at noon, walk up the hill and select from a variety of sandwiches at the deli. In the evening enjoy an all-you-can-eat outdoor western dinner after knocking back a cold one from the outdoor deck connected to the bar. A short path that begins beside the bar leads to the historic landing of Menor's Ferry, where the National Park Service offers rides across the Snake River to the house of a former homesteader. One evening after dinner we walked to the landing and exchanged greetings with rafters and kayakers as they floated down the Snake.

Rooms: One-bedroom cabins can accommodate up to four persons. Two-bedroom units hold up to six. All cabins have a full bath and full kitchen (no microwave).

Wheelchair Accessibility: One cabin has a boardwalk ramp and a bathroom with a wide doorway, a high toilet, grab bars, and a roll-in shower.

Reservations: Dornan's Spur Ranch Log Cabins, P.O. Box 39, Moose, WY 83012. Phone (307) 733-2522; fax (307) 733-3544. A deposit of three nights' stay is required during high season, and a deposit of one night's stay is required for the low season. All cancellations result in a $50 charge plus forfeit of deposit if received less than thirty days prior to arrival.

Rates: Rates are seasonal. High-season rates apply Memorial Day weekend to September 30 and Christmas through New Year's Day with a three-night minimum: one-bedroom cabin with one to two persons ($175), with three to four persons ($205); two-bedroom cabin with up to six persons ($250). Low-season rates for October 1 to Memorial Day weekend with a one-night minimum: one-bedroom cabin with one to two persons ($125); with three to four persons ($150); two-bedroom cabin with up to six persons ($175).

Location: South end of Grand Teton National Park, at Moose Junction. The cabins are 12 miles north of Jackson, Wyoming.

Season: Open year-round.

Food: A chuckwagon outdoor restaurant serves breakfast ($10.00), lunch ($8.00–$11.00), and all-you-can-eat dinner ($16.00–$19.00); Saturday and Sunday, prime rib or twelve-ounce steak ($23.00) during summer months. A bar/restaurant serves salads, pizza, and pasta for lunch and dinner (hours vary); inside and outside seating are available for both the chuckwagon restaurant and the bar/restaurant. Groceries are available at the store.

Transportation: Air service is available to Jackson, Wyoming, where rental vehicles are available.

Facilities: Grocery; bar/restaurant; wine store; outdoor restaurant; gift shop; fly-fishing store; gas station; and a sports shop with sporting equipment and bicycle, canoe, and kayak rentals. A National Park Service visitor center is nearby.

Activities: Hiking, fishing, scenic and whitewater float trips on the Snake River, canoeing, kayaking, mountain biking. Winter activities include cross-country skiing, downhill skiing, and snowmobiling.

FLAGG RANCH RESORT

P.O. Box 187 • Moran, WY 83013 • (307) 543-2861 • www.flaggranch.com

Flagg Ranch Resort encompasses a modern log-style main lodge building, ninety-two nearby modern log cabin rooms, a service station, and a campground with hookups. Registration for the cabins is just inside the front door of the main lodge, which itself has no accommodations. The main lodge is quite attractive, with a small lobby separated from the dining room by a large double-sided stone fireplace. In addition to the dining room and lobby, the main lodge houses a gift shop, tour desk, grocery, lounge, and front desk. Flagg Ranch Resort is located at the north end of John D. Rockefeller Jr. Memorial Parkway, 2 miles south of the south entrance to Yellowstone National Park and 5 miles north of the north entrance to Grand Teton National Park.

Thirty wooden buildings constructed in 1995 with metal roofs and log-style exteriors house ninety-two cabin-style rooms. The cabin complex sits on a bluff that overlooks the Snake River Valley, although the river itself is visible from only a few of the cabin patios. The buildings, constructed as either duplexes or quads, are clustered in a natural setting of rocks, dirt, weeds, grass, and wildflowers behind a large parking area that is approximately a quarter mile from the main lodge. The buildings are nicely spaced, and the cabins are insulated, so you are unlikely to be bothered by noise from guests in an adjoining cabin. A series of cement walkways lead from the parking area, where two-wheeled luggage carts are kept. The cabins are far enough from the main lodge and restaurant that many guests drive between the two locations.

All the cabins are rented in one of two classifications: view and nonview. View cabins rent for $10 per night extra and are in the back of the complex nearest the bluff and most distant from the parking area. View rooms each have a patio facing the Snake River Valley. All ninety-two cabins are the same size, with some having one king bed and others two queen beds. Each cabin has a private bathroom with a combination shower-tub (with the exception of three wheelchair-accessible cabins), gas heat, a vaulted ceiling, and a finished interior that is similar to that found in a large and nicely furnished motel room. Each cabin also has a coffeemaker and telephone. None of the rooms has air-conditioning, a television, or a kitchenette. Cabins have a covered cement patio with rocking chairs.

The cabins at Flagg Ranch are modern, clean, and comfortable. Each is identical in interior size and

Flagg Ranch, which is believed to have been a favorite camping spot for both native tribes and fur trappers, was established between 1910 and 1916 at its present location by an early guide and pioneer in this area. The ranch is the oldest continually operating resort in the upper Jackson Hole area. It has served as both a dude ranch and a lodging facility, offering overnight accommodations to early trappers and present-day travelers. The ranch name is derived from the flag that flew from the Snake River Military Station, once located here.

furnishings, so you are only required to choose between a view or nonview cabin and between two queen beds or one king bed. We don't know about your bedding preference, but we suggest you spring for a view room that has larger windows and a patio that faces nature instead of your neighbor. The slight difference in cost is especially worthwhile if you arrive early and will be spending considerable time in your cabin. Keep in mind that cabins with a view are most distant from the parking lot, but with the availability of luggage carts, the difference in distance isn't really a problem. We enjoyed sitting on the patio, reading a book, and being able to see the beauty of the Wyoming landscape uninterrupted by other cabins. A trail behind the cabins leads along the edge of the bluff and down to the Snake River.

Flagg Ranch offers modern, comfortable lodging at a convenient location between Yellowstone and Grand Teton National Parks. The cabins are relatively large, and the main lodge building has an attractive western decor. Several activities are available for guests, including interpretive tours to Yellowstone and Grand Teton National Parks, guided trail rides, scenic float trips, and whitewater rafting trips. With prior notice,

Flagg Ranch will furnish transportation to the ranch (fee charged) from several locations including the Jackson airport and Teton Village. Check with the ranch for information. The road between the town of Jackson and Flagg Ranch is open during winter months, although the lodge is closed. Snowcoaches from Yellowstone provide transportation between Flagg Ranch and the Old Faithful area, where Old Faithful Snow Lodge is open during winter months.

Rooms: Doubles, triples, and quads. All rooms have a private bath with a combination shower-tub.

Wheelchair Accessibility: Three nonview cabins nearest the parking area have a roll-in shower and are ADA compliant. The main lodge and restaurant are wheelchair accessible.

Reservations: Flagg Ranch Resort, P.O. Box 187, Moran, WY 83013. Phone (800) 443-2311 or (307) 543-2861; fax (307) 543-2356. A deposit of one-night's stay (or two-nights' stay for multiple nights) is required. A cancellation notice of six days is required for a full refund, less a $25 cancellation fee.

Rates: Nonview ($175), view ($185). Rates quoted are for two adults. Children seventeen and under stay free.

Location: North end of John D. Rockefeller Jr. Memorial Parkway, 2 miles south of the south entrance to Yellowstone National Park.

Season: Mid-May through mid-October.

Food: A full-service restaurant offers a breakfast buffet ($12.00), lunch ($8.00–$9.00), and dinner ($13.00–$24.00). Alcoholic beverages are served in the dining room. A children's menu is available. A cocktail lounge adjacent to the dining room serves appetizers. Groceries are available at a small store in the main lodge.

Transportation: The nearest scheduled air service is in Jackson, Wyoming.

Facilities: Restaurant, cocktail lounge, gift shop, grocery store, gas station, coin laundry, small National Park Service visitor center.

Activities: Hiking, whitewater rafting, float trips, trail rides, guided fishing trips, interpretive tours to Yellowstone National Park and Grand Teton National Park.

Pets: Pets are permitted in the cabins at an additional fee of $10 per day, per pet.

JACKSON LAKE LODGE

Grand Teton Lodge Company • P.O. Box 250 • Moran, WY 83013 • (307) 543-3100
www.gtlc.com

Jackson Lake Lodge includes a very large central lodge building flanked by numerous multiple-unit wooden buildings that house cottage units hidden from view by surrounding trees. Overnight rooms are also on the third floor of the lodge. The three-story concrete lodge sits on a bluff overlooking a large willow meadow and Jackson Lake, both of which are highlighted by the spectacular Teton Mountain Range. Registration is just inside the main entrance. The lodge building has a large second-floor lobby with two corner fireplaces, many comfortable chairs and sofas, Native American artifacts scattered throughout, and a two-story wall of windows offering a picture-perfect view of the Tetons. The lodge also has a dining room, grill, cocktail lounge, gift shop, apparel shop featuring fine western and adventure wear, and T-shirt shop—all on the second floor; an art gallery on the third-floor balcony has tables and chairs and a great view. A large parking lot is just behind the lodge, and plentiful parking is near each of the cottage units. Arriving guests can use the entrance drive to register and, for guests who will be staying in the lodge, drop off luggage. An elevator is in the lodge. Jackson Lake

Lodge is located on the east side of Jackson Lake, 5 miles northwest of Moran Junction, about 35 miles north of the town of Jackson.

The lodge offers four basic types of rooms: view rooms, lodge rooms, cottages, and suites. All rooms have heat, a telephone, a hair dryer, a coffeemaker, a ceiling fan, and a private bath, but no television or air-conditioning. Cottages comprise the vast majority of the 385 rooms at the Jackson Lake complex. The thirty-seven rooms in the main lodge, all on the third floor, are similar except for the view. Rooms on the west side of the building, with large windows that provide great views of the Tetons, cost $80 more per night than rooms on the east side. The more costly view rooms also have a small refrigerator, a wet bar, and down comforters on the beds. All the rooms in the lodge have two queen beds and are quite large and attractively decorated, but none has a balcony. The main lodge building has one suite with a sitting area furnished with a sofa and chairs, one king-size bed, a whirlpool bathtub, a wet bar, and a full-size refrigerator. The suite offers a panoramic view of the mountains.

The Amoretti Inn, the original lodge constructed in 1922 at this site, included a main lodge building and thirty cabins. The lodge, which stood near where the 900 building of the current lodge is located, boasted of indoor plumbing in its log cabins. The name was changed to Jackson Lake Lodge in the late 1920s. The old lodge continued to provide overnight rooms until the new Jackson Lake Lodge was completed in June 1955. The current lodge was designed by Gilbert Stanley Underwood, who also designed Yosemite National Park's Ahwahnee. The old cabins were moved to Colter Bay, where they were renovated and remain in use.

The 347 cottage rooms each have two queen beds, comfortable furniture, and a full bath. The cottages are quite roomy (bigger than rooms in the main lodge), most have a vaulted beamed ceiling, and they were renovated in 2008 and 2009. They are attractively decorated and considerably nicer than a typical motel room. Most of the cottages are in a series of one-story wood-frame buildings of eight to twenty rooms that back up to one another. The buildings are in a nicely landscaped area with lots of vegetation including fir and aspen trees. Many cottages have a front porch but do not offer a mountain or lake view. Most odd-numbered cottages in the 100 and 200 buildings do not have a front porch and are less desirable. One two-story and five one-story buildings offer cottages with a private back patio or balcony and rent for $10.00 extra per night. Cottages 123 and 125 in this category each have a patio that offers a partial view of the Tetons. Three two-story cottage buildings offer forty-six units with a private balcony or patio that faces the Tetons. Other than three corner suites in one of the buildings, these are the premiere cottage units and rent for $60 to $70 per night more than cottages with a back patio but no mountain view. Rooms on the second floor each have a balcony and a vaulted interior ceiling, while first-floor rooms have a regular ceiling and a back patio fronted by a small grassy area. There are no elevators in the two-story cottage buildings. Three suites in one of the two-story view buildings have a double-size room; two bathrooms, one with a whirlpool tub and one with a shower; and a king-size bed plus a Murphy bed. One of these suites (room 911) has a full kitchen and wraparound balcony.

Staying in a nonview room in the main lodge allows you to enjoy a great view of the Tetons by walking down one flight of stairs to the second-floor lobby. If you want to splurge for a room with a view, we suggest you choose one of the view cottages, which have a private balcony or patio facing the mountains. One of the great pleasures of staying in one of these units is sitting on your back patio or balcony and enjoying the magnificent panorama of Jackson Lake against a background of the Tetons. The mountain-view cottages each have a large back window that allows a similar view. The back patio or balcony, along with the ease of getting your luggage into the room, makes these a better choice than the view rooms in the lodge.

Jackson Lake Lodge is a place to enjoy spectacular scenery and abundant wildlife. The highlight of visiting the lodge is sitting in the upstairs lobby and looking out enormous windows at America's most beautiful mountain range. All rooms in the complex are relatively large and comfortable. Several choices are available for dining, and the main dining room on the second floor has large western-theme murals and large windows with views that rival those of the lobby. The cocktail lounge, on the opposite side of the lobby from the dining room, has two walls of windows with views of the Tetons. The lodge offers more stores than are typically found in a national park lodge. A variety of activities are available, including swimming in a heated pool, horseback riding, float trips, and park bus tours.

Rooms: Doubles, triples, and quads. All rooms have a private bath.

Wheelchair Accessibility: Wheelchair-accessible rooms are in both the lodge and the cottages. In the lodge, one non-view and one view room are ADA compliant. An elevator operates from the registration area on the lower floor to the third floor, where lodge rooms are located. Eighteen cottage units, some of which offer a mountain view, each have ramp access and are ADA compliant with a combination shower-tub.

Reservations: Grand Teton Lodge Company, P.O. Box 250, Moran, WY 83013. Phone (800) 628-9988, (307) 543-3100. If staying two or more nights, a two-night deposit is required. A seven-day cancellation is required for deposit refund less a $30 fee.

Rates: Main lodge: nonview ($199); view ($279); cottages/patios: nonview ($199–$209); view ($269-$279); suite ($459–$650). Rates quoted are for two persons. Each additional person is $10 per night. Children eleven and under stay free.

Location: Jackson Lake Lodge is located on the eastern shore of Jackson Lake, 5 miles northwest of Moran Junction, about 24 miles north of the town of Moose.

Season: Mid-May through early October.

Food: The main dining room serves a breakfast buffet ($14.00), breakfast menu ($5.00–$10.00), lunch ($9.00–$18.00), and dinner ($20.00– $38.00). Next door, the Pioneer Grill, with U-shaped counters, serves breakfast ($5.00–$8.00), lunch ($9.00–$11.00), and dinner ($9.00–$20.00). A pool grill with sandwiches, pizza, and ice cream is open for lunch during July and August. An all-you-can-eat barbecue ($22) is offered Sunday through Friday evenings, weather permitting. A cappuccino/espresso cart is open during the morning hours in the lobby.

Transportation: The nearest airport is 28 miles south, in Jackson, Wyoming, where rental vehicles are available. A free shuttle operates several times a day between Colter Bay, Jackson Lake Lodge, and the town of Jackson. Reservations suggested (800-628-9988).

Facilities: Dining room, grill, cocktail lounge, gift shops, apparel shop, newsstand, tour desk, outdoor heated swimming pool, service station, stable, medical clinic, conference facilities.

Activities: Horseback riding, swimming, Snake River float trips, hiking, evening ranger/naturalist programs, boat cruises on Jackson Lake, bus tours to Yellowstone National Park and through Grand Teton National Park.

Pets: Pets are allowed in some cottages.

JENNY LAKE LODGE

P.O. Box 240 • Moran, WY 83013 • (307) 733-4647 • www.gtlc.com

Jenny Lake Lodge features a main log lodge building on a grassy area and thirty-seven log cabins. The complex is located at the base of the Tetons, near beautiful Jenny Lake. The main lodge building, with hardwood floors and vaulted ceilings, houses the registration desk, the dining room, and a cozy lobby with stuffed furniture and a large stone fireplace. Lobby and some dining room windows provide good mountain views. A wooden front deck has chairs and benches that face the mountains. A few of the cabins are freestanding, but most are duplex units. The cabins are nicely spaced in an area of pine trees. The facility is quaint, quiet, well maintained, and expensive. Unlike cabin rates at most other national park facilities, the rates here include breakfast, a five-course dinner, the use of bicycles, and, for those so inclined, horseback riding. Lunch is also served for an extra charge. Jenny Lake Lodge is located in the middle of Grand Teton National Park, about 20 miles north of Jackson, Wyoming.

Jenny Lake Lodge has been awarded four diamonds by the American Automobile Association, indicating that it is one of the more upscale lodging units in the United States, let alone in a national park. For example, each cabin is named for a wildflower and has an original watercolor painting of the respective flower. The beds are covered with handmade quilts and down comforters, and robes are provided in each cabin.

Two types of cabin accommodations are available at the lodge. Each cabin has a log-beamed vaulted ceiling, hardwood floors, heat, a ceiling fan, a small refrigerator, a coffeemaker, a hair dryer, a telephone, and a private bath with a combination shower-tub, but no air-conditioning or television. Thirty-one one-room cabins vary somewhat in decor, view, and bed configuration, which ranges from one queen-size bed, to a queen-size plus a twin, to one king-size bed. Each cabin has a covered front porch with two rocking chairs. Some of the cabins face the mountain range and offer good views from the front porch. Six suites each have a woodstove (wood provided) and sofa bed in the

Jenny Lake Lodge is the descendant of a small 1920s dude ranch called Danny Ranch on the same site. Five cabins and a portion of the original main lodge building remain as part of the existing complex, which gained its current name in 1952. The original log building now houses the lodge dining room. Cabins have been modernized and added to over the years. A major restoration was undertaken in the late 1980s, and four new cabins were added in 1993.

sitting area or living room and an in-wall safe. Five of the suites have two rooms, a living room, and a bedroom. One suite consists of one very large room with a whirlpool tub and a large private patio. The suites have either a king or two queen beds.

At Jenny Lake Lodge guests enjoy the sights and activities of Grand Teton National Park in luxury. You can relax, hike, bike, and sightsee while staying at the national park lodge that is nearest to the beautiful Tetons. The rustic nature of the lodge and cabins provides a taste of the West, but with style. Two meals a day, bicycles, and horseback riding are included; the chef will cook any fish you catch; and a valet will take care of your laundry for a nominal charge. You can take the free shuttle to Jackson Lake Lodge and enjoy the swimming pool or to the town of Jackson for a day of shopping. Fly into Jackson and the staff will, with prior notice, pick you up. The downside to Jenny Lake Lodge is the expense, for it is one of the most costly lodging facilities in any national park. For the price of a night at Jenny Lake Lodge, you can stay two nights and eat well a short distance up the road at sister facility Jackson Lake Lodge. On the other hand, if cost isn't a factor, Jenny Lake Lodge is your place to enjoy the beauty of the Tetons in comfort.

Rooms: Singles, doubles, triples, and quads. All cabins have a full bathroom.

Wheelchair Accessibility: Two cabins each have ramp access and a bathroom with grab bars and a combination shower-tub. The registration building, which includes the dining room, is wheelchair accessible with ramp access.

Reservations: Grand Teton Lodge Company, P.O. Box 240, Moran, WY 83013. Phone (800) 628-9988 or (307) 733-4647. Up to a three-day deposit is required for stays of three days or more. Sixty-day cancellation is required for a refund less a $40 fee.

Rates: Cabin: one person ($450); two persons ($550); suites: one or two persons ($725–$785). Each additional person is $150 a day. Children two years and under stay free with an adult. Breakfast and dinner are included in the price of a cabin.

Location: Midsection of Grand Teton National Park, approximately 20 miles north of Jackson, Wyoming.

Season: End of May to early October.

Food: A cozy dining room serves breakfast, lunch, and a five-course dinner. Breakfast and dinner are included in the price of a room. Lunches range from $9.00– $11.00. Nonguests are charged $70 per person for dinner.

Transportation: Daily air service is available from Denver, Colorado, and Salt Lake City, Utah, to Jackson, Wyoming, where rental vehicles are available. Free shuttles are available to take guests to Colter Bay, Jackson Lake Lodge, and the town of Jackson.Pickup at the Jackson airport is available for a fee.

Facilities: Dining room, stables, bicycles, gift shop, concierge service. Guests have free use of the swimming pool at Jackson Lake Lodge. A National Park Service visitor center is 3 miles away.

Activities: Hiking, fishing, horseback riding, Snake River float trips, bicycling. Guided walks and evening campfire programs originate at the National Park Service visitor center.

SIGNAL MOUNTAIN LODGE

P.O. Box 50, Inner Park Road • Moran, WY 83103 • (307) 543-2831

www.signalmountainlodge.com

Signal Mountain Lodge is a medium-size commercial and lodging complex with seventy-nine cabin units plus support structures that include a registration building, a separate restaurant/gift shop, a marina with rental boats, and a gas station/convenience store. The back side of the registration building houses a comfortable and generally uncrowded lounge with couches, stuffed chairs, tables, a stone fireplace, and large windows that offer excellent views of Jackson Lake and the Teton Range. A separate and somewhat smaller room in the front of the building has a television, a small library, computers with Internet access, and a collection of

■   ■   ■

Today's Signal Mountain Lodge was a small fishing camp that went through several owners before being purchased in 1932 by Charles Wort, a homesteader who had plans to make this a fishing resort. His dream was at least partially fulfilled by his two sons. The Worts sold the lodge in 1940 in order to build an upscale hotel that continues to welcome guests in the town of Jackson. The new owners financed construction of the current guest cabins, convenience store, and registration building during the forty years they owned the property.

■   ■   ■

games and puzzles. The adjacent building houses an attractive restaurant and a grill, both of which offer lake and mountain views. The same building also includes a cocktail lounge, T-shirt shop, and nice gift shop. Signal Mountain Lodge is in a scenic location 7 miles west of the Moran national park entrance station and about 4 miles south of Jackson Lake Lodge.

The lodge offers five types of cabins that are constructed two, three, or four to a building with the exception of one large freestanding unit. All of the cabins have a covered porch with chairs or a picnic table, carpeting, electric heat, a telephone, and a full tiled bathroom with a combination shower-tub, but no television or air-conditioning. The cabins are within easy walking distance of the registration building, restaurant, and store. The least expensive rooms are one-room rustic cabins with beds that range from one double to two doubles plus a sofa bed. Five of the units with one double bed have a gas fireplace. The two-room rustic cabins can accommodate from four to six guests with bedding that ranges from two to three double beds. Both one- and two-room rustics are priced according to the beds available in the cabins. Some of the cabins have

a good view of the lake, while other cabins have views obstructed by trees or other cabins. Two-room rustic cabins 136, 138, 142, 143, and 144 sit a short distance from the lakeshore and offer great lake views from the porches. Two-room cabin 102 sits on a hill and offers a partial mountain view. One-room cabins 129, 146, and 147 provide partial lake views. Avoid one-room cabin 107 and two-room cabin 112, which each have a porch directly on the road.

Sixteen larger Country Rooms offer more modern motel-style lodging with two queen beds or one king, a small refrigerator, a microwave, and a coffeemaker. Three Deluxe Country Rooms, all in the same building, have a living room and separate bedroom with one king bed. These units also have a gas fireplace. All but one of the Country Rooms sit back from the lake and offer minimal views. Country Room 137 is sandwiched between two two-room cabins and enjoys a private porch that offers a good lake view. We would choose this over the other twelve units in this classification. Twenty-eight Lakefront Retreats are constructed four units to a building, with two units up and two unit units down. These large two-room units have a living room–kitchen with a sofa bed, a microwave, a two-burner stove, a coffeemaker, a refrigerator, and limited cookware and utensils. A separate bedroom has either two queen beds or a king. These sit directly on Jackson Lake and are the only accommodations at Signal Mountain Lodge that offer excellent views of both Jackson Lake and the Tetons. The upper units of each building are closer to parking, offer better views, and are priced $10 per night more than the bottom units. Request upper Lakefront unit 152 or lower unit 151, both of which offer the best views.

Larger groups can be accommodated in a family bungalow with two units that is available for rent either separately or as a whole. One unit has a bedroom with two queen beds, as well as a separate kitchen–living room equipped with a sofa bed, a microwave, a stove top, an oven, a coffeemaker, a full-size refrigerator, and limited cookware and utensils. The attached one-room unit has a king bed, sofa bed, small refrigerator, microwave, and coffeemaker. The building has a large deck with chairs and a picnic table. One large "Home Away from Home" cabin has three rooms including a bedroom with two queen beds, a living/dining room with a sofa bed and gas fireplace, and a kitchen with limited cookware and utensils. This unit also has a laundry area.

Signal Mountain Lodge is a quiet facility situated directly on Lake Jackson in a beautiful area of Grand Teton National Park. Rooms here are more rustic and less expensive than at nearby Jackson Lake Lodge, but the vistas are equally impressive. The cabins are similar to those at Colter Bay, but the Signal Mountain complex is much smaller. All the cabins are close to the lake, allowing guests to walk a short distance to enjoy a swim or rent a canoe or kayak. The adjacent campground is a nice place to take a walk. The location approximately midway between the town of Jackson and Yellowstone National Park makes this a good base from which to explore Grand Teton National Park.

Rooms: Doubles, triples, and quads. Several rooms with a sofa bed can accomodate up to six persons. All rooms have a private bath.

Wheelchair Accessibility: No cabins are designated as wheelchair accessible. A few cabins have ramp access, but bathrooms have not been modified to facilitate wheelchair accessibility. The restaurant, grill, and lounge are wheelchair accessible.

Reservations: Signal Mountain Lodge accepts reservations only by phone. Phone (307) 543-2831 Monday through Friday from 8:00 a.m. to 5:00 p.m. MST. The reservation line is open twenty-four hours daily from May through early October. A deposit of one night's stay is required. Cancellation notice of seven days is required for refund of deposit less an administrative fee of $10 per room per night of the stay that is canceled (to a maximum of $50 per room).

Rates: One-room rustic log cabins ($123–$156); one-room rustic log cabin with a fireplace ($157); two-room rustic log cabins ($170–$180); Country Rooms ($160); Deluxe Country Rooms ($212); Lakefront Retreats ($236–$254). one-room family bungalow ($170), two- room family bungalow ($248); Home Away from Home ($302). Rates are by the room and not the number of occupants. Rollaways are $15 per night with a maximum of one per unit.

Location: On Jackson Lake, 7 miles west of Moran Junction and 35 miles north of Jackson.

Season: Mid-May to mid-October.

Food: The Peaks Restaurant serves dinner only ($19–$36). The adjacent Trapper Grill offers breakfast ($7.00–$10.00), lunch and dinner ($8.00–$16.00). Food from the grill is also served in the lounge and on the outside deck. Limited groceries, beer, and wine are available in the convenience store. Eleven miles north, Leeks Pizzeria serves pizza, pasta, and sandwiches.

Transportation: The nearest scheduled air service is in Jackson, Wyoming, where rental vehicles are available.

Facilities: Restaurant, grill, cocktail lounge, gift shop, clothing store, convenience store, laundromat, and gas station. Marina with powerboat, canoe, and kayak rentals.

Activities: Boating, canoeing, kayaking, fishing, hiking, guided fishing trips, guided sailboat tours, evening naturalist programs, float trips.

Pets: Pets are permitted in all of the units except the upper Lakefront Retreats for a charge of $10 per pet, per night.

TRIANGLE X RANCH

2 Triangle X Ranch Road • Moose, WY 83012 • (307) 733-2183 • www.trianglex.com

Triangle X Ranch, the only operating dude ranch in a national park, includes all the buildings you would expect in a working ranch, as well as twenty freestanding log or wood-frame cabins that provide overnight accommodations. The ranch offers excellent views of the Teton Mountain Range from a rise overlooking Jackson Hole. Its authenticity and scenic location have resulted in the ranch serving as a location for several movies, including John Wayne's first picture and the classic western *Shane*. One of the ranch's many buildings includes the dining room plus an adjacent living room with a fireplace. All of the cabins are within a short walking distance of the dining room. During the peak season of June through August the Triangle X requires a minimum stay of one week beginning and ending on Sunday. Reduced minimum stays are required during other times of the year. The ranch is particularly appealing to people who enjoy horseback riding, which is the main activity for guests. Triangle X Ranch is on the eastern side of Grand Teton National Park, 25 miles north of Jackson, Wyoming, just off U.S. Highways 26, 89, and 191. It is 6 miles south of Moran Junction.

A total of twenty log or wood-frame cabins each have electricity, heat, and a private bathroom with a combination shower-tub, but no telephone or television. Cabins are available with one, two, and three bedrooms.

■   ■   ■

Triangle X Ranch has served as home to four generations of the same family. The ranch was purchased in the summer of 1926 by John S. Turner, who started construction of his home and welcomed guests the same summer. The ranch was self-sufficient, with refrigeration provided by ice cut from nearby ponds and stored in piles of sawdust. In the late 1920s Turner sold the property to a land company owned by John D. Rockefeller, who eventually donated the property to the federal government. Today the grandsons of John Turner operate the ranch as a concessionaire of the National Park Service.

■   ■   ■

The two- and three-bedroom units each have two full bathrooms. In general, most bedrooms have either two twin beds or one queen bed. While all cabins have a very rustic exterior, the interiors are quite nice, with paneled walls and heavy pine furniture. Most of the ceilings are slightly vaulted. Each cabin has a covered front porch with chairs, and most enjoy views of the Tetons.

Triangle X Ranch is the place to stay if you want an overall western experience in a national park. Here you can enjoy mountain scenery, horseback riding, and evening activities with a western theme. With each guest spending an entire week at the ranch, it is a certainty you will make new friends during your stay. Three meals a day, each announced by the ringing of a dinner bell, are served family-style and included in the price of a room. A typical dinner includes a main entree, a green salad, several vegetables, home-baked bread, and a dessert. Daily horseback riding (except for Sunday) is included in the price of your stay. Each guest is assigned his or her own horse at the beginning of the week's stay. Each evening has a different scheduled activity, including square dancing, ranger talks, cookouts, and campfire gatherings. Triangle X offers float trips and pack trips at extra cost.

Children five to twelve receive special attention at Triangle X. They eat in a separate dining room from teenagers and adults, and their activities, including horseback riding, are especially designed for their age group.

Winter brings a much different environment with different activities. The required stay is reduced to two nights, and a shuttle service is available without charge to and from the Jackson Hole airport and Jackson Hole Ski Resort. Triangle X provides complimentary cross-country skis and snowshoes. In addition, guided snowmobile trips can be arranged (fee charged). An outdoor hot tub is available for guests. Winter is accompanied by more formal gourmet meals including dinners with three to four courses and several entree choices.

Rooms: One to three persons in a one-bedroom unit; three to five persons in a two-bedroom unit; five to six persons in a three-bedroom cabin. All cabins have a private bath with a combination shower-tub.

Wheelchair Accessibility: One cabin has ramp access to the front door and a bathroom with a wide doorway, grab bars, and a roll-in shower. The dining room building also has ramp access.

Reservations: Triangle X Ranch, 2 Triangle X Ranch Road, Moose, WY 83012. Phone (307) 733-2183; fax (307) 733-8685. Minimum stay of one week from early June to late August, four days at other times during the summer season; a two-day minimum is required during the winter season. Required deposit of 35 percent of total cost. Credit cards are not accepted during the summer season. When a cancellation occurs, a refund is given if the cabin can be filled.

Rates: All rates are per person per week. One-bedroom cabin (one person $2,120, two persons $1,755, three persons $1,500); two-bedroom cabin (three persons $1,880, four persons $1,630, five persons $1,500); three-bedroom cabin (five persons $1,680, six persons $1,500). Prices reduced prior to early June and after late August. Winter rates are $120 per night per person. A 15 percent service charge is added to all bills. Summer rates include three meals a day, horseback riding, and all ranch activities.

Location: East side of Grand Teton National Park, 25 miles north of Jackson, Wyoming. The ranch is 6 miles south of Moran Junction, on U.S. 26, 89, and 191.

Season: Summer season: late May to the first week in November. Winter season: December 26 to mid-March.

Food: Three daily family-style meals are served in the ranch dining room. Meals are included in the quoted rates for both summer and winter seasons.

Transportation: Scheduled airlines serve Jackson, Wyoming, where rental vehicles are available. Salt Lake City, Utah, is the nearest large airport. Triangle X provides shuttle service from the Jackson airport for $40 per trip.

Facilities: Corrals, dining room, laundry, gift shop.

Activities: Summer—horseback riding, breakfast and dinner cookouts, square dancing, fishing, hiking. Optional services offered (fee)—float trips, guided-fishing trips, pack trips (minimum of four days), and hunting trips (ten days). Winter—cross-country skiing, snowmobiling, snowshoeing, wildlife viewing, relaxing in the outdoor hot tub. Downhill skiing is available at three resorts in the area.

Yellowstone National Park

P.O. Box 168 • Yellowstone National Park, WY 82190 • (307) 344-7381 • www.nps.gov/yell

Yellowstone National Park, the world's first and probably best-known national park, comprises nearly 3,400 square miles of lakes, waterfalls, mountains, and some 10,000 geysers and hot springs. The park has almost 300 miles of roads. Most of the major attractions are near Grand Loop Road, which makes a figure eight in the park's central area. The road's east side provides access to canyons, mountains, and waterfalls, while the west side leads to areas of thermal activity. Most of the park is in the northwestern corner of Wyoming, with overlapping strips in Montana and Idaho. **Park Entrance Fee:** $25 per vehicle, $20 per motorcycle, or $12 per person, good for seven days. This entrance fee also covers Grand Teton National Park and the connecting parkway.

Lodging in Yellowstone National Park: Yellowstone has nine separate lodging facilities scattered about the park. One is near the north entrance, one is in the northeast section, one is in the canyon area, two are in Lake Village on the north shore of Lake Yellowstone, one is 20 miles inside the south entrance, and three are in the Old Faithful area. The lodges offer a wide choice of accommodations that range from rustic cabins without a private bathroom to a modern upscale lodge with handcrafted furniture. Likewise, prices range from what you are likely to pay for a Motel 6 in rural America to the price of a nice hotel room in a major city. Much of Yellowstone's lodging consists of cabins in four categories. In ascending order of quality and cost, cabins are classified as Budget (rustic, small, no private bathroom), Pioneer (rustic, small, private bathroom), Frontier (small or midsize, nicer interior, private bathroom), and Western (nicest, larger than Frontier, private bathroom). The cabins are generally quite old, but the interiors have often been refurbished. In general, we find the cabins to have nicer interiors than indicated by the exterior appearance.

Mammoth Hot Springs Hotel and Cabins, near the north entrance, offers a historic hotel plus rustic cabins, both of which have rooms with and without private bathrooms.

Roosevelt Lodge Cabins, in the northeast section of the park, has rustic cabins with and without private bathrooms. Roosevelt is the park's smallest lodging facility and offers some of the least expensive accommodations in Yellowstone.

Canyon Lodge and Cabins, the park's largest lodging facility is centrally located midway between the east and west entrances. Canyon includes two modern lodge buildings with a total of eighty-one rooms plus three categories of cabins, each with a private bathroom.

Lake Village, on the east side of the park, has two separate but nearby lodging facilities. Lake Yellowstone Hotel and Cabins provides 110 recently renovated Frontier Cabins plus an elegant historic hotel that was completely redone in the early 1990s. Nearby, Lake Lodge Cabins has 186 cabins that range from rustic to reasonably modern.

Grant Village, near the park's south entrance from Grand Teton National Park, has six relatively modern motel-type buildings with nearly 300 rooms. This is our least favorite place to stay.

The Old Faithful Area has three different lodging facilities, including the famous Old Faithful Inn, with 327 rooms including many in the original structure, or "Old House," plus larger and more upscale rooms in two newer wings. Nearby, less well-known Old Faithful Lodge Cabins offers cabins with and without private bathrooms at relatively inexpensive rates. Old Faithful Snow Lodge and Cabins, behind its more famous sister hotel, has two classes of cabins plus one hundred rooms in one of the newest and nicest hotels in the park. The cabins at Snow Lodge are larger and less closely clustered compared to the cabins at Old Faithful Lodge Cabins.

Yellowstone National Park

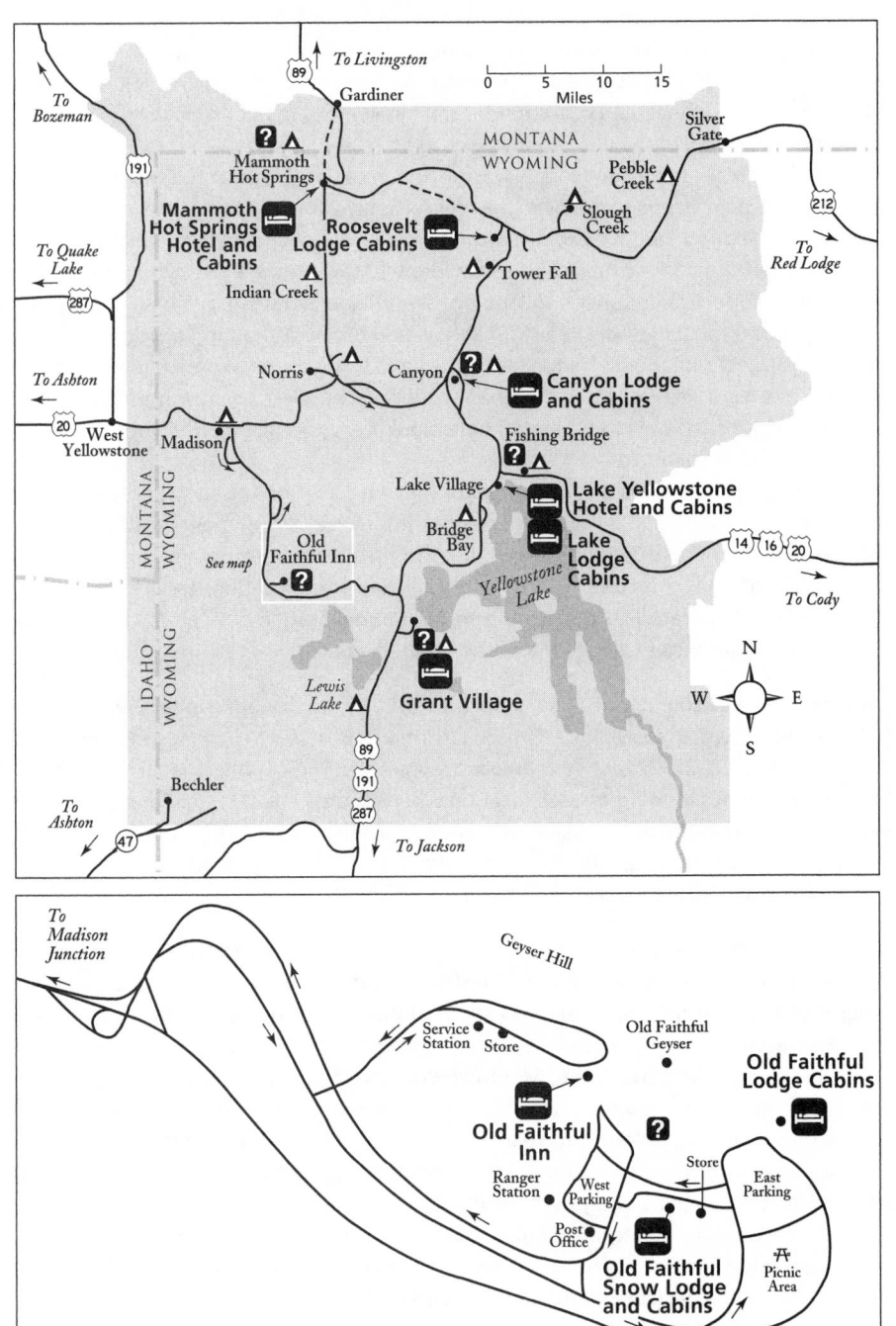

When choosing a lodging facility, remember that Yellowstone encompasses a very large area and visiting different sections of the park can entail unexpectedly long driving times. Distances are substantial, but planning to visit another area of the park on the basis of mileage alone will almost certainly result in underestimating the travel time required. Traffic can be heavy, animal watching causes bottlenecks on the roads, and the park seems to be in an endless cycle of road repair that often slows traffic to a standstill. Thus, consider staying in more than one location, especially if you will be visiting for more than a couple of days.

Three good choices for a stay of a week are the areas of Old Faithful, Mammoth, and Lake Village. Every first-time visitor to Yellowstone will certainly want to spend time in the Old Faithful area, which offers a good base for exploring the park's geyser country. Staying at Mammoth offers time to learn about the park's history and to explore what was once an Army fort for soldiers who protected Yellowstone. Either Canyon Village or Lake Village can serve as a base for exploring the park's canyon country and viewing beautiful Yellowstone Falls. Although Canyon Village is nearer canyon country, our choice would be to stay in the Lake Village area, which enjoys a more relaxed atmosphere. Lake Yellowstone Hotel is probably our favorite place to stay in the park. If you are planning a short visit and want to stay in a single place, Canyon Village offers the most convenient location to all the park's features.

Yellowstone is very busy, so it is important to make reservations as early as possible. If you are unable to obtain a reservation when you first call, it may pay to call periodically, because openings may become available due to cancellations. You may be able to obtain a room as a walk-in, although you aren't likely to have much choice regarding the location, facility, or cost. All nine lodging facilities are operated by the same firm, so the registration desk at any of the lodges can determine whether vacancies exist at any of the other locations.

Reservations for All Accommodations Inside the Park: Yellowstone National Park Lodges (operated by Xanterra Parks & Resorts), Reservations Office, P.O. Box 168, Yellowstone National Park, WY 82190. Phone (888) 297-2757; www.TravelYellowstone.com. The concessionaire requires a deposit equal to the first night's lodging at each location where you will be staying. Cancellation notice of forty-eight hours during the summer season required for refund of deposit. Fourteen days' advance notice required for cancellation of winter reservations. If traveling in an off-season, be sure to inquire about seasonal specials, such as Early Bird, Fall, and Winter Kickoff specials.

Transportation: Scheduled airlines serve Bozeman, Montana, on the northwest side; West Yellowstone, Montana (closed in winter), on the west side; Cody, Wyoming, on the east side; Jackson, Wyoming, south of Grand Teton National Park, and Billings, Montana, which is 129 miles to the northeast. Rental vehicles are available at all five locations. Scheduled shuttle service is available to the park from Bozeman and Livingston, Montana. Bus service operates between Cody and the park. No public transportation system operates within Yellowstone National Park, although narrated bus tours along the upper and lower loop roads are scheduled from various lodging locations in the park. Heavy traffic, poor road conditions, crowded overlooks, and seemingly continual repairs can make driving in Yellowstone an aggravating affair.

Snowcoaches operate during winter months between Old Faithful and West Yellowstone (three hours one-way), Mammoth (four hours one-way), and Flagg Ranch (three and a half hours one-way). Within the park, only Old Faithful Snow Lodge and Mammoth Hotel are open during winter months. The road from Livingston to Mammoth and then on to Cooke City is open year-round. All other roads in the park are closed. Transportation is available between Jackson and Flagg Ranch during winter months. Most of the transportation mentioned above operates only once per day.

CANYON LODGE AND CABINS

Yellowstone National Park, WY 82190 • (307) 344-7331 • www.TravelYellowstone.com

Canyon Lodge and Cabins is Yellowstone's largest lodging complex and includes a registration building, hundreds of cabins, and two modern lodge buildings that are part of a large commercial center. The Canyon Village center also includes a large general store/coffee shop, a registration building, a restaurant, a cafeteria, a lounge, a sporting goods store, a gas station, a post office, gift shops, and a new National Park Service visitor education center. This is a busy commercial center, but most overnight rooms are far enough away that you will be able to enjoy a relatively quiet stay. It is also large enough that you will have a hike, or you may prefer driving, to the restaurant, depending on the location of your cabin. Canyon Village takes its name from the Grand Canyon of the Yellowstone River, a half mile away. The village is near the park's center, 42 miles from the east entrance and 40 miles from the west entrance at West Yellowstone.

Canyon Lodge and Cabins has four classes of accommodations. All of the rooms have heat and private baths but no telephone, television, or air-conditioning. Adequate parking is near all the rooms. The least expensive and most plentiful lodging at Canyon are almost 400

Pioneer and Frontier Cabins built in the 1950s. These cabins are constructed either six or eight to a building and clustered in two large loops behind the registration building and commercial center. Cabins in both categories are essentially identical except for various upgrades that are often relatively minor. Each cabin has a very small bathroom with a shower. The cabins come in two sizes, regardless of category, with two twins in small units and usually two doubles in larger units. A Pioneer Cabin with two double beds is larger than the more expensive Frontier Cabin with two twin beds. A cabin might be upgraded to the more expensive category because of new carpet, new beds, or a new roof. In many instances it is difficult to determine which type of cabin you are in other than by the price. We found that even housekeeping employees have difficulty determining if a cabin is Pioneer or Frontier without looking at the rate card on the door.

One hundred Western Cabins are constructed four or six units to a building. These units were constructed in 1969 and extensively refurbished from 2005 to 2007. Western Cabins are quite a bit larger and nicer compared to cabins in the other two categories. Each

■ ■ ■

Canyon Lodge is within walking distance of the North Rim of the Grand Canyon of the Yellowstone. A half-mile trail leads from cabin P26 to the North Rim's Grandview Point. From here North Rim Trail leads either 1 mile northeast to Inspiration Point or 1 mile southwest to the Lower Falls. The entire North Rim Trail, which begins at South Rim Drive Bridge and ends at Inspiration Point, is slightly less than 3 miles, and a portion of it is paved. A variety of trails are also on the south side of the canyon.

■ ■ ■

Western Cabin has two queen beds, a bathroom with a combination shower-tub, a coffeemaker, and upgraded furniture.

Two newer rustic-style lodge buildings with steep shake roofs and dormers offer eighty-one nearly identical rooms, each with two double beds (except for seven wheelchair rooms and two rooms on the fourth floor of Dunraven), a carpeted floor, attractive pine furniture, and a bathroom with a combination shower-tub. The rooms have coffeemakers and electric heat, but no air-conditioning, telephone, or television.

Public telephones, vending machines, and ice machines are in each of the two buildings that are adjacent to one another and connected by a short walkway. Adequate parking is near the entrance to each building. The oldest of the two, Cascade Lodge, was constructed in 1993 and has thirty-seven rooms on three floors. The newer Dunraven Lodge was completed in 1999 and has forty-four rooms on four floors. Dunraven is built on a small hillside and entered on the second floor. The first floor has rooms on only one side. Only Dunraven has an elevator, and an attractive lobby with a steepled ceiling is on the second floor. The lobby is for use by guests of both lodge buildings. The rooms in these two lodges are by far the nicest accommodations in the Canyon complex.

If you are traveling on a tight budget, select a Pioneer cabin with two double beds. This will put you in one of the larger units at relatively low cost. For those seeking more upscale accommodations, we would choose either of the lodge units over a Western Cabin. Of the two, you might want to select the newer Dunraven Lodge because it has an elevator. Try for second- or third-floor rooms on the south side (odd-numbered rooms) that face the woods rather than the parking lot. Dunraven rooms on the fourth floor are somewhat smaller than rooms on the other floors. Rooms on the third floor of Cascade, especially 305 and 307, are larger and offer views of the woods.

Canyon Lodge and Cabins is the most convenient place to stay if you plan to explore Yellowstone from a single base. It is a large complex, and many of the cabins show their age. However, the strategic location at the center of Yellowstone may trump any negatives, especially if you plan to spend most of every day touring this large park. The lodge is situated in the canyon district, one of the park's most scenic areas. Canyon Village, in which the lodge is located, has anything you will need after a long day of sightseeing. A restaurant, cafeteria, coffee shop, and picnic shop offer an array of meals and prices. You will also find gift shops, a sporting goods store, and a large general store with books, supplies, gifts, and groceries. An exceptional National Park Service visitor education center is across the parking lot from the registration building .

Rooms: Doubles, triples, and quads. All rooms have a private bath.

Wheelchair Accessibility: A total of seven ADA-compliant rooms are in the two lodge buildings. Each room has one queen bed or a double bed plus a twin bed and a bathroom with a roll-in shower. Five Western Cabins with one double bed plus a twin bed are ADA compliant with a combination shower-tub in the bathrooms.

Rates: Pioneer Cabins ($70); Frontier Cabins ($96); Western Cabins ($149); lodge rooms ($164). Each additional person is $11 per night. Children eleven and under stay free.

Location: Near the middle of Yellowstone National Park, 40 miles from the west entrance at West Yellowstone.

Season: June through the last week in September.

Food: Several eating options are available in the Canyon commercial center, which is a long walk from the two lodge buildings and many of the cabins. A dining room offers a breakfast buffet ($12), lunch ($13), and dinner ($13–$23). A less expensive cafeteria serves three meals a day with dinner costing from $7.00–$17.00. The picnic shop serves sandwiches, salads, drinks, and ice cream. A coffee shop in the general store serves breakfast, salads, sandwiches, hamburgers, ice cream, and beverages. A lounge serves appetizers.

Facilities: Restaurant, cafeteria, picnic shop, coffee shop, lounge, gift shop, laundry, general store with groceries, sporting goods store, post office, gas station, stables, National Park Service visitor education center.

Activities: Horseback riding, hiking, narrated excursions, evening ranger programs.

Grant Village

Yellowstone National Park, WY 82190 • (307) 344-7311 • www.TravelYellowstone.com

Grant Village includes a registration building, two restaurants, and six modern two-story lodge buildings, each with approximately fifty rooms. A general store, service station, and National Park Service visitor education center are nearby. The wooden lodge buildings, constructed from 1982 to 1984, sit staggered across a hillside above the south shore of the West Thumb of Yellowstone Lake. Adequate parking is directly in front of each building. There are no elevators, but assistance with luggage can be requested at the registration building. Grant Village is located in the south end of Yellowstone, in the West Thumb area. It is the southernmost lodging facility in the park, 20 miles north of the south entrance to Yellowstone.

The lodge buildings and rooms are similar to what you are likely to find in a newer Holiday Inn Express or Comfort Inn. Rooms on both floors of each building are entered from long central corridors. Although half the rooms in each of the six lodge buildings face toward the lake, views are obscured by pine trees. All of the rooms have electric heat, a coffeemaker, a hair dryer, a telephone, and a private bath. About half the bathrooms have a shower only, while the remainder offer a combination shower-tub. None of the rooms have air-conditioning, a television, or a balcony. All rooms except those with one double bed are of decent size, although probably somewhat smaller than a typical motel room. Each building has a small first-floor lobby with tables and chairs. Rooms in the two older buildings, B and C, were recently remodeled and rent for a slight premium.

Other than opting for one of the lodge buildings with a remodeled room, the building you are assigned really doesn't matter much. Building A is closest to the dining room, so this may be a factor. Ask for a room with two double beds, because the few rooms with one double bed (other than ADA rooms) are quite a bit smaller. You might also consider asking for a room that doesn't face a parking lot. The eight corner rooms in buildings A, D, E, and F enjoy an extra side window.

Grant Village primarily appeals to people traveling between Grand Teton and Yellowstone after a long day of driving and sightseeing in one of the two parks. In other words, it is a place to spend a night rather than a base from which to explore the park. Being away from the park's heavily visited tourist areas means the village is quiet and free from the traffic and crowds found in much of the rest of Yellowstone. In addition, it is only 19 miles from the park's main attraction, Old Faithful. Stay at Grant Village and you can beat the crowds by arriving at Old Faithful early the next morning. Three eating establishments with varying menus and prices are only a short walk from the lodge buildings. The Grant Village dining room near Lodge A is in an unusual building, with windows that offer lake views and a high vaulted ceiling supported by large beams. A small cocktail lounge is just off the entrance area. An informal and less expensive restaurant, Lake House, is directly on the lake and serves a buffet breakfast and pizza and pasta for dinner. Large floor-to-ceiling windows on three sides of the building provide excellent lake views. A general store near the registration building houses a grill that serves breakfast, sandwiches, ice cream, and beverages.

Rooms: Doubles, triples, and quads. All rooms have a private bath with shower or combination shower-tub.

Wheelchair Accessibility: Two rooms on the first floor of each building have either one queen bed or one double bed, a roll-in shower, and are ADA compliant.

Rates: Mid-range room ($138); high-range remodeled room ($143). Rates are quoted for two adults. Each additional person is $11 per night. Children eleven and under stay free.

Location: At the south end of the park, 20 miles north of the south entrance.

Season: The end of May through the last week in September.

Food: Grant Village Dining Room serves a breakfast buffet (11.00), breakfast menu items ($6.00–$9.00), lunch ($8.00–$10.00), and dinner ($19.00–$29.00) in an attractive building. Lake House serves a breakfast buffet ($8.25), a dinner buffet ($12.00), and a dinner menu ($7.00–$14.00). A grill in the general store serves breakfast, salads, sandwiches, and beverages. The store also has a good offering of groceries.

Facilities: Dining room, restaurant, cocktail lounge, grill, general store, gift shop, service station, boat ramp, post office, laundry, National Park Service visitor center.

Activities: Hiking, fishing, narrated bus tours, evening ranger programs at the campground amphitheater.

LAKE LODGE CABINS

Yellowstone National Park, WY 82190 • (307) 344-7311 • www.TravelYellowstone.com

Lake Lodge Cabins is a complex consisting of a large log building with a registration desk and support services, plus 186 wood cabins situated on a hill overlooking the lodge. No guest rooms are in the main registration building, which has a cafeteria, a gift shop, a cocktail lounge, and a large lobby area with two impressive gas fireplaces. The main building has a long covered front porch with chairs and overlooks Yellowstone Lake. The

entire complex sits back from the lake, and the cabins offer no lake views. Parking is near each cabin unit. The lodge is located at Lake Village, in the eastern section of Yellowstone National Park. It is 30 miles from the park's east entrance station.

Lake Lodge Cabins offers two types of cabin accommodations. All of the cabins have heat and private bath with shower, with some of the Western Cabins having a combination shower-tub. There is no air-conditioning, telephone, or television in any of the cabins. Most of the cabins are constructed four to a building, although a few buildings have two units and others have six. The least expensive alternative is the eighty-six Pioneer Cabins that sit in an area devoid of trees. The smallest Pioneer Cabins have one double bed; larger units have two double beds. These cabins look very rustic on the outside, but the interior is fairly nice, with paneled walls and carpeting. Cabins D11 through D20 have been extensively refurbished with a new foundation, a new interior, and the removal of lowered ceiling tiles to reveal the original vaulted ceiling. These refurbished cabins rent for the same price as Pioneer units that have not been renovated.

One hundred Western Cabins are identical to those at Canyon Lodge and Cabins. All are the same size and come with two double beds or two double beds plus a twin bed. These cabins are quite a bit larger and cost twice as much as the Pioneer Cabins. The layouts differ from building to building, but a majority of Western Cabins have windows in two walls. Western Cabins in loops A, B, and J have been extensively renovated with brighter interiors, upgraded furniture, and new bathrooms with shower-tub combinations. These rent for slightly more than other Western Cabins. Western Cabins toward the rear of the complex (units in loops G, H, and J) are spaced farther apart and surrounded by trees.

■　　■　　■

Lake Lodge was constructed during the 1920s to provide mid-level accommodations to travelers who didn't want to tent camp but who couldn't afford the more expensive hotels. The East Wing was added as a dining area (currently the cafeteria) in 1926, and the West Wing was built as a dance hall (now an employee recreation hall) in the same year. The front porch of Lake Lodge was added in 1929.

■　　■　　■

Lake Lodge Cabins provides both modestly priced and more upscale accommodations in a section of the park that is scenic and relatively quiet. Recently renovated Pioneer Cabins are quite nice and an excellent value because they rent for the same price as other cabins of the same class. If you desire a larger room, try for a renovated Western Cabin. This is the nearest lodging complex to Fishing Bridge and Bridge Bay Marina. Guests can enjoy a leisurely stroll across a wide grassy area to beautiful Yellowstone Lake, frequently in the presence of a grazing buffalo or two. Dining options range from a relatively inexpensive cafeteria in the registration building to an elegant dining room in adjacent Lake Yellowstone Hotel. Make reservations as early as possible if you want to eat dinner in the hotel dining room.

Rooms: Doubles, triples, and quads. A few rooms have a single bed for a fifth person. All cabins have private baths.

Wheelchair Accessibility: Two renovated Western Cabins are ADA compliant and have large showers.

Rates: Pioneer Cabins ($66); Western Cabins ($138–$149). Rates quoted are for two adults. Each additional person is $11 per night. Children eleven and under stay free with an adult.

Location: On the north shore of Yellowstone Lake, in the east-central section of Yellowstone National Park. The lodge is approximately 30 miles from the east park entrance and 43 miles from the south entrance.

Season: Mid-June to mid-September.

Food: A cafeteria is open for breakfast ($4.00–$8.00), lunch/dinner ($6.00–$17.00). A nearby general store has limited groceries and a lunch counter that serves breakfast, salads, sandwiches, soups, ice cream, and beverages. Nearby Lake Yellowstone Hotel has a lovely dining room and a small deli.

Facilities: Gift shop, laundry, cafeteria, cocktail lounge. A general store is a short walk from the lodge. Nearby Lake Yellowstone Hotel offers additional facilities.

Activities: Hiking, fishing. Nearby Bridge Bay Marina offers boat tours on Lake Yellowstone, boat rentals, and narrated tours.

LAKE YELLOWSTONE HOTEL AND CABINS

Yellowstone National Park, WY 82190 • (307) 344-7311 • www.TravelYellowstone.com

Lake Yellowstone Hotel and Cabins comprises a three- and four-story hotel building, an adjacent two-story annex, and 110 closely clustered cabin units that are located behind the hotel. The hotel, annex, and cabins offer a total of 304 rooms. The large hotel is the oldest public lodging facility in the park today. An extensive renovation returned the hotel to its 1920s appearance. The first floor houses the registration desk, lobby, dining room, lobby bar, gift shop, and a few rooms. The wonderful lobby and sunroom, with some of the hotel's original wicker furniture, has large windows that overlook Yellowstone Lake. The 1920s-era dining room has large windows on the south and west walls. Although most guests first enter the hotel from the large back parking lot, driving under the hotel's front portico provides more convenient access for registration and dropping off luggage. Lake Yellowstone Hotel and Cabins is located in the east-central portion of Yellowstone National Park, on the north shore of Yellowstone Lake. It is 30 miles from the east entrance to the park.

The main hotel, often called Lake Hotel, has 158 rooms in two wings, one on each side of the main lobby. The hotel's only elevator is in the East Wing, and bell service is available. All of the rooms are attractively decorated and each has heat, a full tiled bathroom, a fan, a coffeemaker, bathrobes, a hair dryer, and a telephone, but no air-conditioning or television. Room size and beds vary, but the largest rooms are in the three-story West Wing, while the best lake views are from end rooms of the East Wing. The East Wing elevator makes it easy to haul luggage to fourth-floor rooms that enjoy the best views and where nobody is walking on a floor above. We recommend even-numbered rooms 430 to 460. Bedding ranges from one to three queen-size beds, although a few rooms have two double beds. Other than one second-floor suite, all rooms in the hotel, regardless of size and bedding, are priced according to whether they face the lake or are on the back side of the hotel. Rooms on the lake side rent for an extra $10 per night, which is money well spent. The Presidential Suite on

■ ■ ■

Construction on Lake Yellowstone Hotel began in 1889 in an area once populated by native tribes, fur trappers, and mountain men. The first guests arrived two years later. Additions engineered by the architect of Old Faithful Inn in the early 1900s nearly tripled the number of rooms at the hotel to 210. The East Wing, with 113 additional rooms, was completed in the early 1920s, and the sunroom was added in 1924. The hotel had fallen into disrepair by the 1980s, when a decade-long renovation was initiated to return the building to its glory years of the 1920s.

■ ■ ■

the corner of the second floor has a queen bed in each of two large bedrooms, two full bathrooms, and a large living room with a wet bar and refrigerator stocked with snacks and sodas. In the West Wing, room 100 with one queen bed is a good choice. In general, requesting a room with two queen beds means you are likely to end up with a larger room at no additional cost.

The two-story annex, which was once used as employee housing, has thirty-six rooms that are nearly as nice as rooms in the main hotel but rent for $65 less per night. Annex rooms have heat, a telephone, a coffeemaker, a hair dryer, bathrobes, and a private bathroom with a combination shower-tub (except for four wheelchair-accessible rooms that each have a roll-in shower), but no air-conditioning or television. A small lobby with several stuffed chairs is on the first floor. Beds in annex rooms consist of either one or two doubles. Rooms with two double beds are generally larger but rent for the same price. None of the rooms in the annex offers particularly good views, although those on the east side provide views of pine trees, while rooms on the west side overlook the parking lot. The annex rooms probably offer a better value than rooms in the main hotel, especially if you can get a larger room with two double beds on the east side. If you book a room in the annex, this is what you should request.

The Frontier Cabins were built in the 1940s and renovated from 2002 to 2005. They are closely clustered in an area devoid of trees behind the hotel and away from the lake. Most of the cabins are constructed as duplex units, with rooms that back up to one another. The remaining cabins are freestanding units. All the cabins are approximately the same size and have a nicely finished interior with carpeting, two double beds, and a private bathroom with a shower. If you decide to book a cabin, request freestanding units 49, 50, or 51, which sit at the end of the complex and face the lake and trees. In addition, you will avoid noise from guests in an adjoining room.

Lake Yellowstone Hotel and Cabins is our favorite place to spend several nights in Yellowstone National Park. It is in a peaceful setting on a beautiful lake, and you can't go wrong with any of the lodging. The hotel captures the ambience of an earlier period, with a bright, airy sunroom that is a pleasant place to read a book or talk with friends, while stealing occasional glances at the lake. A pianist or string quartet entertains here most evenings. The hotel has a delightful dining room and a small deli and is a short distance from neighboring Lake Lodge Cabins, which offers laundry facilities and a relatively inexpensive cafeteria. If you are unable to secure a room on the lake side of the hotel, or if you prefer not to pay $200 per night, consider an Annex room that is just as nice as a hotel room, only without the view and atmosphere. The Frontier Cabins, especially the freestanding units, offer the best value at this location. Choosing a cabin makes it easier to transport luggage because parking is close to each of these units. The Annex is immediately adjacent to the hotel, and the cabins are nearby, so staying in the Annex or cabins allows guests to enjoy the hotel's sunroom and dining room.

Rooms: Doubles, triples, and quads. A few rooms sleep up to six. All rooms, including cabins, have private bathrooms.

Wheelchair Accessibility: Four first-floor rooms in the Annex and five Frontier Cabins are ADA compliant. The dining room in the main hotel is wheelchair accessible, with ramp access into the building.

Rates: Frontier Cabins ($128); Annex ($143); hotel—back ($206), front ($216), suite ($565). Children eleven and under stay free. Each additional person is $11 per night.

Location: East-central section of the park, on the north shore of Yellowstone Lake. The hotel is 30 miles from the park's east entrance.

Season: From mid-May to early October.

Food: A 1920s-era hotel dining room serves breakfast ($6.00–$1100), lunch ($9.00–$13.00), and dinner ($17.00–$39.00). A breakfast buffet ($13.00) is served daily. A children's menu is available. A deli on the first floor is open from 10:30 a.m. to 9:00 p.m. for sandwiches, soups, and beverages. A cafeteria at nearby Lake Lodge Cabins serves three meals a day. A general store close to the hotel has limited groceries and a counter that serves breakfast, sandwiches, soups, salads, ice cream, and beverages.

Facilities: Clinic, dining room, lobby bar, small deli, gift shop, post office. Nearby is a general store. Lake Lodge Cabins has a cafeteria and laundry facilities.

Activities: Hiking, fishing, photo tour, sunset tour, narrated park tours, evening music in the hotel lobby. Nearby Bridge Bay Marina offers boat tours on Lake Yellowstone, boat rentals, and fishing guides.

MAMMOTH HOT SPRINGS HOTEL AND CABINS

Yellowstone National Park, WY 82190 • (307) 344-7311 • www.TravelYellowstone.com

If you have ever wanted to stay at an old Army fort, then Mammoth Hot Springs Hotels and Cabins is your place. The hotel is adjacent to buildings that were once part of a small military post that served as headquarters for the U.S. Army when it was in charge of this park. Some of the original Army buildings are still in use as housing and administrative offices for personnel of the National Park Service. The current lodging complex at Mammoth comprises a four-story hotel plus 115 cabin units that together provide a total of 212 rooms.

Registration for all lodging is in the first-floor lobby of the hotel. Bell service is available at the front desk. The cabin units each have their own parking area and are clustered along the roads and in grassy areas behind the hotel. Mammoth Hot Springs Hotel and Cabins is located near the north entrance to Yellowstone National Park, 5 miles south of Gardiner, Montana.

The lodging complex offers various types of rooms, both in the hotel and in the cabins. Ninety-seven hotel rooms each have steam heat and a telephone, but no air-conditioning or television (with the exception of the suites). An elevator is near the registration desk. The hotel has sixty-eight rooms with a private bath that rent

for about $30 per night more than twenty-nine rooms without a private bath. Community bath and shower rooms are on each floor. Rooms without a bath have two double beds. Regular hotel rooms with a bath have two double beds or a double bed plus a single bed. Some bathrooms have a tub, some have a shower, and some have both. Corner rooms 230, 231, 330, and 331 each have a full bath and rent for the same price but are quite a bit larger than other rooms with a bath. The hotel has two suites, one each on the third and fourth floors. These are about the size of two regular rooms and have a bedroom plus separate sitting room. The suites each have a television and coffeemaker, and guests receive a gift basket and a newspaper. The fourth-floor suite has two bathrooms, one with a shower-tub combination. The third-floor suite has one bathroom with a shower but no tub.

The cabin units, both with and without a private bath, are either freestanding or duplex units. All cabins have nearly identical living space (not counting the small bathroom in the Frontier cabins), finished interiors, two double beds, a sink with hot and cold water, and a covered front porch with chairs. Frontier cabins, all of

The hotel and cabins currently operating at Mammoth are only the latest chapter in a long history of lodging in this area. The first crude hotel in the park was built at Mammoth in 1871. The much larger and more elaborate National Hotel was constructed here in 1883. An annex that was added to the National Hotel in 1911 serves as the main lodging section of today's Mammoth Hot Springs Hotel. The remainder of the old National Hotel was torn down. The current hotel's front section containing the lobby, a map room, and a gift shop was added in 1936 and 1937, one year before the first ninety-six cabins were completed behind the hotel.

which were completely remodeled from 2005 to 2008, have a shower and toilet and rent for about $30 extra per night compared to Budget cabins without a bath. Four of the Frontier cabins with one queen bed each have a large hot tub on a private porch and rent for approximately $100 extra per night. These hot tubs can be rented by the hour during winter months. All of the cabins front either on a road or around a grassy area. The latter are preferred, and we recommend Budget cabins C26, C27, and C30. Frontier cabins B14, B15, B16, C46, and C49 are recommended if you desire a private bath. Each of these cabins is freestanding, fronts on a grassy area, and enjoys morning sun. A13 and A14, one Frontier and one Budget cabin, are in a duplex building. This is a good choice for a family who needs more than one cabin since both rooms will have access to a bathroom without being charged for two cabins with a bath.

Mammoth Hot Springs Hotel and Cabins is located in a unique and interesting section of Yellowstone National Park. It's fun to walk through the surrounding area and view the historic buildings of this former Army post. A National Park Service visitor center in one of the old military buildings has exhibits on the park's early history. Trails to the upper and lower terrace areas begin near a picnic area just down the road from the hotel. Mammoth is a handy location for the many visitors who are planning a trip to Lamar Valley in an attempt to view the park's elusive wolves. Staying here allows guests the flexibility of eating in a large art deco–style dining room or at a lower-cost grill on the opposite side of the same building. We prefer the cabins listed above to rooms in the hotel. The cabins allow you to relax on your own front porch, and parking beside each cabin makes loading and unloading luggage less of a chore. The major downside of staying at Mammoth is its location at the extreme north end of the park, some distance away from Old Faithful and many of Yellowstone's other popular sites. Choosing to stay only at Mammoth will result in substantial amounts of driving while going to and from other features of the park. This isn't an issue if you will be utilizing several lodging locations during your visit.

Rooms: Doubles, triples, and quads. Many hotel rooms and cabins have private baths.

Wheelchair Accessibility: The hotel has a ramp to the elevator that provides access to all floors. Two rooms in the hotel and four cabin units, each with a roll-in shower and one queen bed, are ADA compliant. The restaurant across the street from the hotel is wheelchair accessible, with access through the grill on the opposite side of the building.

Rates: Budget Cabins ($75); Frontier Cabins ($107); Frontier Cabins with hot tubs ($211); hotel rooms without a bath ($85); hotel rooms with a bath ($115); suites ($427). Rates quoted are for two persons except suites, which are for up to four. Each additional person is $11 per night. Children eleven and under stay free. Special packages are offered during the winter season.

Location: North end of Yellowstone National Park, 5 miles south of Gardiner, Montana.

Season: Summer season is from early May to early October. Winter season is from mid-December to early March. During winter months, only the hotel is open. The hot tub cabins are open to rent by the hour.

Food: A large dining room across the street from the hotel offers breakfast ($6.00–$10.00), lunch ($7.00–$12.00), and dinner ($13.00–$26.00). A children's menu is available. A grill next to the dining room offers breakfast items, a variety of fast food, soups, salads, and ice cream. A general store sells ice cream, beverages, limited groceries, and alcoholic beverages.

Facilities: Restaurant, cocktail lounge, espresso bar in lobby, grill, gift shop, general store, post office, National Park Service visitor center. Winter season: ski shop, ice-skating rink, and skate and snowshoe rental.

Activities: Walks along the boardwalk that winds through the hot springs area, walking among the historic buildings at Mammoth (printed guide available), hiking, evening programs. Winter activities include ice skating, guided snowshoe touring, cross-country skiing, snowmobiling, guided snowmobile touring, snowcoach rides.

OLD FAITHFUL INN

Yellowstone National Park, WY 82190 • (307) 344-7311 • www.TravelYellowstone.com

Old Faithful Inn is America's most famous national park lodge. Think of national parks, and both Yellowstone and this historic hotel will almost certainly come to mind. The large lobby, with log beams and a vaulted ceiling that soars 77 feet above the first floor, has multiple overhanging balconies. A mezzanine with chairs, tables, and sofas wraps around the entire second floor. Oddly shaped logs are used as decoration and for support of the railings and log beams. A huge clock projects from the front of a massive, four-sided stone fireplace that highlights the lobby. An attractive restaurant and lounge are entered from the back of the lobby. The hotel is well maintained, and all of the facilities, including the rooms, are clean and comfortable.

The inn doesn't directly face Old Faithful, but arriving guests are likely to discover that the famous geyser is the first thing they see as they drive up to the front door to unload their luggage. Good views of Old Faithful are obtained from several locations in the hotel, including the large second-floor porch and a few of the lodging rooms. All of the lodging rooms are in the older main section and the two attached wings.

The Northern Pacific Railroad financed the construction of Old Faithful Inn, which provided lodging for the large number of tourists coming to this area by train. The hotel that would cost approximately $140,000 was to replace the Upper Geyser Basin Hotel, which had been lost to fire. Old Faithful Inn was constructed in three phases: the original Old House along with the dining room, kitchen wings, small guest room wings, and the magnificent seven-story lobby was completed in 1903. The East Wing was constructed from 1913 to 1914, while the Y-shaped West Wing was added in 1927. Numerous modifications have taken place over the years, including an expansion of the lobby (timber columns supporting the balconies replaced the old north wall), additions to the dining room, and construction of the cocktail lounge.

No cabins or separate buildings are part of the hotel, although two other lodging facilities with cabins are nearby. The registration desk for Old Faithful Inn is to the left as you enter the lobby. Bell service is available to assist with luggage. A large parking area is in front of the hotel, a relatively short walk from the entrance. Lodging rooms are on three floors in the Old House (the original structure) and the East Wing, and on four floors in the West Wing. One elevator is in each wing, but these are relatively slow during busy times, so you may end up climbing several flights of stairs depending upon where your room is located. Old Faithful Inn is in the southwest portion of Yellowstone National Park, 30 miles from the entrance station at West Yellowstone.

The inn offers 327 rooms that vary in size, views, bathroom facilities, and configuration. Accommodations range from recently restored Old House rooms without private bath in the original central log building to relatively large rooms with a private bath in each of the wings. Room rates vary accordingly. All of the rooms have heat, but none have air-conditioning or television. Only the rooms in the east and west wings have telephones. Pay phones are in the hotel wings.

The least expensive rooms in Old Faithful Inn are in the original Old House section of the building. Although these rooms tend to be dark, and can also be noisy if they are located close to the busy lobby, the log or rough-hewn wood hallways and interior walls provide the ambience of a rustic national park lodge. These rooms received extensive restoration from 2006 to 2008. Most of the eighty-nine rooms in the Old House are without a private bathroom. Guests in these rooms must use one of the community bathrooms located on each corridor of this section of the building. Rooms in the Old House are all different and interesting. Some are small with one queen bed, while others are quite large with two rooms and up to three queen beds. First-floor rooms have interior log walls, while rooms on the second and third floors have walls of rough-hewn pine. Bathrooms often have claw-foot tubs, but none have a shower. A few have pull-chain toilets. If requesting an Old House room, keep in mind that there are no showers on the first floor, and guests staying in first-floor rooms without a bath are required to use second-floor shower rooms. Some of the best Old House rooms are without a private bathroom, such as corner room 229, which offers the best view of the Old Faithful geyser, and room 46, a large, rustic corner room with corner window seats. Room 243 has a unique shape and is entered from a short private stairway. The best rooms with a bath are 8 and 108, both of which have two bedrooms. Room 127 is large, offers a view of the geyser basin, and has a unique bathroom. President Clinton stayed in room 127 during his visit to Old Faithful. It is best to avoid rooms 1 through 6, which are in a hallway with a bathroom that is heavily used by nonguests.

Rooms in the East Wing are generally larger with either one or two double beds. These rooms also have tiled bathrooms, a coffeemaker, and a hair dryer. Rooms 1012, 1020, 1024, and corresponding rooms on the second and third floors offer good views of Old Faithful geyser. Three L-shaped mini-suites in this wing each have two queen beds and a sitting area with a coffeemaker, daily newspaper, and refrigerator stocked with snacks. Six two-room suites with windows facing Old Faithful each have two queen beds and a separate sitting room. The suites offer the same amenities as described for the mini-suites, including upgraded bathrooms.

Recently renovated West Wing rooms have a nice tiled bathroom, a coffeemaker, a hair dryer, and bedding that ranges from one queen to two doubles. Rooms facing the front of the hotel (even-numbered rooms) are somewhat larger and more expensive than rooms on the opposite side of the hallway. Although they entail a longer walk from the elevator and lobby, we like corner rooms 2073 and 2074, and corresponding rooms on the third and fourth floors. These rooms are at the end of the corridor and subject to less noise and foot traffic. They also provide additional light and better views by having windows on two walls.

Old Faithful Inn is the classic national park lodge in which every visitor to Yellowstone should stay at least one night. That first entry into the marvelous lobby often brings a child's sense of wonderment to the most tired traveler. Guests gather on the porch over the front portico for an excellent view of the Old Faithful geyser. The inn is convenient to the Upper and Lower Geyser basins and a good base for exploring thermal activity in this section of the park. Be aware that, during the summer, the inn is a busy place and the Old Faithful area is congested during the day. Both guests and visitors constantly roam the lobby, mezzanine, and second-floor porch, so if you are seeking quiet, this isn't the place. On the other hand, you've got to see Old Faithful, so you might as well do it from where you are staying.

Rooms: Doubles, triples, and quads. A few rooms in the Old House can sleep up to six persons. Most but not all rooms have a private bath.

Wheelchair Accessibility: Four wheelchair-accessible rooms each have a bathroom with a wide doorway and a combination shower-tub with grab bars. Two of the rooms have two single beds, and the other two rooms have a double plus a single bed.

Rates: Old House rooms; one room without a private bath ($93); two rooms without a private bath ($176 for up to six persons); one room with a private bath ($119); two rooms with a private bath ($206 for up to four persons). West Wing rooms; ($159–$202 depending on location and remodeling). East Wing rooms ($202–$228 depending on location). Semi-suites ($397); suites ($502). Most rates quoted are for two persons. Semi-suites and suites are quoted for four persons. Each additional person is $11 per night. Children eleven and under are free when staying with an adult.

Location: Southwest section of Yellowstone National Park, 30 miles from the entrance station at West Yellowstone.

Season: The second week in May through the second week in October.

Food: A dining room on the main floor serves a breakfast buffet ($11.00), a breakfast menu ($5.00–$9.00), a lunch buffet ($13.00), a lunch menu ($8.00–$9.00), a dinner buffet ($29.00), and dinner ($16.00–$33.00); reservations are required for dinner. A children's menu is available. The deli offers sandwiches, fast-food items, and ice cream; the bar sells sandwiches and appetizers; a lunch counter in the adjacent general store serves breakfast, salads, sandwiches, hamburgers, soup, ice cream, and beverages. Other eating facilities, including a cafeteria, are nearby.

Facilities: Dining room, mezzanine lounge, mezzanine espresso shop, deli, bar, tour desk, gift shop. Many additional facilities, including a gas station, gift shops, stores, and restaurants, are in the immediate area.

Activities: Walking through nearby geyser area, guided tours of the inn, narrated bus tours, hiking.

OLD FAITHFUL LODGE CABINS

Yellowstone National Park, WY 82190 • (307) 344-7311• www.TravelYellowstone.com

Old Faithful Lodge Cabins consists of a rustic lodge building plus ninety-seven cabins, mostly constructed two to four to a building. The main lodge was built in the late 1920s and has no overnight accommodations. The cabins are behind and to one side of the main lodge, which houses the registration desk. The impressive lobby area has large windows that provide an excellent view of Old Faithful. A big stone fireplace is surrounded with chairs and tables for eating, visiting, and viewing. The main building also has a food court, ice cream shop, bake shop, and gift shop. Old Faithful Lodge Cabins is in the southwest section of Yellowstone National Park, 30 miles from the west entrance at West Yellowstone. It is a short walk from the better-known Old Faithful Inn.

The lodge offers cabins in two classifications, Budget and Frontier. All of the cabins were remodeled in 2002 and have finished interiors, heat, electricity, and carpeted floors, but only Frontier Cabins have a private bathroom. Keep in mind that the cabins are not insulated, so the small electric heaters may prove inadequate when the outside temperature is low, as may be the case in the spring and fall. The cabins are clustered closely together behind the main lodge in an area with much paving and few trees. A few of the cabins front

Boardwalks and unpaved paths meander through Upper Geyser Basin, near Old Faithful Lodge Cabins. A boardwalk that begins near the lodge leads around Old Faithful geyser and through a large area of pools, geysers, and hot springs. One path is designated for both people and bicycles. One 3-mile loop leads to Morning Glory Pool and returns to the lodge. Both shorter and longer trails are in the basin area.

on a river, while several others face the geyser basin. Most, however, offer no particularly good views. Cabins in either classification are the best values in the Old Faithful area.

The least expensive rooms in the Old Faithful area are thirty-five Budget Cabins, which have a hot-and-cold water sink but no bathroom facilities. Toilets and sinks are in two community bathrooms and also in the main lodge building. Shower facilities are only in the community bathroom nearest the lodge office. Bedding in Budget Cabins is a double bed plus a twin bed or two double beds. Cabins in this classification are all the same size, so units with two doubles have less floor space for you and your belongings. All except two Budget Cabins are constructed as duplex units with connecting doors, a feature that may appeal to families. If you plan to choose a cabin without a bath, we suggest units 221 through 225, which sit on a small bluff overlooking the river in the back of the complex. These offer more privacy and a good view but are some distance from the showers. Budget cabins 200, 201, 203, 205, 207, and 209 are nearest the geyser basin, but trees obstruct views of Old Faithful. Budget Cabins 226 and 235 are the only freestanding units in this classification, which means you will probably enjoy more quiet. Both are away from the river but close to a community bathroom.

Sixty-one Frontier Cabins are mostly constructed as duplex units. These units have a sink in the room and a private bathroom with a toilet and shower. Bedding is one double or a double plus a twin. The Frontier Cabins with a double and a twin are somewhat larger in size but priced the same as cabins in the same class with one double bed. Essentially, most of the Frontier Cabins are the same size as Budget Cabins but have a private bathroom. Frontier units 114, 141, and 144 are the only freestanding cabins in this classification. Cabin 114 faces Old Faithful geyser but is in the front of the complex and is subject to a heavy traffic flow.

Old Faithful Lodge Cabins offers basic but relatively inexpensive accommodations near Old Faithful geyser and the geyser basins. This lodge is in essence a low-cost alternative to the two other nearby lodges. The cabin rooms here are certainly not as nice as those in Snow Lodge or Old Faithful Inn, but they are convenient to the thermal areas of this section of the park. The interior of the main lodge was extensively renovated from 2007 to 2008 and is a comfortable place to relax and watch Old Faithful do its regular business. The food court serves relatively inexpensive lunch and dinner items, while a small bakery sells muffins, cinnamon rolls, and other baked goods, as well as coffee. More upscale meals plus snacks are available at the other two lodges, while a nearby general store offers sandwiches, soups, and other light items.

Rooms: Doubles, triples, and a few quads. More than half the cabins have a private bath.

Wheelchair Accessibility: One double-size Frontier Cabin, 228, is ADA compliant with a roll-in shower. One Budget Cabin has ramp access.

Rates: Budget Cabins ($65); Frontier Cabins ($107). Rates quoted are for two persons. Each additional person is $11 per night. Children eleven and under stay free with an adult.

Location: Southwest section of Yellowstone National Park, 30 miles from the entrance station at West Yellowstone.

Season: Mid-May to mid-September.

Food: A large food court offers the same menu for lunch and dinner ($6.00–$10.00). Two snack shops serve bakery goods, packaged sandwiches, ice cream, yogurt, and espresso. Upscale dining and snacks are available at the two nearby lodges. Two general stores each have a lunch counter and sell limited grocery items.

Facilities: Food court, snack shops, tour desk, gift shop. Many stores and restaurants are in the immediate vicinity.

Activities: Walking through the geyser area, hiking, ranger-guided walks, narrated tours.

OLD FAITHFUL SNOW LODGE AND CABINS

Yellowstone National Park, WY 82190 • (307) 344-7311 • www.TravelYellowstone.com

Old Faithful Snow Lodge and Cabins consists of a single three-story main lodge building plus thirty-four wooden cabins that are located near, but not immediately beside, the lodge. The lodge offers a dining room, grill, cocktail lounge, gift shop, and an impressive two-story lobby with huge wood beams and a large gas fireplace. A second-floor mezzanine with chairs and a table overlooks the lobby. Craftsmen created many of the furnishings in the lobby, lounge, and restaurant. Lamps and chandeliers throughout the building and the guest rooms feature animal motifs. Even much of the woodwork includes inlaid animal figures. The rustic design of the lodge fits in well with better-known Old Faithful Inn, which is nearby. Old Faithful Snow Lodge and Cabins is in the Old Faithful area of Yellowstone, 30 miles from the west entrance at West Yellowstone. The lodge is across a large parking area from Old Faithful Inn. Plenty of parking is available near the lodge and beside the cabins. Registration for the lodge and the cabins is at the main desk of the lodge building.

Snow Lodge is the first full-service hotel (dining rooms, lobby, gift shop, etc.) built in Yellowstone National Park since Canyon Lodge was completed in 1911 (and has since burned). The complex has one hundred similar but not identical rooms that are all rented at the same rate. The new lodge building replaces the previous Snow Lodge that was demolished in 1998. Each room in the new lodge has one double plus a twin or two double beds. Heavy wooden shutters swing out to cover the windows. A padded window seat is in a few of the rooms. All rooms have a full bath with a combination shower-tub, bathrobes, a telephone, a coffeemaker, and heat, but no air-conditioning.

The complex is in a relatively quiet section of the Old Faithful area, but the location does not lend itself to great views from any of the rooms. There are elevators in the lodge, and bell service is available to assist with luggage. We recommend that you try to book rooms 2037, 2039, 2041, and the three corresponding rooms on the third floor, which are larger but rent for the same rate as all other rooms in the lodge. Rooms on the second floor have larger windows than third-floor rooms.

Two categories of cabins are rented at Snow Lodge. All the cabins sit in a gravel area of sparse vegetation. The least expensive are the ten Frontier Cabins with one or two double beds. Cabins 706 and 707, each with one double bed, are quite a bit smaller than the other eight Frontier Cabins. They all rent for the same price, so try to get two doubles if you book a Frontier Cabin. These cabins are roomy and nicely finished. They do not have a porch. Each cabin has a private bath with a shower but no tub. Twenty-four Western Cabins are somewhat larger and nicer than the Frontier units. These are constructed four to a building; each cabin has a small covered porch, two queen beds, and a full bath with a combination shower-tub. We believe the Frontier Cabins with two double beds are a better value than the Western Cabins.

Old Faithful Snow Lodge and Cabins offers something for everyone. Those on a tight budget can choose an inexpensive Frontier Cabin. Others willing to spend more can sleep in one of Yellowstone's nicest lodging units. Although the lodge doesn't have the aura of nearby Old Faithful Inn, the Snow Lodge is a first-class place to stay. The location of Snow Lodge is both an advantage and a disadvantage. While the lodge is convenient to the boardwalks and trails of the area's geyser basins, the lodge rooms and public areas do not enjoy any really good views of the thermal features that make this area so popular. For those seeking quiet, Snow Lodge is away from the high-traffic areas of Old Faithful. While the lobbies of Old Faithful Inn and Old Faithful Lodge Cabins are often full of people and noise, the lobby at Snow Lodge is generally uncrowded and quiet. The lodge is one of only two Yellowstone lodging units (Mammoth is the other) open during the winter.

■   ■   ■

Old Faithful Snow Lodge and Cabins and Mammoth Hot Springs Hotel are the only two facilities that offer winter accommodations. Reservations should be made well in advance of your planned arrival. Only Mammoth is accessible by car. Old Faithful Snow Lodge is accessible only by over-the-snow vehicles from West Yellowstone, Mammoth, and Flagg Ranch on the south end. Cross-country skiing, snowshoeing, and ice skating (Mammoth) are popular activities. Ski rentals, waxes, trail maps, and other equipment are available at both locations. A winter visit to Yellowstone is a unique experience.

■   ■   ■

Rooms: Doubles, triples, and quads. All rooms have a private bath.

Wheelchair Accessibility: Five first-floor rooms in the lodge, each with one double plus one twin bed, are ADA compliant with a roll-in shower. One Western Cabin with two queen beds and a tub-shower combination is ADA compliant.

Rates: Frontier Cabins ($94); Western Cabins ($140); Snow Lodge rooms ($191). Rates quoted are for two persons. Each additional person is $11 per night. Children eleven and under stay free.

Location: Southwest section of Yellowstone, 30 miles southeast of the west entrance at West Yellowstone.

Season: Summer season is from early May to mid-October. Winter season is from mid-December to mid-March. No roads are open to the Old Faithful area during winter months.

Food: An exceptionally attractive dining room with a western motif has a large gas fireplace and handcrafted furniture. The dining room serves a breakfast buffet ($12.00), a breakfast menu ($7.00–$12.00), and dinner ($17.00–$32.00). Lunch is served only when Old Faithful Inn is closed for the season. A grill serves breakfast ($4.00–$6.00) and fast food for lunch/dinner ($5.00–$8.00). Another dining room, a cafeteria, and a general store with limited groceries and a grill are nearby.

Facilities: Dining room, grill, cocktail lounge, gift shop, laundry facilities, and bicycle rental. Other nearby facilities include a clinic, general store, National Park Service visitor center, and post office. Winter sports equipment rental is available during winter months.

Activities: Hiking, walking through the nearby geyser area, guided walks, biking, and narrated tours. Winter activities include snowcoach tours, guided ski tours, cross-country skiing, snowshoeing, and snowmobiling.

ROOSEVELT LODGE CABINS

Yellowstone National Park, WY 82190 • (307) 344-7311 • www.TravelYellowstone.com

Named for an area that served as a favorite campsite for President Theodore Roosevelt, Roosevelt Lodge Cabins includes a log registration and dining building and an adjacent small store. These two structures are surrounded on three sides by rustic wood cabins that were constructed mostly in the 1920s. The main building has a registration desk flanked on one side by a lobby with a large stone fireplace and on the other side by a family-style dining room. Rocking chairs line a covered porch across the front of the building. The lodging complex is situated on a hill surrounded by pine trees and overlooking a valley with a background of mountains. The

relatively isolated location places the lodge away from the congestion that plagues other such facilities in the park. Roosevelt Lodge Cabins is in the northeast corner of Yellowstone National Park, 23 miles southeast of the north entrance near Mammoth and 29 miles west of the northeast entrance to Yellowstone.

Roosevelt Lodge Cabins provides a total of eighty wood-frame cabins in the smallest lodging complex in Yellowstone National Park. All overnight accommodations are in the freestanding cabins, which have vaulted ceilings, shake roofs, and wood floors. None has air-conditioning, a television, a telephone, or a porch. The cabins are closely clustered in an area of trees, grass, gravel, and weeds, surrounded by hills. They are near a small store and the log registration building that houses the dining room. Parking is in front of the dining room and beside or near each cabin.

The least expensive units at Roosevelt Lodge Cabins are sixty-six Rough Rider Cabins, which have no water or private bathroom. The concessionaire supplies complimentary manufactured (Presto) logs for the woodstove that serves as the only source of heat. Three modern community bathrooms with toilets, sinks, and showers are scattered among the cabins. Most of the Rough Rider Cabins are small freestanding buildings with wood floors and one double bed. The interior has adequate space for luggage and other belongings. These cabins come in different sizes and have small screened windows to provide ventilation and outside light, which results in relatively dark interiors. Some Rough Rider units are in larger cabins that have either two or three double beds. Rough Rider Cabin 5, with three double beds, is the only cabin in the complex with two rooms. Keep in mind that all cabins in the Rough Rider

■   ■   ■

The location of Roosevelt Lodge Cabins has served as a home for previous lodging facilities. John Yancy, an early entrepreneur to this area, built the Pleasant Valley Hotel in 1884 near the site where today's Old West Cookout takes place. Yancy died in 1903, and the hotel burned three years later. This same year saw the construction of the Roosevelt Tent Camp, which had wood-floored, candy-striped canvas tents. The current lodge was completed in 1920, and the cabins were added during the same decade.

■   ■   ■

■   ■   ■

Roosevelt Lodge Cabins is well-known for its "Roosevelt's Old West Cookout." Participants depart for Pleasant Valley from the Roosevelt Corral each day in a wagon or on horseback. Different rates are charged depending on whether you choose the wagon ride, the one-hour horseback ride, or the two-hour horseback ride. The cookout includes an all-you-can-eat steak dinner plus entertainment and is very popular, so reservations should be made well in advance, especially if you choose one of the two horseback rides. Reservations for the cookout can be made at the same time you reserve a room.

■   ■   ■

classification rent for the same price regardless of size and bedding.

Fourteen Frontier Cabins with a private bath and heat have nicely finished interiors. They are the same size as the larger Rough Rider Cabins and have a much nicer interior appearance than you would expect from viewing the cabin exterior. Each Frontier unit (other than two wheelchair Frontier Cabins) has two double beds and four windows that let in more exterior light than the smaller Rough Rider units. The Frontier Cabins are in a small cluster among the Rough Rider Cabins.

The choice between the two types of cabins will depend primarily on how much you are willing to pay for a private bathroom and a heater. If you don't think they are worth $43 extra, request a less expensive Rough Rider Cabin. Rough Rider Cabin 5 is a bargain, with two rooms and three double beds. This unit also has a front porch and is the end unit in a row of cabins. We especially like the location of Rough Rider Cabin 115, bordered on two sides by a creek. Cabins 109, 111, 113, and 114 are also on the creek but not in quite as good a location as 115. These are five smaller cabins, each with one double bed. You might also consider requesting a Rough Rider Cabin with two double beds, in which case you are likely to end up with one of the larger cabins in this classification. Rough Rider units 80, 88, and 89 each have three double beds and are near the bathroom and the creek. None of the Frontier Cabins is preferable to any other, although all have finished and comfortable interiors that make them considerably nicer than most of the Rough Rider Cabins. Frontier Cabins generally fill quickly and must be reserved well in advance.

Roosevelt Lodge Cabins offers basic accommodations at nominal cost in a quiet area near the Lamar Valley, where wolves are frequently sighted. The Frontier Cabins are comfortable, and the Rough Rider Cabins are among the lowest-cost accommodations in the park. The main registration and restaurant building, of log construction, has an attractive lobby with a hardwood floor and a large stone fireplace. A lobby bar in one corner serves alcoholic beverages beginning in the late afternoon. The covered porch is a great place to sit in a rocking chair and watch the sun rise, spend part of an afternoon, or relax after an evening meal. The informal country-style dining area specializes in BBQ ribs and fish. Horseback riding and stagecoach rides are available at the nearby corral.

Rooms: Doubles, triples, and quads. A few cabins hold up to six adults. Most of the cabins do not have a private bath.

Wheelchair Accessibility: Two Frontier Cabins are each ADA compliant with a roll-in shower. The restaurant is wheelchair accessible via a ramp to the front door of the registration building, which also has a bathroom that is wheelchair accessible.

Rates: Rough Rider Cabins ($64); Frontier Cabins ($107). Rates quoted are for two persons. Each additional person is $11 per night. Children eleven and under stay free.

Location: Northeast section of Yellowstone, 23 miles southeast of the north entrance.

Season: Mid-June through early September.

Food: A dining room serves breakfast ($6.00–$9.00), lunch ($7.50–$9.00), and dinner ($9.00–$26.00). An Old West Cookout via horseback ($69 for one hour, $84 for two hours) or covered wagon ($58) is offered each evening, rain or shine. Limited groceries are sold at a small store.

Facilities: Store, dining room, lobby bar, gift counter, stables, gas station.

Activities: Hiking, guided trail rides, fly-fishing guide service, stagecoach rides, half-day and full-day guided tours to Lamar Valley.

INDEX OF LODGE NAMES

ABOUT THE AUTHORS

David and Kay Scott have spent thirty summers touring America's national park areas including six summers devoted to staying in and experiencing America's national park lodges. The initial 1996 lodge trip allowed them to gather information for the first edition of this book. Five subsequent lodge trips, the latest in 2008, provided material to update and expand the content for the current edition.

David and Kay are also the authors of Globe Pequot's *Guide to the National Park Areas: Eastern States* and *Guide to the National Park Areas: Western States.* They have discussed national park travel on numerous radio programs and have appeared twice on NBC's *Today,* once from Yellowstone National Park and again from Grand Canyon National Park. Their articles about national park lodging have appeared in major newspapers including the *Miami Herald, Orlando Sentinel, Minneapolis Tribune, Oklahoman, San Diego Union,* and the *Atlanta Journal Constitution.* David and Kay live in Valdosta, Georgia, where David is a professor emeritus of finance at Valdosta State University and Kay is retired from the public schools. David is also the author of two dozen finance books including *Wall Street Words* and *The American Heritage Dictionary of Business Terms.*